The Fantasy
Football
Guide
2000

The Fantasy Football Guide 2000

TENTH EDITION

Joseph Korch

Adams Media Corporation
Holbrook, Massachusetts

Published by
Adams Media Corporation
260 Center Street, Holbrook, MA 02343
www.adamsmedia.com

ISBN: 1-58062-291-7

ISSN: 1520-0299

Printed in Canada.

J I H G F E D C B A

Cover photo by Al Bello/Allsport

*This book is available at quantity discounts for bulk purchases.
For information, call 1-800-872-5627.*

CONTENTS

ACKNOWLEDGMENTS

My rite of spring is a little bit warped.

It's not the first crocus, the first robin sighting or the melting Northwoods snow that signals my spring. It's the Pro Bowl — that meaningless showcase of NFL talent in a plush Hawaii setting. When the Pro Bowl ends, book season begins.

Time to pore through a mountain of information; time to begin Chapter 1 of *The Fantasy Football Guide*.

Before the lengthening days and warming temperatures begin cutting ribbons of open water on the Menominee River behind my house, my spring ritual is under way. Get the sports section of the daily newspaper out, then come home and work on the book. Head 14 miles back to town to cover a ballgame or a track meet, and then return home to tackle a few more player evaluations.

Writing this book is a castle to climb, but that's no problem — just scale it one step at a time. Before I know it, the ice is out on the river and a chapter is finished. A couple of weeks later, the buds are starting to swell, and another chapter is finished. About the time my two dogs begin attracting wood ticks, a third chapter is complete.

When Wisconsin's spring fishing opener arrives (the first Saturday in May), I'm wrapping up the final chapters of the book. It's so close to finality, I can taste that first walleye fillet, that first pan-fried brook trout.

Now that it's complete, I can breathe a sigh of relief, spool up some new fishing line on my reels, and thank the people most responsible for giving me the opportunity of a lifetime.

Thanks to Ed Walters and the folks at Adams Media Corporation for believing in this book. This year's edition (No. 10) is, unquestionably, the finest yet. And to my literary editor, Jim Donovan, who brought this book to the attention of Adams Media.

Thanks again to Peter Grennen, who always does a great job of copyediting. And to Gene Brissie, who came up with the idea for this book 10 years ago: Look at it now . . . we've come a long way in a mighty-fast decade.

Thanks to my brother, Rick, who made the book possible. After starting *The Fantasy Football Guide* from scratch and writing the first four editions from 1991 to 1994, Rick could no longer write it when he accepted a public relations position with the Jacksonville Jaguars during their inaugural 1995 season. So he gave me the opportunity of a lifetime.

Thanks again to my mom, my best friend of all: Your extensive knowledge of the English language has always kept me on my toes.

And the biggest thanks always goes to you, the reader, for making all of this possible. Keep those suggestions coming — and please send for my free Draft Day Update, which will be written in August. That will provide you with the most up-to-date fantasy rankings. If your fantasy draft or auction is held more than two weeks before the regular-season opener, let me know, and I'll e-mail the update to you.

INTRODUCTION

Why buy a book on fantasy football?

Try taking your home computer to bed with you.

Your Internet connection won't accompany you on your summer vacation.

Some fantasy football magazines are pretty good, but after a couple of days of reading they're ready for the recycle bin once you pull out the player rankings.

The *2000 Fantasy Football Guide* is a fine addition to your bookcase.

A Draft Day Update will arrive in your mailbox before the season starts in order to keep you abreast of developments in summer camp and the preseason, along with final rankings by position and overall.

The *2000 Fantasy Football Guide* is better than ever.

Why?

■ First and foremost, I think this year's rankings will be the most accurate in the the book's 10-year history. My reputation is banking on it, and so is the fate of my teams in three completely different fantasy leagues.

■ And there are the new additions. There's much more information on fantasy auctions and keeper leagues. If you haven't played in an auction league, you don't know what you've been missing. It's an opportunity to buy any player, regardless of draft position, as long as you're willing to spend the fictional dough. A separate ranking has been added to provide dollar values for player auctions.

■ And, yes, the Internet is definitely an excellent way to get up-to-the-minute information that can help your draft. That's why I have included a new chapter listing the best sites on the Internet — where to get good information during the season.

■ This book contains the most comprehensive statistics in its 10-year history.

■ Finally, if you have some overriding questions as you prepare for your draft, I'll ask and answer what I believe to be the 10 key questions regarding fantasy football in the new millennium.

After last season, there are plenty of questions to answer. Many fantasy players were penalized for drawing a low number in their draft. The first round turned into a land mine of franchise-wrecking injuries, while the middle rounds made or broke fantasy franchises. Terrell Davis, Jamal Anderson, Fred Taylor, Brett Favre, Antonio Freeman and Curtis Martin all had disappointing fantasy seasons. But Stephen Davis, Tony Gonzalez, Steve Beuerlein, Wesley Walls and Rich Gannon were all mid-round picks who carried their teams to fantasy titles. And Kurt Warner probably wasn't even drafted in most fantasy leagues.

I'll steer you in the direction of some possible fantasy sleepers to consider in the middle and late rounds — and some of the big-name players to stay away from.

I'll fill you in on all of the offseason changes and update you on the players who are coming back from 1999 injuries.

Each team is broken down and evaluated by fantasy position, with the best players to draft singled out.

Please send for my free Draft Day Update, which will be mailed to you just before the start of the NFL season. It's a perfect companion for your draft, an eight-page newsletter that contains updated rankings based on training camp and preseason developments. Other books charge for this type of offer, but you won't pay a thing for this valuable information.

If your draft is held several weeks before the regular season starts, E-mail me and I'll send you an updated cheatsheet.

Most of all, good luck with your team . . . or teams, for those of you who, like me, can't get enough so you enter more than one league.

Joseph Korch
May 16, 2000

Chapter 1
HOW TO PLAY

It's not who wins the game, it's how they scored the points, that matters. Play fantasy football, and you'll soon find yourself watching every highlight show and surfing Internet sites in search of scoring summaries. The fate of your favorite NFL team remains vital, but that's totally out of your control. The fate of your fantasy team, however, rests largely within your grasp. Combine elements of skill, guts, hunches, timing, fortune and just plan dumb luck, and you have a game that has captivated the attention of football fans by the millions. It's a game that will inject a tidal wave of emotions into your weekends. One minute, you'll be clenching your fist in satisfaction because Edgerrin James just scored a touchdown. The next minute, you'll be cursing because Robert Smith, your other starting running back, has just been replaced in the red zone by the Vikings' goal-line back, Leroy Hoard.

This book will tell you how to play fantasy football, and it details many of the variations, such as scoring, player transactions and playoffs. But this book is flexible. It's your league, so set it up the way you want.

You will want anywhere from four to 16 people to form a fantasy football league, with each player getting his own franchise (in some cases, two players share a franchise). Each player will stock his team with players, set weekly lineups and play games. First you will have to decide on a commissioner and a deputy commissioner (who will decide on any possible disputes that may involve the commissioner, if that person has a team in the league).

Your league may want to set a franchise fee, just as the NFL does when it expands. All of the money goes into a pot, which can include transaction fees. At the end of the season, the money is awarded to the top teams. It's up to you and your friends to decide how to split the pot. Leagues often award teams money for each weekly win and the highest weekly point total.

You will decide on a length for your league's season and then decide upon a schedule so the teams can play head-to-head during the season (see the Appendix for suggested schedules).

Team owners will gather before the start of the NFL season for the annual fantasy draft. There they will select players from actual NFL rosters in the following positions: quarterback, running back, wide receiver, tight end and kicker.

In other variations, you may want to choose a team defense, a coach, sackers, interceptors or other variations for your league (but remember, the more complicated your scoring method, the more time-consuming it will be to tabulate scoring). Every team will have the same roster size. A roster often consists of two quarterbacks, four running backs, four wide receivers, two tight ends and two kickers.

Teams will be allowed to pick up, drop and trade players after the draft, although your league will have to set rules beforehand so that nobody gains an unfair advantage.

Each team will submit a weekly lineup to the commissioner before a set deadline. The lineup usually consists of one quarterback, two running backs, two wide receivers, one tight end and one kicker, although there are many variations (which are described later in this chapter).

Teams will meet in head-to-head competition and score points according to a predetermined scoring method. Results and standings will be posted (or mailed/faxed to all teams) by the commissioner. The season ends with playoffs and the championship game.

So there you have it — the basics of fantasy football. Now it's time to get a little more complicated and go a little deeper into how to play fantasy football.

JOINING A LEAGUE

For a fee, you can join any one of a lot of established leagues that award large prizes. *USA Today* has a large league in which people can draft, play and trade players by calling a toll-free 800 number. Other leagues are held by *The Sporting News*, the Sportsbuff Network and many metropolitan newspapers. Check *Pro Football Weekly*, *USA Today*, *The Sporting News, Fantasy Football Weekly* or any of the many other pro football preview magazines for advertisements of fantasy football leagues.

These are called "play-by-mail" leagues. They usually cost between $9 and $99 per year for each team, and they often have complex scoring methods that they manage with the help of computers, so you don't have to tabulate your team's scoring. The level of competition is also noticeably higher than that in most friendly leagues.

Most play-by-mail leagues conduct their fantasy football drafts through the mail or by entering numbers that correspond to players on a Touch-Tone telephone. Team owners rank the players in the order they want to draft them. Each service has its own method of making sure each team gets the players it values most.

Some leagues offer phone drafts, in which every team owner gets on a conference phone call with the other members. But this method is more expensive, because drafts usually take two hours or more. E-mail offers a viable alternative method of conducting drafts, submitting line-ups and distributing results.

Inevitably, some of the players you draft will underachieve, either due to injuries, poor play or the emergence of a teammate who forces them onto the bench. As a result, you will want to play the free-agent wire often. However, it usually costs several dollars for every roster move. You might even receive a few phone calls from other team owners in the league suggesting possible trades.

The best way to decide if you want to join a national fantasy league is to write or call for information, read it and then talk on the telephone to the people who run the games to determine if you can trust them. The biggest and most successful leagues can usually be trusted. These leagues usually post scores and standings on the Internet, as well as list up-to-date statistics, trade updates, lists of available free agents and injury reports. Many of them also offer statistics services to handle your league's weekly scoring and eliminate the hassle that many league commissioners go through. Again, that costs money.

Compared to friendly leagues, weekly and year-end prizes (such as a car or $10,000) are the main reason for fantasy football players to join these leagues. Obviously, they can be quite profitable to the winners (who also get to brag that they are a "national champion").

STARTING A LEAGUE

Number of Teams

The best way to get involved in fantasy football is to start your own league with a group of your friends. The number of players in your league is up to you, but it should range from four to 16. Eight and 10 are the most common numbers of teams.

Remember, there are only 31 starting quarterbacks in the NFL. Since every fantasy team has two quarterbacks on its roster, if your league has more than 15 teams, some will have a real backup quarterback as their backup quarterback (and the same for kickers). Imagine the impact of this scenario should your starter get injured.

You will also want to have an even number of teams, because it makes scheduling easier with everybody playing head-to-head every weekend, eliminating the need for byes in your league's schedule.

The most important thing to remember in starting a league is to decide the rules first. You don't want to get into the middle of the season and have teams disputing the rules. Obviously, the rules can get complicated, so you might want to decide on the many options in this book before a situation arises in which it's too late to choose one.

Make your league's rules definitive. If there are any gray areas, there will be trouble. The best rules are the simplest ones, but you have to cover all the possible areas that can fall open to debate.

But be willing to change your rules from year to year, such as adding a new scoring variation. Too many leagues resist change over a period of years — the old "why change it if it works?" line. But change for the better should always be welcome and makes each year a little bit more fun. In 1994, the NFL made quite a few rules changes, such as adding a two-point conversion. In 1999, instant replay returned. Your league should consider changing some of its rules every year, too. Rules variations are discussed near the end of this chapter.

Commissioner and His Duties

The commissioner is the Paul Tagliabue of your league. He manages the league, although he does not set the rules. Every team owner should have equal say in making the rules.

The commissioner should have the time and organizational skills to do the job. The duties of the league commissioner are to coordinate Draft Day, record rosters, keep track of roster changes, handle fees paid by teams (entry fees and player transaction fees), record the starting lineups, tabulate the scoring, distribute weekly results to the team owners and serve as the league treasurer. Don't underestimate the magnitude of this responsibility.

In some leagues, playing rosters are distributed so that every team owner knows what players the other teams have activated for that game. Thus, each weekend you can keep track not only of how your players are doing but also of how your opponents' players are doing.

After compiling the weekly scores, the commissioner should revise the weekly standings, add up the total points (offensive and defensive) for every team, list all player transactions made the previous week and distribute them to every owner.

Your league should select a responsible person, perhaps somebody who does not have a team in the league. If the commissioner also has a team in the league, you should have a deputy commissioner to help settle disputes that involve the commissioner.

HOW TO PLAY

The fantasy league commissioner should be paid at least enough to cover league expenses. If he has a team in your league, the other owners might want to waive his franchise entry fee to compensate him for his services. Either one is a good method.

Size of Rosters

Most rosters consist of approximately 14 players: two quarterbacks, four running backs, four wide receivers, two tight ends and two placekickers. One of the most common variations is for a roster to include one defensive team.

There are a lot of other variations, however, which are open to a league's preference. They are listed elsewhere in this chapter. Other books and magazines tell you to draft a number of players ranging anywhere from 12 to 26. But pick the number you feel is right. It's your league, and you get to set the rules.

In most leagues, about half of the players on a roster "play" during any particular week. That is, in the aforementioned 14-player roster, the active or "starting" lineup consists of one quarterback, two running backs, two wide receivers, one tight end and one kicker.

Putting Together a Roster

Your responsibilities as a fantasy team owner are much like those of the general manager and head coach of an NFL team. The general manager assembles the team, and the coach is the on-field leader. But first you have to put your coaching duties aside while the general manager's aspect comes to life.

There are two ways to form your roster: through a draft right before the beginning of the NFL season and, during the season, through a supplemental draft and/or by picking up free agents (and dropping one of your players to keep your roster the same size).

Franchise Entry Fee

Just like in the NFL, most leagues have a franchise entry fee (which ranges from $10 to $1,000 or more). The fees are collected, held and paid out at the end of the season to the best teams in the league. If a franchise entry fee is charged, leagues should also charge a fee for all roster transactions made during the course of the season. These entry fees usually cost more than other types of sports pools, but the entire fantasy football season lasts longer, too.

In most states, however, fee-based fantasy sports leagues that pay prize money are illegal. In the state of Texas, players in a fantasy football league were actually charged with felony gambling one year. And in 1991, the state of Florida ruled against fantasy sports leagues, saying they involve a form of gambling. Florida attorney general Bob Butterworth, in a nonbinding opinion requested by the state attorney, said fantasy leagues involve more chance than skill, violating state statute. Nothing has happened in other states in the last few years, but there's always the chance that it could happen.

The NFL frowns upon fantasy football because of its so-called association with gambling, but the league appears to be softening its stance. In 1998, the Fantasy Football Expo was held under the auspices of the Minnesota Vikings at the Minneapolis Metrodome. And NFL Properties, the NFL's marketing division, has licensed a board game called "Fantasy Football," and the league is looking for other ways to make a buck off fantasy football — all of which make the NFL somewhat hypocritical. Most fantasy players play for fun, not for money. It has been said many times that fantasy football players are the only people in the world who would spend $100 (for newsletters, books, etc.) to make $10.

So it is unnecessary to charge an entry fee if team owners want to play just for fun. That's the idea.

Scheduling

Most fantasy football seasons — the regular season and playoffs — begin at the start of the NFL's regular season and end on the final week of the regular season.

Many leagues choose to end their season a week early in order to avoid the last week of the NFL's regular season, when playoff teams often rest some of their top scorers. Some leagues also have a special fantasy playoff league that runs through the Super Bowl. That is for those fantasy leaguers who can't get enough.

Since there are 17 weeks in every NFL season (16 games and one open date per team), you will want to shorten your regular season to 13, 14 or 15 weeks, and then use the remaining two or three weeks for the playoffs, provided that your league intends to have playoffs. The schedule is determined by the same order of your player draft. Team 1 plays Team 2, Team 3 plays Team 4, and so on. The order changes every week until each team has played the others once, and then the schedule is repeated.

In leagues with eight or more teams, you may wish to split the teams into divisions of equal size, with teams playing those in their own division twice and the teams in the other division once. Or, if your league has 16 teams, you may wish to split into four four-team divisions. The disadvantage of splitting into divisions is that one division might have most of the good teams, which could result in teams with better records than those in the other division not making the playoffs.

Here is a typical schedule for a 10-team league in which each team plays every other twice:

Team #	1	2	3	4	5	6	7	8	9	10
Week #										
1	2	1	4	3	10	7	6	9	8	5
2	4	5	8	1	2	9	10	3	6	7
3	6	3	2	5	4	1	8	7	10	9
4	9	10	6	7	8	3	4	5	1	2
5	2	1	5	9	3	7	6	10	4	8
6	5	7	4	3	1	10	2	9	8	6
7	10	6	7	8	9	2	3	4	5	1
8	4	3	2	1	10	9	8	7	6	5
9	3	5	1	9	2	8	10	6	4	7
10	5	4	8	2	1	10	9	3	7	6
11	8	9	10	6	7	4	5	1	2	3
12	7	8	9	10	6	5	1	2	3	4
13	3	7	1	5	4	8	2	6	10	9
14	6	4	5	2	3	1	9	10	7	8
15	10	6	7	8	9	2	3	4	5	1
16	Playoffs									
17	Championship Game									

For schedules of leagues of different sizes, see the Appendix.

Not every league will last the entire season. For example, an eight-team league that plays 14 weeks (with each team playing each other twice) and then has two weeks of playoffs will end with one week remaining in the NFL's regular season. If your league is set up that way, I suggest you start your league the first week of the NFL season and end it before the final week of regular-season play. It's possible that not every NFL team will have every player signed by the season opener (because of holdouts), but too many playoff-bound teams rest their top players in the final week of the regular season so they don't get injured before the playoffs start. Even the weaker teams sometimes start rookie or backup quarterbacks in the last game to see what these players can do.

Thus, there are often a lot of fantasy players in the final week or two who either had to play backups rather than their starters or who received no points from their starters because they played little, if at all.

In Week 1, all games count. In Week 17, you could be in your league championship with your key players sitting out in order to rest up for the real playoffs. Keep this in mind when forming your schedule.

The NFL will again use a schedule of 16 games in 17 weeks (one open date) for every team this season. In an eight-team league with each team playing each other twice and two weeks of playoffs, you may wish to fill the remaining week by reverting back to the schedule for Week 1 before starting the playoffs. That would eliminate the round-robin competition, but it would lengthen the season to run the same as the NFL regular season. This method may, however, give unfair advantages to some teams who might play weaker teams for the added week or two. That's one reason why luck is such a big part of fantasy football.

Playoffs

In some leagues, the traditional head-to-head style of play, with opposing teams facing off week-to-week, determines the league champion by virtue of the best won-lost record. Or, in the traditional format for fantasy baseball, cumulative season statistics (most points scored) are used to determine the winner. But fantasy leagues can — and should — use a playoff system, with the best teams advancing to the playoffs in a single-elimination format. The team with the best record plays the fourth-best team, and the second- and third-best teams play each other. The two winners then face off in the fantasy championship. Some leagues utilize wild cards to keep more teams alive in the late-season playoff hunt, and other leagues include every team in the playoffs.

Tiebreaker — If two or more teams are tied with the same record at the end of the regular season, use a tiebreaker to determine which team goes to the playoffs. There are several methods you could choose (but the method should be decided upon before the start of the season).

Option 1 — Head-to-head competition. If both teams are tied in head-to-head competition (usually one victory each), the next tiebreaker is point differential in head-to-head competition. This system is closest to the one the NFL uses. If teams are still tied, go to Option 2.

Option 2 — Most points scored during the regular season. This system better reflects how a team fared during the entire regular season and lessens the possibility that a team that got lucky in head-to-head games will advance.

Payoffs

Your league should decide before the start of the season how it will

HOW TO PLAY

split the money paid for the franchise entry fee.

Payment is usually made to the league champion and the runner-up. Your league may wish to split some of the money among the third- and fourth-place teams that also made the playoffs. A typical breakdown might be 50 percent of the pot to the league champion, 25 percent to the second-place finisher, 15 percent to the third-place team and 10 percent to the fourth-place owner. Some leagues also give a "booby prize" to the worst team, or to the team that allowed the most points. Another option is a "Toilet Bowl," in which the non-playoff teams compete for consolation honors and a little bit of cash. It's best to spread the money around as much as possible. Players usually are not in it for the money as much as they are to have fun and enjoy camaraderie with other football fans. But more payouts keep interest going through the entire season — even for the last-place team.

A payoff to the team that scored the most points during the regular season is also wise, because the highest-scoring team is the league's best team, regardless of the luck factor that goes into any one week.

Some leagues also hold back a portion of the entry fees to throw a year-end party to formally recognize the league champion and distribute the money. That's easy to do if your league is a close-knit group of players.

SCORING

Nowhere else in fantasy football are there more variations from league to league as there are in the scoring systems. The many different possibilities are endless. Three systems are most commonly used (each with its own variations). Remember that the more complicated the system, the harder it is to determine scores each week.

You can get the official NFL scoring results out of most daily newspapers (or even more quickly on the Internet), but there will occasionally be discrepancies or missing statistics. The best daily sources are *USA Today* and major metropolitan newspapers. The NFL's official web site, nfl.com, posts game stats within hours after games are over. Some of the other top web sites are: espn.com, cbssportsline.com and cnnsi.com.

Some NFL players line up at more than one position, so your league will need to clarify the position at which any of these players will be played. Last year, Minnesota's Jim Kleinsasser started the season at tight end and finished it at fullback. And Pittsburgh's Kordell Stewart was switched from quarterback to wide receiver late in the season. Select one publication to act as your league's official source, and use its designation for players' positions. *Pro Football Weekly* and *Fantasy Football Weekly* are the best sources for this, because they list depth charts each week. You may be surprised to learn that depth charts on nfl.com are not as up to date as they should be.

Selecting a Scoring System

The best way to decide which scoring system your league should use is to poll the team owners and determine which one is most popular. The Basic System is used by most fantasy leagues, but, because luck is such a big factor in it, two other systems have become popular because they utilize performance more than luck to determine the league winner.

A. The Basic System

The most widely used scoring method is the basic one — teams receive points only when one of their activated players for that week scores points in an NFL game. When a player scores a touchdown, you get six points. When a kicker converts a field goal it's worth three points, and an extra point is worth one point.

For example, if Mike Alstott dives over the goal line from the one-yard line, you get six points. And if Fred Taylor runs 80 yards for a touchdown, you also get six points. It's the same way with placekickers — a 20-yard field goal is worth the same as a 55-yarder.

Scoring by Position

Quarterbacks
1. Three points for each touchdown pass thrown.
2. Six points for each touchdown scored rushing.
3. Six points for each touchdown scored receiving.
4. One point for each two-point-conversion pass.
5. Two points for each two-point-conversion run or catch.

Running Backs, Wide Receivers and Tight Ends
1. Six points for each touchdown scored rushing.
2. Six points for each touchdown scored receiving.
3. Three points for each touchdown pass thrown.
4. Two points for each two-point-conversion run or catch.

Kickers
1. Three points for each field goal.
2. One point for each extra point.

Miscellaneous Scores
1. Running backs and wide receivers get six points for a touch-

HOW TO PLAY

down on a punt or kickoff return.

Variations to the Basic Scoring System — One of the biggest faults with the Basic Scoring System in fantasy football is that it rewards those players who pound the ball over from the goal line while ignoring those players who got the ball to the goal line.

For example, last season, Arizona's Mario Bates rushed for just 202 yards but scored nine touchdowns, while Minnesota's Robert Smith rushed for 1,015 yards but just two TDs. My personal favorite was a game several years ago in which Chiefs running back Barry Word rushed 19 times for 112 yards but didn't score, while his teammate Christian Okoye carried the ball 11 times for only five yards — but he scored two TDs.

That is why so many leagues use variations in their scoring systems. Your league can change the scoring method any way it wants. Here are some of the most popular variations to the Basic Scoring System.

Passing touchdowns — Most leagues give six points to the receiver (he got the ball into the end zone) and three to the quarterback (after all, he got the ball to the receiver). But some leagues divide the points equally, with three points given to both the quarterback and the receiver (or running back) who scores. The thinking here is that the NFL gives only six points for a touchdown, so the credit should be divided equally between the two players involved. Leagues that give six points for a rushing touchdown and then split the points for a passing touchdown do so for another reason — it's harder to score on the ground. I don't necessarily believe that, however. And some leagues give six points to quarterbacks for TD passes (a few leagues award four points per touchdown pass), though I think that is too much because it results in nearly twice as many points scored by quarterbacks as running backs or receivers. Reducing the value of a TD pass to three or four points places nearly equal value among the three positions.

Varied-point systems — Some leagues award 10 points for scoring a touchdown (rushing or receiving), five for passing touchdowns and field goals, two points for extra points and 10 points for all defensive scores, regardless of their nature. The only difference is higher points per game, so why not just go with one, three and six points? If you use a varied-point system, do not devalue the kicking game. Points scored on field goals should be half of those scored on touchdowns. For example, don't award 10 points for a touchdown and only three for a field goal.

Yardage — Bonus points can be awarded for yards gained by running backs and receivers, passing yards or even for long plays (for example, double points for scoring plays of 50 yards or more). Many leagues award three bonus points to a running back with a 100-yard rushing game, a receiver (wide receiver, tight end or running back) with a 100-yard receiving game and a quarterback with a 300-yard passing game. Some also give three bonus points for scoring plays of 40 yards or more (rushing or receiving), two points for a passing touchdown of 40 yards or more and two bonus points for field goals of 50 yards or more.

Defensive scores — In many leagues, teams draft entire defensive units from NFL teams and then award six points for every score made by that defense in a game on a touchdown return of a fumble, interception or a blocked kick. Two points are awarded for a safety.

Sacks — Leagues that draft defensive players usually award one or two points for a sack.

Interceptions — Teams can subtract one point for each interception thrown by a quarterback or add one point for interceptions made by a team defense.

Remember, the more complicated the scoring, the harder it will be to tabulate your league's scores.

B. The Distance System

Some leagues award points according to the length of the scoring plays. This system favors the gamebreakers — players who score on long plays — rather than those who score from a yard out. In doing so, it eliminates much of the luck factor.

There are a variety of ways to give points for long-distance scoring. The following is one of the most common methods:

PASSING FOR A TOUCHDOWN

Length of Touchdown	Points
1 – 9 yards	1
10 – 19 yards	2
20 – 29 yards	3
30 – 39 yards	4
40 – 49 yards	5
50 – 59 yards	6
60 – 69 yards	7
70 – 79 yards	8
80 – 89 yards	9
90 – 99 yards	10

RUSHING AND RECEIVING FOR A TOUCHDOWN

Length of Touchdown	Points
1 – 9 yards	2
10 – 19 yards	4
20 – 29 yards	6
30 – 39 yards	8
40 – 49 yards	10
50 – 59 yards	12
60 – 69 yards	14
70 – 79 yards	16
80 – 89 yards	18
90 – 99 yards	20

FIELD GOALS

Length of Field Goal	Points
Under 20 yards	2
20 – 29 yards	3
30 – 39 yards	4
40 – 49 yards	5
50 – 59 yards	6
60 and over	7

Extra points are worth one point each (except two-point conversions).

Here is one of the most popular Distance Scoring Systems:

Yardage of play	0–9 Points	10–39 Points	40-plus Points
QB pass for TD	6	9	12
RB run for TD	6	9	12
WR/TE catch for TD	6	9	12
QB run/catch for TD	12	18	24
RB catch/pass for TD	12	18	24
WR/TE run/pass for TD	12	18	24
K run/catch/pass for TD	12	18	24
ST/Defense return for TD	12	18	24
Fake field goal for TD	12	18	24

Yardage of Play	17–39	40–49	50-plus
Field Goal	3	5	10

Safety = 12 points
Point after touchdown = 1 point

C. The Performance System

Scoring under this method is based on yards gained, not points scored. The major advantage is that less luck is involved, and the true stars will stand out over the course of the season. Every year, there are several players who rack up impressive yardage statistics but can't find the end zone. Frank Sanders of Arizona is notorious for catching a lot of passes and seldom scoring (last year, he had 79 catches for 954 yards and just one TD).

Here is the most common scoring method for the Performance System (although leagues can make their own variations):

SCORING BY POSITION
Quarterbacks, Running Backs and Wide Receivers
1. One point for every 20 yards passing.
2. One point for every 10 yards rushing.
3. One point for every 10 yards receiving.

Kickers
1. Three points for each field goal.
2. One point for each extra point.
3. If a kicker passes, runs or catches for yardage, he is awarded the points that any other position players would receive for the same play.

Points are not deducted for negative yardage. The following is a detailed chart for the Performance Scoring System just described.

Passing Yardage	Points
0 – 19 yards	0
20 – 39 yards	1
40 – 59 yards	2
60 – 79 yards	3
80 – 99 yards	4
100 – 119 yards	5
120 – 139 yards	6
140 – 159 yards	7
160 – 179 yards	8
180 – 199 yards	9
200 – 219 yards	10
220 – 239 yards	11
240 – 259 yards	12
260 – 279 yards	13

HOW TO PLAY

280 – 299 yards	14
300 – 319 yards	15

and so on.

Rushing Yardage	Points
0 – 9 yards	0
10 – 19 yards	1
20 – 29 yards	2
30 – 39 yards	3
40 – 49 yards	4
50 – 59 yards	5
60 – 69 yards	6
70 – 79 yards	7
80 – 89 yards	8
90 – 99 yards	9
100 – 109 yards	10
110 – 119 yards	11
120 – 129 yards	12

and so on.

Pass Receiving Yardage	Points
0 – 9 yards	0
10 – 19 yards	1
20 – 29 yards	2
30 – 39 yards	3
40 – 49 yards	4
50 – 59 yards	5
60 – 69 yards	6
70 – 79 yards	7
80 – 89 yards	8
90 – 99 yards	9
100 – 109 yards	10
110 – 119 yards	11
120 – 129 yards	12

and so on.

Another favorite performance method to award points is to develop a scoring system that includes statistics for the following categories: quarterback — pass-completion percentage, passing yards, passing touchdowns and negative points for interceptions; running backs — rushing yards, rushing average and touchdowns; wide receivers and tight ends — receptions, receiving yards, yards per reception and touchdowns; and kicking — field goals and points subtracted for missed field goals. For defense, a system of 1–10 points is awarded for points allowed (example: 10 points for a shutout), or 1–5 points for rushing or passing yards allowed (5 points for less than 100 yards rushing or 200 yards passing allowed). Defenses are also awarded points for sacks and interceptions. Leagues that use this type of scoring system usually devise it themselves.

Whatever scoring system you use, don't go with one that awards so many points that your game scores are 110–96. Use one with realistic scores somewhere in the range of real NFL scores.

D. The Combined System

This is the scoring system that is the most fair, and it is getting more popular every year. It is a combination of the Basic Scoring System and the Performance Scoring System. Players receive points when they score, as well as for yardage gained and/or the length of scoring plays.

This system negates some of the luck factor that is so prevalent in the Basic Scoring System, and it is not so heavily determined by yardage, either. In other words, the value of players is weighted more evenly in this system. Superstars are often no better than goal-line scorers in the basic method, and they're no better than players who gain a lot of yards but rarely score in the performance system.

Points are tabulated according to whatever parts of the Basic, Performance and Distance Scoring Systems are used. For example, a player can be awarded six points for a touchdown scored, three more points if it came on a play of 40 or more yards (some leagues use 50 yards as the barrier), and three more points if he gained 100 yards in the game. Or a quarterback can get three points for a touchdown pass, two or three more for a scoring pass over 40 (or 50) yards and two or three more for 300-yard games.

In fact, the analyses of players in this book are based on the Combined Scoring System more than any of the others.

E. The Rotisserie System

As in fantasy baseball, some league champions are the teams with the most points scored during the season. This method certainly rewards the best team overall, but it eliminates the week-to-week competition, which is the most exciting aspect of fantasy football once the season gets under way.

The team that scores the most points is justifiably the best team in

HOW TO PLAY

a league, but it is very possible (and even likely) that it won't win the league championship based on weekly play.

What makes the fantasy-football-to-the-NFL correlation closer than the rotisserie-baseball-to-the-major-leagues correlation is that the highest-scoring team is not always the Super Bowl champion or the winner of a fantasy league.

THE DRAFT

The draft is the most exciting event of fantasy football and, more than anything else, it is what determines how well your team will fare.

Now it's time to stock your team. Your league will conduct a draft that is very much like the NFL draft, except that, instead of drafting college players, you are actually picking players from current NFL teams.

Some leagues, called "keeper leagues," continue from year to year with basically the same teams, which allows owners to keep a few of the players from the previous year's roster. It's an interesting option that a lot of leagues use, but the drawback is that everybody should have a chance to draft Peyton Manning, Terrell Davis and Randy Moss. Keep that in mind.

Preparing for Draft Day

Study, study, study. This book will help you immensely as you prepare for your fantasy football draft, because its emphasis is on player evaluation. But you also need to study NFL rosters and have some knowledge of each team's depth charts (which are included in this book) — who starts and who doesn't. The majority of owners in every league do their homework and prepare for Draft Day. But there are always one or two owners in every league who do not, and they are usually the ones at the bottom of the standings.

Remember, a league of eight teams will include only about 120 out of the approximately 500 skill-position players on NFL rosters. That leaves you with a lot of players from which to choose, making your draft picks the most crucial aspect of putting together your team.

You need to know more than just the players on your favorite team. You need more than last year's NFL statistics or a list of the All-Pro and Pro Bowl teams. You really need to know something about every team in the league — and not just who's good, but rather who gets the ball and scores the points. You also need to know your league's rules and draft accordingly (see Draft Strategy).

Do not go strictly on last year's statistics, because many players are inconsistent, and their numbers will go up and down from year to year. Be sure to know whether or not a player's 1999 statistics were truly indicative of his abilities. Last year's statistics don't necessarily indicate what may happen this season. For example, Emmitt Smith's numbers vary somewhat from year to year, but he's always among the league's top rushers. But, while Kurt Warner, Steve Beuerlein and Stephen Davis had great seasons last year, that does not mean they'll do it again this year. The same holds true for players such as Olindo Mare, Patrick Jeffers and Olandis Gary.

And it's just the same for players coming off bad seasons. Jerry Rice (getting old, poor quarterbacking), Jake Plummer (poor play), Wade Richey (low-scoring team), and Terrell Davis (injury) all had sub-par seasons in 1999 for different reasons. But all four of them are very capable of having good or great seasons in 2000.

Injuries have a lot to do with a player's performance, and injuries to other players often determine whether or not some players will get a chance to perform or not.

Remember, the success of your entire season largely depends on how you do in the draft. Don't take your draft lightly.

When to Hold Your Draft

It is necessary to hold your draft on a day in which every team can be represented. Do not allow an owner of one team to draft players for the owner of another team who cannot attend the draft. If a team is not represented at the draft, it must make its selections by telephone or from the pool of players that remains after the draft.

You will want to hold your draft as close to the start of the NFL season as possible. The best day is anytime from Tuesday through Saturday during the week before the NFL season starts, which is after the date that teams make their final cuts to 53 players.

A quiet environment might be the best spot to hold your draft, since you will want to be able to think. But, for some reason, bars and restaurants seem to be the most-used locations.

If your league's commissioner owns a team, you might want to have an outside friend act as the recording secretary for your draft, since the commissioner will be drafting. You need somebody to keep track of the draft order, record everyone's picks as they are made, maintain time limits between picks and leave the commissioner free to concentrate on his draft.

You might also want to have large boards made up to record the picks so everyone can see them during the draft and will know what players are no longer available.

Some leagues (especially those that have 14-week regular seasons and two weeks of playoffs) hold their drafts one week into the NFL season and then start their leagues at the same time NFL teams are playing their second game so they can run their leagues the remainder of the NFL season, rather than end a week before the NFL playoffs start. This gives them the advantage of seeing how certain players (especially rookies) are doing and helps sort out neck-and-neck battles for starting positions. Last year, fantasy players weren't sure who would be the starting tailback in Washington, but Stephen Davis won the starting job over Skip Hicks late in the preseason. Davis was a mid- to late-round pick in most fantasy drafts, and he had an excellent season.

Draft Order

The draft begins with each team owner drawing a number. Teams then draft players in order. In succeeding rounds, teams draft players in the reverse order. Therefore, the person with the last pick in the first round gets the first pick in the second round, giving him two picks in a row.

That's why the owner with the last pick shouldn't panic, because it all evens out in the long run. The person with the first pick in the first round does not choose again until the last pick in the second round. Then he gets two picks in a row, because, as the third round begins, he gets the first pick again. At that point, the draft returns to the original first-through-last order.

The third and fourth rounds (and all pairs of succeeding rounds) work just like the first two rounds until every owner has filled his team roster at every position up to your league's roster limit.

Here's how it works:

Team 1 — 1st pick
Team 2 — 2nd pick
Team 3 — 3rd pick
Team 4 — 4th pick
Team 5 — 5th pick
Team 6 — 6th pick
Team 7 — 7th pick
Team 8 — 8th pick
Team 8 — 9th pick
Team 7 — 10th pick
Team 6 — 11th pick
Team 5 — 12th pick

Team 4 — 13th pick
Team 3 — 14th pick
Team 2 — 15th pick
Team 1 — 16th pick
Team 1 — 17th pick
and so on.

Some leagues redraw the draft order every two rounds so that owners don't pick from the same two positions throughout the draft.

You may want to set a time limit on each team when selecting a player in order to keep the draft moving. A one-minute limit should be sufficient if team owners have done their homework and are prepared for the draft. In contrast to the NFL draft, where teams get 15 minutes to make their first-round pick and less in succeeding rounds, it seems as if the late picks in fantasy football are the hardest to make. That's when you are trying to fill out a position, draft players with different bye weeks, where you are looking for sleepers and players with potential and don't want to make a mistake. The early-round picks usually go quickly, because owners are more familiar with the big-name players.

Some leagues like to have their draft order set well in advance of the draft so players can conduct mock drafts beforehand. At the least, it will give you the opportunity to assess who may be available for your first few picks.

About two hours are normally needed to complete a draft for an eight- or 10-team league, but the time goes by quickly. And it's a lot of fun.

Drafting Players

The most important factor in fantasy football that determines who wins and who loses — other than luck — is the draft. The team with the best players scores the most points. The team with the most points wins games. So you want to put together the best (meaning highest-scoring) team possible.

You can draft players from any position in any order, but I suggest that you strongly consider taking a running back and wide receiver with your first two picks (or, possibly, two running backs or two receivers). Forget about the tight ends and placekickers until the middle rounds — you want to get as many of the high-scoring players as possible early on. Kickers also score a lot of points, but high-scoring kickers are a dime a dozen. High-scoring running backs and receivers are a precious commodity.

There is a big disparity between the best players and the very good players at the running back and wide receiver positions, and not as much difference between the best kickers.

Depending on which draft pick you have and which players are available, you might want to wait until the third or fourth round before drafting a quarterback. There's only one Fred Taylor and Randy Moss, but Kurt Warner wasn't even drafted in most of last year's fantasy leagues. Often, quarterbacks drafted in late rounds finish the season among the league leaders in touchdown passes (such as Steve Beuerlein in 1999). So be willing to change your strategy. You never know who might still be on the board when it's your turn to draft.

With few exceptions, you should draft two running backs and two wide receivers with four of your first five picks, because quality players at those positions are hardest to find. The pool is a bit deeper for quarterbacks. If your roster has two quarterbacks who throw between 15 and 20 touchdown passes, you can play the matchups from week to week and still get reasonably good production. Don't be fooled when other fantasy team owners are drafting quarterbacks in the first two rounds. With the exception of Peyton Manning, Kurt Warner and Brett Favre, you're better off taking a running back and a wide receiver first. Don't wait too long to draft a quarterback, however.

Due to injuries, there's no such thing as a sure bet (remember Terrell Davis, Jamal Anderson and Fred Taylor last year). But there is a sharp drop-off in production between top-level running backs such as Marshall Faulk and top-flight players such as Corey Dillon and Robert Smith, who pile up the yardage but seldom score. You'll need two solid backs and two good receivers to have a good fantasy season, and there aren't many out there. Several of the teams in your league will have a poor No. 2 back and a weak link at receiver, and they're likely to be the teams out of playoff contention. Address those two positions first at your draft.

On the other hand, there is not a lot of difference between the best placekickers, most of whom will score more than 100 points. Every team in your league will end up with a decent kicker, so the difference is not very much between them. And few tight ends — Wesley Walls, Tony Gonzalez and maybe Shannon Sharpe — are worth an early pick. If you don't get one of them, draft a second running back, second wide receiver and first quarterback (and perhaps a third running back and third wide receiver) before picking any other tight end, because they are unlikely to score many points.

Don't draft your second quarterback too early, even if a good one is available; instead, take a running back or wide receiver you will use a lot during the season. Of course, any quarterback's susceptibility to injuries warrants having a good backup quarterback on a fantasy football team — much as the Jets had a pretty good backup to Vinny Testaverde in Ray Lucas — but you are better off drafting players who will play and score points for you than having a good player on your team whom you probably will not play much.

And, if your league uses team defenses, don't draft your defensive team until the last round or two, because picking a defense is basically a crapshoot anyway. If you get three touchdowns all season by your team defense, you have done well.

After the draft, the commissioner should give every team owner a copy of each team's roster.

Player Auctioning

As they say, real fantasy football players stock their fantasy football teams the old-fashioned way — they buy them. Established leagues often like to use this method, in which players are bid for in an auction rather than drafted, because it adds another dimension to the draft.

Every team spends the same amount of money to make up, or buy, their teams. This is true free agency in fantasy football, because you do actually own the player. Also, in an auction, every team has equal opportunity to get every player.

Once an order is determined for choosing the players to be bid on, owners bid until one owner has outbid the others for a particular player. The best players obviously go for the most money (as much as 40 or 50 percent of a team's limit). Since only a few players in the league are worth that percentage of a team's "salary cap," you have to be sure you make that choice wisely. Choosing players with good potential for a smaller cost will enable you to outbid other teams for some of the most-sought-after players.

One risky but potentially rewarding strategy is to open bidding on players you don't want, and then try to drive the price up. The idea is to start a bidding war for players who don't interest you and by doing so burn a big chunk of your opponents' salary caps. The key is knowing when to pull out of the bidding so that you don't get stuck with that player.

In the late stages of your auction, several quality players can be had for a bargain price — provided you have saved some of your salary cap.

The auction continues until each team owner fills out his roster, and the cost of those players must not exceed the league's salary cap.

For example, one of the longest-running fantasy football leagues in the country has a $100 limit per team. Players such as Randy Moss and Edgerrin James cost more than $40 each, whereas players such as Rich

Gannon and Ed McCaffrey can be had for $2–$5. The objective is to fill out an entire roster with $100 (this league has 12 players per team). Most of the teams try to buy one or two superstars and then fill out their rosters with cheaper players with good potential. But, since every team starts with the same bankroll, the most important thing is to budget carefully.

A regular draft is somewhat shorter than an auction, but an auction is certainly more exciting. But it's not recommended for beginning fantasy players; wait a year or two before taking the plunge into an auction.

Draft Strategy

■ The rules that your league uses concerning its scoring method dictate largely the players you want to draft. If your scoring reflects only those scores made by NFL players every week, you will want to draft players who score the most points. For example, Leroy Hoard can be more valuable than Curtis Martin. But if your fantasy league rewards teams with running backs who rush for 100 yards in a game or quarterbacks who throw long touchdown passes, you will want to take other factors into consideration.

If your league's scoring system gives quarterbacks six points for each touchdown pass thrown, by all means try to draft a quarterback first. And if your league gives bonus points for distance scoring, you will want to go with the gamebreakers — running back Fred Taylor rather than Hoard, wide receiver Marcus Robinson rather than Terrance Mathis, and kicker Todd Peterson rather than Adam Vinatieri.

■ The most important factor in drafting is projecting a player's performance for the upcoming year. So don't place too much emphasis on last year's statistics. On the average, only about three of the top 10 scorers among running backs and wide receivers finish in the top 10 the following year. Quarterbacks are easier to judge, with about 70 percent finishing in the top 10 in successive years.

That is why this book lists statistics for the last five years of every player's career (not just three). If you study players' entire careers, you will see that a lot of players who were injured or had subpar seasons last year will be much better draft picks than you might have thought on first glance. Also, try not to pick based strictly on 1999 statistics; a lot of players who had career years will never reach those marks again.

You also will want to know which of the 1999 rookies who didn't see a lot of playing time last year are ready to break out in 1999. The five quarterbacks drafted in the 1999 first round — Tim Couch, Akili Smith, Donovan McNabb, Cade McNown and Daunte Culpepper — will in all likelihood play more than they did last year. And running back Ricky

Williams is bound to surpass his disappointing 1999 production.

■ Do not draft too many players from one division. During the weeks that teams have a bye (see the 2000 NFL schedule in the Appendix), you will not be able to play these players, and if too many of your best players are from the same division, you will have to play too many backups on those weekends, almost guaranteeing that you will lose a game or two. So spread your picks around. Also, for the same reason, be sure to pick your two quarterbacks and two kickers from teams that have different bye weeks. A good suggestion is to draft your top three players (quarterback, running back and wide receiver) from three different divisions so you'll always have two of them on the bye weeks.

■ Don't draft too many players from your favorite team. If they have an off year, they will very quickly become your least-favorite players. Be objective, and even take players from a team you do not like, because they will help you win in fantasy football. And don't pass over players just because they have past reputations as troublemakers. Jeff George has had a couple of good seasons in recent years.

■ Don't draft too many players from bad teams. Most owners want the bulk of their players from good teams, because they'll have more scoring opportunities. Corey Dillon (Cincinnati), Errict Rhett (Cleveland) and Duce Staley (Philadelphia) are perfect examples of players who would probably accumulate some excellent statistics if they played on better teams.

■ Know which players are holding out, both veterans and rookies. Because of the advent of a salary cap for both rookies and veterans, there are fewer holdouts than in past years. But some players — Carl Pickens is notorious — will invariably try to get bigger salaries, so be aware of them.

■ Consider a player's age. Last year, several players seemed to grow old quickly, such as Jerry Rice, Dan Marino and Ben Coates.

■ Be aware of which players might lose their starting jobs in 2000. Some of these players are quarterbacks Tony Banks, Jim Harbaugh and Brian Griese, running backs Adrian Murrell and Antowain Smith, and wide receivers Bert Emanuel and Jermaine Lewis.

■ Because of free agency, know the players that switched teams who could be due for good years. Some of these players include quarterbacks Jeff Blake (New Orleans) and Trent Dilfer (Baltimore); running backs James Stewart (Detroit), Raymont Harris (New England) and Errict Rhett (Cleveland); and wide receivers Joey Galloway (Dallas), Jake Reed and Joe Horn (New Orleans), Curtis Conway (San Diego), Shawn Jefferson (Atlanta) and Eddie Kennison (Chicago). Look for Rhett's statistics to tumble because he signed with a weaker team than the one he played for last year.

■ Know the injury status of players you are thinking about drafting. Among the best players coming off 1999 injuries are quarterbacks Steve Young (San Francisco) and Vinny Testaverde (New York Jets); running backs Terrell Davis (Denver), Jamal Anderson (Atlanta) and Fred Taylor (Jacksonville); wide receivers Herman Moore (Detroit), Curtis Conway (now with San Diego) and Yancey Thigpen (Tennessee) and tight end Shannon Sharpe (now with Baltimore). See the Injury Report in Chapter 11.

■ Don't put too much emphasis on preseason statistics, because they can be very misleading.

■ Know which teams have changed their offenses. For example, if a team goes to a one-back offense, the backups and fullbacks will not see much action. A new offensive coordinator could jump-start an attack or cripple it (remember Pittsburgh in 1998 and the Vikings early in 1999). And be aware of possible changes due to the unprecedented coaching carousel. Of the seven teams with new coaches, the Cowboys, Saints and Patriots figure to undergo the most dramatic face-lifts.

■ Know which rookies have the best chance of contributing right away. A few rookies to keep an eye on are quarterbacks Chad Pennington (New York Jets) and Chris Redman (Baltimore); running backs Thomas Jones (Arizona), Ron Dayne (New York Giants), Shaun Alexander (Seattle) and Jamal Lewis (Baltimore); wide receivers Peter Warrick (Cincinnati), Plaxico Burress (Pittsburgh), Sylvester Morris (Kansas City), Travis Taylor (Baltimore) and R. Jay Soward (Jacksonville); tight end Bubba Franks (Green Bay); and kicker Sebastian Janikowski (Oakland).

■ When drafting, no matter what round it is, have two or three players in mind. That way, if somebody else picks the player you wanted, you will be able to make a comparable choice. In the middle rounds, many players should be ranked about even; what you are looking for is the so-called "sleeper" in every round. There's always one.

■ If you don't think a player you want will be available in the next round, now's the time to draft him.

Here's what a typical roster might look like for the 2000 season:

Round 1 — Fred Taylor, RB, Jacksonville Jaguars
Round 2 — Isaac Bruce, WR, St. Louis Rams
Round 3 — Brad Johnson, QB, Washington Redskins
Round 4 — Mike Alstott, RB, Tampa Bay Buccaneers
Round 5 — Ed McCaffrey, WR, Denver Broncos
Round 6 — Rickey Dudley, TE, Oakland Raiders
Round 7 — Curtis Enis, RB, Chicago Bears

Round 8 — Al Del Greco, K, Tennessee Titans
Round 9 — Elvis Grbac, QB, Kansas City Chiefs
Round 10 — Troy Edwards, WR, Pittsburgh Steelers
Round 11 — Jonathan Linton, RB, Buffalo Bills
Round 12 — O. J. McDuffie, WR, Miami Dolphins
Round 13 — David Sloan, TE, Detroit Lions
Round 14 — John Carney, K, San Diego Chargers
Round 15 — Buffalo Bills defense

In this typical roster, players were chosen from all six divisions, which is the ideal spread. And, even though some of the players play for losing teams, they'll still put up some pretty good numbers. But note that most of the players play for winning teams.

ROSTER CHANGES AND TRANSACTIONS

As in the NFL, you are able to make changes in your roster during the season. Just because you didn't have a good draft doesn't mean you have to suffer through the season with a bad team. And when one of your players is lost to his NFL team because of an injury, you also can replace him on your roster with another player. Fine-tuning your roster is a must after the season begins.

The winner of most fantasy football leagues is not necessarily the owner who drafted the best team, but the one who did the best job working the waiver wires during the season. In fact, the first roster changes you make after the draft might be the most critical to your team's success. That's when you will be able to answer most of the questions you had on Draft Day — who will be the featured running back on a particular team, for example — and when you will be able to identify emerging players.

There are always talented players — primarily rookies and second-year pros who didn't play much the previous year, as well as players who come out of nowhere to have good seasons — who will be overlooked in your league's initial draft and who would be a valuable addition to a fantasy team. Remember Kurt Warner, Stephen Davis, Marcus Robinson, Patrick Jeffers, Tyrone Wheatley and Derrick Mayes last year? This is how teams catch up to the preseason favorite. In other words, don't just draft a team and sit back to see how you will do. Be active.

Some leagues do not allow roster transactions of any kind after the draft. That's wrong. A fantasy league is supposed to be fun, and flexible roster changes allow every team the opportunity to improve during the season.

There are three commonly used methods to make roster changes: trades, holding a league-wide supplemental draft and the open-waiver system in which every team is allowed to pick up and drop players at any time.

Many leagues charge a small transaction fee for any personnel move. This usually lowers the incentive to make wholesale roster changes and helps to increase the pot for the payoff.

Your roster size may never exceed the limit; for every player you add, you must drop a player. Once you drop a player, he is eligible to be picked up by any team.

Too many fantasy leagues set too many restrictive deadlines and rules for transactions (as well as for drafting, setting weekly lineups and many other aspects of fantasy football). Be flexible. The idea is to have fun and allow every team an equal opportunity to win. You need to be sure the rules are not stretched or broken, but they should not hinder the idea of fantasy football, which is to provide enjoyment to football fans.

Remember, NFL teams change their rosters and lineups constantly throughout the season. So should you. But don't "overmanage." You want to be continuously looking for players to add to your roster, but be careful not to give up on your players too soon. Some players need time to develop, just as you knew when you drafted them. In 1999, Patrick Jeffers barely even played the first four games of the season, but he finished with 12 touchdown catches. Often it's wiser to bench a player rather than cut him, because he might pay dividends down the stretch.

Trades

Trading players is one of the most fascinating aspects of pro football. Fans spend weeks, if not years, trying to determine which team got the best of a trade. Remember the two big trades of the 1980s involving Eric Dickerson and Herschel Walker? This year, only time will tell if the Seahawks were wise in trading Joey Galloway to the Cowboys.

In fantasy football, however, trades are usually a rare occurrence. In fact, some leagues do not allow them at all because of the possibility that two team owners would get together and make a trade that helps one team at the expense of another (especially at the end of the season).

If your league allows trades, you will want to set some safeguards. For example, set a deadline just as the NFL does. The NFL does not allow trades after the sixth week of the season, but you will want to set your fantasy league's deadline a little later. Do not allow one team to trade a player or players for "future considerations," for obvious reasons. You can also make trades contingent on the approval of the commissioner or the other team owners to guard against hanky-panky.

Two-for-one trades (in which one team offers two players for one very good player) are allowed, as long as each team obeys the league's roster limit. The team receiving two players must drop another player on its roster, while the team receiving one player must pick up another player.

In professional sports, the commissioners have the power to veto trades that are not "in the best interests of the league," and your commissioner and team owners should have the same power. If the commissioner has a team in the league, a simple majority of owners can veto a trade involving his team.

Waivers

In the NFL, teams are free to drop or waive players at any time and pick up or sign players at any time, and this is my suggestion. Teams should be able to improve their roster at any time. In a league of eight teams with 14 players per roster, only 112 out of approximately 500 skill-position players (quarterbacks, running backs, wide receivers, tight ends and kickers) will be on a fantasy roster. That leaves a lot of good players undrafted; thus, there should be no limit on the number of roster changes per team.

Under this method, the first team to pick up a player from the unclaimed pool of NFL players gets him. All he has to do is notify the league commissioner (and pay the appropriate fee, if there is one). For each player obtained via waivers, a player must be released.

Some leagues specify a certain night for transactions. Other leagues allow transactions by teams in order of record, from worst to first.

Every year there are several players whose midseason addition helps fantasy teams. Kurt Warner, Tyrone Wheatley, Marcus Robinson, Muhsin Muhammad and Kevin Johnson weren't drafted in many 1999 leagues, but the shrewd fantasy owners who got them via the waiver wire were handsomely rewarded. Work the waiver wires carefully and you could come up a winner.

The first two weeks of the season are an important time in the fortunes of your team. Keep an eye on players who come out of nowhere, surprise starters and even rookies who were not expected to start or play much.

Supplemental Drafts

A fantasy league can also decide to hold a supplemental draft after four weeks (or even eight weeks) to supplement rosters with players not chosen in the preseason draft (those players on current rosters during the season). Team owners are able to drop as many players on their rosters as they want and replace them with new players.

The supplemental draft is conducted just like the preseason draft except that the order changes. Like the system used in the NFL, teams draft in reverse order of their won-lost records (that is, the team with the worst record drafts first and so on, to the team with the best record). Ties are broken by total points scored (with the team with the fewest points scored considered the weaker team). The draft then reverses order in the second round and continues back and forth until every owner has made the changes he wants to make.

Any player not on a fantasy team is available to be picked up from the supplemental pool. This is especially effective in allowing every team an almost equal opportunity to grab the latest hotshot player in the NFL, as compared to total free agency, in which the first team owner to contact the commissioner gets the player.

Not every team may wish to take part in the supplemental draft, especially if an owner is happy with his team.

If the teams in your league originally acquired players through an auction, you should hold a supplemental draft/auction at some point during the season to allow all teams to bid for new players.

No Transactions

If a league does not allow teams to make transactions, or if a deadline is put on all transactions, you still should allow teams to replace players who are injured.

The simplest way to do this is to allow teams to replace only those players who are actually placed on injured reserve by their NFL teams. No team should be forced to play without a player at a position or be without a capable backup. Players lost to a fantasy team because of trades or waivers would not qualify to be replaced unless your league's rules specify otherwise.

Leagues that do not allow transactions often have larger roster sizes, which gives each team the chance to stock enough players in the draft to get through the entire season.

Injured Reserve

What do you do when one of your top players is injured and placed on injured reserve? In most leagues, you would either keep him on the bench until he is healthy again (thus taking up space that could be occupied by a healthy player), or you could drop the injured player and add another one at the same position. However, if you drop the player, he would be free to be picked up by any team when he is reactivated.

Thus, your league might want to allow teams to have an injured reserve list, so any player who is placed on injured reserve by his NFL team would be retained by the fantasy team and temporarily replaced by a pickup. Then, when the injured player is playing again in the NFL, the fantasy team would either have to activate him and drop the substitute player (or another player) or drop the player on injured reserve (for example, if the substitute player is doing better).

In the NFL, when a player is put on injured reserve, he is not permitted to play for the rest of the season. Many teams leave injured players on their rosters (inactive week after week) in hopes they will return later in the season. It's the same in fantasy football — if you have a deep enough roster, that is.

LINEUPS

The most enjoyable week-to-week aspect of fantasy football is setting your lineup in advance of each weekend's action.

Now it's time to play coach. You are Tony Dungy or Tom Coughlin. You don't decide what plays to use, but rather what players to use, and that's how you score points. If drafting is the most important part of fantasy football, then "starting" the right players is the most important decision you make once the season starts. One of the most frustrating moments of fantasy football is knowing that a player you didn't start for a particular week scored a touchdown — or even two! And it's equally frustrating to start a player who doesn't even suit up because of an injury.

Whom to Play
The starting lineup usually consists of:
    1 Quarterback
    2 Running Backs
    2 Wide Receivers
    1 Tight End
    1 Kicker
    1 Team Defense (optional)

Lineup variations: There are a number of variations that your league will have to decide upon before the start of the season. For example, one popular national fantasy league recommends 1 quarterback, 2 running backs,

3 wide receivers, 1 tight end, 1 kicker, 1 special-teams player (kick return-er), 1 linebacker and 1 defensive back (or one team defense in place of the special-teams player and two defensive players). But, since NFL teams have only six skill-position players on offense, your league should, too.

Those on your team who do not "play" sit on the bench for a week (or, in some cases, all season).

Because of the advent of H-backs, run-and-shoot offenses and three- and four-wide-receiver formations, some NFL teams do not use tight ends and others use them basically for blocking.

One fantasy league allows teams the option of drafting one extra wide receiver in place of a tight end and/or playing one extra wide receiver rather than a tight end any particular week. Instead of drafting four wide receivers and two tight ends, teams pick five wide receivers and only one tight end and have the option of playing either three wide receivers or two wideouts and one tight end each week. A rule requires that each team play its tight end for at least half of the games. That adds an interesting element of strategy of deciding when to start a tight end.

Many leagues start a third receiver instead of a designated tight end, and consider tight ends to be receivers.

Setting a Deadline

Be sure to set a deadline for teams to submit their starting lineups for each week, but set it as late as possible. You might want to have a deadline set for 7:00 p.m. Friday or 6:00 p.m. Saturday so that your phone is not ringing off the hook Sunday as you are sitting down to watch the NFL pregame shows on television. In the event of Thursday or Saturday games, you will need to adjust your deadlines — even if some teams don't have players involved in those games. All rosters should be turned in before the first game played each week.

Your league might want to allow teams the option to call in a lineup change anytime before 1:00 p.m. EST Sunday, when games begin, if the commissioner can be reached (or if he has a phone-answering machine). This allows teams to make last-minute changes in the event of player injury. It's not as complicated at it may seem, as it might be used only a few times in the course of the season by all of the teams combined.

Once the deadline has passed, changes cannot be made — even in the event of injuries to a player before a game. If the commissioner has a team in the league, he must turn in his lineup to another league member to guard against cheating. If a team does not turn in a lineup, its lineup from the previous week will be automatically used.

For leagues that have an early lineup deadline, one option is to allow teams to make one lineup change anytime until the kickoff of Sunday's first game. That allows players to get late-breaking news and injury updates from the Sunday morning pregame shows and adjust their lineups accordingly.

Before choosing your lineup, consider several factors, such as injuries, opposing defenses, whether your players are playing at home or on the road, and weather. The final factor to consider is which players are hot and which ones are cold. But the most important factor is not to put a player in your starting lineup after he has had a big game. You want to put him in at the right time — check the matchups and anticipate when he is due to have a big day.

Quite often, players who are not listed on the official NFL injury list on Friday afternoon do not play in that weekend's games; thus they can't score any points for their teams. But every team is under the same disadvantage — whether it be fantasy football or real football.

Problem No. 1: One question I am often asked is whether you should play your best players against a strong defense or if you should play weaker players who are going up against easier defenses. For example, do you start Ricky Williams against the Rams, who have a strong run defense, or should you go with Warrick Dunn against the Cardinals, who have a weak run defense?

I prefer to start the better players, because the best players tend to play better against good teams. I offer no basis for this other than that it works for me. Besides, take a look at the Super Bowl. That's when the best players play against the best the NFL has to offer — and the truly great players always shine in the end.

However, my rule does not hold hard and fast. For example, I might go with Charlie Batch against the Vikings (who have a bad pass defense) rather than Jon Kitna against the Jaguars (who are strong against the pass). In other words, when dealing with the tier of players just below the stars, it might be better to go with the player facing the weaker competition.

Also, you might want to take into consideration whether or not a player is playing at home or on the road. In 1991, the Cowboys' Emmitt Smith scored 10 of his 13 touchdowns in the friendly confines of Texas Stadium and only three of them on the road. Then, in 1993, Smith had both of his three-touchdown games on the road. Detroit's Barry Sanders typically ran better at home or on other carpeted surfaces than on natural grass. Most teams perform better at home and so do their players, but it's not necessarily a sure thing. So go with your hunch and hope that it pays off.

Problem No. 2: Should you start a player who is listed as probable, questionable or doubtful on the official NFL injury report (which is released every Wednesday afternoon and updated Friday afternoon)? There's nothing more frustrating during a fantasy football season than activating a player for a game and then seeing him stand on the sidelines in street clothes — or not starting him and watching him score three touchdowns! Both of those things have happened to every fantasy football player.

Injuries are constant in the NFL; thus depth is very important for a fantasy football team. You will be playing a guessing game, however, just as NFL head coaches have to guess whether or not their opponent is going to start a player who is listed as injured.

In the NFL, teams are supposed to list players with a 75 percent chance of playing as probable, 50 percent chance of playing as questionable and 25 percent chance of playing as doubtful. But not every team follows that guideline. Some list too many players (the Broncos last year were fined for submitting inaccurate injury reports), some don't list enough players and some don't list an injured player in an attempt to throw off their opponents.

Here's a comparison of the weekly injury reports with how they usually turn out:

Category	Chances of Playing	Reality
Probable	75%	90%
Questionable	50%	60%
Doubtful	25%	10%

So, if a player is listed as probable, in all likelihood he'll play. And you should play him unless you have an equally talented, healthy reserve. If he's questionable and you have a pretty good backup, consider playing the backup. And if the player is doubtful, go with your best backup, even if he has little chance of scoring. Then sit back and watch your "benched" star score two touchdowns!

How to Get Around the Byes
in the NFL Schedule

As you know, NFL teams no longer play every week during the season. In 2000, every NFL team will again have one bye, or one week off, during the course of the season — a 16-game schedule in 17 weeks for every team. Thus you will have to work around these byes when you draft your players and make up your weekly lineups.

The byes mean that every player on your fantasy team will have one week off in which you will not be able to play him, and at least one team has a bye every week of the NFL regular season.

The byes don't present much of a problem, as was originally anticipated when they started in 1990, because fantasy leagues that provide for good depth are able to deal with them.

Still, don't ignore the byes. Don't just say, "Well, it's only one week." In most leagues, most teams will have about a .500 record, and the difference between making and not making the playoffs could be that one week in which your best players couldn't play.

The byes affect every team the same and balance out over the entire season. So, while you will have to bench Edgerrin James one game this season and play somebody like Donnell Bennett, remember that your opponents have the same predicament. It's really no worse than having one of your players injured for a week when he will have to sit out a game anyway. You just have to live with it — just as the real team's coach does when one of his players is injured and out for one game.

After all, you have about as many players on the bench as you normally play, so you still should be able to play a good player, especially if you drafted well before the season started (or made good roster moves).

Be sure to select a method of dealing with the byes before the start of your season. Here are the most commonly used options:

Option 1: When players on your team have a bye, you simply start other players, just as if the players whose teams do not play that week are injured.

The most important thing is not to draft too many players who have the same bye week (this no longer includes four of the teams in a division). Ideally, you should select your top three players (usually a quarterback, running back and wide receiver) from teams with three different bye weeks.

Option 2: Expand each team's roster. Instead of a 14-man roster, you can go to a 19-man roster, adding one player at each position — quarterback, running back, wide receiver, tight end and kicker — during the draft. The bigger roster allows for more flexibility and substitution in all weeks. But since you will find that even on a 14-man roster some players will never "play," an expanded roster is not really necessary to handle the byes. And larger rosters mean fewer players will be available for all teams to pick up during the season.

Option 3: Allow coaches to place idle players on an "Inactive List" and pick up a replacement player for one week. But chances are that you already will have a better player sitting on your bench than you can pick up (or you had better make a roster transaction right away and pick up that player for good).

Option 4: Players receive the same points during the week their teams have a bye as they will score the following week. That way your best players could play in every game. The biggest disadvantage with this carryover method is that it delays the fantasy results for a week. Also, if the player does not score the second week, the "goose egg" goes down on the scorecard twice.

Option 5: Allow teams to "rent" a player for one week at no charge in order to fill in for someone who is sitting during a bye week. Rented players must not be on any roster in your league. Limit player renting to secondary positions such as kicker, tight end and defense. This eliminates the need to use up a roster space for a backup at these positions.

What is the effect of the byes on fantasy league scoring? In my league one year, the average number of points for both teams in the seven weeks without byes was 56.5 points. During the seven weeks when four NFL teams did not play, the average score was 55.8. In fact, the three highest-scoring weeks in my league that year came during weeks with the byes (although the two lowest-scoring weeks also came on bye weeks). So the byes proved to be negligible, because the backup players were just as capable of scoring as those players who normally would have started. The next year, it was the opposite — 57.8 points per game during the non-bye weeks and only 47.9 points during the bye weeks. In other words, it has been my experience that open dates have a minimal effect over the course of a year.

TABULATING THE SCORES

Since the team with the highest score in head-to-head competition each week wins, a fun part of fantasy football is tabulating the scoring. This can be a real task, however, if your league has a complicated scoring method. The league commissioner usually has the headache of putting together the stats every week, and he needs a reliable source every Monday and Tuesday to get NFL box scores from every game.

Here's my method for tabulating the scores for a game (the sample is from the championship game from a league I'm in). We used a basic scoring method of six points for touchdowns rushing, receiving and defensive scores, three points for a touchdown pass thrown and field goals, two points for a safety or a two-point conversion, one point for extra points.

Boone's Farm	**Nutcracker**
QB — Manning: 0	QB — Favre: 33
RB — T. Allen: 6	RB — E. Smith: 6
RB — Montgomery: 0	RB — A. Smith: 0
WR — Scott: 0	WR — R. Ismail: 0
WR — Moulds: 0	WR — Robinson: 0
TE — Williams: 6	TE — Dudley: 6
K — Christie: 31111	K — Hollis: 11
D — Miami: 0	D — Denver: 0
TOTAL: 19	TOTAL: 20

Some leagues prefer to use the following designations for scores: T for touchdowns scored, P for touchdowns thrown (worth three points), F for field goals, X for extra points and S for safeties. That's simple enough, but I just write down the actual point value for each player.

What's Going On?

One of the most frustrating times for a fantasy football player is not knowing how you and your opponent are doing on Sunday afternoons. Unless your league is set up in such a way that you know what players your opponent has started, you might not even be able to tabulate his scoring.

The hardest part is trying to find out who is doing the scoring when you're watching Sunday afternoon games. You may have to wait until Monday morning when your newspaper hits your doorstep, although Fox now runs a fantasy statistics ticker across the bottom of the screen during halftime and postgame shows. The Internet offers another option for determining scores.

For most fantasy players, it's always "Who scored the Seahawks' touchdown?" Or "How'd Marshall Faulk do? Did he score two touchdowns again? Did he get 100 yards?" That's the fun — and frustration! — of fantasy football.

ESPN's excellent "Prime Time" show on Sunday evenings shows every significant scoring play and is eagerly watched by fantasy football players.

Computer Software Packages

Many services advertised in daily newspapers and other sports publications supposedly offer easy-to-use computer software packages to manage fantasy football leagues and tabulate scoring. Some of these allow leagues many different options to customize your own rules, rather than restricting you to one set of rules. Most packages are compatible with PC computers, although some work on Macintosh computers. The cost for these packages ranges from $40 to $200 or more. Look in *Pro Football Weekly*, *The Sporting News* and NFL preview magazines for these kinds of ads.

Breaking Ties

Occasionally, the score of a game between two fantasy football teams will end in a tie. Unless your league decides that ties are OK, there are two commonly used methods of breaking ties.

Option 1: Add the scores of the players on each team's reserve list (those players not activated that week). This will usually break the ties (if a tie remains, use Option 2). This is the best method, as the team's backups should determine a winner and a loser. When a winner is determined, the winning team receives the victory and the loser gets a loss in the standings. But only the points that led to the tie should be added to the cumulative points in the standings (in other words, the points scored by the backups are not added to the team's points in the standings).

Option 2: Teams can list their reserves in the order they would want them used in a tiebreaker. For example, teams would probably list their backup kicker first, and the team with the kicker that scored the most points would win. If this method is used, you might want only field goals to count for kickers, as it better reflects NFL overtimes (in which there are no extra points).

In some leagues, every game has a home team and an away team. In a tiebreaker, using this method, if the home team's first reserve scores, the home team wins the game. If he fails to score, the visiting team's first player has the opportunity to break the tie. If neither player scores, the tiebreaker goes to the next players on the reserve lists (home team, then visiting team) until the tie is broken.

This method is more luck than anything, whereas Option 1 truly awards the team with the best backups (for that week, anyway). Besides, in an average season, there won't be more than two or three ties anyway, and owners shouldn't have to spend all that time determining the order of their reserves, when they probably won't be used.

WHAT DO YOU NEED TO WIN?

In a combined scoring system (a combination of the Basic, Distance and Performance Scoring Methods) an average score of 36 points per game will usually win most games and make you your league's champion for the regular season. With a bad game in the play-offs, however, all could be for naught.

Thirty-six points is not a lot. It could break down this way:

QB — 33	WR — 6
RB — 6	TE — 0
RB — 3	K — 33111
WR — 6	Defense — 0

That's all it takes — a good game by just a few of your players. Your quarterback throws two touchdown passes; one running back scores a touchdown while the other has a 100-yard game; both of your wide receivers score a touchdown; your kicker hits two field goals and three extra points (not much at all); and your tight end and defense don't get any scores. That's it.

Some weeks, most of your players will be hot, and you will score upward of 50 or 60 points. Some other weeks, you might score only in the teens — and still win. It's also very possible that you can score a lot of points but your opponent's players will be even hotter and score more points — and thus beat you in a 59–56 shootout.

VARIATIONS

Every league has its own special rules that make it different from the others. Here are some of the most common variations for fantasy football.

Drafting a Defense

Remember, pro football isn't just offense. The most common variation is to draft a team defense to be used as an eighth player. Unlike the skill-position players, a fantasy team drafts an entire NFL team's defense. When any member of the team's defense scores a TD, whether on an interception, a fumble recovery or a blocked kick, six points are awarded to the fantasy team. And when a defense scores a safety, two points are awarded.

Other possible scoring methods include rewarding defenses for holding opposing offenses under 300 total yards, under 100 yards rushing or under 200 yards passing. Different point totals are assigned to each category. See Chapter 8 on Defenses.

Drafting Individual Defensive Players

Some leagues, those with the most complicated rules and scoring methods, actually draft an entire defense — three linemen, four linebackers, two cornerbacks and two safeties. Points are awarded for tackles, assists, sacks and interceptions.

An option here is to subtract defensive points from your opponent's score rather than adding the defensive points to your team's score.

Remember, though, this method gets very complicated — and very few newspapers list statistics for tackles and assists. And, since statistics for tackles are unofficial anyway, they are not really an accurate measure of players' abilities. For example, the leading tacklers for the Raiders, Buccaneers and Ravens usually have close to 200 tackles a season, while teams like the 49ers, Colts and Jaguars, which decide tackles much more conservatively, have a leading tackler with only about 100 tackles every year.

Drafting a Special Team

Another fantasy variation is to draft kick returners or a team's entire special-teams unit (punt and kickoff returners). Six points are awarded whenever a player returns a kickoff or a punt for a touchdown or scores off a fake punt or a fake field goal. (In some leagues, when you draft a team, you get all of its scores, whether scored by its defense or its special teams.)

Drafting a Coach

Each team can draft an NFL coach as an extra player and be awarded three points every time his team wins a game in the NFL.

Re-Drafting for Playoffs

OK, so the regular season is over and you haven't had enough. Fantasy football is in your blood and you want more. So go ahead and do it all over again during the NFL playoffs.

In the week immediately following the end of the regular season, hold a draft just as you did before the start of the season. Some leagues hold their draft the week between the four wild-card games and the first round of the divisional playoffs, because the wild-card teams will all play an extra game if they advance to the Super Bowl. I don't particu-

play an extra game if they advance to the Super Bowl. I don't particularly buy this reasoning; drafting players from a wild-card team is taking a chance, since it's unlikely that one of those teams makes it to the Super Bowl. Most are out of the playoffs after another week.

By the end of the regular season, every fantasy owner should have a good feel for what players are scoring well, but the most important aspect is knowing which teams will go the furthest in the playoffs, because players can produce points only as long as their teams advance in the playoffs. That's why shrewd drafting is essential. Drafting a kicker from a team that goes far in the playoffs is especially important, because a kicker is the surest bet to score points every week. Al Del Greco literally carried fantasy playoff teams last winter, because he scored points in four games.

Unlike the regular season in fantasy football, a fantasy league held during the NFL playoffs does not feature head-to-head competition. Rather, the champion is determined by the team that scores the most points overall through the Super Bowl.

Some leagues hold their fantasy league playoffs this way but allow teams to "protect" one or two players from their rosters before beginning a new draft. Other leagues allow players to be drafted by more than one team. Scoring is the same as the method used during the fantasy season, unless you want to make alterations.

Keeper Leagues

In rotisserie baseball, owners retain the rights to players on their fantasy teams from the previous year. You can do that in fantasy football, too, by allowing each team to keep a specified number of players from the previous season's roster.

The best part about keeper leagues is that they are more like the NFL, where teams basically stay the same except for some changes (even teams with a new head coach don't turn over half of the previous year's roster). Keeper leagues provide a sense of continuity from year to year. They allow fantasy owners to form a team identity, and they probably foster more trades throughout the season.

But remember, if you have a keeper league, you are eliminating the single most exciting part of fantasy football — the draft — because every team no longer has the opportunity to draft players like Peyton Manning, Marshall Faulk and Randy Moss; they will already be on another owner's team. In effect, you are eliminating the first two or three rounds of your draft, because the top players won't be available.

SOURCES

There are several good sources for fantasy football league players to get in-depth game scores and summaries, weekly statistics, depth charts, rosters and injury updates. Here are the best:

Game Summaries and Box Scores

Good sources for game statistics are daily newspapers, with *USA Today* being the best. Also check out the top web sites: nfl.com, espn.com, cbssportsline.com and cnnsi.com.

Statistics

Most metropolitan daily newspapers print individual statistics by conference, usually in the Thursday sports sections. *USA Today* runs stats by conference for each team on Wednesday and Thursday (one conference each day). *Pro Football Weekly* runs the longest lists of individual statistics, as well as the most complete team statistics and rankings. And the NFL's official web site, nfl.com, is loaded with stats.

Depth Charts

Pro Football Weekly and *Fantasy Football Weekly* are the only national publications that list complete depth charts weekly. Their depth charts come from each NFL team's news releases and are updated weekly.

Rosters

The best place to find rosters for use in the draft is any one of the reputable NFL preview magazines on the newsstands (the best being *Pro Football Weekly's Preview 2000*, *Street and Smith's* and *The Sporting News*) and on the Internet.

Injury Updates

Most daily newspapers list the official weekly NFL injury report in the agate section of Thursday's sports section. Remember that the "official" NFL injury report is not 100 percent accurate. Check your Saturday and Sunday newspapers, as well as the NFL pregame shows, for last-minute updates.

NFL News

You will also need to know the latest news about what's going on around the NFL — what lineup changes are about to occur, who's playing well and when a player is about to come off the injured reserve list. The best sources for NFL news are *USA Today, The Sporting News* and *Pro Football Weekly* and on the Internet.

Television

Six years ago, Rick Korch, the original author of this book (who now works for the Jacksonville Jaguars), co-hosted the first nationwide television show ever on fantasy football. The show, now called "NFL Players Fantasy Football," is seen in millions of homes on Fox Sports Net and other regional sports networks. The show is now in its seventh year with host Brady Tinker and former NFL stars Tony Dorsett and Bob Golic. Check your TV guide for this year's schedule.

A second television show, "Fantasy Football Weekly," featuring Paul Charchian, the publisher of *Fantasy Football Weekly* magazine, started in 1999 and will have even wider distribution in 2000, including 10 of the top 20 markets and 40 cities overall. It's a good one, too, with some sound analysis.

Radio

The folks at *Fantasy Football Weekly* magazine also started their own radio show, called "Fantasy Sports Weekly," which will be aired on the Westwood One/CBS Radio Network usually from 9:00-11:00 a.m. Saturdays. Again, check in your market to see if and when it is aired.

Chapter 2

PLAYER EVALUATIONS

The player evaluations in this book are intended as a guide to help you draft and put together your fantasy team before and during the season. But go ahead and make your own decisions. It's your team and you should have the biggest say-so in the makeup of it.

In writing the player evaluations, I have taken into consideration such factors as player performance over an entire career (not just last year's statistics), injury status, holdouts, the improvement and decline of players, age, changes in teams' game plans (and the players' roles in them), supporting cast, the movements of free agents and the 2000 drafts of every team.

But, since this book went to press in late spring, you will need to consider other factors, such as injuries suffered during training camp, depth chart changes and in-season coaching changes (for making roster transactions). However, the most significant changes that occur after press time are the many players who are released by their teams after June 1 so that their prorated signing bonuses don't all count under this year's salary cap (50 percent of the remaining prorated bonus counts against the 2001 cap). A number of players will still change teams before the start of the season, and a few could have a big impact on fantasy football.

Players are ranked at each position with their evaluations, and there is also a separate chapter with the rankings (as well as a checklist) of all the top players at each position. Also in that chapter, I rank the top players regardless of position. This is the list I will use going into my fantasy football draft (updating it, of course, with what happens during the preseason).

Since each fantasy football league differs in size and makes its own rules, it is difficult to make exact evaluations and suggestions. For example, a starting player in a 12-team league might be a backup in an eight-team league. So this book will mainly focus on average leagues — those with 8–10 teams that draft two quarterbacks, four running backs, four wide receivers, two tight ends and two kickers (and start one quarterback, two running backs, two wide receivers, one tight end and one kicker).

Tips for Choosing Players for Your Draft
Here are some general tips for any scoring method:
■ Don't draft only big-name players.

■ Remember that other players draft foolishly when a panic occurs. Just because everybody else is drafting kickers or quarterbacks, that doesn't mean you have to follow the trend. Be like an NFL coach — don't stray from your game plan.

■ Be careful when considering injury-prone players. If one of your top draft picks misses a large portion of the season, your team will suffer.

■ Know the status of players going into the season — who's injured and who's holding out. This is very important, because you don't want to draft a player who can't play.

Here's an example of your drafting strategy for the Basic Scoring System:

■ Round 1 — Draft the player who will score the most touchdowns. Remember, in most leagues quarterbacks are awarded only three points for each touchdown pass thrown, and since quite a few of them can throw 20 touchdowns in a season, a running back or wide receiver who scores more than 10 to 15 touchdowns is very valuable — and very rare. (Suggested pick: Edgerrin James, Fred Taylor, Marvin Harrison, Randy Moss, Marshall Faulk, Terrell Davis, Emmitt Smith, Antonio Freeman, Eddie George or Cris Carter.) Kurt Warner, Peyton Manning and Brett Favre are the only quarterbacks who should go high in your draft, either in the first round or early Round 2.

■ Round 2 — Again, try to draft a running back or wide receiver who can score 10 or more touchdowns in a season. Don't panic and take a quarterback yet unless you can get one of the three mentioned above. (Suggested pick: Isaac Bruce, Dorsey Levens, Joey Galloway, Jamal Anderson, Curtis Martin, Jimmy Smith, Eric Moulds or Marcus Robinson.)

■ Round 3 — This is when you draft the best three-point player, a quarterback, or the best six-point player that is still available. It's also a good round to consider taking tight end Tony Gonzalez.

■ Rounds 4–5 — If you already have a quarterback, running back and wide receiver, take another running back, because there is little depth in the NFL at that position (there are a lot of good ones but only a few great ones). But consider drafting another high-scoring wide receiver or a tight end such as Wesley Walls, Rickey Dudley or Shannon Sharpe.

■ Rounds 6–8 — You will want to have all seven of your starting positions filled by the end of the eighth round (with the possible exception of kicker, which you can adequately fill in rounds nine or 10), which allows you to draft one strong backup player (who will still play

PLAYER EVALUATIONS

a lot if a starter is playing badly). You might want to take your backup quarterback here, but not too early, because you might use him only once or twice all season. Also try to get one of the top tight ends.

■ Rounds 9–12 — Draft your backups, but try to get players who can step into your lineup if a starter is injured or playing poorly. Take the best available players, keeping in mind that you don't want to take too many players who have the same bye week. Draft seriously in the late rounds, because these players often are the determining factor between winning and losing. Also consider taking a rookie as your fourth running back or wide receiver in these rounds, because he may develop into an integral player on your team by the end of the season. Draft a defense in one of the final two rounds. The last round is also when you will want to gamble on a pick.

Rounds 6–10 are the most important of your draft. They are the ones that separate the contenders from the pretenders. Since most people will draft approximately the same in the early rounds, this is where you will pick up the players who will mean the difference between winning and losing. Pick some up-and-coming stars here, and if they come through, so will your team.

Basic Scoring System — This scoring system is the hardest to draft for, because luck more than skill determines how well your team will do.

■ Draft players solely on ability to score points.

■ Draft high-scoring running backs and wide receivers first.

■ Do not draft quarterbacks first (with the possible exception of Kurt Warner, Peyton Manning and Brett Favre).

■ Unless you have a chance for Tony Gonzalez, Wesley Walls, Rickey Dudley or Shannon Sharpe, don't draft a tight end until the middle or late rounds of the draft.

Performance Scoring System — This is the easiest scoring method to draft for, because it eliminates the luck factor more than the other methods do — players are awarded points based purely on yards gained.

■ Draft players strictly on their potential for gaining yards.

■ Since quarterbacks pass for 300 yards more often than running backs or wide receivers accumulate 150 yards, go for a quarterback first.

■ Draft running backs and wide receivers in Rounds 2–5. Remember to take into consideration a running back's ability to gain yards receiving.

■ Draft your second quarterback no later than the end of Round 8 (and earlier if there's a good one on the board).

■ Draft tight ends who gain yards rather than those who catch short touchdown passes at the goal line.

■ Fill all of your starting positions by the end of Round 8.

Distance Scoring System — This method is a combination of the two above, since players are awarded points for scoring plays and the length of them. In other words, the longer the touchdown (or field goal), the more points awarded.

■ Focus on players who have big-play, long-distance abilities.

■ In the first round, draft either a running back or one of the top wide receivers. You want players who score from a long way out, rather than those players who see the ball mainly near the goal line (such as Mario Bates and Leroy Hoard).

■ In the second round, take your first wide receiver or one of the very top quarterbacks.

■ Wait until the third round before drafting a quarterback, and try to get one who throws to big-play receivers.

■ In the fourth round, draft the best available running back or receiver or one of the top three tight ends.

■ Go for a kicker in Round 5, one who has a strong leg and plays for a team that will give him a lot of opportunities for field goals.

■ Fill all of your starting positions by the end of Round 8.

Combined Scoring System — This method — which is the most used — combines many of the features of the above three systems, rewarding players who can score, score from long distances and pick up a lot of yardage.

■ In the first round, draft either a running back, a wide receiver or one of the top three quarterbacks.

■ In the second round, draft whichever of the two positions you didn't get in the first round or one of the top three quarterbacks.

■ By the third round, you should have a quarterback, running back and wide receiver.

■ Try to draft one of the top four tight ends by the end of the fifth round, and have your second running back and wide receiver by the end of the sixth round.

■ Don't draft a kicker too quickly, as there are at least a dozen every year who score 100 points. You will be better off stockpiling running backs and wide receivers.

Chapter 3

QUARTERBACKS

KURT WARNER

It's a rather unsettling feeling realizing that the next MVP quarterback could be a second-string NFL unknown who played Arena League football just a few years ago. But, from now on, Kurt Warner's dream season will make fantasy players look a little more closely at the depth charts before making their late-round picks. With so little certainty at the position, those late-round picks often become your every-week starters.

From year to year, only a small handful of the same quarterbacks produce big numbers. The others who rank among the league leaders are late bloomers, unearthed sleepers or recycled goods. Predicting

QUARTERBACKS   57

which of these projects will blossom into 25-touchdown passers requires imagination and insight ... and a little luck.

An innovative offensive coordinator can develop a bust into a Pro Bowler, so consider drafting a high risk/high reward quarterback from one of these teams. Brian Billick has a proven reputation for getting the most out of quarterbacks, and he appears to be tapping the potential of Tony Banks. Other teams with young quarterbacks who could blossom this season include Minnesota, Chicago, Philadelphia and Tampa Bay. Several veterans who struggled last season have new coordinators and could come back strong in 2000. They include Brett Favre, Drew Bledsoe and Kerry Collins. A change of scenery might do wonders for talented Jeff Blake. If he stays healthy, Rob Johnson will make Bills fans quickly forget about Doug Flutie. As for Ryan Leaf and Kordell Stewart, just remember that 95 percent of the game is mental, and maybe one of these days they'll get it. Following last year's disaster, there's only one way for Jake Plummer to go, but the Cardinals' shaky offensive line could get him killed.

Among last year's injured quarterbacks, Vinny Testaverde is completely recovered from his Achilles heel injury and is a much safer pick than Steve Young, who might be one hit away from retirement (if he returns at all).

Warner and Steve Beuerlein are unlikely to match last year's phenomenal numbers, but they're not one-year wonders, either. They should rank with Peyton Manning, Favre, Brad Johnson, Rich Gannon, and possibly Jon Kitna among the league leaders in touchdown passes.

Draft Tips for Choosing a Quarterback

■ Look at past performances, especially for the last two or three seasons.

■ Look for quarterbacks who play for passing teams. They'll throw the most touchdown passes (especially near the goal line). The key is to get a quarterback who will throw 20 or more touchdown passes a season. And he doesn't necessarily have to play for a winning team; quarterbacks often throw touchdown passes with their struggling team hopelessly behind in the second half.

■ Consider a quarterback's running abilities. With zone blitzes popular and speed rushers prevalent, quarterbacks are getting chased out of the pocket more than ever. Steve McNair is unsurpassed in his running ability. Other mobile quarterbacks include Donovan McNabb, Plummer, Blake, Gannon, Damon Huard and Stewart. Since a rushing TD is worth six points in the Basic Scoring System, players such as

McNair (eight rushing TDs in 1999) are very valuable. Rushing yards are also very important in the Performance Scoring System.

■ Do not draft a quarterback from a team in which the situation is unsettled. Be sure that the first one you draft is going to start (and is healthy, too). If you are going to gamble, do it with your second quarterback.

■ If your league uses a scoring method that rewards yardage or distance, try to get a quarterback who has a big-play receiver on his team, such as Manning with Marvin Harrison, Favre with Antonio Freeman, Beuerlein with Muhsin Muhammad and Patrick Jeffers, Gannon with Tim Brown, and Johnson with Eric Moulds.

■ Don't worry about drafting a quarterback from a losing team (if he's a good one). If his team lacks a running game, chances are he will throw a good percentage of touchdown passes, and that's what counts.

■ Make sure you have a quality backup who can take over if your starting quarterback is injured (or when your starter is out with a bye).

■ Forget about this year's rookie quarterbacks, because none of them is likely to start more than a few games this season.

■ Keep an eye on training camp developments so that you can sort out preseason battles. Are the Vikings certain that Daunte Culpepper is ready to start this year after not having played at all in '99? Is Cade McNown ready to take the reins of the pass-happy offense in Chicago, or might Jim Miller be the opening-day starter? Are second-year players Tim Couch, Shaun King, Akili Smith and Donovan McNabb ready to emerge? Is Miami's Damon Huard good enough to start in the NFL? The Broncos don't appear to be sold on Brian Griese, at least in the short term, so will Gus Frerotte compete for the starting job? Will Baltimore's Tony Banks pick up where he left off, or will he revert to the careless play of his first three seasons? How long will the Steelers go with Kordell Stewart before turning to Kent Graham? Will San Diego's Ryan Leaf ever mature, or is he one of the all-time busts? Will Brett Favre, Drew Bledsoe and Jake Plummer recover from disappointing 1999 seasons? Who will be the starter in San Francisco?

1   KURT WARNER / RAMS

YEAR	ATT.	COMP.	YARDS	TDS	300+	TD-R	GP/GS
1998	11	4	39	0	0	0	1/0
1999	499	325	4353	41	9	1	16/16

Comments: Warner is the NFL's ultimate rags-to-riches poster boy. He surprised everyone except himself in 1999 with a performance that earned him league and Super Bowl MVP honors. Thrust into a starting role when Trent Green blew out his knee late in the preseason, Warner directed the third-highest-scoring offense in NFL history. He threw more touchdown passes (14) for more yards (1,217) in his first four starts than anyone in NFL history. With uncanny accuracy, poise and skill in reading defenses, Warner led the league in touchdown passes (41), completions (325), completion percentage (65.1) and passer rating (109.2). He became the second player in NFL history to throw 40 or more touchdown passes. Warner set team records in virtually every passing category. Finally, his nine 300-yard passing games tied the NFL single-season record.

The skinny: Think Warner is a flash-in-the-pan? Think again ... he'll rank among the league leaders in 2000.

2 PEYTON MANNING / COLTS

YEAR	ATT.	COMP.	YARDS	TDS	300+	TD-R	GP/GS
1998	575	326	3739	26	4	0	16/16
1999	533	331	4135	26	2	2	16/16

Comments: So much for the sophomore jinx. After two great seasons in which he hasn't missed a game, Manning already ranks with Brett Favre as perhaps the two most reliable and durable quarterbacks. Following his rookie season, it's no surprise that in 1999 Manning led the AFC in passer rating and touchdown passes. He didn't have a bad game all season, and in nine games, Manning completed at least one pass that covered more than 40 yards. In 1998, he provided everything the Colts could have hoped for and more from the No. 1 pick in the draft. After a slow start, he showed steady improvement and ranked second in the AFC with 26 TD passes. Manning led the league with 28 interceptions, but he was the only quarterback to take every snap in 1998. He set league rookie passing records in virtually every category. Manning has thrown at least one touchdown pass in 29 of his 32 games.

The skinny: Manning will rank among the league passing leaders for many more years to come.

3   BRETT FAVRE / PACKERS

YEAR	ATT.	COMP.	YARDS	TDS	300+	TD-R	GP/GS
1995	570	359	4413	38	7	3	16/16
1996	543	325	3899	39	2	2	16/16
1997	513	304	3867	35	2	1	16/16
1998	551	347	4212	31	4	1	16/16
1999	585	341	4091	22	6	0	16/16

Comments: In 1999, Favre turned the clock back six years to the mistake-prone early days of his career, when he tried to force plays that weren't there. A severely sprained thumb in his throwing hand, combined with a bad habit of trying to win games by himself, led to an alarming 23 interceptions and just 22 touchdown passes. In 1998, Favre threw 31 touchdown passes, ran for another and led the NFL with 4,212 passing yards. From 1995 to '97, he threw 112 touchdowns for 12,179 passing yards en route to an unprecedented three consecutive MVP Awards. He holds every Packers passing record and is the only player in NFL history to throw 30 or more TD passes in five seasons. Favre is deadly in the red zone, where he threw 24 touchdowns and no interceptions in 1997. His 39 scoring passes in 1996 were the third most in NFL history. He now has eight consecutive seasons with 3,000 passing yards, three seasons with 4,000 passing yards, and an NFL quarterback record of 125 consecutive starts.

The skinny: Favre is still the most durable player in fantasy football, and he'll bounce back strong with more Favre-like numbers.

4   STEVE McNAIR / TITANS

YEAR	ATT.	COMP.	YARDS	TDS	300+	TD-R	GP/GS
1995	80	41	569	3	0	0	6/2
1996	143	88	1197	6	1	2	9/4
1997	415	216	2665	14	0	8	16/16
1998	492	289	3228	15	0	4	16/16
1999	331	187	2179	12	1	8	11/11

Comments: McNair throws a low-risk pass and he's a high-risk runner to defend. In 1999, despite only 11 starts because of injuries and the fact that he failed to throw a touchdown pass for six straight games, McNair's eight touchdown runs made him a productive fantasy starter. His season high was five TD passes vs. Jacksonville. In 1998, McNair improved all of his numbers but completed just two passes of 40 yards or longer. He became the franchise's fourth player ever to pass for 3,000 yards in a season, and he led NFL quarterbacks with 559 rushing yards, including a spectacular 71-yard bootleg that ranks as the fourth longest in NFL history for quarterbacks. The Oilers broke in McNair gradually in his first two seasons, and he posted a 4–2 record and a 96.0 passer rating. In each of his five seasons, McNair has thrown more touchdowns than interceptions.

The skinny: McNair is a solid fantasy starter because of his wheels, not his arm.

5 BRAD JOHNSON / REDSKINS

YEAR	ATT.	COMP.	YARDS	TDS	300+	TD-R	GP/GS
1995	36	25	272	0	0	0	5/0
1996	311	195	2258	17	0	1	12/8
1997	452	275	3036	20	2	0	13/13
1998	101	65	747	7	1	0	4/2
1999	519	316	4005	24	4	2	16/16

Comments: Durability is the only concern with Johnson. He held up for the entire 1999 season, so he produced career-best numbers and made the Redskins glad they gave up first-, second- and third-round draft picks to get him. He completed a team-record 316 passes for 4,005 yards, the second most in team history. Johnson's 24 touchdown passes tied for fourth in the NFL, and his 471 passing yards in Week 15 set a single-game team record. Productive but injury prone in Minnesota in '98, Johnson fractured his fibula, lost the starting job to a red-hot Randall Cunningham, then he fractured a finger. In 1996 and '97, Johnson led the Vikings to five fourth-quarter comeback wins and threw a TD pass in 15 consecutive games. In '97, he tied for third in the NFC with 20 touchdown passes (11 in the fourth quarter, to lead the NFL), despite missing the last three games with a neck injury. He is 25–14 as a starter.

The skinny: Barring an injury, Johnson will match or exceed last year's production. But, if he falters, Jeff George will take over quickly.

6   STEVE BEUERLEIN / PANTHERS

YEAR	ATT.	COMP.	YARDS	TDS	300+	TD-R	GP/GS
1995	142	71	952	4	0	0	7/6
1996	123	69	879	8	0	0	8/4
1997	153	89	1032	6	0	0	7/3
1998	343	216	2613	17	0	0	12/12
1999	571	343	4436	36	5	2	16/16

Comments: Beuerlein's 1999 season was even more incredible considering he was sacked 50 times and played most of the season with a hernia. His 36 touchdown passes were the league's second most and tied for sixth in NFL history, and his league-high 4,436 passing yards rank 11th in NFL history. Over the final six games, Beuerlein threw 20 TD passes and just three interceptions. In 1998, Beuerlein moved into the starting lineup in Game 5 and had a career year. He ranked fifth in the NFC in touchdown percentage (5.0) and in passer rating (88.2), and his 63 percent completion rate tied for the league lead. A competent backup earlier in his career, Beuerlein stepped up and delivered in place of the injured Kerry Collins in 1996 and '97. In 1994, Beuerlein was the second-worst-ranked passer in the NFC. But, in 1993, his first full season as an NFL starter, he set career highs in every major category. He has started 28 consecutive games.

The skinny: Beuerlein's performance last season was no fluke; he's thriving at the helm of coach George Seifert's offense. Still, don't expect 36 TD passes this time around. He's not *that* good.

7   VINNY TESTAVERDE / JETS

YEAR	ATT.	COMP.	YARDS	TDS	300+	TD-R	GP/GS
1995	392	241	2883	17	2	2	13/12
1996	549	325	4177	33	5	2	16/16
1997	470	271	2971	18	3	0	13/13
1998	421	259	3256	29	1	1	14/13
1999	15	10	96	1	0	0	1/1

Comments: An entire Jets season came crashing down in the 1999 opener when Testaverde ruptured his Achilles tendon in the second quarter. He's on track for a full recovery this year. The 1986 Heisman Trophy winner once threw an NFL-record 35 interceptions in a season, but in 1998 he finally reached his potential. He replaced an injured Glenn Foley in Week 3 and set a Jets single-season mark with an AFC-high 29 TD passes. In

1997, Testaverde reverted to his mistake-prone past (15 interceptions) and played his way out of Baltimore's plans. He had an excellent year in 1996, when he ranked second in the NFL with 33 TD passes and 4,177 passing yards. In 1994, Testaverde led the Browns to their best season in years, but he threw more interceptions than TDs for the seventh time in eight seasons.

The skinny: Testaverde will rank among the AFC leaders in touchdown passes.

8 MARK BRUNELL / JAGUARS

YEAR	ATT.	COMP.	YARDS	TDS	300+	TD-R	GP/GS2
1995	346	201	2168	15	2	4	13/10
1996	557	353	4367	19	6	3	16/16
1997	435	264	3281	18	3	2	14/14
1998	354	208	2601	20	2	0	13/13
1999	441	259	3060	14	3	1	15/15

Comments: A three-time Pro Bowler, Brunell has certainly lived up to Jacksonville's expectations, but he's never quite lived up to fantasy football expectations. He runs less for the sake of self-preservation, and the Jaguars run more and rely less on Brunell's arm. Last season, Brunell had the AFC's fourth-highest passer rating, but nine AFC quarterbacks threw more touchdown passes. Brunell posted good numbers in 1998 — he tied for fifth in the AFC with 20 touchdown passes despite missing nearly four games due to an ankle injury. Heading into the 1997 season, fantasy players drooled over Brunell, but injured knee ligaments limited his production. From 1995 to '97, Brunell scored on nine touchdown runs. In a spectacular 1996 season, he produced 4,763 combined rushing and passing yards, the fifth most in league history.

The skinny: Brunell is a top-level quarterback in the NFL, but he's just a marginal starter in fantasy football.

9 DREW BLEDSOE / PATRIOTS

YEAR	ATT.	COMP.	YARDS	TDS	300+	TD-R	GP/GS
1995	636	323	3507	13	2	0	15/15
1996	623	373	4086	27	4	0	16/16
1997	522	314	3706	28	3	0	16/16
1998	481	263	3633	20	4	0	14/14
1999	539	305	3985	19	4	0	16/16

Comments: Defenses kept a fierce pass rush on Bledsoe in 1999, and he cracked along with the rest of the Patriots. He did get off to a great start, with 13 touchdown passes and four interceptions in the first eight games. But, over the final eight games, he threw only six touchdown passes and 17 interceptions. It was a huge step back from Bledsoe's previous three seasons. In 1998, he completed 15 passes of 40 yards or more and tied for fifth in the AFC with 20 touchdown passes. He cemented his standing in the upper echelon of fantasy quarterbacks with a 28-touchdown-pass season in 1997. Bledsoe came of age in 1996, when he threw 27 TD passes and led the league in pass attempts (623) and completions (373). No quarterback ever threw as many passes as Bledsoe did in 1994 (691 attempts). He has 25 career 300-yard passing games, he owns the team's top six single-season passing yardage totals, and he has missed just six games in seven seasons.

The skinny: If the line and running game improve, as expected, Bledsoe will return to form this season.

10 JON KITNA / SEAHAWKS

YEAR	ATT.	COMP.	YARDS	TDS	300+	TD-R	GP/GS
1997	45	31	371	1	0	0	3/1
1998	172	98	1177	7	0	1	6/5
1999	495	270	3346	23	0	0	15/15

Comments: Kitna found a comfort zone and starred for nine games in 1999. Then he began making mistakes when opponents blitzed extensively. The result was an up-and-down season that offered much promise but didn't cement Kitna's status as Mike Holmgren's long-term solution. He threw the AFC's third-most touchdown passes (23), but he also tied for the third-most interceptions (16). Kitna has good size, a strong arm and playmaking potential. While watching his nephew play at Central Washington, former Seattle coach Dennis Erickson discovered Kitna. He spent the 1996 season on the Seattle practice squad, led Barcelona to the 1997 World League title and started the final five games with Seattle in '98. Kitna has five fourth-quarter comebacks and a 12–9 record as a starter.

The skinny: While the jury's still out, Kitna appears headed for stardom and a big 2000 season.

11 RICH GANNON / RAIDERS

YEAR	ATT.	COMP.	YARDS	TDS	300+	TD-R	GP/GS
1995	11	7	57	0	0	0	2/0
1996	90	54	491	6	0	0	4/3
1997	175	98	1144	7	1	2	9/6
1998	354	206	2305	10	1	3	12/10
1999	515	304	3840	24	2	2	16/16

Comments: All Gannon ever really needed was a chance. In 1999, his 12th NFL season, he excelled in his first full year as a starter. His mobility and accuracy are a perfect fit for the Raiders' West Coast offense. Gannon completed just one 50-yard-plus pass, and it was on a screen play. But he had the AFC's second-best passer rating, and his 24 touchdown passes tied for fourth in the NFL and were a career high. He rushed for 298 yards (fifth most among quarterbacks) and two touchdowns. With the Chiefs in 1998, he rushed for 168 yards and three TDs in 12 games (10 starts). In 1997, Gannon replaced an injured Elvis Grbac and won five of six starts. He signed with Kansas City after being out of football all of 1994. Gannon has amassed 14,998 career passing yards and more than 1,500 rushing yards.

The skinny: Gannon should be able to prove that his 1999 production was no fluke.

12 ROB JOHNSON / BILLS

YEAR	ATT.	COMP.	YARDS	TDS	300+	TD-R	GP/GS
1995	7	3	24	0	0	0	1/0
1996	0	0	0	0	0	0	2/0
1997	28	22	344	2	0	1	5/1
1998	107	67	910	8	0	1	8/6
1999	34	25	298	2	0	0	2/1

Comments: The job is now Johnson's to lose, and he has played well every time he has had an opportunity. Strong-armed and mobile, he has thrown 10 touchdown passes and just three interceptions in seven starts with the Bills. In 1999, Johnson replaced Doug Flutie for the final regular-season game, and in the playoffs he led the Bills on a potential game-winning drive before being beaten on the Music City Miracle. Seldom does a quarterback who plays as well as Johnson did in 1998 lose his job during an injury. But Doug Flutie found the magic while the Johnson-led Bills were 3–3 (Flutie was 7–3 as a starter). The Bills traded first- and fourth-

QUARTERBACKS

round draft picks for Johnson, who made a fortune because of one excellent start for Jacksonville in 1997, when he completed 20 of 24 passes.

The skinny: Johnson should make the most of his second chance to lead the Bills' offense.

13 TROY AIKMAN / COWBOYS

YEAR	ATT.	COMP.	YARDS	TDS	300+	TD-R	GP/GS
1995	432	280	3304	16	2	1	16/16
1996	465	296	3126	12	1	1	15/15
1997	518	292	3283	19	2	0	16/16
1998	315	187	2330	12	1	2	11/11
1999	442	263	2964	17	1	1	14/14

Comments: Aikman performed well in 1999, considering the way he was inhibited by an injury-depleted receiving corps and a conservative passing game. He always ranks among the league leaders in the passing categories that help the Cowboys but don't help fantasy players. In 1998, he had the NFC's fourth-highest passer rating but just 12 TD passes in 11 games. His touchdown production increased in 1997 because the Dallas running game ground to a halt. Aikman set a career high with 518 pass attempts, and he threw his most touchdown passes since his career-high total of 23 in 1992. Aikman is the most accurate postseason quarterback in NFL history, but he needed eight NFL seasons to surpass 100 career touchdown passes. He ranks third in NFL career completion percentage (61.58), and ninth with a career passer rating of 82.68.

The skinny: Aikman has thrown 20 touchdown passes just once in his career, which means he's a fantasy backup and nothing more.

14 ELVIS GRBAC / CHIEFS

YEAR	ATT.	COMP.	YARDS	TDS	300+	TD-R	GP/GS
1995	183	127	1469	8	3	2	16/5
1996	197	122	1236	8	0	2	15/4
1997	314	179	1943	11	1	1	10/10
1998	188	98	1142	5	0	0	8/6
1999	499	294	3389	22	1	0	16/16

Comments: Grbac made huge strides in 1999. In a ball-control offense, he threw 22 touchdown passes, the fourth most in the AFC. For the first time in his three years as a starter, Grbac remained healthy. Four of his touchdown passes covered 70 or more yards. He easily shattered his own single-season records and piled up the third-most passing yards (3,389) in franchise history. Grbac's horrendous 1998 season mirrored the collapse of the Chiefs. He missed four games after suffering a shoulder injury, and his passer rating of 53.1 was among the league's worst. In 1997, Grbac provided the Chiefs with the steady, low-risk play they had sought from one of the most sought-after free agents. With San Francisco in 1995, Grbac replaced an injured Steve Young and completed 127 of 183 attempts for 1,469 yards, eight touchdowns and three interceptions.

The skinny: Grbac will be hard-pressed to repeat last year's numbers, but he's a borderline fantasy starter and a great backup.

15 CHRIS CHANDLER / FALCONS

YEAR	ATT.	COMP.	YARDS	TDS	300+	TD-R	GP/GS
1995	356	225	2460	17	1	2	13/13
1996	320	184	2099	16	0	0	12/12
1997	342	202	2692	20	0	0	14/14
1998	327	190	3154	25	1	2	14/14
1999	307	174	2339	16	2	1	12/12

Comments: Chandler is still like fine china — quality that's fragile. When he stays healthy, the passing game clicks and the Falcons usually win. But last season Chandler missed four games and left four others early due to injuries. His touchdown percentage was the NFC's fourth best, and he ranked 11th in the NFL with an 83.5 passer rating. Injury-prone throughout his career, Chandler remained healthy throughout most of the 1997 and '98 seasons. In 1998, he ranked sixth in the NFL with 25 touchdown passes, and he ran up a streak of 27 consecutive regular-season games with at least one scoring pass in 1998 and '99. Tired of a nomadic NFL career that included six teams in 10 seasons, Chandler signed with Atlanta in '97 after two fine but injury-plagued seasons in Houston, where he threw 33 touchdown passes.

The skinny: Chandler is good enough to be a fantasy backup but too injury-prone to be a solid fantasy starter.

16 JAKE PLUMMER / CARDINALS

YEAR	ATT.	COMP.	YARDS	TDS	300+	TD-R	GP/GS
1997	296	157	2203	15	2	2	10/9
1998	547	324	3737	17	2	4	16/16
1999	381	201	2111	9	1	2	12/11

Comments: It's hard to fathom a worse 1999 season for Plummer. A sprained thumb slowed his preseason, and a fractured finger on his throwing hand almost eliminated his practice time and sidelined him for four regular-season games. Plummer finished with the league's worst passer rating (50.8), and his 24 interceptions led the league. In Plummer's defense, the Arizona offensive line was in a state of flux and the ground game was practically nonexistent. In just 38 NFL games, he has led the Cardinals to 11 fourth-quarter comeback wins, and he has eight touchdown runs. In 1998, Plummer threw 20 interceptions and 17 touchdown passes. He gave the Cardinals much reason for optimism with an outstanding rookie 1997 season in which he threw 15 touchdown passes in just 10 games.

The skinny: Plummer's numbers will improve when he develops patience and when the team upgrades the offensive talent around him.

17 JEFF BLAKE / SAINTS

YEAR	ATT.	COMP.	YARDS	TDS	300+	TD-R	GP/GS
1995	567	326	3822	28	1	2	16/16
1996	549	308	3624	24	2	2	16/16
1997	317	184	2125	8	1	3	11/11
1998	93	51	739	3	1	0	9/2
1999	389	215	2670	16	1	2	14/12

Comments: The Saints gave Blake his badly needed new lease on life with a free-agent contract. He played fairly well throughout six seasons in Cincinnati, though he took much of the blame for the team's dismal records. In 1999, Blake struggled early, was benched in favor of rookie Akili Smith, and then finished strong after Smith was injured. His touchdown percentage ranked eighth in the NFC and his passer rating ranked ninth. His 93-to-62 touchdown-to-interception ratio is the best in Bengals history, but he posted a 21–31 record in 52 consecutive starts between 1994 and '97. Blake lost his confidence and his starting job in 1997. His 1995 Pro Bowl season included a club-record 567 pass attempts and an AFC-high 28 TD passes. In 1994, he went from being an unknown to the NFL's biggest surprise at quarterback.

The skinny: The Saints have surrounded Blake with enough weapons that he could come back strong in 2000.

18 CHARLIE BATCH / LIONS

YEAR	ATT.	COMP.	YARDS	TDS	300+	TD-R	GP/GS
1998	303	173	2178	11	0	1	12/12
1999	270	151	1957	13	0	2	11/10

Comments: Consistency and low risk are trademarks of Batch's play. In his first two seasons, he has avoided the mistakes that normally plague young quarterbacks. He has 24 touchdown passes, just 13 interceptions and the highest passer rating (83.8) in Lions history among quarterbacks with 500 or more attempts. In 1999, a fractured thumb on his throwing hand slowed his fast start and sidelined him for five games, but he still produced 13 touchdown passes and two TD runs. In 1998, Batch took over the starting job in the third game of his pro career and lived up to the promise of a second-round draft pick. He ended the season with 136 straight passes without an interception, a streak that tied Bernie Kosar's NFL rookie record. His 229 rushing yards ranked second among NFC quarterbacks.

The skinny: An improved ground game will help Batch achieve a career year in 2000.

19 TIM COUCH / BROWNS

YEAR	ATT.	COMP.	YARDS	TDS	300+	TD-R	GP/GS
1999	399	223	2447	15	0	1	15/14

Comments: In 1999, Couch led NFL rookies in completions, attempts, yards, touchdown passes and passer rating. And he did it despite getting sacked 56 times while playing for the league's worst team, a team that had virtually no ground game support. He was prone to a rookie tendency of forcing plays when nothing was there, leading to sacks. Couch's 15 touchdown passes were the ninth most in the AFC, and his statistics compare favorably with the rookie seasons of four of the six all-time passing yardage leaders. Couch's 233 completions rank third all-time among NFL rookies. His good mobility produced 260 rushing yards, including a 40-yarder that broke a franchise record for quarterbacks.

The skinny: Couch will succeed, but on this strugging team he'll be hard-pressed to improve much on last year's production.

20 TONY BANKS / RAVENS

YEAR	ATT.	COMP.	YARDS	TDS	300+	TD-R	GP/GS
1996	368	192	2544	15	2	0	14/13
1997	487	252	3254	14	1	1	16/16
1998	408	241	2535	7	0	3	14/14
1999	320	169	2136	17	1	0	12/10

Comments: Last season, Banks proved the value of good coaching for a quarterback. The Ravens considered trading Banks early in the year, then turned to him as a last resort. Brian Billick's offense took off with Banks at the helm, and the team won six of its final nine games. Careless and mistake-prone in three seasons with the Rams, Banks led the AFC with a 5.3 touchdown percentage, and he threw 17 TD passes and just eight interceptions. He finished as the AFC's sixth-best passer. Previously in his career as a Ram, Banks regressed in 43 consecutive starts. In 14 starts in 1998, he threw just seven TD passes but 14 interceptions. In his first two seasons, he had more fumbles (36) than TD passes (29). Banks burst onto the NFL scene with a strong 1996 rookie season. His 15 TD passes matched his interception output.

The skinny: Banks is no guarantee, but he's a good fantasy back-up with a big upside.

21 KERRY COLLINS / GIANTS

YEAR	ATT.	COMP.	YARDS	TDS	300+	TD-R	GP/GS
1995	433	214	2717	14	2	3	15/13
1996	364	204	2454	14	1	0	13/12
1997	381	200	2124	11	1	1	13/13
1998	353	170	2213	12	2	1	11/11
1999	332	191	2316	8	2	2	10/7

Comments: Collins certainly injected excitement into the 1999 Giants offense — he averaged nearly 300 passing yards per game in six late-season starts, and the Giants hadn't had a 300-yard passer in six years. Collins passed for 2,316 yards and eight touchdowns in six games. However, he continued his careless play with 11 interceptions and 11 fumbles. In 1998, Collins benched himself, was shipped out of Carolina and then burned his bridges in New Orleans. Collins completed less than half of his passes for four touchdowns and 10 interceptions with the Saints. In 1996, Collins posted a 9–3 record as a starter, threw just nine interceptions and led the Panthers to the NFC championship game, but in '97 he lost his confidence and ranked last in the NFL with a 55.7 passer rating and threw 21 interceptions.

The skinny: Collins is liable to throw 20 touchdown passes and 20 interceptions this season.

22 CADE McNOWN / BEARS

YEAR	ATT.	COMP.	YARDS	TDS	300+	TD-R	GP/GS
1999	235	127	1465	8	1	0	15/6

Comments: An innovative plan broke in McNown gradually in his rookie season of 1999, then he got his chance with six mid- and late-season starts. Coach Dick Jauron inserted McNown to run one and two series of downs early in the season, and his overall performance was inconsistent but promising. He often tried to force plays that weren't there, but he connected on nine pass plays of 30 or more yards and formed a big-play chemistry with wideout budding star Marcus Robinson. The Bears' second-leading rusher with 160 yards, McNown was one of just three rookie quarterbacks in the 1990s to throw four touchdown passes in one game. He approached Jim McMahon's rookie passing records.

The skinny: Clearly the Bears' quarterback of the future, McNown will certainly play often in 2000 — even if Jim Miller were to win the starting job.

23 BRIAN GRIESE / BRONCOS

YEAR	ATT.	COMP.	YARDS	TDS	300+	TD-R	GP/GS
1998	3	1	2	0	1	0	1/0
1999	452	261	3032	14	0	2	14/13

Comments: The Broncos say Griese is their starting quarterback, but in the offseason they inquired about the availability of Steve Young and signed Gus Frerotte. In 1999, Griese was a surprise starter over Bubby Brister when the season began, and he started eight games before missing three due to an injured shoulder. In 14 games (13 starts), Griese became the eighth NFL quarterback since 1970 to pass for 3,000 yards in his first season as a starter. But his inexperience showed, and he certainly failed to generate fourth-quarter comebacks as his predecessor, John Elway, had. Griese, who produced two 300-yard passing games last season, ranked near the middle of the AFC with a 75.6 passer rating. But his 3.1 touchdown percentage was among the league's lowest.

The skinny: It's a good bet that Frerotte will replace Griese in the starting lineup at some point this season.

24 DAMON HUARD / DOLPHINS

YEAR	ATT.	COMP.	YARDS	TDS	300+	TD-R	GP/GS
1997	DNP						
1998	9	6	85	0	0	0	2/0
1999	216	125	1288	8	0	0	16/5

Comments: The front-runner for Miami's starting job in 2000, Huard actually outplayed Dan Marino last season. He replaced an injured Marino for five midseason starts and won four of them with safe passing and good mobility. Huard had thrown only nine passes in two previous seasons before being pressed into service in the second series of Game 5 at New England. He completed 24 of 42 passes for 240 yards and two touchdowns, broke a 25-yard run and led Miami to victory. Huard's eight-to-four touchdown-to-interception ratio offers promise, but he's still unproven.

The skinny: Don't expect big numbers from Huard and the Dolphins' offense in 2000.

25 SHAUN KING / BUCCANEERS

YEAR	ATT.	COMP.	YARDS	TDS	300+	TD-R	GP/GS
1999	146	89	875	7	0	0	6/5

Comments: Throw underneath, hand the ball off and minimize mistakes. King filled his role to a T when he was handed the keys to the offense for the final five games of 1999, his rookie season. King's passer rating of 82.4 was the best among the five rookie quarterbacks who played last year (though King played the least). King, who won four of his five regular-season starts and one of two playoff games, has already done well at aspects of the game that often puzzle young quarterbacks. He accurately passes to his backs and receivers in short and intermediate routes, he finds the seams of zones, and he's at his best in the fourth quarter (when his 1999 passer rating was 132.6).

The skinny: King has thrown only 146 regular-season passes, and the Bucs aren't yet convinced he's their short-term answer. But having Keyshawn Johnson as his top receiver can't hurt.

26   AKILI SMITH / BENGALS

YEAR	ATT.	COMP.	YARDS	TDS	300+	TD-R	GP/GS
1999	153	80	805	2	0	1	7/4

Comments: Smith's performance was the worst of the five highly regarded rookie quarterbacks who played in 1999. A training camp hold-out and season-ending severe toe sprain stunted his development, though he showed glimpses of his potential with a big arm and fairly good accuracy. In Week 5, Smith made his first NFL start and led the team to its first victory with two touchdown passes — one on a game-winning drive. But he finished with six interceptions, two TD passes and a bad 55.6 passer rating. Smith displayed good mobility with 114 rushing yards, a 6.0-yard average and one touchdown in seven games played.

The skinny: The jury is still out on Smith, but don't draft him, because his growing pains are bound to be severe on this losing team.

27   DONOVAN McNABB / EAGLES

YEAR	ATT.	COMP.	YARDS	TDS	300+	TD-R	GP/GS
1999	216	106	948	8	0	0	12/6

Comments: In 1999, McNabb struggled as you would expect from a rookie on a losing team that lacked offensive firepower. When the Eagles struggled through a 2–7 record, McNabb became the starter in Game 10 and won three of his seven starts. The No. 2 pick in the 1999 draft, McNabb posted a respectable 8-to-7 touchdown-to-interception ratio. His 60.1 passer rating ranked him fourth among the five rookie quarterbacks who played in 1999. McNabb has a big gun (though he seldom went deep last year) and great wheels. His 313 rushing yards led NFC quarterbacks, and his 6.7-yard average per rush was the NFL's best.

The skinny: Another year of growing pains awaits McNabb. At best, he could develop into a worthy midseason waiver pickup.

QUARTERBACKS

28   JEFF GARCIA / 49ERS

YEAR	ATT.	COMP.	YARDS	TDS	300+	TD-R	GP/GS
1999	375	225	2544	11	3	2	13/10

Comments: Garcia was the new navigator on a sinking 49ers ship last season. He replaced the injured Steve Young in Week 3, lost his starting job, regained it and showed steady improvement with a strong finish. In the final five games, Garcia completed 121 of 182 passes for eight touchdowns, just three interceptions and a passer rating of 98.3. During that span, he burned Cincinnati for 437 passing yards and logged two other 300-yard efforts. A former Canadian Football League star, Garcia spread the ball around the offense well in his 10 starts last season.

The skinny: Garcia isn't a long-term answer in place of Steve Young, but he'll be the man until rookies Giovanni Carmazzi and Tim Rattay are ready.

29   KORDELL STEWART / STEELERS

YEAR	ATT.	COMP.	YARDS	TDS	300+	TD-R	GP/GS
1995	7	5	60	1	0	1	10/2
1996	30	11	100	0	0	5	16/2
1997	440	236	3020	21	2	11	16/16
1998	458	252	2560	11	0	2	16/16
1999	275	160	1464	6	0	2	16/12

Comments: Stewart made no progress in 1999, his third season as the Steelers' starting quarterback. He threw just six touchdown passes in 11 starts, and just two of his completions covered 40 or more yards. He was moved to wide receiver for the final five games. A first-round pick in nearly every 1998 fantasy draft, Stewart was a bitter disappointment on a team with a new offense. With just 11 touchdown passes and 18 interceptions, Stewart saw his passer rating plummet to 26th in the NFL. It was a monumental fall for the player who in 1997 was the No. 1 producer in most fantasy leagues. He became the first NFL quarterback ever to throw for 20 or more touchdowns and run for at least 10. In 1996, the Steelers utilized Stewart as a runner, receiver and third-down quarterback, and he scored eight times. Stewart blossomed into an all-purpose star as a rookie in 1995.

The skinny: Stewart has one final chance to succeed at quarterback in Pittsburgh, but don't bet on it.

30 JIM HARBAUGH / CHARGERS

YEAR	ATT.	COMP.	YARDS	TDS	300+	TD-R	GP/GS
1995	314	200	2575	17	1	2	15/12
1996	405	232	2630	13	0	1	14/14
1997	309	189	2060	10	1	0	12/11
1998	293	164	1839	12	0	0	14/12
1999	434	249	2761	10	2	0	14/12

Comments: Harbaugh finished an uninspiring 1999 season on a high note. When the Chargers switched to a no-huddle offense for the final seven games, he completed 60.9 percent of his passes for five touchdowns and 241 passing yards per game. The Chargers had traded for Harbaugh to obtain veteran stability while Ryan Leaf gains experience. Harbaugh struggled through three straight injury-plagued seasons from 1996 to '98. He surprised nearly everyone with an excellent 1995 season that earned him Comeback Player of the Year honors. He led the NFL in passer rating (100.7), the second-highest such mark in team history. He is the Bears' all-time leader in passing attempts and completions.

The skinny: Harbaugh is one Ryan Leaf outburst from returning to the starting lineup, but his best days are behind him.

31 DAUNTE CULPEPPER / VIKINGS

YEAR	ATT.	COMP.	YARDS	TDS	300+	TD-R	GP/GS
1999	0	0	0	0	0	0	0/0

Comments: As a rookie first-round draft choice in 1999, Culpepper did not throw a pass, and he saw action in only one game, as he backed up Jeff George and Randall Cunningham. But 2000 is a new season, and with those two quarterbacks gone, Vikings head coach Dennis Green has handed the job to the inexperienced Culpepper. He put up very strong numbers in college at Central Florida, but usually against lesser competition. If he struggles, the Vikings won't hesitate to yank him and insert journeyman Bubby Brister.

The skinny: Culpepper is an enormous risk — both in fantasy football and for the Vikings, a perennial playoff team.

TOP BACKUPS

1b STEVE YOUNG / 49ERS

YEAR	ATT.	COMP.	YARDS	TDS	300+	TD-R	GP/GS
1995	447	299	3200	20	5	3	11/11
1996	316	214	2410	14	0	4	12/12
1997	356	241	3029	19	0	3	15/15
1998	517	322	4170	36	0	6	15/15
1999	84	45	446	3	0	0	3/3

Comments: The twilight of Young's fabulous career took a big hit in 1999, a Week 3 concussion that ended his season and raised retirement questions. When healthy, he's still one of the best fantasy players. With 36 touchdown passes and six TD runs in 1998, Young was the top fantasy player in most scoring systems. He set team single-season records for TD passes and passing yards. Young's 1997 season was phenomenal considering the season opener, when he suffered his third concussion in 10 months. He returned in Week 3 and finished with a combined 22 touchdown passes and runs and an NFL-best 104.7 passer rating. Young also took a beating in 1996, when he was sidelined by concussions, a groin injury and a chin laceration. In 1994, Young did everything in leading the 49ers to the Super Bowl title. He led the NFL with 35 TD passes, compiled an all-time-record 112.8 passer rating and scored seven TDs running. Young has 4,239 career rushing yards.

The skinny: Because of his health concerns, Young is no longer worth an early draft pick. But you never know.

2b TRENT DILFER / RAVENS

YEAR	ATT.	COMP.	YARDS	TDS	300+	TD-R	GP/GS
1995	415	224	2774	4	1	2	16/16
1996	482	267	2859	12	1	0	16/16
1997	386	217	2555	21	0	1	16/16
1998	429	225	2729	21	0	2	16/16
1999	244	146	1619	11	1	0	10/10

Comments: If anyone can successfully recycle Dilfer, it's Ravens coach Brian Billick. Dilfer, who was signed to back up Tony Banks, is better suited for Billick's vertical passing game than Tampa Bay's ultra-conservative attack. In 1999, Dilfer lost and regained his starting job, then was sidelined by a fractured clavicle. In 10 starts, he failed to generate much offense. From 1997 to '98, only three NFC quarterbacks threw more touchdown passes than Dilfer. After three ugly seasons, he had turned jeers into cheers with a surprising Pro Bowl season in 1997. His 21 touchdown passes set a Buccaneers record, and his 82.8 passer rating was the franchise's second-best mark ever. The Buccaneers' No. 1 draft pick in 1994, Dilfer had the lowest passer rating (60.1) and touchdown percentage in the NFL in his second season.

The skinny: Dilfer definitely needs a change of scenery, and he conceivably could replace Banks sometime this season.

3b JEFF GEORGE / REDSKINS

YEAR	ATT.	COMP.	YARDS	TDS	300+	TD-R	GP/GS
1995	557	336	4143	24	3	0	16/16
1996	99	56	698	3	0	0	3/3
1997	521	290	3917	29	2	0	16/16
1998	169	93	1186	4	1	0	8/7
1999	329	191	2816	23	2	0	12/10

Comments: After signing as a free agent, George will back up Brad Johnson in Washington, but don't be surprised if he takes over as the starter at some point. With Minnesota in 1999, George helped salvage a sinking ship when he replaced Randall Cunningham after six games and led the Vikings into the playoffs. A good fit for a wide-open, deep passing game, George threw the NFC's fourth-most touchdown passes (23) in just 11 games. A season earlier, the Raiders voided his five-year contract after two seasons because he struggled early, was sidelined by a Week 5 groin injury and pronounced himself unable to play late in the season. His terrific 1997 production was overshadowed by a Raiders season of underachievement. He led the NFL in passing yards and ranked second with 29 touchdown passes. With Atlanta in 1996, George started three games, then had a much-publicized argument with then-coach June Jones and didn't play again. In 1995, George became the first Falcon to pass for 4,000 yards.

The skinny: George's chances are pretty good to play — and play well — but he'd be only an in-season fantasy pickup, which is where his value lies.

4b GUS FREROTTE / BRONCOS

YEAR	ATT.	COMP.	YARDS	TDS	300+	TD-R	GP/GS
1995	396	199	2751	13	1	1	16/11
1996	470	270	3453	12	1	0	16/16
1997	402	204	2682	17	0	2	13/13
1998	54	25	283	1	0	0	3/2
1999	288	175	2117	9	2	0	9/6

Comments: The Broncos signed Frerotte in the offseason to push starter Brian Griese and immediately step in should Griese struggle. Last season, Frerotte backed up Charlie Batch in Detroit and played well in six games when Batch was injured. He engineered two game-winning drives in relief of Batch, and posted season statistics (his passer rating was the NFC's sixth best) that were far better than his career numbers. In 1998, Frerotte was injured in the season opener, then he lost his starting job to Trent Green and played poorly in his only three appearances. The Redskins were disappointed in Frerotte's play in 1997, but fantasy owners got as much as or more than expected — 17 touchdown passes and two TD runs.

The skinny: Frerotte is a capable backup and occasional fill-in, but he's of little value as a fantasy player unless he were to win the starting job in training camp.

5b JAY FIEDLER / DOLPHINS

YEAR	ATT.	COMP.	YARDS	TDS	300+	TD-R	GP/GS
1995	0	0	0	0	0	0	1/0
1996	DNP						
1997	DNP						
1998	7	3	41	0	0	0	5/0
1999	94	61	656	2	1	0	7/1

Comments: Fiedler was signed by the Dolphins to challenge Damon Huard for the starting job, but he's really just a career backup. Last season, he was signed by the Jaguars to compete for the No. 3 quarterback role and he worked his way up to No. 2 on the depth chart. When Mark Brunell went down, Fiedler started the regular-season finale and completed 28 of 39 passes for 317 yards and a touchdown. In all, he stuck to a low-risk game plan and completed 61 of 94 passes in seven games. He spent his first two seasons with Philadelphia and part of '98 with the Vikings. A Dartmouth graduate, Fiedler picks up offenses quickly and makes few mistakes.

The skinny: Fiedler is the safety valve should Huard struggle, but don't expect big numbers. In Jacksonville, he was a product of the system.

6b BUBBY BRISTER / VIKINGS

YEAR	ATT.	COMP.	YARDS	TDS	300+	TD-R	GP/GS
1995	170	93	726	4	0	0	9/4
1996	DNP						
1997	9	6	48	0	0	0	1/0
1998	131	78	986	10	1	1	7/4
1999	20	12	87	0	0	0	2/0

Comments: The journeyman Brister is now in Minnesota, where he will take over if and when second-year pro Duante Culpepper shows signs of trouble. Brister isn't very good anymore, but if he quarterbacks the Vikings, he's sure to put up pretty good numbers with Cris Carter and Randy Moss as his receivers. In 1999, he failed miserably in his opportunity to replace John Elway in Denver and was replaced before the regular season even kicked off. He played in only two games all year. In 1998, Brister subbed for Elway in seven games and the Denver offense never skipped a beat. His touchdown percentage (7.6) and passer rating (99.0) were exceptional, and he was 4–0 as a starter.

The skinny: In reality, Brister is nothing but a journeyman and backup quarterback who might just get his opportunity once again.

7b DOUG FLUTIE / BILLS

YEAR	ATT.	COMP.	YARDS	TDS	300+	TD-R	GP/GS
1987	25	15	199	1	0	0	
1988	179	92	1150	8	0	1	11/91/1
1989	91	36	493	2	0	0	5/3
1998	354	202	2711	20	2	1	13/10
1999	478	264	3171	19	1	1	15/15

Comments: Flutie's size disadvantage caught up with him in 1999, and he's now the backup. The 5-foot-10 Flutie had a league-high 23 passes batted down last year, as defenses kept him inside the pocket to contain his mobility. Flutie threw 16 interceptions — tied for the third most in the AFC. Five games into the '98 season, he replaced the injured Rob Johnson and played too well to give the starting job back when Johnson returned. In 13 games (10 starts), Flutie tied for fifth in the AFC with 20 touchdown passes, and the team went 7–3. Not bad for a 36-year-old who hadn't played in the NFL in nearly nine years. After four shaky seasons with the Bears and Patriots in the late 1980s, Flutie bolted for the Canadian Football League, where, in eight seasons, he threw 270 touchdown passes and was the league's outstanding player six times.

The skinny: Flutie would make a good in-season pickup if Johnson were to get injured.

8b KENT GRAHAM/ STEELERS

YEAR	ATT.	COMP.	YARDS	TDS	300+	TD-R	GP/GS
1995	0	0	0	0	0	0	2/0
1996	274	146	1624	12	1	0	10/8
1997	250	130	1408	4	1	2	8/6
1998	205	105	1219	7	0	2	11/6
1999	271	160	1697	9	0	1	9/9

Comments: Graham was signed to replace Mike Tomczak as veteran insurance for starter Kordell Stewart. In 1999, Graham posted adequate if unspectacular numbers with the Giants and was benched after nine starts. In 1998, he directed the Giants to a 5–1 finish. He threw seven touchdown passes in six starts after the Giants gave up on Danny Kanell. In 1997, Graham struggled in Arizona, where he threw just four touchdown passes in 250 attempts, then was injured and lost his starting job to Jake Plummer. Graham's completion percentage was under 50 percent with the Giants from 1992 to '94. He seldom passes downfield.

The skinny: Stewart hears Graham's footsteps; by midseason, he'll probably take Graham's place on the bench.

9b TRENT GREEN / RAMS

YEAR	ATT.	COMP.	YARDS	TDS	300+	TD-R	GP/GS
1995	DNP						
1996	DNP						
1997	1	0	0	0	0	0	1/0
1998	509	278	3441	23	2	2	15/14
1999	Injured						

Comments: Green got off to a phenomenal start in the 1999 preseason, then wrecked his knee, missed the entire regular season and watched Kurt Warner become the NFL's MVP. Green certainly won't regain his starting job in St. Louis, and he may be on the trading block. Of all the surprises at quarterback in 1998, Green was the least predictable. A career third-stringer with the Redskins, he got his chance when Gus Frerotte was injured in the season opener. Green threw just seven touchdown passes through six games, then he caught fire and threw 16 TD passes and just four interceptions in the final nine games. Green doesn't have a great arm, but he does have mobility and poise.

The skinny: Green's chances for success hinge on a Warner injury or a trade.

10b NEIL O'DONNELL / TITANS

YEAR	ATT.	COMP.	YARDS	TDS	300+	TD-R	GP/GS
1995	416	246	2970	17	4	0	12/12
1996	188	110	1147	4	2	0	6/6
1997	460	259	2796	17	1	1	15/14
1998	343	212	2216	4	1	0	13/11
1999	195	116	1382	10	2	0	8/5

Comments: O'Donnell is a perfect fit for the Titans' short passing game and run-oriented offense. He won't beat a defense often, but he doesn't make many mistakes. When Steve McNair missed five games in 1999 because of a back injury, O'Donnell stepped in and threw eight touchdown passes and four interceptions. O'Donnell's 1998 numbers in Cincinnati (15 touchdowns, four interceptions and a 61.8 completion percentage) were impressive for 13 games, but the Bengals won just two of them. With the Jets in 1997, he tied an NFL opening-day record with five touchdown passes, but he lost the confidence of coach Bill Parcells and was benched. He was a complete bust for the Jets in an injury-plagued 1996 season.

The skinny: O'Donnell isn't a bad late-round insurance pick if you draft McNair as your starter.

11b WARREN MOON / CHIEFS

YEAR	ATT.	COMP.	YARDS	TDS	300+	TD-R	GP/GS
1995	606	377	4228	33	4	0	16/16
1996	247	134	1610	7	0	0	8/8
1997	528	313	3678	25	1	1	15/14
1998	258	145	1632	11	0	0	10/10
1999	3	1	20	0	0	0	1/0

Comments: Moon barely played in 1999 because of Elvis

Grbac's surprising durability. He's still a formidable backup, capable of carrying an offense in a pinch. With Seattle in 1998, Moon started 10 games before the team turned to promising young Jon Kitna. Moon holds single-season passing-yardage marks for the Seahawks, Vikings and Oilers. In 1997, he took over for an injured John Friesz at halftime of the season opener and proceeded to direct the NFL's top-rated passing attack. He smashed Seattle records for single-season completions and yards and became the oldest player ever to score a touchdown. In 1995, Moon led the NFL in pass attempts (606) and ranked second in TD passes (33). The owner of virtually all of the Houston Oilers' passing records, Moon is the NFL's third all-time passing-yardage leader with 49,117 yards and he's tied for fourth with 290 TD passes.

The skinny: Moon could still make a good midseason waiver pickup in the event of an injury to Grbac.

12b   JIM MILLER / BEARS

YEAR	ATT.	COMP.	YARDS	TDS	300+	TD-R	GP/GS
1995	56	32	397	2	0	0	4/0
1996	25	13	123	0	0	0	2/1
1997	DNP						
1998	DNP						
1999	174	110	1242	7	2	0	5/3

Comments: Poll a group of Bears fans, and the majority will tell you Miller should start over Cade McNown when the 2000 season begins. Both head into camp in an open battle, but McNown will probably get the nod. In 1999, Miller replaced the injured McNown for three midseason starts, and he sparked the Bears with pinpoint passing. His numbers ranked among the league's best backups. Miller hadn't played since 1996, when he was benched after a lackluster season-opening performance in Pittsburgh. He played poorly in place of the injured Neil O'Donnell in 1995.

The skinny: Miller is a good bet to get some playing time at some point in the season, and he does have a firm grasp of the offense.

13b RANDALL CUNNINGHAM / VIKINGS

YEAR	ATT.	COMP.	YARDS	TDS	300+	TD-R	GP/GS
1995	121	69	605	3	0	0	7/4
1996	DNP						
1997	88	44	501	6	0	0	6/3
1998	425	259	3704	34	4	1	15/14
1999	200	124	1475	8	2	0	6/6

Comments: Cunningham appeared to lack intensity and leadership in 1999, and he failed to recapture his magic of 1998. He was benched when the Vikings started out 2–4. In the offseason, Cunningham rejected a request to re-sign at a much lower salary and was not going to be retained. In his 1998 dream season, Cunningham replaced an injured Brad Johnson in Week 2 and proceeded to direct the most prolific offense in NFL history. He threw the second-most TD passes in the league (34), led the NFL with a 106.0 passer rating and completed nine pass plays of 50 or more yards. It was a career year for a 13-year veteran who the year before had scraped off the rust collected from a year out of football and posted fairly good numbers in a backup role. Cunningham was the league's fifth-ranked passer in 1992, when he rushed for 549 yards and five TDs.

The skinny: Cunningham is likely to be waived after June 1 and signed by another team for a backup role.

14b JASON GARRETT / GIANTS

YEAR	ATT.	COMP.	YARDS	TDS	300+	TD-R	GP/GS
1995	5	4	46	1	0	0	1/0
1996	3	3	44	0	0	0	1/0
1997	14	10	56	0	0	0	1/0
1998	158	91	1206	5	0	0	8/5
1999	64	32	314	3	0	0	5/2

Comments: Garrett is what you want in a backup — a heady, poised player who seldom makes mistakes. He has a 6–3 record as a starter (he started two games last season), and he has thrown just five interceptions in 294 career pass attempts. The backup to Troy Aikman in Dallas from 1995 to '99, Garrett is now the Giants' No. 2 quarterback, backing up Kerry Collins after signing as a free agent in the offseason. Aikman had kept Garrett on the bench for 47 of 53 games until 1998, when he started five games and compiled respectable numbers —

a touchdown pass per game and a passer rating of 84.5.

The skinny: Garrett is a competent backup who won't threaten to take Kerry Collins's starting job.

15b RYAN LEAF / CHARGERS

YEAR	ATT.	COMP.	YARDS	TDS	300+	TD-R	GP/GS
1998	245	111	1289	2	0	0	10/9
1999	DNP						

Comments: Just when you start to think Leaf might finally be maturing, he does something stupid to set his career back further. He missed the first seven games of 1999 due to a shoulder injury, then he served a four-week suspension for an argument with general manager Bobby Beathard. Following offseason shoulder surgery, Leaf was on track to become this season's starter. He'll work with his fifth quarterback coach in three seasons. The No. 2 pick in the 1998 draft, Leaf ranked last in the NFL as a rookie with an abysmal 39.0 passer rating. Off the field, he was hotheaded and moody. Leaf threw 15 interceptions and just two touchdown passes in 10 games (nine starts) before the Chargers had seen enough and benched him.

The skinny: It's too early to call Leaf one of the all-time-biggest NFL busts, but the clock is ticking.

LOOKING BACK AT QUARTERBACKS

The Best — Kurt Warner (Rams)
Sure Bets — Peyton Manning (Colts), Brett Favre (Packers)
Top Sleepers — Jeff Blake (Saints), Rob Johnson (Bills), Charlie Batch (Lions), Troy Aikman (Cowboys), Tim Couch (Browns)
Possible Busts — Tony Banks (Ravens), Rich Gannon (Raiders)
Coming On — Jon Kitna (Seahawks), Rob Johnson (Bills)
Comeback Candidates — Jake Plummer (Cardinals), Vinny Testaverde (Jets), Steve Young (49ers)
Back to Earth After a Great 1999 — Kurt Warner (Rams), Steve Beuerlein (Panthers)
In for a Career Year — Rob Johnson (Bills), Charlie Batch (Lions), Steve McNair (Titans), Kerry Collins (Giants)
Top Rookies — Chad Pennington (Jets), Chris Redman (Ravens),

Giovanni Carmazzi (49ers)

1999 Injured Players Who Will Be a Factor in '00 — Vinny Testaverde (Jets), Steve Young (49ers)

1999 Rookies Who Will Come On — Tim Couch (Browns), Cade McNown (Bears), Akili Smith (Bengals), Donovan McNabb (Eagles)

Top Players on New Teams — Jeff Blake (Saints), Trent Dilfer (Ravens), Gus Frerotte (Broncos)

Will Struggle on a New Team — Jay Fiedler (Dolphins)

Late-Round Gambles — Jeff Blake (Saints), Kerry Collins (Giants), Cade McNown (Bears), Kordell Stewart (Steelers), Troy Aikman (Cowboys)

Could Be Replaced — Tony Banks (Ravens), Daunte Culpepper (Vikings), Brian Griese (Broncos), Cade McNown (Bears), Shaun King (Buccaneers)

Best Backups — Jeff George (Redskins), Warren Moon (Chiefs), Trent Dilfer (Ravens), Trent Green (Rams), Doug Flutie (Bills), Neil O'Donnell (Titans), Gus Frerotte (Broncos),

Backups Who Will Play the Most — Trent Dilfer (Ravens), Jeff George (Redskins), Gus Frerotte (Broncos), Jay Fiedler (Dolphins), Doug Flutie (Bills), Kent Graham (Steelers), Jim Miller (Bears)

Best of the Rest

Moses Moreno, Chargers
Matt Hasselback, Packers
Doug Pederson, Eagles
Shane Matthews, Bears
Scott Mitchell, Bengals
Mike Tomczak, Lions
John Friesz, Patriots
Billy Joe Tolliver, Saints
Eric Zeier, Buccaneers

Ray Lucas, Jets
Jonathan Quinn, Jaguars
Dave Brown, Cardinals
Jeff Lewis, Panthers
Ty Detmer, Browns
Scott Zolak, Patriots
Bobby Hoying, Raiders
Glenn Foley, Seahawks

Chapter 4

RUNNING BACKS

EDGERRIN JAMES

The dubious award for having one of the early picks in a 1999 fantasy draft may have been a blown-out knee and a season of frustration. Unless, of course, you took a chance on Stephen Davis in a middle round, then picked up Tyrone Wheatley on waivers a couple weeks into the season.

Injuries and successful reclamation projects knocked the running back position upside-down in 1999. The top four rushers in '98 were Terrell Davis, Jamal Anderson, Garrison Hearst and Barry Sanders. Davis, Anderson and Hearst spent the '99 season on crutches, and

Sanders retired — at least temporarily. It's a good thing fantasy players were able to count on most of the other top backs for production at the most critical position.

If the 1999 season proved nothing else, it showed that depth is crucial to fantasy success. It's bad luck when you lose your first-round pick to a season-ending injury; it's bad drafting when your backup runners are benchwarmers who contribute little or nothing to your team. The plethora of 1999 injuries offers another reason why running back is the most important position in fantasy football. Runners take more of a pounding than receivers do. The odds of your starting runners staying healthy all season are less than the chance of having your top receivers in the lineup all season. There are so few sure picks at this position that you want to draft both of your starters before the drop-off starts, because there's a huge difference between the top 20 backs and the rest.

The upcoming season promises to be more uncertain than ever at the running back position. Terrell Davis and Anderson might not be 100 percent recovered until the 2001 season. Fred Taylor never seems to stay healthy. Players such as Ricky Williams and Curtis Enis are boom-or-bust guys. Stephen Davis and Corey Dillon are engaged in contract squabbles.

Draft Tips for Choosing Running Backs

■ Look at past performances, especially the last two or three seasons, rather than just last season.

■ Draft running backs from run-oriented teams.

■ In the Basic Scoring Method, look for each team's designated scorers. Players such as Leroy Hoard and Mario Bates may not gain a lot of rushing yards, but they do get into the end zone quite a bit. A consistent scorer is the first priority.

■ In the Performance Scoring Method, draft runners strictly by their ability to gain yards rushing and receiving. The combination of the two categories often equals one very good player, such as Marshall Faulk, Edgerrin James, Eddie George, Dorsey Levens and Warrick Dunn. But don't discount backs who are primarily receivers, such as Larry Centers, Tiki Barber and Jon Ritchie.

■ In the Distance Scoring Method, look for backs who score consistently and do so on long runs (or pass plays), such as Edgerrin James, Marshall Faulk, Napoleon Kaufman and Fred Taylor. Under this scoring method, scatbacks are often better picks than big backs. Forget about the big backs who score touchdowns only from short range (such as Bates and Hoard).

■ Try to determine who will be the featured running backs for the Chiefs, Patriots, Bills, Dolphins, Chargers and Browns. None of those teams entered training camp with settled situations.

■ Remember to draft rookies who might break into the starting line-up, such as Thomas Jones, Ron Dayne, Jamal Lewis and J. R. Redmond. Several rookies always have big years. It's up to you to figure out which ones will do it in 2000.

■ Consider drafting big, durable backs rather than smaller scat-backs, who often come out in goal-line situations and might be more injury-prone.

■ Make sure you have capable backups who can take over if one of your starters is injured or out of the lineup on a bye.

■ Know what is going on during training camp. Are Stephen Davis and Corey Dillon headed for holdouts? How well are Terrell Davis and Jamal Anderson running in the preseason, and will they be close to 100 percent recovered for the regular season? Will Ricky Williams run better with a blocking fullback and a better supporting cast? Will Antowain Smith and Jonathan Linton share carries, or will one step up as Buffalo's every-down back? Will the Chiefs settle on one ballcarrier or continue their committee approach? Do the Dolphins and Patriots have anyone good enough to carry the load? Will Jerome Bettis continue to get the bulk of the carries, or will Richard Huntley push him out of the Steelers' starting lineup? Is Jermaine Fazande good enough to carry the Chargers' ground game? Will Shaun Alexander steal some carries away from Ricky Watters in Seattle? Is Curtis Enis running better now that he's two years removed from knee surgery?

1 EDGERRIN JAMES / COLTS

YEAR	RUSH	YARDS	TDS	REC	YARDS	TDS	100+	GP/GS
1999	369	1553	13	62	586	4	10	16/16

Comments: Nobody's questioning the Colts now for passing on Ricky Williams to make James the fourth pick in the 1999 draft. James was the best back in the AFC last season, and his rookie impact rivals that of the game's all-time greats. He led the NFL with 1,553 rushing yards, the fourth-highest ever total by a rookie. James also led the league with 10 100-yard rushing games — a rookie record. He reached the 100-yard mark in his first two games but scored just two touchdowns through five games. Then he went on a rampage and finished in a tie for the league lead with 17 touchdowns. An exceptional all-around back with power and breakaway speed, James had one fault last season — eight fumbles. He led AFC running backs with 62 receptions, and his 2,139 combined yards from scrimmage were more than everyone in the league except the man he replaced in the Colts' backfield, Marshall Faulk.

The skinny: James is as close to a sure pick as you'll ever find from a second-year player.

2 FRED TAYLOR / JAGUARS

YEAR	RUSH	YARDS	TDS	REC	YARDS	TDS	100+	GP/GS
1998	264	1223	14	44	421	3	6	15/12
1999	159	732	6	10	83	0	3	10/9

Comments: A hamstring injury prevented Taylor from ranking among the league's top backs in 1999. He missed six games and was hobbled most of the season, but he still produced three 100-yard games, six TDs and a 4.6-yard average per carry. In Taylor's first three starts as a rookie in 1998, he broke off runs of 52, 49 and 77 yards. Taylor moved into the starter's role four games into the season, and he finished sixth in the AFC with 1,223 rushing yards. He scored 17 touchdowns to tie Randy Moss for the third most ever by an NFL rookie, and Taylor actually produced more yards (1,644) than Moss (1,317) and more 100-yard games. Taylor, who is an explosive runner and an excellent receiver, made five runs of 46 or more yards (and he caught a 78-yard touchdown pass) as a rookie.

The skinny: Taylor is the every-down back on the league's best rushing team, so here comes an MVP-type season. Also, look for him to get the ball more often, in a Marshall Faulk–type role. However, he has to learn to play when he's nicked.

3 MARSHALL FAULK / RAMS

YEAR	RUSH	YARDS	TDS	REC	YARDS	TDS	100+	GP/GS
1995	289	1078	11	56	475	3	1	16/16
1996	198	587	7	56	428	0	1	13/13
1997	264	1054	7	47	471	1	4	16/16
1998	324	1319	6	86	908	4	7	16/15
1999	253	1381	7	87	1048	5	7	16/16

Comments: Faulk was so quick in 1999 that he sent coaches scrambling for more speed in the offseason. He smashed Barry Sanders's record with 2,429 yards from scrimmage in a season. Faulk led the league's 1,000-yard rushers with a 5.5-yard average per catch, and he led the NFL's backs with 87 receptions for a fine 12-yard average per catch. He tied for fourth in the league with 12 touchdowns. It's hard to believe that the Rams obtained Faulk in the 1999 offseason in exchange for second- and fifth-round draft picks. The only player with at least 900 rushing and receiving yards in 1998, Faulk led the NFL with a Colts-record 2,227 yards from scrimmage. From 1996 to '97, the Lindy Infante era diminished Faulk's impact. He averaged just 16.5 carries per game in 1997, though he produced eight touchdowns and 1,054 rushing yards. In 1994, he rushed for 1,282 yards, the most ever by a Colts rookie. Faulk has 63 touchdowns and five 1,000-yard seasons in his six-year career.

The skinny: Faulk will churn out another MVP-type season.

4 TERRELL DAVIS / BRONCOS

YEAR	RUSH	YARDS	TDS	REC	YARDS	TDS	100+	GP/GS
1995	237	1117	7	49	367	1	3	14/14
1996	345	1538	13	36	310	2	6	16/16
1997	369	1750	15	42	287	0	10	15/15
1998	392	2008	21	25	217	2	11	16/16
1999	67	211	2	3	26	0	0	4/4

Comments: Even before suffering a torn ACL in Week 4 of the 1999 season, Davis found almost no running room against stacked fronts. His offseason recovery went well, but Davis will need improved quarterbacking to spread opposing defenses. In his first four seasons (1995–98), he scored more touchdowns (61) than any player in NFL history. Only two players ever scored more touchdowns in a season than Davis did in 1998, when he set team records with 23 touchdowns and 138 points. He trampled defenses for 2,008 yards, the league's third-highest single-season total. In 1997, Davis led the AFC with a team-record 1,750 rushing yards, and he tied for the NFL scoring title among nonkickers with 15 touchdowns and three two-point conversions. He is especially valuable in combined scoring leagues, because he had 11 100-yard games in 1998 (seven straight), 10 in '97 and seven in 1996. The 196th player (and 21st running back) chosen in the 1995 draft, Davis became the lowest-drafted player in NFL history to rush for 1,000 yards.

The skinny: Davis will rank among the top backs, but don't expect a return to his 1998 production.

5   EMMITT SMITH / COWBOYS

YEAR	RUSH	YARDS	TDS	REC	YARDS	TDS	100+	GP/GS
1995	377	1773	25	62	375	0	11	16/16
1996	327	1204	12	47	249	3	4	15/15
1997	261	1074	4	49	234	0	2	16/16
1998	319	1332	13	27	175	2	7	16/16
1999	329	1397	11	27	119	2	9	15/15

Comments: While most NFL running backs wear down in five or six years, Smith is as good as ever after 10 seasons. He is the second player in NFL history to rush for 1,000 yards in nine straight seasons. Smith's 13 touchdowns tied for third in the NFL in 1999, though his scoring production dwindled after he suffered a fractured hand in Game 8. And his nine 100-yard games were the second most of his career. Considered to be washed-up fantasy poison in 1998, Smith produced 15 touchdowns and seven 100-yard games. By contrast, he was a fantasy franchise-wrecker in 1997, when he appeared to lose a step and scored just four touchdowns. Smith had a career year in 1995, when he set the NFL single-season touchdown record with 25, and his career-best 1,773 rushing yards made him the only player in history to rush for 1,400 or more yards in five consecutive seasons. Smith now ranks third in NFL history with 13,963 rushing yards and first with 136 career rushing touchdowns.

The skinny: There's no drop-off in sight, and the Cowboys' retooled offense will only help spread defenses for Smith.

6   EDDIE GEORGE / TITANS

YEAR	RUSH	YARDS	TDS	REC	YARDS	TDS	100+	GP/GS
1996	335	1368	8	23	182	0	4	16/16
1997	357	1399	6	7	44	1	8	16/16
1998	348	1294	5	37	310	1	6	16/16
1999	320	1304	9	47	458	4	7	16/16

Comments: It was bound to happen — George is just too good to continue averaging seven touchdowns a season, as he did from 1996 to '98. He tied for third in the NFL with 13 touchdowns last season, then he added two TD runs in the Super Bowl. George was utilized more in the team's passing game in 1999, and he caught a career-high 47 passes, four for scores. He was the AFC's third-leading rusher, and his 1,730 yards from scrimmage represented a personal best. In 1998, George became the fifth back in NFL history to rush for 1,200 yards in each of his first three seasons. He logged six 100-yard rushing games, including five straight.

In 1997, his eight 100-yard games were the most by an Oiler in 17 years. He earned NFL Offensive Rookie of the Year honors in 1996 with the ninth-best rushing total by a rookie in NFL history. Only five runners in NFL history outrushed George in their first four seasons.

The skinny: It will happen again. George will score more than 10 touchdowns in 2000.

7 DORSEY LEVENS / PACKERS

YEAR	RUSH	YARDS	TDS	REC	YARDS	TDS	100+	GP/GS
1995	36	120	3	48	434	4	0	15/12
1996	121	566	5	31	226	5	0	16/1
1997	329	1435	7	53	370	5	6	16/16
1998	115	378	1	27	162	0	1	7/4
1999	279	1034	9	71	573	1	3	16/14

Comments: Levens was the most valuable player on a team of underachievers in 1999. He produced 1,607 yards from scrimmage, third most in the NFL, despite missing two games due to a fractured rib. Levens led the Packers with 10 touchdowns, tied for fourth among NFC backs. He was the club's third-leading receiver with 71 catches, and he moved into third place in team history with his second career 1,000-yard season. A fractured fibula ruined Levens's 1998 season in the second game. He returned for the final five games but averaged just 3.3 yards per carry. In 1997, Levens erased any doubts about being an effective every-down back. When Edgar Bennett blew out his Achilles tendon in the preseason, Levens took over and produced the most total yards from scrimmage (1,805) in Packers history. Levens became a big part of the offense in 1995, his second season, when he scored seven touchdowns.

The skinny: Levens is one of the few backs in the league you can count on for fantasy production.

8 JAMAL ANDERSON / FALCONS

YEAR	RUSH	YARDS	TDS	REC	YARDS	TDS	100+	GP/GS
1995	39	161	1	0	0	0	0	16/0
1996	232	1055	5	49	473	1	3	16/12
1997	290	1002	7	29	284	3	2	16/15
1998	410	1846	14	27	319	2	12	16/16
1999	19	59	0	2	34	0	0	2/2

Comments: Anderson took the hopes of an entire team's season crashing down with him when he tore an ACL in his leg on the third play of Game 2 last season. Offseason rehabilitation went well, and he should be close to 100 percent by September. In 1998, Anderson helped carry the Falcons into the Super Bowl with an unstoppable season. He smashed single-season team records for rushing yards, touchdowns and 100-yard rushing games. Anderson won the NFC rushing title with 1,846 yards, led the league with 12 100-yard games, and he set the NFL record for single-season carries (410). In 1997, he helped carry out coach Dan Reeves's commitment to a strong ground game when he rushed for seven touchdowns, caught three TD passes and even threw a TD pass. In 1996, Anderson virtually came out of nowhere to finish sixth in the NFC with 1,055 rushing yards. From 1996 to '98, Anderson broke 79 runs for 20 yards or more.

The skinny: Runners often need two years to completely recover from knee surgery, so don't expect 1998-like numbers from Anderson.

9   STEPHEN DAVIS / REDSKINS

YEAR	RUSH	YARDS	TDS	REC	YARDS	TDS	100+	GP/GS
1996	23	139	2	0	0	0	0	12/0
1997	141	567	3	18	134	0	0	14/6
1998	34	109	0	21	263	2	1	16/12
1999	290	1405	17	23	111	0	6	14/14

Comments: It pays to pay attention to training camp develop-ments. A career backup and injury fill-in, Davis took Skip Hicks's start-ing job in the 1999 preseason, then proceeded to lead the NFC with a franchise-record 1,405 rushing yards. The team's starting fullback for most of the 1998 season, Davis learned how to run hard inside. He led the league's nonkickers in scoring with 104 points and in rushing touch-downs (17), despite missing the final two regular-season games due to an ankle sprain. He even broke a 76-yard touchdown run in Game 7. In 1998, Davis started 12 games (11 at fullback) and contributed more with his blocking and receiving than with his running. In 1997, he served as a successful change-of-pace back in place of starter Terry Allen. Davis played in one-third of the Redskins' offensive plays that season and ranked second on the team with 567 rushing yards.

The skinny: A repeat of last season? Perhaps 1,000 yards and 10 touchdowns are more realistic from Davis.

10   CURTIS MARTIN / JETS

YEAR	RUSH	YARDS	TDS	REC	YARDS	TDS	100+	GP/GS
1995	368	1487	14	30	261	1	9	16/15
1996	316	1152	14	46	333	3	2	16/16
1997	274	1160	4	41	296	1	3	13/13
1998	369	1287	8	43	365	1	8	15/15
1999	367	1464	5	45	259	0	6	16/16

Comments: Martin kept the Jets' offense from completely crumbling when Vinny Testaverde went down in the 1999 season opener. He approached his career highs in every major category and became the fourth rusher in pro history to rush for 1,000 yards in each of his first five seasons. Martin set a team rushing record with 1,464 yards, third most in the league. In 1998, he started slowly but finished strong, with seven touchdowns in his final eight games. In three previous seasons, Martin rushed for 3,799 yards to rank fourth on the Patriots' career rushing list. In 1995 he set a team record with 15 TDs, then he broke his own record with 17 TDs and a two-point conversion for 104 points in 1996. Martin ran wild in the final 10 games of '95 to earn Rookie of the Year honors. A third-round steal (he was the 10th running back drafted), he led the AFC in rushing with 1,487 yards. In five seasons, he has missed just five games and has scored 50 touchdowns.

The skinny: With Keyshawn Johnson gone, the Jets will rely on Martin to carry the load more than ever.

11   MIKE ALSTOTT / BUCCANEERS

YEAR	RUSH	YARDS	TDS	REC	YARDS	TDS	100+	GP/GS
1996	96	377	3	65	557	3	0	16/16
1997	176	665	7	23	178	3	0	15/15
1998	215	846	8	22	152	1	2	16/16
1999	242	949	7	27	239	2	2	16/16

Comments: Alstott is the ultimate power runner, a battering ram with sure hands. He surpassed Warrick Dunn as the Buccaneers' best ball-carrier in 1999. Alstott scored all seven of the team's rushing touchdowns, and he led the team with nine scores. He ranked eighth in the NFC with 949 rushing yards, though his six lost fumbles have made him a marked man among ball-stripping defenders. In 1998, he led the team with nine touchdowns and led all NFL fullbacks with 846 rushing yards. He tied for fifth in the NFC with 10 touchdowns in 1997, then he added two more in the playoffs. His memorable second- and third-effort one-yard touchdown run that year is his trademark. In 1996, Alstott caught 65 passes, the second most among rookies and among NFL running backs.

The skinny: Alstott is a great goal-line runner on a Super Bowl contender, two reasons why he'll rank among the highest scoring backs.

12   JAMES STEWART / LIONS

YEAR	RUSH	YARDS	TDS	REC	YARDS	TDS	100+	GP/GS
1995	137	525	2	21	190	1	0	14/7
1996	190	723	8	30	177	2	1	13/11
1997	136	555	8	41	336	1	1	16/5
1998	53	217	2	6	42	1	2	3/3
1999	249	931	13	21	108	0	2	14/7

Comments: Stewart was the top free-agent prize among running backs this year. He's a good fit for the Lions' plans of building a power ground game behind a huge offensive line. Stewart, who has a nose for the end zone, shared the AFC rushing lead with 13 touchdowns in 1999. He ranked ninth in the AFC with 931 rushing yards, despite missing two games due to a foot injury and starting just seven games when Fred Taylor was injured. Off to a great start in 1998 with three touchdowns, Stewart suffered a season-ending ACL tear in Week 3. In 1997, Stewart became the fourth player in NFL history to rush for five touchdowns in a game. He ranked fifth among AFC running backs with 10 touchdowns in 1996, despite missing three late-season games due to a sprained toe.

The skinny: Stewart will post solid numbers for as long as he stays healthy, but he's never been very durable.

13   RICKY WATTERS / SEAHAWKS

YEAR	RUSH	YARDS	TDS	REC	YARDS	TDS	100+	GP/GS
1995	337	1273	11	62	434	1	4	16/16
1996	353	1411	13	51	444	0	6	16/16
1997	285	1110	7	48	440	0	2	16/16
1998	319	1239	9	52	373	0	4	16/16
1999	325	1210	5	40	387	2	4	16/16

Comments: Watters could be hearing footsteps from rookie first-round pick Shaun Alexander this season, though he'll still get the bulk of the carries. In 1999, Watters was a fantasy aggravation for seven score-less weeks, but he finished with typically effective numbers: 1,597 yards from scrimmage, four 100-yard rushing games and seven TDs. His average per carry (3.7 yards last year) is on a slow decline, however. That Watters is the only NFL player to ever rush for 1,000 yards on three different teams speaks highly of his play and poorly of his selfishness. He has rushed for 1,000 yards in five consecutive seasons. In 1996, his career year, Watters led the NFL with 1,855 yards from scrimmage. With just three seasons with Philadelphia, he ranks fourth in franchise history in rushing yards (3,794) and rushing touchdowns (31). Watters is third among active rushers with 9,083 yards, and he's one of six backs in NFL history to average at least 100 yards from scrimmage per game.

The skinny: Watters is beginning a slow, steady decline in fantasy production, but he's still the man until Alexander proves otherwise.

14 COREY DILLON / BENGALS

YEAR	RUSH	YARDS	TDS	REC	YARDS	TDS	100+	GP/GS
1997	233	1129	10	27	259	0	4	16/6
1998	262	1130	4	28	178	1	4	15/15
1999	263	1200	5	31	290	1	5	15/15

Comments: Dillon wants either a long-term contract or out of Cincinnati, so there's a chance of a holdout in September. He's coming off a Pro Bowl season in which he rushed for 1,200 yards, the second most in team history. His 4.6-yard average per carry was the best among the AFC's 1,000-yard rushers. Running behind a weak offensive line in 1998, Dillon took a pounding and gained 1,130 yards despite knee, hip, toe and back injuries. In 1997, Dillon patiently waited for his chance, then he made the most of it. He seldom played in the first nine games but finished with 1,129 rushing yards to lead all rookies and rank sixth in the AFC. In Game 14, Dillon broke Jim Brown's NFL single-game mark for rushing yards by a rookie (246), the fifth-highest total in NFL history. He is the 11th player in league history to rush for 1,000 yards in his first three seasons.

The skinny: Dillon will have another big season; the question is where he'll play.

15 DUCE STALEY / EAGLES

YEAR	RUSH	YARDS	TDS	REC	YARDS	TDS	100+	GP/GS
1997	7	29	0	2	22	0	0	16/0
1998	258	1065	5	57	432	1	1	16/13
1999	325	1273	4	41	294	2	5	16/16

Comments: Imagine what Staley could do if defenses weren't solely geared toward stopping him. The ultraproductive Staley isn't very fast or big, but he fights for every yard he gets. In 1999, he led the Eagles in rushing, touchdowns and yards from scrimmage, and he was the team's second-leading receiver with 41 catches. His 1,273 rushing yards ranked seventh in the NFL, though he tailed off somewhat after a six-week midseason stretch that included four 100-yard rushing games. In 1998, Staley was the entire offense in a dreadful Eagles season. The team's rushing and receiving leader, he accounted for 35 percent of the club's yards from scrimmage. He won a preseason battle with Charlie Garner for the starting job and finished as the NFC's sixth-leading rusher. As a rookie in 1997, Staley backed up Ricky Watters and played little on offense.

The skinny: Touchdowns will still be hard to come by until the Eagles surround Staley with enough talent to divert some attention.

16 RICKY WILLIAMS / SAINTS

YEAR	RUSH	YARDS	TDS	REC	YARDS	TDS	100+	GP/GS
1999	253	884	2	28	172	0	2	12/12

Comments: Enormous expectations, a turf toe, a poor supporting cast and a bad attitude contributed to Williams's frustrating start as a rookie in 1999. Expected to make a huge immediate impact, he failed to score until Game 10, then he missed four games due to his toe injury. Except for a midseason back-to-back stretch in which he rushed for 111 and 179 yards, his rookie season was pretty much a bust. Williams ranked 10th in the NFC with 884 rushing yards, but he averaged just 3.5 yards per carry and fumbled six times. In the offseason, the Saints surrounded Williams with playmakers and a blocking back.

The skinny: Look for a monumental leap in production from Williams in his sophomore season.

RUNNING BACKS

17 TYRONE WHEATLEY / RAIDERS

YEAR	RUSH	YARDS	TDS	REC	YARDS	TDS	100+	GP/GS
1995	78	245	3	5	27	0	0	13/1
1996	112	400	1	12	51	2	0	14/0
1997	152	583	4	16	140	0	1	14/7
1998	14	52	0	0	0	0	0	5/0
1999	242	936	8	21	196	3	2	16/7

Comments: All Wheatley has ever needed is a chance to play every down. Written off by the Giants and Dolphins, he was signed by the Raiders midway through the 1999 preseason. Though he shared playing time with Napoleon Kaufman, Wheatley got the bulk of the carries and ranked eighth in the AFC with 936 rushing yards. Running with devastating power, Wheatley quickly became the team's best goal-line option and ranked fourth among AFC backs with 11 touchdowns. A 1995 first-round pick, he had been a huge bust in his first four pro seasons. In 1998, he played in five games and was buried deep on the Giants' bench. In 1997, his best season, he rushed for 583 yards, second on the Giants, and he tied for second in rushing touchdowns with four.

The skinny: Wheatley will prove that his breakthrough 1999 season was no fluke.

18 ROBERT SMITH / VIKINGS

YEAR	RUSH	YARDS	TDS	REC	YARDS	TDS	100+	GP/GS
1995	139	632	5	7	35	0	2	9/7
1996	162	692	3	7	39	0	3	8/7
1997	232	1266	6	37	197	1	6	14/14
1998	249	1187	6	28	291	2	5	14/14
1999	221	1015	2	24	166	0	4	13/12

Comments: Smith was an aggravation to basic scoring league owners in 1999. They watched him ramble up and down the field and then get replaced by Leroy Hoard in the red zone. Smith logged his third straight 1,000-yard season, but he didn't score until the final two games. A true gamebreaker, Smith broke four runs of 40 yards or more in 1998, and he scored a career-high eight touchdowns. He stayed healthy for all but two and a half games in 1997 and, as a result, ranked among the top backs. His 1,266 rushing yards broke Terry Allen's five-year-old team record and ranked fifth in the NFC. Injury-prone for his first four pro seasons, Smith has missed just seven games from 1997 to '99. His 4.7-

yard career average per carry is the best in Vikings history.

The skinny: Smith is bound to score at least seven or eight touchdowns unless Hoard is re-signed by the Vikings.

19 TIM BIAKABUTUKA / PANTHERS

YEAR	RUSH	YARDS	TDS	REC	YARDS	TDS	100+	GP/GS
1996	71	229	0	0	0	0	0	4/4
1997	75	299	2	0	0	0	1	8/2
1998	102	422	3	8	138	1	2	11/3
1999	138	718	6	23	189	0	2	11/11

Comments: If only this guy could stay healthy. Biakabutuka was in the midst of a breakthrough 1999 season when he suffered a high ankle sprain in Game 6. Before the injury, he became the first player in NFL history to break two touchdown runs of over 40 yards in two consecutive games. After the injury, he played in five games and averaged just 3.1 yards per carry, though overall his 5.2-yard average tied for second among players with 600 or more rushing yards. Biakabutuka showed signs of resurrecting his disappointing career late in 1998. In the final four games, he rushed for 377 yards and three TDs. Biakabutuka was thought to be a franchise back when he was drafted in the first round in 1996. But he spent much of his rookie season in street clothes due to an injury and most of the 1997 season on the bench.

The skinny: Biakabutuka has the talent to be a great back, but injuries may prevent him from ever being one.

20 CURTIS ENIS / BEARS

YEAR	RUSH	YARDS	TDS	REC	YARDS	TDS	100+	GP/GS
1998	133	497	0	6	20	0	0	9/1
1999	287	916	3	45	340	2	0	15/12

Comments: Enis struggled through the year-after-knee-injury blues in 1999 when he lacked explosiveness and plodded his way to a 3.2-yard rushing average. Despite ranking ninth in the NFC with 916 rushing yards, his longest run of the season covered just 19 yards, and he never had a 100-yard game. Enis ranked third on the team with 45 receptions. He suffered a slight tear to his rotator cuff late in the season but is back at full strength. His 1998 rookie season couldn't have been much rockier. After a lengthy holdout, Enis showed promise, but he alienated teammates with selfish behavior. Before injuring his knee in Week 9, his first start, he showed signs of being the power runner the team had expected when they made him the fifth pick in the 1998 draft.

The skinny: Enis will be much improved, with a better average per carry, more yards and more touchdowns in 2000.

21 JEROME BETTIS / STEELERS

YEAR	RUSH	YARDS	TDS	REC	YARDS	TDS	100+	GP/GS
1995	183	637	3	18	106	0	0	15/13
1996	320	1431	11	22	122	0	10	16/12
1997	375	1665	7	15	110	2	10	15/15
1998	316	1185	3	16	90	0	6	15/15
1999	299	1091	7	21	110	0	2	16/16

Comments: Bettis is no longer an unstoppable battering ram, but the Steelers' deteriorating offensive line is largely to blame. Coming off a preseason knee injury, he started slowly but ran hard and finished strong when the team was playing out the string in 1999. Bettis will share carries with change-of-pace back Richard Huntley this season. In his somewhat disappointing 1998 season, Bettis rushed for 1,185 yards, but his 3.8-yard average and three touchdowns fell short of expectations. In 1997, the Steelers rode "The Bus" for 1,665 rushing yards, and his nine touchdowns tied for fifth among AFC running backs. In 1996, Bettis was obtained in a draft-day trade and resurrected his career with 1,431 rushing yards and 11 rushing touchdowns. The Rookie of the Year with the Rams in 1993, Bettis ranks fourth among active NFL rushers with 8,462 career yards, and he has 39 career 100-yard rushing games.

The skinny: The Bus isn't ready for the scrap heap, but he's sharing his routes now, which will further hurt his production.

22 CHARLIE GARNER / 49ERS

YEAR	RUSH	YARDS	TDS	REC	YARDS	TDS	100+	GP/GS
1995	108	588	6	10	61	0	1	15/2
1996	66	346	1	14	92	0	0	15/1
1997	116	547	3	24	225	0	1	16/2
1998	96	381	4	19	110	0	1	10/3
1999	241	1229	4	56	535	2	3	16/15

Comments: So much for the theory that Garner is too fragile to play every down. He held up for the entire 1999 season and was the league's third-most-productive back with 1,764 yards from scrimmage. And he became the fifth sub-190-pound running back since 1988 to rush for 1,000 yards. He averaged 5.1 yards per carry, ranked eighth in the league with 1,229 rushing yards and was the team's third-leading receiver. The quick, agile Garner was riddled with knee, ankle, thigh, rib and thumb injuries in his five seasons with the Eagles, so he was released in the 1999 offseason. A preseason ankle sprain ended his hopes of winning the starting job in 1998. He did stay injury-free in 1997, and his 547 rushing yards ranked second on the team. In 1995, Garner had the highest average per carry (5.4 yards) among all NFL ballcarriers who had at least 100 attempts.

The skinny: Garner will play every down, and he'll produce. There's no telling whether or not he'll hold up.

23 ERRICT RHETT / BROWNS

YEAR	RUSH	YARDS	TDS	REC	YARDS	TDS	100+	GP/GS
1995	332	1207	11	14	110	0	4	16/16
1996	176	539	3	4	11	1	0	9/7
1997	31	96	3	0	0	0	0	11/0
1998	44	180	0	11	65	0	0	13/1
1999	236	852	5	24	169	2	4	16/10

Comments: Rhett gets the hard yards, not the big gains. He averaged 3.6 yards per carry with Baltimore last season, just above his career average. Rhett had four 100-yard games, including three straight, before his production tailed off after he suffered a rib injury. He ranked 11th in the AFC despite missing six starts. In 1998, Rhett started the first two games and rushed for 136 yards in 24 carries, then he watched from the bench as Priest Holmes emerged. It was similar to Rhett's relatively inactive final two seasons in Tampa Bay. In 1996, he benched himself by holding out the first seven games due to a contract dispute. Rhett followed up a big rookie season in 1994 with an even better one in '95. He ranked seventh in the NFL with 1,207 rushing yards and tied for fourth in the league in rushing touchdowns with 11.

The skinny: Rhett will start for the Browns, but he may hear footsteps from promising rookie Travis Prentice.

24 JONATHAN LINTON / BILLS

YEAR	RUSH	YARDS	TDS	REC	YARDS	TDS	100+	GP/GS
1998	45	195	1	1	10	0	0	14/0
1999	205	695	5	29	228	1	0	16/2

Comments: Linton proved to be a hard runner but not an every-down answer in 1999. He led the Bills in rushing despite playing behind Antowain Smith most of the season. Linton averaged just 3.4 yards per carry, and his longest of 208 carries covered just 18 yards. However, he finished with a touchdown in each of the final four regular-season games, and he proved to be a pretty good pass receiver. Linton scored six touchdowns and a two-point conversion to rank third on the team in scoring. He was the team's top receiving back with 29 catches.

The skinny: Don't be surprised if Linton becomes the Bills' short-yardage and goal-line back.

25 J. J. JOHNSON / DOLPHINS

YEAR	RUSH	YARDS	TDS	REC	YARDS	TDS	100+	GP/GS
1999	164	558	4	15	100	0	1	13/4

Comments: Johnson at least began to stabilize a revolving door at the Dolphins' tailback position in 1999. Four different tailbacks started for the Dolphins, and Johnson had the only 100-yard rushing day of the bunch. In Game 10, he made his first start and rushed for 106 yards and a touchdown. He led the team with 558 rushing yards and four rushing touchdowns. Hobbled by calf and hamstring injuries, Johnson missed three games and broke just one long run, a 34-yarder in the regular-season finale.

The skinny: Johnson doesn't appear to be durable enough to hold up as the every-down back, but he's the best Miami has.

26 RICHARD HUNTLEY / STEELERS

YEAR	RUSH	YARDS	TDS	REC	YARDS	TDS	100+	GP/GS
1996	2	8	0	1	14	0	0	1/0
1997	DNP							
1998	55	242	1	3	18	0	0	16/1
1999	93	567	5	27	253	3	0	16/2

Comments: A restricted free agent, Huntley was in demand in the offseason, but the Steelers chose to re-sign him (a rarity in Pittsburgh these days). A quick, explosive change-of-pace back, Huntley perfectly complements powerful Jerome Bettis. Huntley's 6.1-yard average per carry led the NFL (among runners with 400 or more yards) last season. A third-down back and kickoff returner, he led the team with eight touchdowns, and he produced nine runs and receptions which covered 20 or more yards. Huntley earned a roster spot in the 1998 preseason with a 9.4-yard rushing average, then he played in every game. A fourth-round pick in 1996, Huntley seldom played in Atlanta. Because Bettis is in the final year of his contract, Huntley could be the starter in 2001.

The skinny: Huntley is prime keeper league material and a good late-round pick.

27

ANTOWAIN SMITH / BILLS

YEAR	RUSH	YARDS	TDS	REC	YARDS	TDS	100+	GP/GS
1997	194	840	8	28	177	0	1	16/0
1998	300	1124	8	5	11	0	3	16/14
1999	165	614	6	2	32	0	2	14/12

Comments: Smith was a disappointment in 1999, and the Bills won't wait long to replace him if he struggles early this season. At times he didn't run hard, though he proved his durability by running with a turf toe late in the season. Smith helped cement his starting job over Jonathan Linton by rushing for 79 yards and two touchdowns in the team's playoff loss. He ranked second on the team with 614 rushing yards and he tied for second with six TDs. In 1998, he tied for seventh in the AFC with eight rushing touchdowns and ranked ninth in the conference with 1,124 rushing yards. As a rookie in 1997, Smith contributed immediately. He led the Bills in touchdowns (eight) and rushing yards (840), and he broke off runs of 54 and 56 yards. But he hasn't progressed much since his rookie season.

The skinny: Smith's shaky starting status makes him a risky mid-round pick.

28 MARIO BATES / CARDINALS

YEAR	RUSH	YARDS	TDS	REC	YARDS	TDS	100+	GP/GS
1995	244	951	7	18	114	0	3	16/16
1996	164	584	4	13	44	0	1	14/10
1997	119	440	4	5	42	0	1	12/7
1998	60	165	6	1	14	0	0	16/1
1999	72	202	9	5	34	0	0	16/2

Comments: A starter in New Orleans early in his career, Bates has carved a niche as a pretty good goal-line back. He scored on one-eighth of his carries in 1999, with his longest score covering just three yards. And he tied for sixth in the NFC with nine rushing touchdowns, the most by a Cardinal in six years. In 1998, he was one of the league's best goal-line backs, with six 1- and 2-yard scores in just 60 carries. With New Orleans in 1997, Bates's playing time diminished after he landed in Mike Ditka's doghouse. In 1995, his best year, Bates scored seven touchdowns and piled up 951 yards to rank 11th in the NFC. He led the Saints in rushing in 1994, '95 and '96.

The skinny: Bates should still get his goal-line carries because rookie Thomas Jones, who will most likely start, isn't very big.

29 LEROY HOARD / CUT BY VIKINGS

YEAR	RUSH	YARDS	TDS	REC	YARDS	TDS	100+	GP/GS
1995	136	547	0	13	103	0	0	12/12
1996	125	492	3	11	133	0	2	11/7
1997	80	235	4	11	84	0	0	12/1
1998	115	479	9	22	198	1	0	16/1
1999	138	555	10	17	166	0	1	15/3

Comments: Hoard scored 10 touchdowns each of the past two seasons for the Vikings, and then was deemed expendable and not re-signed to ease the team's salary cap woes. An excellent goal-line runner, Hoard ranked third in the NFC with 10 rushing scores, and he rushed for 555 yards, the second-highest total of his 10-year career. He has four playoff touchdowns in the past two seasons. In 1996, he filled a huge void in the Vikings' lineup after being waived by Baltimore and Carolina. He finished with 420 yards, three touchdowns and two 100-yard games with Minnesota. He had a good season with Cleveland in 1994, with nine touchdowns and 890 rushing yards. In 1991, Hoard's nine touchdown receptions were the most in one season by an NFL running back since official statistics were first recorded in 1932.

The skinny: Touchdown-makers such as Hoard don't stay unemployed for long.

30 DONNELL BENNETT / CHIEFS

YEAR	RUSH	YARDS	TDS	REC	YARDS	TDS	100+	GP/GS
1995	7	11	0	1	12	0	0	3/1
1996	36	166	0	8	21	0	0	16/0
1997	94	369	1	7	5	0	0	14/1
1998	148	527	5	16	91	1	1	16/10
1999	161	627	8	10	41	0	0	15/1

Comments: Bennett was out of the picture when the 1999 season started, but when Kimble Anders was hurt in Week 2, he moved into the forefront, despite starting just one game. He led the team in rushing for the second straight season with 627 yards. A hard inside runner, Bennett tied for fourth in the AFC with eight rushing touchdowns. In 1998, he failed in his attempt to fill Marcus Allen's huge shoes because he's simply not an every-down back who can threaten a defense. Bennett rushed for a career-high 527 yards and five touchdowns, but he averaged just 3.6 yards per carry and was benched late in the season. A second-round pick in the 1994 draft, Bennett played sparingly in his first three seasons.

The skinny: Bennett is practically a last resort in the team's search for an every-down back this season.

31 WARRICK DUNN / BUCCANEERS

YEAR	RUSH	YARDS	TDS	REC	YARDS	TDS	100+	GP/GS
1997	224	978	4	39	462	3	6	16/10
1998	245	1026	2	44	344	0	2	16/14
1999	195	616	0	64	589	2	0	15/15

Comments: The good news: Dunn led the Buccaneers in receiving with 64 catches in 1999. The bad news: He failed to run hard, couldn't shed a tackle or break a long gainer and averaged only 3.2 yards per rush. He did produce 1,205 yards from scrimmage, but scored just two touchdowns for the second straight season. Dunn was a bitter disappointment to fantasy players in 1998. While he became the Buccaneers' fifth-ever 1,000-yard rusher, it was fullback Mike Alstott who got the ball near the goal line. As a rookie in 1997, he almost immediately proved to be among the most exciting players in the league. He broke loose for seven runs and pass receptions of 40 yards or longer, and he earned Offensive Rookie of the Year and Pro Bowl honors.

The skinny: Don't draft Dunn unless your league uses the performance scoring system.

32 JERMAINE FAZANDE / CHARGERS

YEAR	RUSH	YARDS	TDS	REC	YARDS	TDS	100+	GP/GS
1999	91	365	2	0	0	0	1	7/3

Comments: Bobby Beathard hasn't uncovered many draft finds in recent years, but Fazande could be an exception. A second-round pick in the 1999 draft, the bruising 6-foot-2, 262-pounder enters his second season as the starter. He staked a claim to the starting job in the 1999 season finale, when he plowed for 183 yards and a touchdown in 30 attempts. The only bright spot in an otherwise dismal Chargers ground game, Fazande averaged 4.0 yards per carry — one yard better than the team's average. Despite just three starts, he was the team's leading ground-gainer with 365 yards.

The skinny: Fazande is a sleeper, though the team's quarterback instability is liable to drag the entire offense down to a crawl.

33 NAPOLEON KAUFMAN / RAIDERS

YEAR	RUSH	YARDS	TDS	REC	YARDS	TDS	100+	GP/GS
1995	108	490	1	9	62	0	0	16/1
1996	150	874	1	22	143	1	3	16/9
1997	272	1294	6	40	403	2	6	16/16
1998	217	921	2	25	191	0	4	13/13
1999	138	714	2	18	181	1	?	7/16?

Comments: Kaufman was the lightning in the Raiders' highly effective two-headed backfield in 1999, the quick-strike breakaway threat who complemented Tyrone Wheatley's power well. Nobody who outgained Kaufman averaged more yards per carry, because he is among the league's best breakaway threats. The Raiders' primary ball-carrier in 1998, Kaufman logged four 100-yard games and scored on an 80-yard run. In 1997, he dispelled doubts about his durability as an every-down back. He handled more than three-fourths of the Raiders' carries, never missed a start, and he ranked fourth in the AFC with 1,294 rushing yards. In 1996, he started nine games and led the NFL with an outstanding 5.8-yard average per carry.

The skinny: Kaufman isn't a threat to score more than a few touchdowns because he's too small to be a goal-line back.

34 KEVIN FAULK / PATRIOTS

YEAR	RUSH	YARDS	TDS	REC	YARDS	TDS	100+	GP/GS
1999	67	227	1	12	98	1	0	11/2

Comments: Faulk failed to seize his opportunity to fill a major need in the Patriots' offense in 1999. A lack of durability and poor blitz pickups resulted in a reduced role as a third-down back and a kickoff returner. Faulk started the first two games, but he rushed for just 26 yards in 15 carries. He missed five games due to two separate ankle injuries and made his biggest impact as a kickoff returner, ranking fourth in the AFC with a 24.2-yard average.

The skinny: The 5-foot-8, 197-pound Faulk is better suited for the third-down role than for the starting job.

35 KIMBLE ANDERS / CHIEFS

YEAR	RUSH	YARDS	TDS	REC	YARDS	TDS	100+	GP/GS
1995	58	398	2	55	349	1	0	16/13
1996	54	201	2	60	529	2	0	16/15
1997	79	397	0	59	453	2	0	15/14
1998	58	230	1	64	462	2	0	16/15
1999	32	181	0	2	14	1	0	2/2

Comments: Anders made a living as an outstanding pass-catching fullback for eight NFL seasons. The Chiefs thought they could make him an every-down back in 1999, and he rushed for 142 yards in his second start before suffering a season-ending Achilles heel injury. In 1998, he caught 64 passes (10 in one game) to lead the Chiefs in receiving for the fourth time in five seasons. Anders is the only Chief to catch 50 passes in five straight seasons. He scored a career-high four touchdowns in 1996. From 1995 to '98, Anders had 305 receptions, the most among AFC running backs. However, he has just 17 touchdowns in nine seasons.

The skinny: Watch training camp to see if Anders gets another chance to be Kansas City's every-down back.

36 PRIEST HOLMES / RAVENS

YEAR	RUSH	YARDS	TDS	REC	YARDS	TDS	100+	GP/GS
1997	0	0	0	0	0	0	0	7/0
1998	233	1008	7	43	260	0	4	16/13
1999	89	506	1	13	104	1	2	9/4

Comments: Holmes plays well for stretches, but then he disappears. He replaced an injured Errict Rhett for four late-season starts, and responded with back-to-back 100-yard games that included 72- and 64-yard runs. He had the second-highest average per rush of any back with 500 or more rushing yards in 1999. In 1998, even die-hard football fans were asking "Who?" when Holmes burst upon the scene with 173 rushing yards and two touchdowns in Week 4. Holmes struggled for several games, then he finished strong with 545 yards and five touchdowns in the final six games, including a 227-yard effort against the Bengals in Game 11. He led the team in rushing and receiving.

The skinny: Holmes might play a lot, because he will back up rookie Jamal Lewis, whose surgically repaired knee might not hold up for the entire season.

37 RAYMONT HARRIS / PATRIOTS

YEAR	RUSH	YARDS	TDS	REC	YARDS	TDS	100+	GP/GS
1995	Injured							
1996	194	748	4	5	41	1	3	12/10
1997	275	1033	10	28	115	0	3	13/13
1998	79	228	1	10	68	0	0	8/3
1999	DNP							

Comments: The running-back-starved Patriots took a flyer on Harris, who was a quality back before suffering a broken fibula in 1997. He was clearly a slower runner with Green Bay in 1998 and was replaced in the starting lineup, and he was out of football last season. A hard inside runner with good hands, Harris is the most recent 1,000-yard rusher in Chicago Bears history. He rushed for 1,033 yards and 10 touchdowns in 1997 before suffering the injury in Week 14. In 1996, Harris missed four early-season games but came back with three 100-yard rushing efforts. His 1995 season ended on the second play from scrimmage when he broke his collarbone.

The skinny: Harris is a potential Comeback of the Year story, but more than likely, he will close the curtains on an injury-filled career.

38 OLANDIS GARY / BRONCOS

YEAR	RUSH	YARDS	TDS	REC	YARDS	TDS	100+	GP/GS
1999	276	1159	7	21	159	0	4	11/11

Comments: Lightning struck twice for the Broncos in 1999. Four years after plucking Terrell Davis in the sixth round of the draft, the Broncos stole Gary, also a University of Georgia product, in the fourth round. Inactive the first four weeks of the 1999 season, Gary stepped in for the injured Davis and averaged more than 100 yards per game. Like Davis, Gary lacks great speed, but he hits the hole quickly and runs well inside. Gary piled up 183 and 185 rushing yards in back-to-back games, and he ranked sixth in the AFC with 1,159 yards. Gary tied for eighth in the AFC with seven touchdown runs. The Broncos resisted trade offers for Gary in the offseason, and he could be paired with Davis in the same backfield at times this year.

The skinny: Gary will step aside once Davis returns 100 percent, but the Broncos will find a way to work him into the offense.

39 TERRY KIRBY / BROWNS

YEAR	RUSH	YARDS	TDS	REC	YARDS	TDS	100+	GP/GS
1995	108	414	4	66	618	3	0	16/4
1996	134	559	3	52	439	1	1	14/10
1997	125	418	6	23	279	1	0	16/3
1998	48	258	3	16	134	0	0	9/0
1999	130	452	6	58	528	3	0	16/10

Comments: Kirby was a stopgap starter for the Browns in 1999, a short-term solution. His nine touchdowns led the team and tied for eighth in the AFC. A better receiver than runner, Kirby averaged just 3.5 yards per carry, but he ranked second among AFC backs with 58 catches. The 49ers signed Kirby for insurance three weeks into the 1998 season. In eight games, he contributed 732 rushing, receiving and return yards, three touchdown runs and a TD pass. In 1997, Kirby served as a third-down back and became the first 49ers player to score by rushing, receiving and on a return in the same season. As a Miami rookie in 1993, he tied for the NFL lead among running backs with 75 catches. In seven seasons, Kirby has 304 career receptions and just 723 rushes.

The skinny: Kirby isn't an every-down back, but he is one of the best third-down backs, and he consistently finds the end zone.

40 TIKI BARBER / GIANTS

YEAR	RUSH	YARDS	TDS	REC	YARDS	TDS	100+	GP/GS
1997	136	511	3	34	299	1	1	12/6
1998	52	166	0	42	348	3	0	16/4
1999	62	258	0	66	609	2	0	16/1

Comments: Barber was the only productive running back on the Giants in 1999. Quick and versatile, he excelled in the Giants' spread offense as the third-down back. Only three NFL backs caught more passes than Barber, who set one team record with 231 all-purpose yards in Week 6, and he set another team mark in the season finale with 13 receptions. Barber found his niche as the Giants' third-down back in 1998. He scored on an 87-yard pass play that ranks as the team's sixth-longest play from scrimmage. As a rookie in 1997, he was off to a good start with touchdown runs in each of the first three games before missing four games because of a sprained knee.

The skinny: Barber is worthwhile in a performance league; practically useless in a basic scoring league.

41 CHRIS WARREN / COWBOYS

YEAR	RUSH	YARDS	TDS	REC	YARDS	TDS	100+	GP/GS
1995	310	1346	15	35	247	1	8	16/16
1996	203	855	5	40	273	0	3	14/14
1997	200	847	4	45	257	0	0	15/13
1998	59	291	4	13	66	1	1	9/0
1999	99	403	2	34	224	0	0	16/1

Comments: Warren is arguably the best backup tailback in the league. The Cowboys don't have to change their play calling when he replaces Emmitt Smith. In 1999, Warren finished third on the team with 34 receptions, and he led NFC backups with 403 rushing yards. He was expected to take some of the offensive load off Emmitt Smith's shoulders in 1998, but injuries lessened his impact. Warren became the

Seahawks' all-time-leading rusher on the last play of the 1997 season, then he was waived and signed by Dallas. In his huge 1995 season, Warren ranked second in the AFC with 16 touchdowns and 1,346 rushing yards, and he became the first player in NFL history not drafted in the first two rounds to rush for 1,000 yards in four straight seasons.

The skinny: Warren's contribution is restricted by Smith's exceptional durability.

42 FRED BEASLEY / 49ERS

YEAR	RUSH	YARDS	TDS	REC	YARDS	TDS	100+	GP/GS
1998	0	0	0	1	11	0	0	16/0
1999	58	276	4	32	282	0	0	13/11

Comments: Beasley was a pleasant surprise for the 49ers in 1999, a good blocking fullback with good hands and a burst to break big plays. He greatly helped the team's short passing game, and Charlie Garner's rushing production improved by 15 yards per game with Beasley in the lineup. Beasley averaged 4.8 yards per rush and 8.8 yards per catch, impressive numbers for a fullback. He broke a 44-yard touchdown run in Game 14. Beasley was inactive for the first three games but he scored all four of his touchdowns in the final seven weeks. He was a special-teams player as rookie in 1998.

The skinny: Beasley is an up-and-comer who will play a big role in the 49ers' passing game and get some goal-line carries.

43 ADRIAN MURRELL / REDSKINS

YEAR	RUSH	YARDS	TDS	REC	YARDS	TDS	100+	GP/GS
1995	192	795	1	71	465	2	1	15/9
1996	301	1249	6	17	81	1	5	16/16
1997	300	1086	7	27	106	0	3	16/15
1998	274	1042	8	18	169	2	3	15/14
1999	193	553	0	49	335	0	0	16/12

Comments: The Redskins signed Murrell as insurance in case they fail to re-sign Stephen Davis. Although he is not a reliable short-yardage back who can hammer the line, Murrell is a productive runner. He spent much of 1999 dancing behind an ineffective offensive line, and as a result, his rushing yardage tumbled. From 1996 to '98, Murrell was one of only eight players to rush for 1,000 yards in all three seasons. In 1998, Murrell became only the Cardinals' second 1,000-yard rusher in 13 years, and he was one of eight NFL backs to score 10 or more touchdowns. With the Jets in 1996, he became one of just three rushers in NFL history to rush for 1,000 yards on a team that won only one game.

The skinny: Murrell will start if Davis doesn't sign, so stay tuned.

44 NATRONE MEANS / PANTHERS

YEAR	RUSH	YARDS	TDS	REC	YARDS	TDS	100+	GP/GS
1995	186	730	5	7	46	0	3	10/9
1996	152	507	2	7	45	1	1	14/4
1997	244	823	9	15	104	0	0	14/11
1998	212	883	5	16	91	0	4	10/10
1999	112	277	4	9	51	1	0	7/5

Comments: A shell of his former self, Means signed with Carolina — his home state — in the offseason to replace Fred Lane as Tim Biakabutuka's backup. Means, who hasn't had a 1,000-yard season since 1994, scored three touchdowns in the first five weeks of the 1999 season but then suffered a knee injury and missed nine games. Means's biggest drawback is that he can't stay healthy for an entire season. He was in the midst of a big 1998 season with 878 yards in nine games when he suffered a season-ending foot fracture. With Jacksonville in 1996 and '97, Means was useful but injury prone and replaceable. In 1994, he set the Chargers' single-season rushing record with 1,350 yards. He ranks third on the Chargers' all-time rushing list with 3,885 yards.

The skinny: Given Biakabutuka's injury-plagued past, Means will definitely contribute.

45 TERRY ALLEN / CUT BY PATRIOTS

YEAR	RUSH	YARDS	TDS	REC	YARDS	TDS	100+	GP/GS
1995	338	1309	10	31	232	1	4	16/16
1996	347	1353	21	32	194	0	5	16/16
1997	210	724	4	20	172	1	3	10/10
1998	148	700	2	17	128	0	0	10/10
1999	254	896	8	14	125	1	2	16/13

Comments: Ten years and 7,777 rushing yards have taken their toll on Allen's surgically repaired knees, which showed signs of wear and tear in 1999. His 3.5-yard average per carry was the lowest among the AFC's rushers with 800 or more yards, though the team's offensive line problems didn't open many holes, and he still tied for eighth in the AFC with nine touchdowns. With Washington in 1998, Allen averaged 4.7 yards per carry, but an ankle sprain wrecked the second half of his season and he was released. Coming off his incredible 21 touchdowns in 1996, Allen's injury-plagued, five-touchdown 1997 season was a bitter disappointment for fantasy owners. With Minnesota in 1994, Allen made his second miraculous recovery from a serious knee injury, a feat never before done in the NFL.

The skinny: There's still a place in the league for an aging player like Allen who has a nose for the end zone.

46   AHMAN GREEN / PACKERS

YEAR	RUSH	YARDS	TDS	REC	YARDS	TDS	100+	GP/GS
1998	35	209	1	3	2	0	1	16/0
1999	26	120	0	0	0	0	0	14/0

Comments: Fumble the football, and you won't be on Mike Holmgren's team for long. Green was traded in the offseason to the Packers, where he will serve as a change-of-pace complement to Dorsey Levens. Green played little his first two years with Seattle. But Packers general manager Ron Wolf has coveted him for his explosiveness, so his role will increase this season, as long as he shakes his fumble problems. In 1999, Green was an offensive afterthought and contributed mostly as a kickoff returner. In his 1998 pro debut, he rushed for 100 yards and a touchdown on just six carries. But he didn't get a single carry in seven other games.

The skinny: Green could eventually become the best gamebreaker in the Green Bay offense, though don't expect miracles this season.

47 LAMAR SMITH / DOLPHINS

YEAR	RUSH	YARDS	TDS	REC	YARDS	TDS	100+	GP/GS
1995	36	215	0	1	10	0	0	13/0
1996	153	680	8	9	58	0	1	16/2
1997	91	392	2	23	182	0	0	12/2
1998	138	457	1	24	249	2	1	14/9
1999	60	205	0	20	151	1	0	13/2

Comments: Smith enters a fairly wide-open preseason derby for the starting tailback job in Miami. The backup for Ricky Williams in New Orleans in 1999, Smith ranked second on the team with 205 rushing yards. He impressed the Saints so little in 1998 that they mortgaged their future by trading up in the draft to replace him with Williams. In four seasons with Seattle, Smith settled for part-time duty. He was the Seahawks' leading rusher with 280 yards seven games into the 1997 season, then he broke his ankle and missed four games. In 1996, Smith had become the worst enemy of many a fantasy owner when he outscored star runner Chris Warren eight touchdowns to five.

The skinny: Smith probably won't win Miami's starting job, but he might see decent time as a backup.

48 TONY RICHARDSON / CHIEFS

YEAR	RUSH	YARDS	TDS	REC	YARDS	TDS	100+	GP/GS
1995	8	18	0	0	0	0	0	14/1
1996	4	10	0	2	18	1	0	13/0
1997	2	11	0	3	6	3	0	14/0
1998	20	45	2	2	13	0	0	14/1
1999	84	387	1	24	141	0	0	16/16

Comments: Richardson was the only constant in the Chiefs' running-back-by-committee in 1999. He started at fullback in every game and actually proved to be the most explosive back on the team. Richardson broke four runs of 20 yards or more and led the team with a 4.6-yard average per carry. A punishing lead blocker, Richardson last season proved he could run the ball. After rushing for just 84 yards in his first four seasons, Richardson finished strong, with 284 of his 387 rushing yards in the final five games. He led the team's backs with 24 receptions.

The skinny: The Chiefs will utilize Richardson more for his blocking than his running in 2000.

49 STANLEY PRITCHETT / EAGLES

YEAR	RUSH	YARDS	TDS	REC	YARDS	TDS	100+	GP/GS
1996	7	27	0	33	354	2	0	16/16
1997	3	7	0	5	35	0	0	6/5
1998	6	19	1	17	97	0	0	16/12
1999	47	158	1	43	312	4	0	14/7

Comments: Pritchett gives the Eagles the versatile pass-catching they had expected at the fullback position from Kevin Turner. With the Dolphins in 1999, Pritchett led Miami running backs with five touchdowns. He tied for third on the team with 43 receptions. He started two late-season games at tailback when injuries decimated the position. Pritchett caught 33 passes as a rookie in 1996, but he was primarily a blocking back in 1997 and '98.

The skinny: Pritchett will be a key contributor as a receiver in the Eagles' West Coast offense.

50 LARRY CENTERS / REDSKINS

YEAR	RUSH	YARDS	TDS	REC	YARDS	TDS	100+	GP/GS
1995	78	254	2	101	962	2	2	16/10
1996	116	425	2	99	766	7	1	16/14
1997	101	276	1	54	409	1	0	15/14
1998	31	110	0	69	559	2	0	16/12
1999	13	51	0	69	544	3	0	16/16

Comments: Centers led the Redskins in receiving in 1999, and the team plans to utilize him even more in the passing game this season. Perhaps the best receiving back in NFL history, Centers has had just two high-scoring seasons in his 10-year career. In 1998, he became the Cardinals' career receiving leader with 522 receptions, but he became a salary cap casualty in the offseason. He caught 69 passes that year to top NFC backs and rank second in the league. From 1994 to '96, his 277 catches were unprecedented for a running back. In 1996, Centers stepped up his offensive production by scoring a career-high nine touchdowns. In 1995, Centers set the NFL record for most receptions in a season by a running back (101).

The skinny: Centers may catch 80 passes, but he won't score more than a few touchdowns.

51 MICHAEL PITTMAN / CARDINALS

YEAR	RUSH	YARDS	TDS	REC	YARDS	TDS	100+	GP/GS
1998	29	91	0	0	0	0	0	??/0
1999	64	289	2	16	196	0	1	10/2

Comments: Pittman looks like he's chiseled out of granite, but his physique doesn't translate into football durability. The Cardinals had hoped he would be their long-term answer when he replaced Adrian Murrell in the starting lineup in Game 9. Pittman rushed for 133 yards, including a 58-yard scoring run, and he added a 46-yard reception. Then he suffered turf toe and barely played the rest of the season. A hard but fragile runner, Pittman played just enough as a rookie to show promise.

The skinny: Buff is benched — Pittman will have to settle for a backup role and special-teams play this year.

52 K. ABDUL-JABBAR / CUT BY BROWNS

YEAR	RUSH	YARDS	TDS	REC	YARDS	TDS	100+	GP/GS
1996	307	1116	11	23	139	0	4	16/14
1997	283	892	15	29	261	1	2	16/14
1998	270	960	6	21	102	0	3	15/15
1999	143	445	1	17	84	1	0	13/9

Comments: Abdul-Jabbar's nose for the end zone was knocked off course in 1999. He started the season with the Dolphins, then was benched and traded to the Browns, where he averaged just 3.0 yards per carry and scored just once in 10 games. From 1996 to '98, Abdul-Jabbar produced as so few backs have in their first three seasons, with 33 touchdowns. But, at 5 feet 10, 205 pounds, Abdul-Jabbar is not a big every-down runner. In 1997, Abdul-Jabbar was like gold to his fantasy owners with an NFL-best 16 touchdowns, but he was a source of frustration for the team with a 3.2-yard average per carry. A third-round pick in 1996, Abdul-Jabbar tied for third in the AFC with 11 rushing touchdowns and became Miami's first 1,000-yard rusher in 18 years.

The skinny: Jabbar could catch on as a goal-line back, but he'll never again be a 1,000-yard rusher.

53 FRED LANE / COLTS

YEAR	RUSH	YARDS	TDS	REC	YARDS	TDS	100+	GP/GS
1997	182	809	7	8	27	0	4	13/7
1998	205	717	5	12	85	0	2	14/11
1999	115	475	1	23	163	0	0	15/5

Comments: The Panthers grew tired of Lane's complaints and off-field troubles and unloaded him to the Colts in the offseason. Talented and durable, Lane will back up Edgerrin James. After leading the Panthers in rushing in 1997 and '98, Lane lost his starting job to Tim Biakabutuka last season and was Carolina's second-leading rusher. An undrafted free agent from tiny Lane College, he came out of nowhere in 1997. But in 1998, Lane was his own worst enemy. He grabbed his crotch during an end zone dance and was suspended for one game after arriving late for a team flight. In 1997, he recorded three consecutive 100-yard games and finished second among NFC rookies with a team-high 809 rushing yards in just seven starts.

The skinny: It's hard to believe that Lane has strayed so far away from his humble roots.

54 JOE MONTGOMERY / GIANTS

YEAR	RUSH	YARDS	TDS	REC	YARDS	TDS	100+	GP/GS
1999	115	348	3	0	0	0	1	7/5

Comments: With his mediocre rookie performance in 1999, Montgomery hardly convinced the Giants that he's their every-down back. The fact that Montgomery led the team with 348 rushing yards speaks volumes about why the team drafted Ron Dayne to carry the ground game. Montgomery got off to a slow start due to a hamstring pull, he missed five midseason games to mend a broken foot bone, and he finished the season with bruised ribs. In his first career start, Montgomery gained 111 yards in 38 carries, and he finished the season with a 3.0-yard average per carry.

The skinny: Montgomery will barely even see the ball in 2000 unless Dayne is injured.

55   SKIP HICKS / REDSKINS

YEAR	RUSH	YARDS	TDS	REC	YARDS	TDS	100+	GP/GS
1998	122	433	8	4	23	0	0	9/5
1999	78	257	3	8	72	0	0	10/2

Comments: Hicks lost the starting job to Stephen Davis in the 1999 preseason, and he did nothing to increase his playing time. He averaged just 3.2 yards per carry for the season and gained only 101 yards in 35 carries in two starts for the injured Davis. Hicks didn't play until the the seventh game of 1998, his rookie season, but in just two months he made veteran Terry Allen expendable and became the team's top back. Displaying speed and a knack for getting into the end zone, Hicks set a team record for touchdowns by a rookie (eight). He averaged just 3.5 yards per carry, but he never fumbled in 122 carries.

The skinny: Hicks should be an instant pickup if Davis goes down.

56   THURMAN THOMAS / DOLPHINS

YEAR	RUSH	YARDS	TDS	REC	YARDS	TDS	100+	GP/GS
1995	267	1005	6	26	220	2	3	14/14
1996	281	1033	8	26	254	0	3	15/15
1997	154	643	1	30	208	1	1	16/16
1998	93	381	2	26	220	1	0	14/3
1999	36	152	0	3	37	1	0	5/3

Comments: Cut after 12 seasons in Buffalo, Thomas signed with the Dolphins, where he joins a crowded yet unimpressive backfield. Sidelined for 11 games in 1999 due to a bruised liver, Thomas had become a third-down specialist in Buffalo. An unselfish mentor for Antowain Smith, he rushed for a career-low 381 yards in 1998. In 1996, he joined Barry Sanders as the only players to gain 1,000 yards in eight consecutive seasons. He led the NFL in combined yards from scrimmage from 1989 to '92, breaking an NFL record held by Jim Brown. In 1992, Thomas gained a career-high 2,113 total yards, the ninth-highest total in NFL history. Thomas ranks ninth all-time with 11,938 rushing yards, and seventh with 11,938 combined yards from scrimmage.

The skinny: Thomas has logged too many miles on his body to be an every-down back, so he'll assume a third-down role.

57 SEDRICK IRVIN / LIONS

YEAR	RUSH	YARDS	TDS	REC	YARDS	TDS	100+	GP/GS
1999	36	133	4	25	233	0	0	14/0

Comments: Irvin is the only constant at a position that was completely overhauled in the offseason. He'll battle rookie Reuben Droughns for the job as James Stewart's backup. As a rookie in 1999, Irvin was the closest the Lions had to a goal-line runner. He scored on three short runs and a 16-yarder to lead the team in rushing touchdowns. A speedy change-of-pace back, Irvin led the team's runners with 25 receptions. His playing time increased later in the season.

The skinny: Irvin will probably be utilized as a third-down back.

58 WILLIAM FLOYD / PANTHERS

YEAR	RUSH	YARDS	TDS	REC	YARDS	TDS	100+	GP/GS
1995	64	237	2	47	348	1	0	8/8
1996	47	186	2	26	197	1	0	9/8
1997	78	231	3	37	321	1	0	15/15
1998	28	71	3	24	123	1	0	16/13
1999	35	78	3	23	163	0	0	16/16

Comments: Once an excellent power running and receiving threat, Floyd is now more valuable as a blocker. In 1999, he was Carolina's goal-line back and an occasional option in the short passing game. He punched in three goal-line touchdowns and ranked sixth with 21 receptions. His role in the 1998 Carolina offense was limited to blocking and an occasional catch and carry. Still an excellent goal-line back, he scored four short-range touchdowns. In 1996, he made a miraculous recovery from reconstructive knee surgery. At the time of his 1995 injury, Floyd was tied for eighth in the NFC with 47 receptions.

The skinny: Three or four scores is about all you should expect from Floyd.

59 GREG HILL / CUT BY LIONS

YEAR	RUSH	YARDS	TDS	REC	YARDS	TDS	100+	GP/GS
1995	155	667	1	7	45	0	2	16/1
1996	135	645	4	3	60	1	2	15/1
1997	157	550	0	12	126	0	0	16/16
1998	40	240	4	1	6	0	1	2/2
1999	144	542	2	11	119	1	1	14/8

Comments: Hill was part of the problem rather than a solution to Barry Sanders's retirement in 1999. Although he led the team in rushing, Hill whined about playing time, often missed the hole and averaged just 3.8 yards per carry. In 1998, the Rams' ground game was so bad that Hill's two-game rushing total nearly stood up as the team's season-high total. He started Games 2 and 3 and rushed for four TDs and 240 yards, but he broke his leg and missed the rest of the year. With Kansas City the previous five seasons, Hill never panned out as Marcus Allen's perennial heir apparent.

The skinny: Hill has never gotten the job done for more than a brief stretch.

60 DEREK LOVILLE / RAMS

YEAR	RUSH	YARDS	TDS	REC	YARDS	TDS	100+	GP/GS
1995	218	723	10	87	662	3	0	16/16
1996	70	229	2	16	138	2	0	12/6
1997	24	124	1	2	10	0	0	16/0
1998	53	161	2	2	29	0	0	16/0
1999	40	203	1	11	50	0	0	10/0

Comments: The Rams traded for Loville to get an experienced backup for Marshall Faulk. Steady but unspectacular, Loville has made just 23 starts in 10 seasons, and he has 1,674 career rushing yards and 21 career touchdowns. Last season, he averaged 5.1 yards per carry in a backup role with Denver. In San Francisco, Loville did a commendable job in 1995, when he displayed good hands with 87 catches and a nose for the end zone. He scored more touchdowns (13) that year than every NFC running back except Emmitt Smith.

The skinny: A injury to Faulk would make Loville a very good waiver pickup.

61 MIKE CLOUD / CHIEFS

YEAR	RUSH	YARDS	TDS	REC	YARDS	TDS	100+	GP/GS
1999	35	128	0	3	25	0	0	11/0

Comments: Cloud got lost in a crowded backfield as a rookie in 1999, and he barely got a chance to show what he could do. A second-round pick in the 1999 draft, Cloud was inactive for five of the first six games. In his best game, he rushed for 58 yards in 11 attempts against the archrival Raiders. At 5 feet 10, 205, Cloud doesn't fit the team's blueprint for a big pounder in the backfield. But he has speed that the Chiefs' other backs lack.

The skinny: Cloud will get a chance in camp, but it's doubtful he'll win the starting job.

62 BYRON HANSPARD / FALCONS

YEAR	RUSH	YARDS	TDS	REC	YARDS	TDS	100+	GP/GS
1997	53	335	0	6	53	1	0	16/0
1998	Injured							
1999	136	383	1	10	93	0	1	12/4

Comments: It was painfully obvious last season that Hanspard hadn't fully recovered from 1998 knee surgery. Hanspard, who broke into the league as a big-play threat in 1997, averaged just 2.8 yards per carry last year. He was tentative and lacked the burst he had as a rookie. Hanspard's excellent rookie season offered promise of an increased workload as a change-of-pace back, but he spent the 1998 season on injured reserve. He sparked the Falcons more than they had hoped when they drafted him in the second round in 1997. He became the first Falcon to return two kickoffs for touchdowns. On offense, he broke off runs of 77, 57 and 53 yards, and he averaged 6.3 yards per carry.

The skinny: Hanspard should be back close to 100 percent, but he won't get all that many carries.

63 TERRELL FLETCHER / CHARGERS

YEAR	RUSH	YARDS	TDS	REC	YARDS	TDS	100+	GP/GS
1995	26	140	1	3	26	0	0	16/0
1996	77	282	0	61	476	2	0	16/0
1997	51	161	0	39	292	0	0	13/1
1998	153	543	5	30	188	0	2	12/5
1999	48	126	0	45	360	0	0	15/2

Comments: The sure-handed Fletcher has proven to be more durable than most 5-foot-8, 196-pound backs. A third-down specialist, Fletcher was the team's third-leading receiver in 1999 with 45 receptions. In 1998, he replaced the injured Natrone Means for the final six games and rushed for the century mark twice. Fletcher finished with five rushing touchdowns in the final seven games and a career-high 543 rushing yards. He caught 61 passes in 1996, but his averages of 7.8 yards per catch and 3.7 yards per rush didn't scare many opponents.

The skinny: Fletcher won't come close to his 1998 output of five touchdowns.

64 LEON JOHNSON / JETS

YEAR	RUSH	YARDS	TDS	REC	YARDS	TDS	100+	GP/GS
1997	48	158	2	16	142	0	0	16/1
1998	41	185	2	13	222	2	0	12/2
1999	1	2	0	0	0	0	0	1/1

Comments: Vinny Testaverde's season-opening injury overshadowed the same fate suffered by Johnson, who tore most of the ligaments in his left leg in the 1999 opener. A good change-of-pace backup to Curtis Martin, Johnson became a fantasy transaction after scoring three touchdowns in the third game of 1998 (one on an 82-yard scoring play), then he scored just once more the rest of the season. As a rookie in 1997, Johnson scored on two rushes, a 66-yard punt return and a 101-yard kickoff return. A fourth-round pick in 1997 Johnson has fine career averages of 12.6 yards per catch, 10.2 yards per punt return and 24.0 on kickoff runbacks.

The skinny: Johnson may be a year away from regaining his old form.

65   RODNEY THOMAS / TITANS

YEAR	RUSH	YARDS	TDS	REC	YARDS	TDS	100+	GP/GS
1995	251	947	5	39	204	2	2	16/10
1996	49	151	1	13	128	0	0	16/0
1997	67	310	3	14	111	0	0	16/1
1998	24	100	2	6	55	0	0	11/0
1999	43	164	1	9	72	0	0	16/0

Comments: Thomas is like the Maytag repairman. Eddie George's backup seldom gets any playing time, so he settled for special-teams play and a few carries now and then in 1999. Thomas rushed for 95 yards on 21 attempts in the regular-season finale because the Titans rested George for the playoffs. A hamstring injury sidelined Thomas for five 1998 games. In 1997, he turned just 67 carries into three touchdowns and a 4.6-yard average. Thomas had a big 1995 season, then lost his starting job when the Oilers drafted George. In '95, Thomas had the second-best season by a rookie running back in Oilers history with 947 rushing yards, despite starting just 10 games.

The skinny: In the unlikely event of an injury to George, quickly add Thomas to your roster.

66   ROB KONRAD / DOLPHINS

YEAR	RUSH	YARDS	TDS	REC	YARDS	TDS	100+	GP/GS
1999	9	16	0	34	251	1	0	15/9

Comments: Konrad shared time at fullback with Stanley Pritchett and made a modest impact as a rookie in 1999. He ranked fifth on the team with 34 receptions, but he ran the ball only nine times. The draft addition of blocking fullback Deon Dyer frees up Konrad to be a receiver out of the backfield and possibly a goal-line back in a jumbo backfield.

The skinny: Konrad could score a few touchdowns, but don't expect miracles.

67   ROBERT HOLCOMBE / RAMS

YEAR	RUSH	YARDS	TDS	REC	YARDS	TDS	100+	GP/GS
1998	98	230	2	6	34	0	0	13/7
1999	78	294	4	14	163	1	0	15/6

Comments: Marshall Faulk's backup is almost a moot job, though

Holcombe managed to sneak quite a few carries in 1999. He scored five touchdowns — four on goal-line carries and one on a one-yard catch — and greatly improved his average per carry from a lousy 2.3 yards as a rookie to 3.8 yards last year. Holcombe showed the Rams so little as a 1998 rookie that they buried him to No. 3 on the depth chart and then traded for Faulk in the offseason. On a team looking for a featured runner, Holcombe had the opportunity to take over as the Rams' No. 1 back, but he rushed for just 230 yards.

The skinny: Holcombe will get a few goal-line carries and some mop-up duty, but not much more, especially since Derek Loville and Trung Canidate are now on the roster.

68 JON RITCHIE / RAIDERS

YEAR	RUSH	YARDS	TDS	REC	YARDS	TDS	100+	GP/GS
1998	9	23	0	29	225	0	0	15/10
1999	5	12	0	45	408	1	0	??

Comments: Ritchie is developing into one of the AFC's best all-around fullbacks. A perfect fit for coach Jon Gruden's West Coast offense, Ritchie is a punishing lead blocker and a solid receiver out of the backfield. In 1999, his second season, he ranked second on the Raiders with 45 receptions. He caught more passes than any other AFC fullback. A third-round pick in the 1998 draft, Ritchie seldom runs the ball, but he certainly helps his teammates run it.

The skinny: Maybe if you're desperate in a 16-team league … otherwise, Ritchie is to be appreciated but not drafted.

69 WILLIAM HENDERSON / PACKERS

YEAR	RUSH	YARDS	TDS	REC	YARDS	TDS	100+	GP/GS
1995	7	35	0	3	21	0	0	15/2
1996	39	130	0	27	203	1	0	16/11
1997	31	113	0	41	367	1	0	16/14
1998	23	70	2	37	241	1	0	16/10
1999	7	29	2	30	203	1	0	16/13

Comments: Henderson is practically useless as a runner, but he's a solid blocker with good hands and durability. He ranked fifth on the team with 30 catches, and he played in every game for the fourth consecutive season. He was re-signed before the 1999 season after unsuccessfully testing the free-agent waters. In 1998, Henderson ranked third on the Packers with 37 catches. His 41 receptions in 1997 ranked fourth on the team. He won the starting job in 1996 training camp and started all but five games.

The skinny: Henderson probably won't ever surpass last season's career-high three touchdowns.

70 GARRISON HEARST / 49ERS

YEAR	RUSH	YARDS	TDS	REC	YARDS	TDS	100+	GP/GS
1995	284	1070	1	29	243	1	0	16/15
1996	225	847	0	12	131	1	0	16/12
1997	234	1019	4	21	194	2	3	13/13
1998	310	1570	7	39	535	2	6	16/16
1999	Injured							

Comments: Hearst suffered another setback in his attempt to return from a broken leg and ligament damage suffered in a playoff loss two seasons ago. He needed a second surgery to improve blood circulation and has been given a 70 percent chance of recovery. In 1998, Hearst rushed for a team-record 1,570 yards and piled up 2,105 yards from scrimmage. He led the team with 10 gains of 30 or more yards, and he led the league with four 70-plus-yard plays. Hearst had scored just five touchdowns in his first four seasons, but he scored six in 1997, his first with the 49ers. With the Bengals in 1996, Hearst's 12 fumbles led the NFL.

The skinny: If Hearst contributes at all this season, it won't be until the latter months.

71 HOWARD GRIFFITH / BRONCOS

YEAR	RUSH	YARDS	TDS	REC	YARDS	TDS	100+	GP/GS
1995	65	197	1	11	63	1	0	15/7
1996	12	7	1	27	223	1	0	16/14
1997	9	34	0	11	55	0	0	15/13
1998	4	13	0	15	97	3	0	14/13
1999	17	66	1	26	192	1	0	16/16

Comments: The Broncos threw a bone to Griffith 43 times in 1999, his most touches in four years. An unselfish, devastating blocker, Griffith occasionally scores because nobody expects him to run the ball. He scored three touchdowns in the 1998 postseason to match his regular-season total. In 1997, his first season with the Broncos, Griffith paved the way for Terrell Davis's AFC rushing title. His spectacular one-handed 15-yard touchdown reception in the AFC title game that season gave the Broncos the lead for good.

The skinny: Don't draft Griffith; draft the guy running behind him.

72 KEN OXENDINE / FALCONS

YEAR	RUSH	YARDS	TDS	REC	YARDS	TDS	100+	GP/GS
1998	18	50	0	1	11	0	0	9/0
1999	141	452	1	17	172	1	0	12/9

Comments: For what it was worth, Oxendine was the leading ground-gainer on the NFC's worst rushing team in 1999. He moved into the starting lineup in place of a tentative Byron Hanspard for nine starts, but scored only one touchdown. His 3.2-yard average per carry was barely tolerable, and Oxendine lost four fumbles. In his best game, he rushed for 85 yards in 19 attempts against the Saints.

The skinny: Oxendine isn't even good enough for a No. 2 role.

73 DE'MOND PARKER / PACKERS

YEAR	RUSH	YARDS	TDS	REC	YARDS	TDS	100+	GP/GS
1999	36	184	2	4	15	0	0	11/0

Comments: Just when the Packers' longtime search for a speedy complementary back ended, Parker blew out his knee in the 15th game of 1999. Parker may not be ready for the 2000 season. Even if Parker comes back this year, he may never be the same, because, at 5 feet 10 and 188 pounds, he can't afford to lose a step. As a rookie in 1999, he provided a speed dimension. In his only start in place of the injured Dorsey Levens, Parker rushed for 113 yards and two touchdowns against the Bears. He led the team's backs with a 5.1-yard average per carry.

The skinny: Forget about Parker until the 2001 season.

74 RON RIVERS / CUT BY LIONS

YEAR	RUSH	YARDS	TDS	REC	YARDS	TDS	100+	GP/GS
1995	18	73	1	1	5	0	0	16/0
1996	19	86	0	2	28	0	0	15/0
1997	29	166	1	0	0	0	0	16/0
1998	19	102	1	3	58	0	0	15/0
1999	82	295	0	22	173	1	0	7/6

Comments: Rivers helped the Lions establish a surprisingly adequate ground game in Barry Sanders's absence early in the 1999 season. But he fractured an ankle in Game 6 and played in just one more game, and the Lions' running game ground to a halt. In seven games, Rivers produced four touchdowns, a 4.3-yard average per carry and 468 combined rushing and receiving yards. In his first four seasons, Rivers backed up Sanders and had to settle for an occasional carry.

The skinny: Rivers still has a future as a backup.

75 BARRY SANDERS / NO TEAM

YEAR	RUSH	YARDS	TDS	REC	YARDS	TDS	100+	GP/GS
1995	314	1500	11	48	398	1	7	16/16
1996	307	1553	11	24	147	0	7	16/16
1997	335	2053	11	33	305	3	15	16/16
1998	343	1491	4	37	289	0	8	16/16
1999	DNP							

Comments: Sanders obviously won't return to the Lions, but he just might unretire and chase Walter Payton's all-time NFL rushing record in another uniform. In 1998, Sanders was fantasy frustration, because he carried the Lions into the red zone and then came out of the game. In 1997, a career year, he won his fourth NFL rushing title with a franchise-record 2,053 yards, the second-best single-season total in NFL history. Despite coming out in most goal-line situations, he still scored an NFC-high 14 touchdowns. In 1996, Sanders claimed his third rushing title with 1,553 yards and tied for seventh in the league with 11 rushing scores. Sanders has 15,269 career rushing yards, 77 career 100-yard games and an unprecedented 10 consecutive 1,000-yard seasons.

The skinny: Give it a shot and take a gamble on Sanders with a late-round pick.

LOOKING BACK AT RUNNING BACKS

The Best — Edgerrin James (Colts)

Sure Bets — Fred Taylor (Jaguars), Marshall Faulk (Rams), Terrell Davis (Broncos)

Top Sleepers — Curtis Enis (Bears), Jermaine Fazande (Chargers), Jonathan Linton (Bills), Richard Huntley (Steelers), Raymont Harris (Patriots)

Possible Busts — Jerome Bettis (Steelers), Charlie Garner (49ers), Antowain Smith (Bills), Warrick Dunn (Buccaneers)

Coming On — Duce Staley (Eagles), Jonathan Linton (Bills), Tim Biakabutuka (Panthers), Tyrone Wheatley (Raiders), Richard Huntley (Steelers)

Comeback Candidates — Terrell Davis (Broncos), Jamal Anderson (Falcons), Robert Smith (Vikings), Raymont Harris (Patriots), Garrison Hearst (49ers)

Back to Earth After a Great 1999 — Stephen Davis (Redskins), Olandis Gary (Broncos), Tyrone Wheatley (Raiders), Charlie Garner (49ers), Mario Bates (Cardinals)

In for a Career Year — Curtis Enis (Bears), Tim Biakabutuka (Panthers), Duce Staley (Eagles)

Top Rookies — Ron Dayne (Giants), Thomas Jones (Cardinals), Jamal Lewis (Ravens), J. R. Redmond (Patriots), Shaun Alexander (Seahawks), Travis Prentice (Browns)

1999 Injured Players Who Will Be a Factor in '00 — Terrell Davis (Broncos), Jamal Anderson (Falcons), Kimble Anders (Chiefs)

1999 Rookies Who Will Come On — Ricky Williams (Saints), Jermaine Fazande (Chargers), J. J. Johnson (Dolphins), Kevin Faulk (Patriots)

Top Players on a New Team — James Stewart (Lions), Errict Rhett (Browns), Adrian Murrell (Redskins), Natrone Means (Panthers), Ahman Green (Packers), Thurman Thomas (Dolphins), Fred Lane (Colts), Derek Loville (Rams), Stanley Pritchett (Eagles)

Will Struggle on a New Team — Errict Rhett (Browns), Thurman Thomas (Dolphins)

Late-Round Gambles — Barry Sanders, Fred Beasley (49ers), Adrian Murrell (Redskins), Richard Huntley (Panthers), Natrone Means (Panthers), Ahman Green (Packers), Raymont Harris (Patriots)

Best Backups — Chris Warren (Cowboys), Adrian Murrell (Redskins), Olandis Gary (Broncos), Richard Huntley (Steelers), Priest Holmes

(Ravens), Natrone Means (Panthers), Fred Lane (Colts), Rodney Thomas (Titans), Ahman Green (Packers)

Top Receivers — Larry Centers (Cardinals), Marshall Faulk (Rams), Fred Taylor (Jaguars), Edgerrin James (Colts), Charlie Garner (49ers), Warrick Dunn (Buccaneers), Kimble Anders (Chiefs), Ricky Watters (Seahawks), Duce Staley (Eagles), Terry Kirby (Browns)

Best Big-Play Threats — Fred Taylor (Jaguars), Edgerrin James (Colts), Marshall Faulk (Rams), Robert Smith (Vikings), Napoleon Kaufman (Raiders), Tim Biakabutuka (Panthers)

Best of the Rest

Anthony Johnson, Panthers
Gary Brown, cut by Giants
Darick Holmes, cut by Colts
Zack Crockett, Raiders
Charles Way, Giants
Amp Lee, cut by Rams
Brian Mitchell, Redskins
Kevin Turner, cut by Eagles
Aaron Craver, cut by Saints
Leeland McElroy, Colts
Richie Anderson, Jets
Mack Strong, Seahawks

Rashaan Shehee, Chiefs
Jay Graham, Ravens
Sedrick Shaw, Bengals
Travis Jervey, 49ers
Edgar Bennett, cut by Bears
Lamont Warren, cut by Patriots
Tony Carter, Patriots
Charles Evans, Ravens
Shawn Bryson, Bills
Stacey Mack, Jaguars
Chris Fuamatu-Ma'afala, Steelers

RUNNING BACKS

Chapter 5

WIDE RECEIVERS

MARVIN HARRISON

  Wide receivers are a little like politicians. They're easy to find but it's hard to find one you can rely on for consistent production. There are 62 starting wide receivers in the NFL, as well as a handful of No. 3 receivers who play enough to be considered starters. Yet only six wide receivers scored 10 or more touchdowns last season. That tells you there are precious few wideouts who can carry your fantasy team — especially in a Basic Scoring league. In performance leagues, shopping for a receiver is much easier because quite a few produce plenty of catches and yardage. In 1999, 26 receivers reached the 1,000-yard mark, and 25 wideouts caught 70 or more passes.

Finding a top-notch receiver isn't as simple as identifying the wide-open passing teams, though that certainly helps to pick high-scoring players. Some receivers excel on struggling offensive teams. Who would've expected that Cleveland's Kevin Johnson would score eight touchdowns and gain nearly 1,000 receiving yards as a rookie on an expansion team that ranked last in the league in points.

A big factor in finding the best receivers is identifying the top quarterbacks. Marvin Harrison will continue to catch bombs, and so will the Rams' Isaac Bruce (as long as he stays on the field).

Draft Tips for Choosing Wide Receivers

■ Look at past performances, especially the last two or three seasons, rather than just last season.

■ Draft receivers from pass-oriented teams, such as the Vikings, Panthers, Packers, Seahawks, Jaguars and Redskins. Forget about running teams like the Titans, Buccaneers, Steelers and Chargers.

■ Draft receivers who are favorite targets of a good quarterback, such as Marvin Harrison, Jimmy Smith, Tim Brown, Keyshawn Johnson and Isaac Bruce.

■ Don't overlook the secondary receivers, such as Ed McCaffrey, Keenan McCardell, Sean Dawkins, Bill Schroeder, Albert Connell, Darnay Scott and Johnnie Morton, because they occasionally score more over an entire season (and certainly in stretches) than the main receiver. Also, if the primary receiver gets injured, the secondary receiver becomes the main target.

■ Remember that in today's era of three- and four-wide-receiver formations, a receiver does not have to be a starter to make a big contribution. Several backup wideouts catch half a dozen touchdown passes each season, which is as many as — or more than — a lot of the good starters will catch.

■ Remember to draft rookies who might break into the starting lineup, such as Peter Warrick, Plaxico Burress, Travis Taylor, Sylvester Morris and Dez White. Usually at least one or two rookies make an immediate impact, and it's up to you to determine who will do it in 2000. With such an outstanding group of rookie receivers (and quite a few teams looking to fill a gaping hole in their starting lineup), several are bound to make an immediate impact.

■ Look for speed receivers who make the big plays, rather than possession receivers (especially in the Performance Scoring System).

■ Make sure you have capable backups who can take over if one of your starters is injured or out of the lineup on a bye.

■ If a team has just made a quarterback change or it looks as if a team will have inconsistent quarterbacking throughout the season, take that into consideration. The Chargers, Steelers, Buccaneers, 49ers and Dolphins look as if they might have unstable quarterback situations this year.

■ Be aware of what is going on during training camp. Keep an eye on the teams with unsettled starting receiver positions. The Ravens, Bengals, Browns, Patriots, Colts, Chiefs, Eagles, Steelers and Buccaneers all have competition at a starting position. Know which rookies are in a good situation to make an immediate impact. What kind of quarterbacking will Randy Moss and Cris Carter have in Minnesota? Does Jerry Rice have another good year left in his aging body? Is Peerless Price ready to step into a starting role and contribute right away? What kind of chemistry will Joey Galloway develop with Troy Aikman? Will Detroit's Herman Moore be the dominant player he once was? With Jeff Blake at quarterback, are Saints receivers headed for career years? Will the Raiders replace James Jett in the starting lineup with a receiver more suited for Jon Gruden's West Coast offense? Who will get the ball to Curtis Conway and Jeff Graham in San Diego? Will Carl Pickens be a cancer or a contributor in Cincinnati?

1 MARVIN HARRISON / COLTS

YEAR	REC.	YARDS	AVG.	TDS	100+	GP/GS
1996	64	836	13.1	8	2	16/15
1997	73	866	11.9	6	0	16/15
1998	59	776	13.2	7	2	12/12
1999	115	1663	14.5	12	9	16/16

Comments: A good but not great player for his first three seasons, Harrison became the best receiver in the NFL in 1999. He led the NFL with 1,663 yards, finished second with a team-record 115 catches, and he tied for second in the league with 12 touchdown catches. Harrison teamed with Peyton Manning to become the NFL's premier passing combination, as they hit on at least one 30-yard pass play in 12 games. Harrison carried fantasy teams in the first 10 games, when he scored all of his touchdowns. Though he was shut out over the final six weeks, he did have four 100-yard games in that span. In 1998, a shoulder separation in Week 13 put a premature end to Harrison's third consecutive solid season. He still led the Colts' wide receivers with 59 catches and tied for the team lead with seven touchdown grabs. Given the Colts' mighty offensive struggles of 1996 and '97, Harrison played exceptionally well. He has proved to be the most productive member of an exceptional crop of receivers from 1996.

The skinny: Harrison's 1999 season was a sign of more to come, especially with Peyton Manning throwing to him.

2 RANDY MOSS / VIKINGS

YEAR	REC.	YARDS	AVG.	TDS	100+	GP/GS
1998	69	1313	19.0	17	4	16/11
1999	80	1413	17.7	11	7	16/16

Comments: The NFL adjusted to the Moss factor in 1999. He still excelled in the face of taller defenders and double teams, but his touchdown total was somewhat less than expected. Moss led the NFC with a Vikings-record 1,413 receiving yards, and he tied a team record with five catches of 50 or more yards. Moss scored 12 touchdowns (one on a punt return), and he threw a TD pass. He made such a huge impact in his rookie season of 1998 that teams were left scrambling to find defensive backs who could guard him. He smashed an NFL rookie record with 17 touchdown catches. Unbelievably, Moss gained 40 or more yards with 14 receptions. He was second in the league in scoring among nonkickers, his 19-yard average per catch led the NFC, and his 1,313 receiving yards were the league's third most. As a rookie, Moss set 28 team records and three league records. In four postseason games, Moss has five touchdown catches.

The skinny: Moss could make any quarterback look good, even unproven second-year player Daunte Culpepper.

3 ANTONIO FREEMAN / PACKERS

YEAR	REC.	YARDS	AVG.	TDS	100+	GP/GS
1995	8	106	13.3	1	0	11/0
1996	56	933	16.7	9	4	12/12
1997	81	1243	15.3	12	3	16/16
1998	84	1424	17.0	14	6	15/15
1999	74	1074	14.5	6	3	16/16

Comments: Freeman is the one playmaker still in Brett Favre's arsenal. An excellent runner after the catch, Freeman last season led the Packers in receiving for the fourth consecutive year. A body catcher, Freeman drops too many passes. But he's undeniably productive, with three straight 1,000-yard seasons and 41 touchdown catches in the past four years. In 1998, Freeman led the NFL with 1,424 receiving yards. His 14 touchdown catches tied for second in the league, he produced seven plays of 40 or more yards, and he led the NFL with 578 yards after the catch. In 1997, Freeman became Green Bay's best big-play threat, with 12 touchdown catches and 1,243 receiving yards. In 1996, Freeman catapulted himself from a virtual unknown to a dangerous, emerging star. He won a starting job in training camp. In his first two games after returning from a fractured forearm, Freeman caught 19 passes for 331 yards and three touchdowns — all while wearing a cast.

The skinny: Freeman will find the end zone at least 10 times in 2000.

4   CRIS CARTER / VIKINGS

YEAR	REC.	YARDS	AVG.	TDS	100+	GP/GS
1995	122	1371	11.2	17	5	16/16
1996	96	1163	12.1	10	1	16/16
1997	89	1069	12.0	13	4	16/16
1998	78	1011	13.0	12	3	16/16
1999	90	1241	13.8	13	5	16/16

Comments: Carter suffered hip and ankle injuries that would've sidelined many players last season, but he still produced one of his best seasons. He led the NFL with 13 touchdown catches, ranked second in the NFC with 90 catches, and had four consecutive 100-yard games. In 1998, Carter led the Vikings with 78 catches, and he ranked fourth in the NFC with 12 touchdown catches. In 1997, he led the league with 13 touchdown catches and tied for the most two-point conversions (three). Carter was a fantasy owner's dream in 1995, when he tied for the NFL lead with 17 touchdown receptions and tied a team record with five 100-yard receiving games. That year he became the second player in NFL history with back-to-back 100-catch seasons, and he had more receptions over a two-year period (244) than anyone in NFL history. Carter ranks second on the all-time touchdown reception list with 114 and fourth in receptions with 924. In the last five years, he has 65 touchdown catches.

The skinny: Carter is the most consistent touchdown-maker in the NFL.

5 ISAAC BRUCE / RAMS

YEAR	REC.	YARDS	AVG.	TDS	100+	GP/GS
1995	119	1781	15.0	13	9	16/16
1996	84	1338	15.9	7	4	16/16
1997	56	815	14.6	5	2	12/12
1998	32	457	14.3	1	2	5/5
1999	77	1165	15.1	12	4	16/16

Comments: The Rams paid extra attention to Bruce's tender hamstrings in 1999, and the result was his first full season in three years. He tied for second in the NFL with 12 touchdown catches and ranked eighth in the NFC in receiving yards and 13th in receptions. Those numbers were in sharp contrast to Bruce's two previous seasons, when he was a maddening, wasted early-round fantasy draft pick. Plagued by a hamstring injury, he played in only five 1998 games. In 1997, hamstring and wrist injuries limited Bruce to 56 catches, though his 233 receiving yards in Week 9 was the league's highest output all season. In 1996, Bruce proved to be no one-year wonder by leading the NFL with 1,338 receiving yards. In 1995, he became the top waiver pickup in fantasy leagues with his stunning season. Bruce logged the fifth-most receptions (119) and the second-most receiving yards (1,781) in NFL history.

The skinny: Like to gamble? Bruce remains one of the game's ultimate high-risk, high-reward players.

6 JOEY GALLOWAY / COWBOYS

YEAR	REC.	YARDS	AVG.	TDS	100+	GP/GS
1995	67	1039	15.5	7	3	16/16
1996	57	987	17.3	7	2	16/16
1997	72	1049	14.6	12	3	15/15
1998	65	1047	16.1	10	4	16/16
1999	22	335	15.2	1	0	8/4

Comments: The Cowboys were so desperate for a No. 1 receiver that they traded two first-round draft picks to get Galloway. A sloppy route runner, Galloway gained just 12 yards after the catch last year, after he had held out for the first half of the season. Nevertheless, he is a true gamebreaker and a threat to score on every play. His own worst enemy in 1999, Galloway held out in an attempt to get his contract renegotiated. He showed up for the final eight games and failed to make much of an impact. Galloway put up good numbers in 1998, despite facing almost constant double-teams. He led AFC receivers with 12 TDs (two on punt returns),

WIDE RECEIVERS

and he gained 40 or more yards with seven of his catches. In 1997, he tied for the AFC lead with 12 TD catches, and he proved his durability by playing with a sprained toe. In 1995, Galloway burst upon the NFL scene as no rookie had in a decade. He became the first rookie in Seattle history (and the 10th in NFL history) to record 1,000 receiving yards.

The skinny: Galloway will thrive catching passes from Troy Aikman, one of the most accurate all-time quarterbacks.

7   JIMMY SMITH / JAGUARS

YEAR	REC.	YARDS	AVG.	TDS	100+	GP/GS
1995	22	288	13.1	3	0	16/4
1996	83	1244	15.0	7	4	16/9
1997	82	1324	16.1	4	6	16/16
1998	78	1182	15.2	8	5	16/15
1999	116	1636	14.1	6	9	16/16

Comments: In a decade of wide receiver dominance, Smith has quietly ranked among the best. From 1996 to '99, he accumulated the most receiving yards (5,386) and the second-most receptions (359) of anyone. Strong enough to break through line jams and fast enough to run by defenders, Smith led the NFL with 116 receptions in 1999. His 1,636 receiving yards were the sixth most in NFL history. Those are hard-to-believe numbers from a player who missed the 1993 season due to complications following an appendectomy and sat out 1994. In 1998, he ranked seventh in the AFC in receptions (12 of which gained 30 or more yards) and fifth in the NFL with 1,182 receiving yards. Smith wasn't even a starter when the 1996 season began, but when it ended he had emerged as one of the AFC's best receivers. He led the conference with 1,244 receiving yards.

The skinny: With all of his catches, Smith is overdue for a season with double-digit touchdowns.

8   ERIC MOULDS / BILLS

YEAR	REC.	YARDS	AVG.	TDS	100+	GP/GS
1996	20	279	14.0	2	0	16/5
1997	29	294	10.1	0	0	16/8
1998	67	1368	20.4	9	4	16/15
1999	65	994	15.3	7	3	14/14

Comments: Moulds didn't dominate the 1999 season as he had the previous year. Slowed by double coverages, a hamstring injury and Doug Flutie's mediocrity, Moulds struggled to get open deep. His longest play covered 54 yards (four of his touchdowns covered 60 yards or more in 1998). Moulds scored a touchdown in five straight games played, but his average per catch plummeted from 20.4 in 1998 to 15.3 past year. In 1998, in one quantum leap, he became the best big-play receiver in the AFC. Moulds led the AFC with a team-record 1,368 receiving yards. He finished the regular season with 100 receiving yards in three of the final five games, then he added 240 receiving yards and a touchdown in the Bills' wild-card loss. Expected to emerge in 1997, his second season, Moulds failed to live up to his first-round ability. He played in every game, yet he caught just 29 passes.

The skinny: The Rob Johnson–to–Moulds connection will be among the AFC's best in 2000.

9   MARCUS ROBINSON / BEARS

YEAR	REC.	YARDS	AVG.	TDS	100+	GP/GS
1997	DNP					
1998	4	44	11.0	1	0	3/0
1999	64	1400	16.7	9	5	16/11

Comments: Tall and fast, Robinson is prototypical of the new breed of receivers who have become the Randy Moss–inspired rage. Robinson's 1999 rags-to-riches story nearly rivals that of MVP Kurt Warner. A college sprinter, Robinson was a project when the Bears drafted him in the fourth round in 1997. He spent his rookie season on injured reserve, then earned MVP honors in NFL Europe. Robinson played sparingly in 1998, and he was on the bubble when the Bears made their final cuts last year. He cracked the starting lineup in place of the injured Curtis Conway in Week 6 and proceeded to pile up 1,400 receiving yards, the NFC's second most. Robinson went over the top of defenders and ran by them for seven touchdown catches of 30 yards or more. With nine touchdowns, he was the first nonkicker to lead the Bears in scoring in 10 years.

The skinny: Robinson is just getting started, and he can't be stopped.

10 KEYSHAWN JOHNSON / BUCCANEERS

YEAR	REC.	YARDS	AVG.	TDS	100+	GP/GS
1996	63	844	13.4	8	0	14/11
1997	70	963	13.8	5	1	16/16
1998	83	1131	13.6	10	4	16/16
1999	89	1170	13.1	8	2	16/16

Comments: The Buccaneers traded two first-round draft picks for Johnson, then made him the league's highest-paid receiver. In 1999, the Jets' loss of Vinny Testaverde hardly affected Johnson, who set career highs for catches and receiving yards. A complete, clutch player with exceptional hands, he's a great downfield blocker. Johnson's statistics certainly matched his ego in 1998, when he elevated himself near the top of the league's receivers. He ranked second in the AFC with 11 touchdown catches and fourth in the AFC with 83 receptions. The first pick in the 1996 draft, the only thing bigger than Johnson's numbers that year was his mouth. He set club rookie records for receiving yards (844) and touchdown catches (eight), but he constantly complained about not getting the ball enough. Only two receivers in NFL history have ever caught more passes than Johnson in his first four seasons.

The skinny: Johnson's numbers didn't suffer despite last year's quarterbacking, so don't expect anything less on the Buccaneers.

11 TIM BROWN / RAIDERS

YEAR	REC.	YARDS	AVG.	TDS	100+	GP/GS
1995	89	1342	15.1	10	6	16/16
1996	90	1104	12.3	9	2	16/16
1997	104	1408	13.5	5	7	16/16
1998	81	1012	12.5	9	3	16/16
1999	90	1344	14.9	6	6	16/16

Comments: Brown has more catches (365) than any NFL receiver over the past four seasons. His 12th season was his second best ever. In 1999, Brown ranked fourth in the league with 90 catches and fifth in the NFL with 1,344 receiving yards. He produced remarkably well in 1998, given the Raiders' quarterback instability. He ranked sixth in the AFC with 81 catches and he tied for fifth in the conference with nine touchdown catches. In 1997, he did everything except score touchdowns, tying Herman Moore for the NFL receiving title with a career-high and franchise-record 104 catches. He ranked second in the league with

1,408 receiving yards and seven 100-yard receiving games. He led the AFC in receiving yardage from 1993 to '95. He has a team-record seven consecutive 1,000-yard receiving seasons.

The skinny: Brown is a performance league superstar and a starter in Basic Scoring leagues.

12 ED McCAFFREY / BRONCOS

YEAR	REC.	YARDS	AVG.	TDS	100+	GP/GS
1995	39	477	12.2	2	0	16/5
1996	48	553	11.5	7	0	16/15
1997	45	490	13.1	8	1	15/15
1998	64	1053	16.5	10	4	15/15
1999	71	1018	14.3	7	4	15/15

Comments: A McCaffrey stiff-arm is a formidable weapon and a big reason why he piles up so many yards after the catch. The 6-foot-5 McCaffrey started the 1999 season strong but faded down the stretch. In the first seven games, he scored six touchdowns (including three in the season opener) and had three 100-yard receiving games. He was held scoreless in the final six weeks. From 1997 to '98, only four receivers caught more touchdown passes than McCaffrey, who tied for the AFC lead in 1998 with 10 touchdown grabs. McCaffrey got downfield for catches of 32 or more yards in nine games that year, and his 16.5-yard average per catch was the AFC's sixth best. In 1997, his eight receiving TDs tied for fifth in the AFC. In 1992, he led the Giants with 49 catches and five receiving TDs.

The skinny: Given the Broncos' mediocre quarterbacking, McCaffrey's production will be solid but unspectacular.

13 MICHAEL WESTBROOK / REDSKINS

YEAR	REC.	YARDS	AVG.	TDS	100+	GP/GS
1995	34	522	15.4	1	0	11/9
1996	34	505	14.9	1	1	11/6
1997	34	559	16.4	3	7	13/9
1998	44	736	16.7	6	4	11/10
1999	65	1191	18.3	9	5	16/16

Comments: Well, it's about time. It took Westbrook only five years to deliver the promise of a first-round pick. In 1999, he remained in the lineup (playing with a fractured wrist) and ranked ninth in the league with 1,191 receiving yards. Only five NFC receivers scored more TDs than Westbrook, who tied teammate Albert Connell with the best average per catch of any NFL receiver with 60 or more catches. Westbrook made a remarkable recovery from a career-threatening ruptured neck disk that shortened his 1998 season. That year, Westbrook led the team with 736 receiving yards and a 16.7-yard average per catch. Westbrook was a model of mediocre consistency with 34 catches in each of his first three pro seasons.

The skinny: Go-to players like Westbrook on explosive teams like the Redskins are exactly whom you want to draft.

14 MUHSIN MUHAMMAD / PANTHERS

YEAR	REC.	YARDS	AVG.	TDS	100+	GP/GS
1996	25	407	16.3	1	0	9/5
1997	27	317	11.7	0	0	13/5
1998	68	941	13.8	6	3	16/16
1999	96	1253	13.1	8	5	15/15

Comments: Muhammad has developed into the league's best possession receiver. At 6 feet 2, 215 pounds, he has the hands to go over defenders and the size to break tackles. In 1999, he led the NFC with 96 receptions, his 1,253 receiving yards ranked seventh in the league, and he had five 100-yard receiving games. Muhammad caught at least four passes in every game played (he missed one to nurse a hamstring injury). In 1998, Muhammad got off to a huge start with three touchdown grabs and more than 100 receiving yards in two of the first four games. He tailed off somewhat but still finished second on the Panthers in receptions, receiving yards and touchdowns. In his first two seasons Muhammad contributed more with his blocking than his pass catching. He was sidelined for three 1997 games due to a broken wrist, and injuries also short-circuited his rookie season in 1996.

The skinny: Injuries are all that can stop Muhammad now.

15 GERMANE CROWELL / LIONS

YEAR	REC.	YARDS	AVG.	TDS	100+	GP/GS
1998	25	464	18.6	3	0	14/2
1999	81	1338	16.5	7	6	16/15

Comments: Crowell gives the Lions a tough decision that every coach could live with — how to keep three excellent receivers on the field at the same time. With Herman Moore injured in 1999, Crowell emerged as one of the league's best young wideouts. Only one active receiver (Jerry Rice) had more catches in his second season than Crowell. A virtual Moore look-alike in pads, the 6-foot-3 Crowell has great speed to complement his height. In 1999, he registered six 100-yard receiving games (only four players had more), and he gained 1,338 receiving yards — third best in team history. As the Lions' No. 3 receiver in 1998, Crowell led the team with an 18.6-yard average per catch. He ranked second among NFC rookies with 25 receptions. Seven of his career scores have covered more than 25 yards.

The skinny: A true home-run hitter, Crowell is just too good to be limited to third-down duty.

16 PATRICK JEFFERS / PANTHERS

YEAR	REC.	YARDS	AVG.	TDS	100+	GP/GS
1996	0	0	0.0	0	0	4/0
1997	3	24	8.0	0	0	10/0
1998	18	330	18.3	2	0	8/1
1999	63	1082	17.2	12	5	15/10

Comments: Jeffers began the 1999 season as the No. 3 receiver on an offense that appeared mediocre. He finished the season as a big part of a dominant receiving duo. He cracked the starting lineup in Game 6 and finished the season with five consecutive 100-yard receiving games. Jeffers, who tied for second in the NFL with 12 touchdown receptions, had eight scores in the final five games. Nine of his touchdown grabs covered 30 or more yards. Jeffers made the most of a one-year contract in 1999, then cashed in with a four-year contract extension. He played little with the Cowboys in 1998, then was traded to the Panthers. Jeffers has great size and good hands, and he runs well after the catch.

The skinny: Jeffers won't score 12 more touchdowns this season, but he's no one-year wonder.

17 HERMAN MOORE / LIONS

YEAR	REC.	YARDS	AVG.	TDS	100+	GP/GS
1995	123	1686	13.7	14	10	16/16
1996	106	1296	12.2	9	5	16/16
1997	104	1293	12.4	8	6	16/16
1998	82	983	12.0	5	4	15/15
1999	16	197	12.3	2	0	8/4

Comments: Two separate knee injuries wrecked Moore's 1999 season. He returned for the final six games but made little impact. An injury in the opener snapped his streak of 107 straight games with a reception. In 1998, Moore was held scoreless for the first eight games before finally developing some chemistry with rookie quarterback Charlie Batch. Moore, who ranked fourth in the NFC with 82 catches, became the fastest player in NFL history to record 600 receptions. His typically outstanding numbers didn't thrill fantasy players in 1997 because they expected more than eight touchdowns. He tied for the league lead with 104 receptions, which tied Jerry Rice's record for consecutive 100-catch seasons (three). He set the NFL single-season reception record with 123 catches in 1995. That year he piled up 1,686 receiving yards, 14 TD catches and a team-record 10 games with 100 receiving yards.

The skinny: Moore will have a huge comeback season.

18 TERANCE MATHIS / FALCONS

YEAR	REC.	YARDS	AVG.	TDS	100+	GP/GS
1995	78	1039	13.3	9	2	14/12
1996	69	771	11.2	7	2	16/16
1997	62	802	12.9	6	1	16/16
1998	64	1136	17.8	11	3	16/16
1999	81	1016	12.5	6	1	16/16

Comments: Mathis was a bright spot on a Falcons offense that was a lost cause in 1999. He fought through common double-teams to catch 81 passes — the most ever by a Dan Reeves–coached club — to tie for 10th in the NFL. His touchdown production and average per catch suffered because the team's nonexistent ground game failed to keep defenses honest. In 1998, Mathis tied for seventh in the NFL with 11 touchdown catches (he added three scores in the postseason). His 17.8-yard average per catch was the league's eighth best (among players with

30 or more catches), and he ranked ninth with 1,136 receiving yards. A true free-agent find, he established himself among the league's elite from 1994 to '96. Mathis had just 93 receptions with the Jets in the first four years of his career, but he posted phenomenal numbers in 1994. He set a team record for catches with 111, then the fourth-highest total in league history.

The skinny: Mathis is well-suited for a No. 2 receiving role on your fantasy team.

19 KEVIN JOHNSON / BROWNS

YEAR	REC.	YARDS	AVG.	TDS	100+	GP/GS
1999	66	986	14.9	8	2	16/16

Comments: The Browns couldn't have asked more from Johnson as a rookie in 1999. The first player drafted in the second round, Johnson developed into a rarity — a big-play threat on a first-year expansion team. Eight of his receptions covered 30 or more yards, and he tied for fifth in the AFC with eight touchdown catches. Johnson led all rookie receivers in receptions, receiving touchdowns and receiving yards. A good practice player who seldom drops passes, Johnson caught at least two passes in every game. Even though the Browns are not a very good team, Johnson does have a very good quarterback in Tim Couch throwing to him.

The skinny: Johnson will only get better, but not until he is surrounded by better talent to help draw away double-teams.

20 JAKE REED / SAINTS

YEAR	REC.	YARDS	AVG.	TDS	100+	GP/GS
1995	72	1167	16.2	9	3	16/16
1996	72	1320	18.3	7	3	16/15
1997	68	1138	16.7	6	5	16/16
1998	34	474	13.9	4	1	11/11
1999	44	643	14.6	2	2	16/8

Comments: Reed became an almost irrelevant piece of the Vikings' passing game the past two seasons, so he left for New Orleans, where he'll be the No. 1 receiver. In 1999, he caught 44 passes in a No. 3 receiving role. A combination of back surgery and Randy Moss slowed Reed's 1998 season, though he did score four touchdowns. In 1997, Reed started out like gangbusters, with 34 catches and four TDs in the first five games. He finished ninth in the NFC with 68 catches and sixth with 1,138 receiving yards. In 1996, Reed's 1,320 receiving yards ranked second in team history. After just 11 catches in his first three seasons, Reed turned promise into production in 1994, with 85 catches for 1,175 yards. He has 12 career catches of 50 or more yards, and 17 100-yard receiving games.

The skinny: With Jeff Blake throwing to him, Reed will return to the 1,000-yard club in 2000.

21 AMANI TOOMER / GIANTS

YEAR	REC.	YARDS	AVG.	TDS	100+	GP/GS
1996	1	12	12.0	0	0	7/1
1997	16	263	16.4	1	0	16/0
1998	27	360	13.3	5	0	16/0
1999	79	1183	15.0	6	4	16/16

Comments: Toomer helped put the forward pass back into the Giants' offense in 1999. In his first season as a starter, he set a single-season franchise record with 79 catches, and he piled up the most receiving yards by a Giant in 32 years. In one game, he caught six passes for 181 yards and three touchdowns. Toomer had been a big disappointment in three previous seasons. The Giants' No. 3 receiver in 1998, he tied for second on the team with five touchdowns. But his biggest pass play covered just 36 yards, and his 7.2-yard punt-return average hardly posed a threat. In 1997, Toomer made his biggest contribution returning punts. He made an immediate impact as an outstanding rookie punt returner in 1996, when he scored on runbacks of 87 and 65 yards.

The skinny: Toomer has developed a good chemistry with Kerry Collins, so his career is just now taking off.

22 ROD SMITH / BRONCOS

YEAR	REC.	YARDS	AVG.	TDS	100+	GP/GS
1995	6	152	25.3	1	0	16/1
1996	16	237	14.8	2	0	10/1
1997	70	1180	16.9	12	6	16/16
1998	86	1222	14.2	6	4	16/16
1999	79	1020	12.9	4	3	15/15

Comments: Smith missed John Elway's presence as much as any

Broncos player in 1999. He ranked fifth in the AFC in receptions and ninth in receiving yards, but he scored just four times. Only one of Smith's receptions covered 35 or more yards, as he became more of a short-range target than he had in the two previous seasons. Smith came on strong with 60 receptions in the final nine games. In 1998, he proved his breakthrough 1997 season was no fluke by catching a career-high 86 passes. Smith tied for third in the NFL in receptions and was fourth with 1,222 receiving yards. In 1997, he was the one NFL receiver who seemingly came out of nowhere to have a huge year. Smith had just two NFL starts in two previous seasons, but he became Elway's big-play receiver in 1997. He tied for the AFC lead with 12 TD catches, and nine of his plays went for 30 yards or longer.

The skinny: Don't draft Smith too early. With just 10 scores in the past two seasons, he's more suited for a fantasy backup role.

23 ROB MOORE / CARDINALS

YEAR	REC.	YARDS	AVG.	TDS	100+	GP/GS
1995	63	907	14.4	5	3	15/15
1996	58	1016	17.5	4	3	16/16
1997	97	1584	16.3	8	8	16/16
1998	67	982	14.7	5	2	16/16
1999	37	621	16.8	5	2	14/12

Comments: Moore is coming off the worst season of his 10-year career, a performance that was hindered by a preseason holdout, a pulled hamstring and poor quarterbacking. Moore did lead the team with five touchdown receptions, and his 71-yard catch was the team's longest in seven years. In 1998, Moore served as a possession receiver rather than a big-play maker. He caught just two passes for 40 or more yards, three fewer than the previous season. In 1997, Moore hooked up with rookie quarterback Jake Plummer for seven touchdown strikes in the final nine weeks. He had a spectacular career season in which he led the NFL with a team-record 1,584 receiving yards and posted eight 100-yard receiving games. Moore ranks 19th in NFL history in receptions (628) and receiving yards (9,368).

The skinny: Moore is probably headed for a 1,000-yard season, but don't expect more than a handful of touchdowns.

24 CARL PICKENS / BENGALS

YEAR	REC.	YARDS	AVG.	TDS	100+	GP/GS
1995	99	1234	12.5	17	5	16/15
1996	100	1180	11.8	12	2	16/16
1997	52	695	13.4	5	1	12/12
1998	82	1023	12.5	5	2	16/16
1999	57	737	12.9	6	2	16/14

Comments: Pickens was a cancer on the Bengals the past two seasons, though his talent and production are undeniable. Last season, he caught 57 passes but relinquished his role as the team's go-to receiver to Darnay Scott. Pickens became the first Bengal to reach 500 career receptions, and he has caught at least one pass in 93 straight games. In 1998, Pickens came back strong from an off year in 1997, but he scored just five times. The magic that once made Jeff Blake–to–Carl Pickens the No. 1 connection in fantasy football was missing in 1997, when Pickens finished with his worst statistics in four years. In 1996, he broke his year-old team single-season reception record with 100 catches. His 17 touchdown grabs in 1995 tied for the league lead, and only three receivers in NFL history have caught more TD passes in a season.

The skinny: Pickens needs a change of scenery, or else he'll never rekindle any of his old magic.

25 TERRELL OWENS / 49ERS

YEAR	REC.	YARDS	AVG.	TDS	100+	GP/GS
1996	35	520	14.9	4	1	16/10
1997	60	936	15.6	8	0	16/15
1998	67	1097	16.4	14	2	16/8
1999	60	754	12.6	4	2	14/14

Comments: Owens was a hot commodity on fantasy draft night last summer. But four months later, he was a huge disappointment — largely due to shaky quarterbacking. A dangerous big-play receiver the two previous seasons, Owens's longest play covered just 36 yards last year. Throughout much of 1998, he played like the NFL's No. 1 receiver this side of Randy Moss, with at least one touchdown in 11 of the final 12 games. Owens tied for second in the NFL with 14 touchdown catches, his 1,097 receiving yards ranked seventh in the NFC, and he led the 49ers with a 16.4-yard average per catch. In 1997, the physical 6-foot-3, 217-pound Owens stepped up in the absence of the injured Jerry

Rice and tied for fifth in the NFC with eight touchdown catches. As a rookie third-round pick in 1996, he ranked second on the 49ers with 520 receiving yards.

The skinny: Don't expect another huge season from Owens until the 49ers find a quarterback.

26 DARNAY SCOTT / BENGALS

YEAR	REC.	YARDS	AVG.	TDS	100+	GP/GS
1995	52	821	15.8	5	1	16/16
1996	58	833	14.4	5	1	16/16
1997	54	797	14.8	5	2	16/15
1998	51	817	16.0	7	2	13/13
1999	68	1022	15.0	7	2	16/16

Comments: Scott has been a model of consistency on some miserable Bengals teams. In 1999, he became the team's No. 1 receiver and set career highs with 68 receptions for 1,022 yards. Scott scored six of his seven touchdowns in a five-game stretch late in the season. In 1998, he developed into the Bengals' big-play receiver. He scored a team- and career-high seven touchdowns, despite missing the first three games of his five-year career. In 1997, he was spinning his fast wheels until Boomer Esiason took over quarterbacking duties. In the final five games, Scott caught 27 passes for 468 yards and four touchdowns. Scott has caught at least 46 passes for five or more scores in six consecutive seasons.

The skinny: You know what kind of production to expect from Scott.

27 WAYNE CHREBET / JETS

YEAR	REC.	YARDS	AVG.	TDS	100+	GP/GS
1995	66	726	11.0	4	0	16/16
1996	84	909	10.8	3	1	16/9
1997	58	799	13.8	3	1	16/1
1998	75	1083	14.4	8	5	16/15
1999	48	631	13.1	3	1	11/11

Comments: A dependable complementary receiver and third-down target, Chrebet now is thrust into the Jets' No. 1 role due to the trading of Keyshawn Johnson. In 1999, Chrebet missed the first five games due to a broken foot. After a slow start, he finished strong with three touchdowns and a 100-yard receiving game in the final five weeks. In 1998, he tied for seventh with eight touchdown catches and he led the Jets with five 100-yard games. In 1997, Chrebet ranked second on the team with 58 catches, despite not starting. A true rags-to-riches story, Chrebet wasn't even drafted in 1995, but he caught more passes in his first two seasons (150) than any player in NFL history. He was discovered because he played collegiate football at Hofstra, where the Jets' year-round training facility is located.

The skinny: Chrebet should be primed for a career year.

28 DERRICK MAYES / SEAHAWKS

YEAR	REC.	YARDS	AVG.	TDS	100+	GP/GS
1996	6	46	7.7	2	0	7/0
1997	18	290	16.1	0	1	12/3
1998	30	394	13.1	3	0	10/6
1999	62	829	13.4	10	2	16/15

Comments: The Seahawks stole Mayes from the Packers in the 1999 preseason for a conditional seventh-round pick. An injury-prone underachiever in his three previous seasons, Mayes stayed healthy last year and led the team in catches and touchdowns. He made a quick impression with seven catches for 137 yards and a touchdown in Week 2, and finished third in the AFC in touchdown catches. In three seasons with the Packers, Mayes was both a tease and a disappointment. In 1998, he was sidelined for six games by a knee ligament sprain. In 1997, he struggled through rib, ankle and shoulder injuries and failed to score. A second-round pick in the 1996 draft, he played sparingly as a rookie. Mayes has great hands.

The skinny: Mayes's fragility makes him a risky pick, but if he stays healthy he'll produce.

29 TERRY GLENN / PATRIOTS

YEAR	REC.	YARDS	AVG.	TDS	100+	GP/GS
1996	90	1132	12.6	6	2	15/15
1997	27	431	16.0	2	1	9/9
1998	50	792	15.8	3	4	10/9
1999	69	1147	16.6	4	4	14/13

Comments: Injuries clouded Glenn's first three pro seasons.

Attitude clouded last season, when he posted big numbers but was suspended for the season finale after missing a game with the flu. Glenn set career highs in receiving yardage and average per catch. He ranked fifth in the AFC in receiving yards, and his 214-yard effort in Week 4 set a team record. Smooth as silk and dangerous as dynamite but fragile as china, Glenn missed four midseason games in 1998 due to a hamstring injury and finished the season on the shelf with a fractured ankle. In 1997, he was slowed by ankle, hamstring and collarbone injuries and played in 10 games. Amid a 1996 rookie class that may be considered among the greatest wide-receiver groups ever, Glenn set an NFL rookie reception record with 90 catches (second in the AFC).

The skinny: Even when he stays healthy, Glenn doesn't find the end zone often enough to warrant an early-round pick.

30 RAGHIB ISMAIL / COWBOYS

YEAR	REC.	YARDS	AVG.	TDS	100+	GP/GS
1995	28	491	17.5	3	1	16/16
1996	12	214	17.8	0	1	13/5
1997	36	419	11.6	2	1	13/2
1998	69	1024	14.8	6	3	16/15
1999	80	1097	13.7	6	3	16/14

Comments: Ismail was the lone constant on a Cowboys receiving corps that was decimated by injuries in 1999. He stepped into Michael Irvin's No. 1 receiving role and set career highs in catches and receiving yards. Ismail tied for eighth in the NFC in catches and he even rushed for 110 yards and a touchdown on 13 carries. Ismail had six 100-yard receiving games in his first six seasons; he had three last season, then added a fourth in the playoffs. He didn't make an impact in the NFL until 1998, when he had five receptions covering 40 or more yards and led the Panthers in receptions, receiving yards and touchdowns. With the Raiders from 1993 to '95, Ismail never developed into the dependable receiver they needed to take the pressure off star Tim Brown.

The skinny: With Joey Galloway drawing double teams, Ismail should thrive as the team's No. 2 receiver.

31   TONY MARTIN / DOLPHINS

YEAR	REC.	YARDS	AVG.	TDS	100+	GP/GS
1995	90	1224	13.6	6	4	16/16
1996	85	1171	13.8	14	4	16/16
1997	63	904	14.3	6	2	16/16
1998	66	1181	17.9	6	5	16/16
1999	67	1037	15.5	5	5	16/13

Comments: Martin's best move in 1999 was dodging federal money-laundering charges that threatened his career. On the field, he provided a desperately needed deep treat. Martin led the Dolphins in receptions, receiving yards and 100-yard receiving games. Ten of his catches covered 25 or more yards. In 1998, his only season in Atlanta, Martin led the team with 66 catches. He averaged 17.9 yards per catch, and 13 of his plays covered 30 or more yards. One of the unexpected fantasy superstars in 1996, Martin tied for the NFL lead with 14 touchdown receptions. From 1995 to '96, Martin had the third-most TD catches (20) and the third-most receptions (175) in the AFC. In 1995, he had a career year with a team-record 90 catches, including a 99-yarder.

The skinny: Martin could be an underutilized player in offensive coordinator Chan Gailey's run-oriented offense.

32   TORRY HOLT / RAMS

YEAR	REC.	YARDS	AVG.	TDS	100+	GP/GS
1999	52	788	15.2	6	2	16/15

Comments: Holt came on strong late in his rookie season, and he showed enough to warrant being the first receiver taken in the 1999 draft. He led NFC rookies in catches, receiving yards and touchdowns. Over the final six regular-season games, Holt caught 25 passes for 429 yards and four touchdowns. He posted his only two 100-yard games in the final four weeks. In the playoffs, he had 20 receptions for 242 yards, including seven receptions for 109 yards and a touchdown in Super Bowl XXXIV. He started 15 games last season and ranked third on the team in catches and receiving yards.

The skinny: The levelheaded Holt will only get better and produce more.

33 JERRY RICE / 49ERS

YEAR	REC.	YARDS	AVG.	TDS	100+	GP/GS
1995	122	1848	15.1	15	9	16/16
1996	108	1254	11.6	8	3	16/16
1997	7	78	11.1	1	0	2/1
1998	82	1157	14.1	9	3	16/16
1999	67	830	12.4	5	2	16/16

Comments: Rice appeared older and and a step slower in 1999, though his numbers don't indicate a big drop-off. No longer capable of carrying the 49ers on his shoulders, Rice posted his lowest numbers (besides his injury-shortened 1997 year) since he was a rookie. In 1998, he returned from two major surgeries the year before to post typical Rice-like numbers. Uncommonly durable throughout his 15-year career, Rice is the only receiver in NFL history to catch 100 passes in three consecutive seasons. He had a career season in 1995, when his 1,848 receiving yards erased Charlie Hennigan's NFL record, and his 122 receptions were one short of Herman Moore's NFL record. He has caught at least one pass in all 209 games during his career. Rice holds NFL records in career receptions (1,206), receiving yards (18,442), receiving touchdowns (169), total touchdowns (180) and 100-yard receiving games (66).

The skinny: Unless Steve Young returns, Rice's numbers will continue to take a dive.

34 QADRY ISMAIL / RAVENS

YEAR	REC.	YARDS	AVG.	TDS	100+	GP/GS
1995	32	597	18.7	3	1	16/2
1996	28	527	18.8	0	0	16/2
1997	8	166	20.8	0	0	3/0
1998	28	590	21.1	0	0	10/1
1999	68	1105	16.3	6	3	16/16

Comments: Coach Brian Billick resurrected more than Tony Banks's struggling career in 1999. He pulled Ismail off the scrap heap and watched the Missile take flight in the Ravens' high-flying offense. Ismail did not catch a pass as a special teamer with the Saints and Dolphins in 1997 and '98. Last season, he caught at least two passes in every game and finished sixth in the AFC with 1,105 receiving yards. Ismail developed chemistry with Banks, and the pair connected on six passes for 258 yards — the 11th-best day in NFL history — in Game

13. In a nine-minute span of the third quarter, Ismail caught touchdown passes of 54, 59 and 76 yards. Ismail never reached his potential in four seasons with Minnesota. In 1994, he led Viking receivers with a 15.5-yard average per catch, but he was more effective as a kickoff returner.

The skinny: Think last season was a fluke for Ismail? Not in this offense.

35   AZ-ZAHIR HAKIM / RAMS

YEAR	REC.	YARDS	AVG.	TDS	100+	GP/GS
1998	20	247	12.4	1	0	9/4
1999	36	677	18.8	8	1	15/0

Comments: Hakim was like lightning in a bottle for the Cinderella 1999 Rams. The team's third receiver, he turned just 36 receptions into eight touchdowns. In Game 3, Hakim scored on all three of his pass receptions, and added an 84-yard punt return for a touchdown to tie a team record for touchdowns in a game. He tied for 11th in the NFC in touchdowns. His 18.8-yard average per catch ranked second among NFC receivers with 35 or more catches. Five of his catches covered 40 or more yards, and Hakim ranked sixth in the NFC with a 10.5-yard punt return average. As a rookie in 1998, Hakim played well when he got his chance late in the season. At only 5 feet 10, 178 pounds, Hakim is an elusive runner after the catch.

The skinny: The Rams will again find a way to utilize Hakim's playmaking, though he probably won't score eight times in 2000.

36   JOHNNIE MORTON / LIONS

YEAR	REC.	YARDS	AVG.	TDS	100+	GP/GS
1995	44	590	13.4	8	1	16/14
1996	55	714	13.0	6	2	16/15
1997	80	1057	13.2	6	3	16/16
1998	69	1028	14.9	2	3	16/16
1999	80	1129	14.1	5	5	16/12

Comments: Morton has developed into one of the league's steadiest receivers, a precise route runner and a reliable possession receiver. In 1999, he tied for eighth in the NFC with 80 catches, and he became the second player in Lions history to gain 1,000 receiving yards in three consecutive seasons. Morton caught 29 passes for three scores in the final four games. In 1998, he scored on the NFL's longest play from scrimmage, a 98-yard catch, but he scored only one other time all season. After two years as the slot man, he flourished in 1997, his first season as an outside receiver. In 1996, he ranked second on the Lions with six touchdown catches and third with 55 receptions. A first-round pick in 1994, Morton struggled early in his career. But in the last 12 games of 1995, he caught 41 passes for 552 yards and eight touchdowns.

The skinny: Morton is much more valuable in performance leagues because of his high production and modest scoring.

37 SEAN DAWKINS / SEAHAWKS

YEAR	REC.	YARDS	AVG.	TDS	100+	GP/GS
1995	52	784	15.1	3	2	16/13
1996	54	751	13.9	1	0	15/14
1997	68	804	11.8	2	1	14/12
1998	53	823	15.5	1	3	15/15
1999	58	992	17.1	7	2	16/13

Comments: Take a career possession receiver from some conservative offenses and put him on a passing team, and you get a career year. Dawkins was a big addition to the Seahawks in 1999. He established personal highs in receiving yards, average per catch and touchdowns, then he added a score in the team's playoff loss. In 1998, Dawkins caught 53 passes from the Saints' weak quarterback corps. With the Colts from 1993 to '97, the 6-foot-4 Dawkins developed into a reliable option, but he never developed into the top receiver the Colts had hoped for when they made him a first-round pick. Dawkins has caught more than 50 passes for six straight seasons, but he had just 13 TD catches before last year.

The skinny: Year Two of Mike Holmgren's offense will bring out another career year from Dawkins.

38 BOBBY ENGRAM / BEARS

YEAR	REC.	YARDS	AVG.	TDS	100+	GP/GS
1996	33	389	11.8	6	0	16/2
1997	45	399	8.9	2	0	11/11
1998	64	987	15.4	5	3	16/16
1999	88	947	10.8	4	2	16/14

Comments: Engram is a dependable possession receiver who moves the chains on a passing team. His 88 receptions in 1999 ranked third in the NFC and second in Bears history. Running short hitch and screen routes, Engram actually gained fewer yards with 24 more catches than he made in 1998. In Week 16, Engram caught 13 passes — the most by a Bear in 35 years. His quality 1998 season was an eye-opener, considering his feeble 8.9-yard average per catch the season before. Engram caught five bombs, and he led the team in every receiving category. His 987 receiving yards ranked 12th in the NFC. Engram gave the Bears plenty of reasons to be excited when he finished the 1996 season with five touchdowns in the final five games, but he did little to excite anybody in '97. He has caught a pass in 33 consecutive games.

The skinny: Engram is a fantasy backup at best because of his modest touchdown production.

39 YANCEY THIGPEN / TITANS

YEAR	REC.	YARDS	AVG.	TDS	100+	GP/GS
1995	85	1307	15.4	5	4	16/15
1996	12	144	20.3	2	0	6/2
1997	79	1398	17.7	7	6	16/15
1998	38	493	13.0	3	1	9/8
1999	38	648	17.1	4	1	10/10

Comments: The Titans' passing game mirrors Thigpen's health. Quarterback Steve McNair failed to throw a touchdown pass in six consecutive midseason games — and Thigpen missed five of them due to an ankle injury. He ranked second on the team with 648 receiving yards and led the Titans with a 17.1-yard average per catch. The fact that Thigpen missed seven games in 1998 and still led the team's wide receivers with 38 catches speaks volumes about his importance. With the Steelers in 1997, he led the NFL in average yards per reception (17.7). He set a Steelers record with 1,398 receiving yards (third most in the NFL), and he posted six 100-yard receiving games. Injuries kept Thigpen on the sidelines throughout most of the 1996 season, a disappointing sequel to 1995, when he set a Steelers record with 85 catches.

The skinny: Let somebody else in your league worry about how long Thigpen will last before getting hurt.

40 KEENAN McCARDELL / JAGUARS

YEAR	REC.	YARDS	AVG.	TDS	100+	GP/GS
1995	56	709	12.7	4	1	16/5
1996	85	1129	13.3	3	3	16/15
1997	85	1164	13.7	5	4	16/16
1998	64	892	13.9	6	2	16/15
1999	78	891	11.4	5	3	16/15

Comments: McCardell excels in his consistency as a possession receiver. A reliable short- and intermediate-route runner, he caught just two passes that covered 30 or more yards last season, when he ranked sixth in the AFC with 78 catches. McCardell's 1998 season was slowed by a shoulder injury, but he tied for 15th in the AFC with 64 catches. In 1997, his 85 receptions were the AFC's second most, and his 1,164 receiving yards ranked fifth in the conference. A No. 3 wideout with Cleveland in 1995, McCardell moved up into a No. 1 receiving role with Jacksonville in 1996. He became the first Jaguar to be voted to the Pro Bowl, and he tied for fourth in the AFC with 85 catches. Over the past four years, McCardell has 312 receptions, the fourth most in the league.

The skinny: McCardell is a first-down maker, not a big touchdown maker.

41 SHAWN JEFFERSON / FALCONS

YEAR	REC.	YARDS	AVG.	TDS	100+	GP/GS
1995	48	621	12.9	2	1	16/15
1996	50	771	15.4	4	0	15/15
1997	54	841	15.6	2	1	16/14
1998	34	771	22.7	2	2	16/16
1999	40	698	17.5	6	1	16/16

Comments: Jefferson finally put the touchdown in his arsenal in 1999, then he bolted for Atlanta in the offseason. He had scored just 18 touchdowns in eight previous seasons, but in 1999, his six TD grabs led the Patriots. Six of Jefferson's catches covered at least 30 yards. In 1998, Jefferson led the NFL with a 22.7-yard average per catch, but he scored only two touchdowns. In 1997, his 841 receiving yards led the team. Jefferson scored on 76- and 64-yard bombs during the regular season, then he added nine catches for 104 yards in a playoff loss. In five seasons with the Chargers, Jefferson caught 162 passes for 2,144 yards but scored just 10 touchdowns.

The skinny: Jefferson is a good fit in Atlanta, a deep threat opposite Terance Mathis. But don't expect more than a few scores.

42 ORONDE GADSDEN / DOLPHINS

YEAR	REC.	YARDS	AVG.	TDS	100+	GP/GS
1998	48	713	14.9	7	1	16/12
1999	48	803	16.7	6	3	16/7

Comments: The 6-foot-2 Gadsden has found a niche as Miami's go-to target near the end zone. In 1999, he led the team with six touchdown catches — five in the final seven weeks — and five of his plays covered 30 or more yards. He led the team with a 16.7-yard average per catch and ranked second in receptions. Fantasy players were asking "Who?" in 1998, when Gadsden came out of nowhere to become Miami's second-best receiver. A free-agent find, he started 12 games and caught 48 passes, tying for the team lead with seven touchdowns.

The skinny: Gadsden's touchdown total could suffer with Damon Huard running the offense.

43 JAMES JETT / RAIDERS

YEAR	REC.	YARDS	AVG.	TDS	100+	GP/GS
1995	13	179	13.8	1	0	16/0
1996	43	601	14.0	4	1	16/16
1997	46	804	17.5	12	1	16/16
1998	45	882	19.6	6	2	16/16
1999	39	552	14.2	2	0	16/11

Comments: Jett is a round peg trying to cram into a square hole, a home-run-hitting deep threat playing in a West Coast offense. Last season, Jett tied for third on the Raiders with 39 receptions — but those were his lowest numbers in his three years as a starter. In 1998, Jett came back to earth after his career took off into fantasy football orbit in '97. His average per catch improved to 19.6 yards, but his touchdown total was cut in half. In 1997, Jett was the most pleasant surprise in fantasy football. He turned more than one of every four receptions into a touchdown and tied for the Raiders' scoring lead with 72 points. An undrafted rookie free agent in 1993, he was a member of the 1992 Olympic Gold Medalist 400-meter relay team.

The skinny: Jett will probably start for one more season in Oakland, but don't expect much.

44 JERMAINE LEWIS / RAVENS

YEAR	REC.	YARDS	AVG.	TDS	100+	GP/GS
1996	5	78	15.6	1	0	16/1
1997	42	648	15.4	6	2	14/7
1998	41	784	19.1	6	2	13/13
1999	25	281	11.2	2	0	15/6

Comments: Lewis became the forgotten man in the 1999 Ravens offense, a smurf-sized misfit for Brian Billick's offense. His production plummeted — both on offense and on special teams. Coming off back-to-back eight-touchdown seasons, Lewis averaged just 11.2 yards per reception, 7.9 yards per punt return and 19.8 yards per kickoff return. That was in sharp contrast to 1998, when nobody in the AFC did more with fewer catches than Lewis. Five of his six touchdown catches covered 46 or more yards, and his 19.1-yard average per catch was the league's fourth best. Entering the 1997 season, few football fans knew who Lewis was, but he shed his anonymity with 2,025 combined yards, despite missing five games due to an ankle injury. His NFL-high 15.6-yard punt-return average included two touchdowns in the same game.

The skinny: If you drafted Lewis last year, you now know better. If you didn't, don't pick him this year, either.

45 TIM DWIGHT / FALCONS

YEAR	REC.	YARDS	AVG.	TDS	100+	GP/GS
1998	4	94	23.5	1	0	12/0
1999	32	669	20.9	7	2	12/8

Comments: A fearless kamikazi with track speed, Dwight was the Falcons' lone big-play threat in 1999. At 5 feet 8, 180 pounds, he really took a pounding. He suffered hamstring, back and knee injuries and missed four games. Dwight cracked the starting lineup midway through the season and led the team with nine touchdowns — seven on pass receptions and one each on a run and a punt return. His 20.9-yard average per catch led all NFL receivers with 30 or more catches, and 10 of his receptions covered 30 or more yards. As a rookie in 1998, Dwight caught a touchdown pass in the season opener but contributed primarily on special teams.

The skinny: The return of Jamal Anderson will only help spread the field for Dwight, but his durability is a concern.

WIDE RECEIVERS

46 CURTIS CONWAY / CHARGERS

YEAR	REC.	YARDS	AVG.	TDS	100+	GP/GS
1995	62	1037	16.7	12	3	16/16
1996	81	1049	13.0	7	4	16/16
1997	30	476	15.9	1	3	7/7
1998	54	733	13.6	3	0	15/15
1999	44	426	9.7	4	1	9/8

Comments: Conway resembles a box of hollow chocolates — he looks great but doesn't meet expectations. The receiver-starved Chargers signed him in the offseason to provide a deep threat, but the question has always been how long he can stay healthy. With Chicago in 1999, Conway was tied for the NFC lead in receiving after five weeks with 29 catches. Then he injured his ankle and missed seven of the next 11 games. Expected to provide big plays and team leadership in 1998, Conway dropped as many bombs as he caught and he went into a shell filled with self-doubt. In 1997, Conway broke his collarbone and missed nine games. The only Bears receiver ever to post consecutive 1,000-yard seasons, Conway set career highs in 1996 with 81 catches for 1,049 yards. He emerged as one of the NFL's most dangerous receivers in 1995 with 12 touchdown receptions.

The skinny: Conway could be the Comeback Player of the Year. More likely, he'll again underachieve.

47 BILL SCHROEDER / PACKERS

YEAR	REC.	YARDS	AVG.	TDS	100+	GP/GS
1996	DNP					
1997	2	15	7.5	0	0	15/1
1998	31	452	14.6	1	1	13/3
1999	74	1051	14.2	5	1	16/16

Comments: Schroeder moved into the starting lineup in 1999 in place of the retired Robert Brooks. He won the starting job with a strong preseason, then proceeded to tie for the team lead with 74 catches. A good strider with shaky hands (he had nine drops last season) and questionable toughness, Schroeder caught at least three passes in every game. For three seasons, fumbled kickoff returns made Schroeder the victim of former coach Mike Holmgren's verbal abuse. He contributed offensively for the first time in 1998, when he caught 31 passes for 452 receiving yards before suffering a season-ending broken collarbone in Game 13.

The skinny: Schroeder is a No. 3 receiver who masqueraded as a starter last season.

48 ALBERT CONNELL / REDSKINS

YEAR	REC.	YARDS	AVG.	TDS	100+	GP/GS
1997	9	138	15.3	2	0	5/1
1998	28	451	16.1	2	1	14/5
1999	62	1132	18.3	7	4	15/15

Comments: Connell moved into the starting lineup and capitalized on his opportunity by turning in a breakthrough 1999 season. He developed into a solid deep threat and produced four 100-yard receiving games and eight plays of 30 yards or more. Connell tied teammate Michael Westbrook with an 18.3-yard average per catch that led the league's receivers with 60 or more catches. He ranked ninth in the NFC with 1,132 receiving yards. A fourth-round pick in the 1997 draft, Connell played little as a rookie. In 1998, he started five games in place of the injured Westbrook and missed two due to a knee injury. He tied for fifth on the team with 28 catches.

The skinny: Connell's 1999 season was no fluke, though at 179 pounds, his durability is a concern.

49 TROY EDWARDS / STEELERS

YEAR	REC.	YARDS	AVG.	TDS	100+	GP/GS
1999	61	714	11.7	5	0	16/6

Comments: Edwards wasn't the big-play receiver as a rookie that the Steelers had hoped when they made him a 1999 first-round pick. But quarterback Kordell Stewart's failure to throw downfield was a big reason why. Edwards did begin to show his potential, though just two of his receptions covered 30 or more yards. He led the team with 714 receiving yards and tied for the lead with 61 catches. Edwards slipped into coach Bill Cowher's doghouse early in the season for poor route running, but he started the final five games. He set the team's rookie reception record and he ranked third among last year's rookies in catches.

The skinny: If and when the Steelers make a quarterback change, Edwards could begin to catch some deep balls from Kent Graham.

50 PEERLESS PRICE / BILLS

YEAR	REC.	YARDS	AVG.	TDS	100+	GP/GS
1999	31	393	12.7	3	1	16/4

Comments: The Bills broke Price in gradually in 1999, his rookie season. With Andre Reed now gone, Price will move into a starting role this time around. Last year, he got off to a slow start but finished with 12 catches in his final three games (including the playoff loss). He played better when he gained a better understanding of the offense late in the season. The Bills' No. 3 receiver in '99, Price tied for fourth on the team with 31 receptions. Price has great speed and good hands, but he tends to get jammed at the line.

The skinny: Price should at least double last year's output.

51 EDDIE KENNISON / BEARS

YEAR	REC.	YARDS	AVG.	TDS	100+	GP/GS
1996	54	924	17.1	9	2	15/14
1997	25	404	16.2	0	0	14/9
1998	17	234	13.8	1	0	16/13
1999	61	835	13.7	4	1	16/16

Comments: Kennison was obtained by the Bears for a fifth-round draft pick to provide outside speed to complement Marcus Robinson. His breakaway speed gives the offense a new dimension with its wide receiver screens. In 1999, Kennison was the Saints' most productive receiver with 61 receptions, and his 90-yard touchdown catch was the longest in franchise history. But his confidence was shot when the Saints obtained him in a 1999 trade with St. Louis. In the two seasons since his outstanding rookie campaign, Kennison ran pass routes tentatively and couldn't catch the ball. Kennison's TD production from 1996 to '97 plummeted from 11 to zero. In 1996, Kennison scored on nine pass plays and two punt returns, and he set team rookie records for most receptions (54) and receiving yards (924).

The skinny: A good fit in this passing offense, Kennison is headed for a career year.

52   JOE HORN / SAINTS

YEAR	REC.	YARDS	AVG.	TDS	100+	GP/GS
1996	2	30	15.0	0	0	9/0
1997	2	65	32.5	0	0	8/0
1998	14	198	14.1	1	0	16/1
1999	35	586	16.7	6	0	16/1

Comments: Horn steps into an ideal situation in New Orleans. He'll compete with Keith Poole for the No. 2 receiving job on a team with strong-armed Jeff Blake at quarterback. Horn was Kansas City's designated deep-route runner and its best big-play threat in 1999, when he provided five catches of 30 or more yards. Horn led Chiefs wide receivers with six touchdown receptions and a 16.7-yard average per catch last year. But he needs to improve his route running and do a better job of coming back for balls. Horn played little on offense in his first three seasons with the Chiefs.

The skinny: Horn is a good late-round sleeper with touchdown potential.

53   DERRICK ALEXANDER / CHIEFS

YEAR	REC.	YARDS	AVG.	TDS	100+	GP/GS
1995	15	216	14.4	0	0	14/2
1996	62	1099	17.7	9	3	15/14
1997	65	1009	15.5	9	3	15/13
1998	54	992	18.4	4	2	15/14
1999	54	832	15.4	2	4	16/15

Comments: Alexander certainly broke big plays in 1999, just not enough for a fantasy team. He scored on 86- and 81-yard catches and on an 82-yard end-around, but those were his only touchdowns all year. Alexander had 11 pass plays of 20 or more yards, and he led the team's wide receivers in catches and receiving yards. He struggled early in 1998, his first season with the Chiefs, but he finished strong with 42 catches for 739 yards and three touchdowns in the final eight games. Alexander's eventful 1997 season with Baltimore included a 92-yard reception, his second consecutive 1,000-yard season, a team-high nine touchdowns and a trip to the doghouse due to dropped passes and lazy work habits. In 1996, he ranked eighth in the AFC with 1,099 receiving yards and tied for 10th in the conference with nine touchdowns.

The skinny: When the Chiefs pass in the red zone, they look to Tony Gonzalez — not Alexander.

54   O. J. McDUFFIE / DOLPHINS

YEAR	REC.	YARDS	AVG.	TDS	100+	GP/GS
1995	62	819	13.2	8	0	16/16
1996	74	918	12.4	8	2	16/16
1997	76	943	12.4	1	3	16/16
1998	90	1050	11.7	7	3	16/16
1999	43	516	12.0	2	0	12/10

McDuffie had an off year in 1999, and a sprained toe put an early end to it. He has nine career 100-yard receiving games — none last season. The toe sprain kept him out of four late-season games, and McDuffie had his fewest receptions in five years. Normally a possession receiver, he was the closest thing the Dolphins had to a big-play threat in 1998. He won the NFL receiving title with 90 catches, but 14 receivers gained more receiving yards. McDuffie's 1997 touchdown production was victimized by a diverse offense in which 11 different players caught a TD pass. From 1995 to '96, his 16 touchdown catches were the sixth most among AFC receivers. McDuffie ranks fourth in team history in catches (401) and receiving yards (4,931), and fifth with 29 TD catches.

The skinny: McDuffie no longer has Dan Marino throwing to him, so don't expect more than a few scores.

55   KEVIN DYSON / TITANS

YEAR	REC.	YARDS	AVG.	TDS	100+	GP/GS
1998	21	263	12.5	2	0	13/9
1999	54	658	12.2	4	1	16/16

Comments: Dyson became part of NFL folklore with the Music City Miracle, his unforgettable game-winning kickoff return against Buffalo in the 1999 playoffs. Unfortunately, the 1998 first-round draft pick has hardly been a miracle during his first two seasons. Last year, Dyson made progress from his rookie season, but he disappeared when the team needed him most — a five-game midseason stretch when No. 1 receiver Yancey Thigpen was injured. Dyson did, however, lead the team in receiving yards and rank second in receptions. As a rookie, he was slow to catch on and slowed by hip and ankle injuries, so he played little early before earning nine late-season starts. He failed to make the impact the team had hoped, especially in the deep passing game.

The skinny: The Titans' power-oriented offense isn't designed to get the ball to Dyson much more than it did last year.

56 CHARLES JOHNSON / EAGLES

YEAR	REC.	YARDS	AVG.	TDS	100+	GP/GS
1995	38	432	11.4	0	0	14/12
1996	60	1008	16.8	3	4	16/12
1997	46	568	12.3	2	1	13/11
1998	65	815	12.5	7	1	16/16
1999	34	414	12.2	1	0	11/11

Comments: Johnson was thrust into a No. 1 receiving role on a bad passing team in 1999, and his longest play covered just 36 yards. Before spraining a knee in Week 11, Johnson was leading the team in receptions. In 1998, he became Pittsburgh's No. 1 wideout and had a career year with a team-high 815 receiving yards and seven TD catches. In 1997, he missed four games due to a knee injury but still ranked second on the team with 46 receptions. A first-round draft pick in 1994, Johnson appeared to be a bust until 1996, when he developed into a deep threat in the Steelers' offense. That year he hit the 100-yard receiving mark four times and became the sixth Steelers receiver to surpass the 1,000-yard receiving mark.

The skinny: Look for a strong comeback season for Johnson as the Eagles improve their West Coast offense.

57 REIDEL ANTHONY / BUCCANEERS

YEAR	REC.	YARDS	AVG.	TDS	100+	GP/GS
1997	35	448	12.8	4	0	16/12
1998	51	708	13.9	7	1	15/13
1999	30	296	9.9	1	0	13/7

Comments: Anthony was a disappointment in 1999, and his prospects for offensive contributions appear to be even dimmer this year. Coming off a solid second season, Anthony had only one good game in 1999, in Week 4 when he caught seven passes for 94 yards and a touchdown. He averaged just 20.7 yards per kickoff return (17th in the NFC) and just 9.9 yards per reception. In 1998, Anthony led the team in receptions, his seven TD catches were the most by a Buccaneer in nine years, and he ranked eighth among NFC kick returners with a 24.3-yard average. As a rookie in 1997, he seldom was able to utilize his deep speed because of line jams.

The skinny: Don't waste a draft pick on Anthony this season.

58 COREY BRADFORD / PACKERS

YEAR	REC.	YARDS	AVG.	TDS	100+	GP/GS
1998	3	27	9.0	0	0	8/0
1999	37	637	17.2	5	1	16/2

Comments: Bradford was a great special-teamer but just a one-dimensional deep threat in the Packers' offense in 1999. He averaged 17.2 yards per catch to tie for fifth among NFC receivers with 35 or more receptions. The team's third wide receiver, Bradford caught a last-second game-winning touchdown pass against Minnesota and made a spectacular one-handed touchdown grab to beat Detroit. But he caught just 37 passes and dropped 10 others. A fifth-round draft pick in 1998, Bradford was primarily relegated to special-teams play as a rookie.

The skinny: Bradford is too erratic to become a starter, so don't expect a quantum leap in production.

59 DAVID BOSTON / CARDINALS

YEAR	REC.	YARDS	AVG.	TDS	100+	GP/GS
1999	40	473	11.8	2	1	16/7

Comments: A native of Humble, Texas, Boston certainly got a taste of humble pie in 1999 when the NFC's worst offense dragged a talented rookie right down with it. Boston was underutilized and made little impact. The eighth player chosen in the 1999 draft, Boston had just one big game, an eight-catch, 101-yard effort in Week 5. Boston has a great combination of size and speed, but just two of his receptions covered 40 or more yards. He ranked third on the Cardinals in receptions and receiving yards, but his 11.8-yard average per catch didn't scare anybody.

The skinny: Look for increased production from Boston, but remember, he still is a No. 3 receiver.

60 TERRENCE WILKINS / COLTS

YEAR	REC.	YARDS	AVG.	TDS	100+	GP/GS
1999	42	565	13.5	4	1	16/11

Comments: The pint-sized Wilkins wore down late last season, but he was an undrafted free-agent find in 1999. He ranked third on the high-scoring Colts with seven touchdowns — four on pass plays, one each on a kickoff and a punt return and another on a fumble recovery. He ranked seventh in the conference in punt returns and ninth in the AFC with a 22.2-yard kickoff-return average. His 2,089 combined yards are the seventh most by a rookie in NFL history. Wilkins, who moved E. G. Green out of the starting lineup, ranked third on the team with 42 catches. But his offensive production tailed off late in the season.

The skinny: Wilkins is best suited for a slot receiver/kick return role rather than a No. 2 receiving position.

61 KEITH POOLE / SAINTS

YEAR	REC.	YARDS	AVG.	TDS	100+	GP/GS
1997	4	98	24.5	2	0	3/0
1998	24	509	21.2	2	1	15/4
1999	42	796	19.0	6	1	15/15

Comments: Poole was the lone playmaker on a pathetic Saints offense in 1999. He is not very big or fast, but he gets open and makes the most of his catches. The average length of his 10 career scores is 35 yards. In 1999, he had the highest average per catch (19.0) of any NFL receiver with 40 or more catches. Poole takes a beating but started every game last season and led the team with six touchdowns. In his only four starts of 1998, Poole caught 12 passes for 185 yards. In 1997, he made both of his touchdown catches in the season finale.

The skinny: Poole has 70 career catches, 10 touchdowns, and, finally, a decent quarterback throwing him the ball.

62 HINES WARD / STEELERS

YEAR	REC.	YARDS	AVG.	TDS	100+	GP/GS
1998	15	246	16.4	0	0	16/0
1999	61	638	10.5	7	0	16/14

Comments: Ward had a breakthrough second season with the 1999 Steelers as a speedy flanker. He had a team-high seven touchdown receptions and tied Troy Edwards for the team lead with 61 catches. Although he excels running after the catch, Ward averaged just 10.5 yards per reception as the team failed to pass downfield. Only one of Ward's catches covered 40 or more yards. A third-round pick in 1998, he made little impact as a rookie.

The skinny: Ward won't match last year's production in his new role as the team's No. 3 receiver.

63 JACQUEZ GREEN / BUCCANEERS

YEAR	REC.	YARDS	AVG.	TDS	100+	GP/GS
1998	14	251	17.9	2	0	12/1
1999	56	791	14.1	3	2	16/10

Comments: Green was the closest thing the Buccaneers had to a big-play threat in 1999. The speedy 5-foot-9 Green is a deep threat and a good complement to Keyshawn Johnson. Last year, Green led the Bucs in receiving yards and average per catch, and four of his plays covered more than 40 yards. During a five-week midseason stretch, he caught 29 passes for 500 yards and three scores. As a rookie in 1998, Green showed signs of being the gamebreaker the team anticipated when it chose him in the second round. A speed demon, he scored on a 95-yard punt return and on pass plays of 44 and 64 yards. However, he was slowed by a turf toe, a thumb injury and a shoulder sprain, and he fumbled four times in the final two games.

The skinny: The power-oriented Bucs will probably underutilize Green's home-run potential.

64 JEFF GRAHAM / CHARGERS

YEAR	REC.	YARDS	AVG.	TDS	100+	GP/GS
1995	82	1301	15.9	4	7	16/16
1996	50	788	15.8	6	3	11/9
1997	42	542	12.9	2	1	16/16
1998	47	600	12.8	2	0	15/15
1999	57	968	17.0	2	4	16/11

Comments: Graham was productive yet erratic in 1999. He led the team in catches and receiving yards, but he scored just two touchdown passes and dropped two potential game-winning touchdown passes. With no other receiving threat to help draw attention on the opposite side of the offense, Graham finished strong, with four 100-yard games in the final six weeks. On a 1998 Eagles team with a horrible passing game, Graham did well to lead the squad with 600 passing yards. Chicago's loss was the Jets' free-agent gain in 1996, when Graham scored six touchdowns with 50 pass receptions, despite missing five games due to injuries. In 1995, he set a Bears single-season receiving record with 1,301 yards.

The skinny: Graham has six touchdowns in the past three seasons, and the Chargers' quarterbacking doesn't promise to increase that in 2000.

65 DEDRIC WARD / JETS

YEAR	REC.	YARDS	AVG.	TDS	100+	GP/GS
1997	18	212	11.8	1	1	11/1
1998	25	477	19.1	4	0	16/2
1999	22	325	14.8	3	0	16/5

Comments: No one in the Jets' offense missed injured quarterback Vinny Testaverde more than Ward did in 1999. The team's deep threat, he practically disappeared because nobody could get him the ball. Ward caught 15 passes in five early-season starts for the injured Wayne Chrebet. But in the other 11 games, he caught just seven passes in the No. 3 receiving role. In 1998, Ward tied for fifth on the team with four touchdowns, including plays of 71, 43 and 36 yards. His 19.1-yard average led the team and tied for fourth in the AFC (25 or more catches).

The skinny: Keyshawn Johnson's departure opens the door for Ward to move into the starting lineup and have a career year.

66 TORRANCE SMALL / EAGLES

YEAR	REC.	YARDS	AVG.	TDS	100+	GP/GS
1995	38	461	12.1	5	0	16/1
1996	50	558	11.2	2	0	16/13
1997	32	488	15.3	1	0	13/7
1998	45	581	15.1	7	2	16/4
1999	49	655	13.4	4	1	15/15

Comments: Small scored one-third of the team's nine touchdowns by wide receivers in the final two weeks of the 1999 season. He scored on catches of 84, 63 and 50 yards and led the team in catches and receiving yards. A free-agent addition, Small started slowly but caught 32 passes in the final eight weeks to help fill a gaping void. With the Colts in 1998, Small tied Marvin Harrison for the team lead with seven touchdown catches. In 1997, Small served as the Rams' third receiver and finished fourth on the team with 32 receptions. He finished the 1994 season with a career game, when he caught six passes for 200 yards — the second-highest receiving-yardage total in New Orleans history.

The skinny: The Eagles' passing game is bound to pick up, so Small should be good for four or five scores.

67   IKE HILLIARD / GIANTS

YEAR	REC.	YARDS	AVG.	TDS	100+	GP/GS
1997	2	42	21.0	0	0	2/2
1998	51	715	14.0	2	1	16/16
1999	72	996	13.8	3	3	16/16

Comments: The Giants expected an explosive playmaker when they made Hilliard the first receiver taken in the 1997 draft. Instead, they got a good possession receiver. In 1999, Hilliard fell just four yards shy of a 1,000-yard season. His 72 catches were the third most in franchise history. Just one of Hilliard's plays covered 40 or more yards, but he caught at least two passes in every game. In 1998, he made a successful recovery from vertebrae fusion surgery (a spine injury sustained in the second game of his pro career had wrecked his rookie season). He caught a pass in every game (four of which were 40 yards or longer), and he ranked second on the team with 51 receptions.

The skinny: Hilliard will catch a lot of passes for a handful of scores in 2000.

68   FRANK SANDERS / CARDINALS

YEAR	REC.	YARDS	AVG.	TDS	100+	GP/GS
1995	52	883	17.0	2	2	16/15
1996	69	813	11.8	4	0	16/16
1997	75	1017	13.6	4	2	16/16
1998	89	1145	12.9	3	5	16/16
1999	79	954	12.1	1	2	16/16

Comments: Sanders's consistency is admirable for the Cardinals but maddening for fantasy players. He's one of the league's best possession receivers, but he seldom scores. In 1999, Sanders tied for 11th in the NFC with 79 catches, and he led the conference with 30 third-down receptions. Sanders caught 13 passes in the season finale, the most by a Cardinals wide receiver in 37 years. In 1998, the sure-handed, 6-foot-2 Sanders led the NFC with 89 catches. Sanders came on strong late in 1997, when he ranked ninth in the NFC with 1,017 receiving yards. A deep threat in 1995, Sanders became more of a possession receiver in '96, when he led the Cardinals' wideouts with 69 catches.

The skinny: Sanders is good for the Cardinals, but he's no good for your fantasy team.

69 J. J. STOKES / 49ERS

YEAR	REC.	YARDS	AVG.	TDS	100+	GP/GS
1995	38	517	13.6	4	1	12/2
1996	18	249	13.8	0	0	6/2
1997	58	733	12.6	4	0	16/16
1998	63	770	12.2	8	2	16/13
1999	34	429	12.6	3	1	16/4

Comments: Stokes represents a huge long-term investment, and he has yet to pay big dividends. He practically disappeared from the 49ers' offense in 1999, when he failed to score until Game 12. The team's No. 3 receiver, Stokes tied for fourth in receptions last season. At 6 feet 4, Stokes has the size and hands to go over defenders for the ball. In 1998, he was a fairly big part of the NFL's No. 1–ranked offense when he showed progress with career highs in receptions, receiving yards, touchdowns and 100-yard games. In 1997, he matured into a productive player and exceeded his two-year reception total with 58 catches. A first-round draft pick in 1995, Stokes was a disappointment in his first two seasons.

The skinny: Stokes's playing time could increase as Jerry Rice's career winds down, but don't expect Rice-like numbers.

70 TROY BROWN / PATRIOTS

YEAR	REC.	YARDS	AVG.	TDS	100+	GP/GS
1995	14	159	11.4	0	0	16/0
1996	21	222	10.6	0	0	16/0
1997	41	607	14.8	6	2	16/6
1998	23	346	15.0	1	0	10/0
1999	36	471	13.1	1	1	13/1

Comments: Brown appears to be the Patriots' No. 2 receiver almost by default this season. A career No. 3 receiver and punt returner, he ranked third on the team with 36 receptions last season. He ranked fifth in the AFC with a 10.7-yard punt-return average, and he averaged 33.9 yards with eight kickoff returns. In 1998, Brown hobbled on a sprained ankle and never made much of an impact on offense. Hardly a household name among fans outside of New England, Brown has good chemistry with Drew Bledsoe. In 1997, he ranked second on the Patriots with six touchdowns and led them with two 100-yard receiving games and three pass plays of 50 yards or more.

The skinny: If the Patriots don't sign a veteran to assume the No. 2 receiving role, Brown could be headed for a career year.

71 MIKE PRITCHARD / SEAHAWKS

YEAR	REC.	YARDS	AVG.	TDS	100+	GP/GS
1995	33	441	13.4	3	0	15/13
1996	21	328	15.6	1	0	16/5
1997	64	843	13.2	2	0	16/15
1998	58	742	12.8	3	0	16/16
1999	26	375	14.4	2	0	14/4

Comments: Pritchard's role in the 2000 Seahawks is likely to increase due to Joey Galloway's departure. A precise route runner who will go over the middle, Pritchard was the team's third and fourth receiver in 1999 and caught just 26 passes. He produced in 1998, but failed to stretch defenses enough to take double teams away from Galloway. In 1997, Pritchard benefited from Seattle's league-best passing offense. He ranked 17th in the AFC with 64 catches, his most since playing in Atlanta's run-and-shoot attack in the early 1990s. From 1991 to '93 in Atlanta, he caught 201 passes, the fifth-most receptions ever by a player in his first three seasons.

The skinny: Pritchard makes catches but not touchdowns.

72 DARRIN CHIAVERINI / BROWNS

YEAR	REC.	YARDS	AVG.	TDS	100+	GP/GS
1999	44	487	11.1	4	1	16/8

Comments: A rookie fifth-round draft pick by an expansion team, Chiaverini was probably the most anonymous player in the league to score four touchdowns in 1999. He ranked fifth among rookie receivers in receptions and sixth in receiving yards. He bounced in and out of the starting lineup in place of the injured Leslie Shepherd and started eight games. In Game 15, Chiaverini caught 10 passes for 108 yards and a touchdown against Jacksonville.

The skinny: A possession receiver rather than a gamebreaker, Chiaverini is well suited for the No. 3 receiving role.

73   JASON TUCKER / COWBOYS

YEAR	REC.	YARDS	AVG.	TDS	100+	GP/GS
1999	23	439	19.1	3	2	15/4

Comments: Tucker was force-fed into the Cowboys' 1999 lineup due to a myriad of injuries. His big-play ability helped the Cowboys overlook his inexperience and mistakes. Tucker was the league's second-best kickoff returner with a 27.9-yard average, despite never breaking one all the way. He became more involved in the offense late in the year and finished with two 100-yard receiving games — including a 90-yard touchdown — in the final two weeks. Tucker averaged 19.1 yards per catch.

The skinny: Tucker is still a project, and his contribution in 2000 will mainly be limited to kick returns.

74   PATRICK JOHNSON / RAVENS

YEAR	REC.	YARDS	AVG.	TDS	100+	GP/GS
1998	12	159	13.3	1	0	13/0
1999	29	526	18.1	3	1	10/6

Comments: The Ravens tapped some of Johnson's potential in 1999, but injuries have marred his first two seasons. He scored on 76- and 52-yard receptions and also caught a 64-yarder to finish with a fine 18.1-yard average per catch. Johnson broke into the starting lineup for six late-season games, but a calf injury dogged him all year. In 1998, he suffered the same fate as many rookie receivers — he struggled to pick up his team's offense and gain playing time. A second-round draft pick and former college sprinter, Johnson caught just 12 passes and contributed mostly as a kickoff returner. He missed three games due to hip and hamstring injuries.

The skinny: Don't draft Johnson, but take a wait-and-see approach. He could be a good midseason pickup.

75 BERT EMANUEL / DOLPHINS

YEAR	REC.	YARDS	AVG.	TDS	100+	GP/GS
1995	74	1039	14.0	5	4	16/16
1996	76	931	12.3	6	3	14/13
1997	65	991	15.2	9	1	16/16
1998	41	636	15.5	2	1	11/11
1999	22	238	10.8	1	0	11/10

Comments: A pricey free-agent acquisition in 1998, Emanuel really struggled the last two seasons and he was released in the spring and signed by Miami, where he joins a deep corps of wideouts. In 1999, he missed five games with injuries and didn't provide much of an impact for a team that went all the way to the NFC Championship game. In '98, he was slowed by a sprained ankle and plagued by 13 dropped passes. His best years were from 1995 to '97 with Atlanta, when he piled up nearly 3,000 receiving yards.

The skinny: Emanuel could be a late-round sleeper if he can bounce back and rejoin the league's better wide receivers.

LOOKING BACK AT WIDE RECEIVERS

The Best — Marvin Harrison (Colts)

Sure Bets — Randy Moss (Vikings), Antonio Freeman (Packers), Cris Carter (Vikings)

Top Sleepers — Joe Horn (Saints), Peerless Price (Bills), Eddie Kennison (Bears), David Boston (Cardinals), Ike Hilliard (Giants), Hines Ward (Steelers)

Possible Busts — Albert Connell (Redskins), Patrick Jeffers (Panthers), Curtis Conway (Chargers), Az-Zahir Hakim (Rams)

Coming On — Marcus Robinson (Bears), Michael Westbrook (Redskins), Muhsin Muhammad (Panthers), Kevin Johnson (Browns), Amani Toomer (Giants), Qadry Ismail (Ravens), Hines Ward (Steelers), Germaine Crowell (Lions), Derrick Mayes (Seahawks)

Comeback Candidates — Jermaine Lewis (Ravens), Herman Moore (Lions), Joey Galloway (Cowboys), Reidel Anthony (Buccaneers), Jake Reed (Saints), O. J. McDuffie (Dolphins), Terrell Owens (49ers)

Back to Earth After a Great 1999 — Patrick Jeffers (Panthers), Marcus Robinson (Bears), Derrick Mayes (Seahawks), Tim Dwight (Falcons), Bill Schroeder (Packers), Albert Connell (Redskins)

In for a Career Year — Eric Moulds (Bills), Joe Horn (Saints), Qadry Ismail (Ravens), Sean Dawkins (Seahawks)

Top Rookies — Peter Warrick (Bengals), Travis Taylor (Ravens), Plaxico Burress (Steelers), Sylvester Morris (Chiefs), R. Jay Soward (Jaguars)

1999 Injured Players Who Will Be a Factor in '00 — Herman Moore (Lions), Curtis Conway (Chargers), Yancey Thigpen (Titans), O. J. McDuffie (Dolphins), Wayne Chrebet (Jets)

1999 Rookies Who Will Come On — Peerless Price (Bills), David Boston (Cardinals), Troy Edwards (Steelers), Marty Booker (Bears), Na Brown (Eagles)

Top Players on New Teams — Joey Galloway (Cowboys), Keyshawn Johnson (Buccaneers), Jake Reed (Saints), Curtis Conway (Chargers), Eddie Kennison (Bears), Shawn Jefferson (Falcons)

Will Struggle on a New Team — Keyshawn Johnson (Buccaneers), Curtis Conway (Chargers)

Late-Round Gambles — Peerless Price (Bills), Sean Dawkins (Seahawks), Keith Poole (Saints), Eddie Kennison (Bears), David Boston (Cardinals), Troy Edwards (Steelers), E. G. Green (Colts), Dedric Ward (Jets), Troy Brown (Patriots), Charles Johnson (Eagles)

Best Deep Threats — Randy Moss (Vikings), Eric Moulds (Bills), Michael Westbrook (Redskins), Marcus Robinson (Bears), Joey Galloway (Cowboys), Germaine Crowell (Lions), Terry Glenn (Patriots), Tim Dwight (Falcons), Qadry Ismail (Ravens), Keith Poole (Saints)

Best Duos — Minnesota's Cris Carter and Randy Moss, Detroit's Herman Moore and Germaine Crowell, Jacksonville's Jimmy Smith and Keenan McCardell, Carolina's Muhsin Muhammad and Patrick Jeffers, Denver's Ed McCaffrey and Rod Smith, Chicago's Marcus Robinson and Bobby Engram, and St. Louis's Isaac Bruce and Torry Holt.

Best of the Rest

Ricky Proehl, Rams	E. G. Green, Colts
Mickael Ricks, Chargers	Kevin Lockett, Chiefs
Jerome Pathon, Colts	Yatil Green, Dolphins
Courtney Hawkins, Steelers	Charlie Jones, Chargers
Will Blackwell, Steelers	Andre Reed, cut by Bills
Lamar Thomas, Dolphins	James McKnight, Cowboys
Andre Rison, cut by Chiefs	Ernie Mills, cut by Cowboys
Chris Calloway, Falcons	Andre Hastings, cut by Saints
Na Brown, Eagles	Eric Metcalf, cut by Panthers
Leslie Shepherd, cut by Browns	Matthew Hatchett, Vikings
Isaac Byrd, Titans	Karl Williams, Buccaneers

Chapter 6

TIGHT ENDS

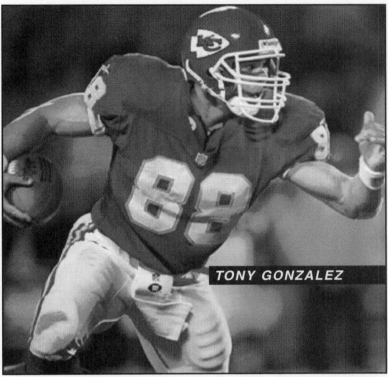

TONY GONZALEZ

Tight ends can pack a punch into your lineup, or they can pack dead-weight, a waste of a roster space. They're worth your attention, because the top 10 percent of the league's tight ends easily outscore the other 90 percent combined. The best tight ends are primary targets; the others toil as blocking specialists or as short-range targets in a controlled passing game. The best tight ends carry your fantasy team for long stretches of the season; the others give you a couple of unexpected scores per season, and waste your time the other 14 weeks.

Tight ends add a dimension to fantasy football, another decision to mull over on draft day — a feast-or-famine possibility. Some fantasy leagues dump the tight end position and replace it with a third wide receiver in the starting lineup. This is a viable option, one that results in somewhat higher scores. But it removes an element of strategy. Should you grab Wesley Walls or Tony Gonzalez in an early round, or focus on running backs and wide receivers and then draft a tight end in a middle round? Eliminating the tight end position greatly reduces the possibility of drafting a player in a late round who rewards his owner with seven or eight touchdowns. Thus, don't do it in your league.

Draft Tips for Choosing Tight Ends

■ Look at past performances, especially the last two or three seasons, rather than just last season.

■ Draft tight ends who play on offenses that spread the ball around, because they are likely to catch more passes. Those teams are Denver, Carolina, Indianapolis, Jacksonville, Tennessee, San Diego, Kansas City, Oakland and the New York Giants. Stay away from teams such as Arizona, Atlanta, Pittsburgh, Cleveland, Seattle and the New York Giants, because they don't throw to their tight ends enough. Draft tight ends who play during goal-line situations and ones who run deep pass patterns, because both are apt to get into the end zone.

■ Many teams start two tight ends — a pass-catching specialist and a blocking specialist. Know which is which.

■ Consider matching a tight end with your quarterback when putting together your team. If the pair hooks up for a touchdown or two on Sunday, that can carry your fantasy team.

■ Take into consideration tight ends on teams that are likely to have a quarterback change or a rookie signal caller during the season. The switching of quarterbacks often means a change in a team's offensive scheme, and thus it could change the production of the player you want to pick. Rookie quarterbacks are seldom adept at looking off their primary target and finding an open tight end.

■ A tight end you draft in the last round won't be much different in terms of scoring capability than one you might draft in the middle rounds, so don't choose one too early. Instead, stock up on other positions.

■ Watch what is going on during training camp. Will the Ravens utilize Shannon Sharpe as much as the Broncos used to? Is Mark Chmura's neck stable enough to support him throughout another season in Green Bay? Who will start for the New York Jets, Miami, Minnesota, Philadelphia, Arizona, Chicago and New England? Is Reggie Kelly, a 1999 second-round draft pick, worth the high price (this year's first-round draft pick) the Falcons paid to get him? Is Ben Coates over the hill, or will a change of scenery give him new life? How will the retooled Saints offense utilize Andrew Glover and Cam Cleeland? Is there anything left in the aging knees of Eric Green and Troy Drayton? Who will replace Jackie Harris as the much-utilized second tight end in Tennessee? Will the Seahawks utilize their tight ends much more than last year, when Mike Holmgren's offense uncharacteristically ignored the position? Was Tony Gonzalez's 1999 performance a fluke or a sign of things to come? Will David LaFleur, who scored seven touchdowns last season, be an even bigger part of the Dallas offense this year?

1 TONY GONZALEZ / CHIEFS

YEAR	REC.	YARDS	AVG.	TDS	100+	GP/GS
1997	33	368	11.2	2	0	16/0
1998	59	621	10.5	2	0	16/16
1999	76	849	11.2	11	0	15/15

Comments: Tall enough to go over defenders, strong enough to break through line jams and fast enough to outrun linebackers, Gonzalez is the most skilled tight end in the game. He reached his full potential in 1999, when he led all tight ends in catches and receiving yards, and he led AFC tight ends with a team-high 11 touchdown catches. He shattered the Chiefs' tight end records and caught the second-most passes in a season by a receiver in team history. In 1998, his only two scores came in the final two games, but he consistently caught passes all season. With 59 catches, Gonzalez smashed the team's 21-year-old tight end record of 48 receptions. The Chiefs broke him in easily in 1997, and he still managed to make a significant impact as a rookie with 33 catches (a team record for rookie tight ends).

The skinny: Gonzalez could be the best tight end in the league for years to come.

2 WESLEY WALLS / PANTHERS

YEAR	REC.	YARDS	AVG.	TDS	100+	GP/GS
1995	57	694	12.2	4	0	16/10
1996	61	713	11.7	10	0	16/15
1997	58	746	12.9	6	0	15/15
1998	49	506	10.3	5	0	14/14
1999	63	822	13.0	12	0	16/16

Comments: George Seifert's pass-happy offense produced a career year from Walls in 1999, his 10th season. He has always been a primary target, and, with 575 Carolina pass attempts, that meant 63 catches for Walls last season. He tied an NFL tight end record with 12 touchdown catches. Walls also led NFC tight ends in receptions and receiving yards. In 1998, the Panthers began opening up their offense, and Walls was the NFC's second-leading tight end with 49 catches, despite a foot injury that sidelined him for the final two games. He was the top tight end in the NFC in 1996 and '97, when he led the Panthers in receptions and touchdown catches. In 1996, his first season as a Panther, Walls caught 10 touchdown passes to tie for second among NFC receivers. In four seasons with Carolina, Walls has earned four Pro Bowl berths. He emerged with the Saints from 1994 to '95, when he caught eight touchdown passes.

The skinny: Walls is the league's most consistent tight end, and the only one who has at least four touchdowns every year since 1994.

3 RICKEY DUDLEY / RAIDERS

YEAR	REC.	YARDS	AVG.	TDS	100+	GP/GS
1996	34	386	11.4	4	0	16/15
1997	48	787	16.4	7	2	16/16
1998	36	549	15.3	5	0	16/15
1999	39	555	14.2	9	0	16/16

Comments: Dudley quieted skeptics with a strong 1999 finish that went a long way toward shedding his underachiever label. Dudley caught just 13 passes for 185 yards and two scores through eight games. Then he caught 26 passes for 370 yards and seven touchdowns in the final eight games. Dudley was the league's third-highest scoring tight end and the Raiders' touchdown catch leader. He followed the same slow-start, big-finish script in 1998, scoring just one touchdown through seven games but coming on strong to finish with a respectable five TDs.

In 1997, Dudley held on to the ball and lived up to his enormous potential, and his seven touchdown catches were the second most among NFL tight ends. That was a big step forward from his rookie season of 1996, when Dudley dropped passes on a regular basis.

The skinny: Dudley requires patience by fantasy owners because of his slow starts, but the end result makes him a fantasy stud.

4 SHANNON SHARPE / RAVENS

YEAR	REC.	YARDS	AVG.	TDS	100+	GP/GS
1995	63	756	12.0	4	2	13/13
1996	80	1062	13.3	10	2	15/15
1997	72	1107	15.4	3	0	16/16
1998	64	768	12.0	10	0	16/16
1999	23	224	9.7	0	0	5/5

Comments: Sharpe reaped the benefits of free agency by signing with the Ravens, who were starved for a short-to-intermediate target to help open up a deep passing game. Sharpe's 1999 season in Denver was ended by a fractured clavicle in Week 5. At the time, he was the team's leading receiver with 23 receptions. The Broncos' all-time reception leader with 552 catches, he had a big 1998 season with 10 touchdown passes to lead all tight ends. He is the only tight end in league history to catch 50 passes in seven straight seasons. In 1997, Sharpe succeeded at everything except scoring touchdowns; he led the tight ends in catches (72), receiving yards (1,107) and 100-yard games (four), but had just three scores. He is among just three tight ends in NFL history to record three 1,000-yard seasons, and he has 15 career 100-receiving-yard games. Sharpe has had more than his share of injuries in 10 pro seasons, but he plays through them to produce like virtually no other tight end. He has scored 44 career touchdowns.

The skinny: The Baltimore offense is tailor-made for Sharpe, so he should again rank among the league's most productive tight ends.

5 DAVID LaFLEUR / COWBOYS

YEAR	REC.	YARDS	AVG.	TDS	100+	GP/GS
1997	18	122	6.8	2	0	16/5
1998	20	176	8.8	2	0	13/13
1999	35	322	9.2	7	0	16/16

Comments: LaFleur was a long shot to lead the Cowboys in touchdown catches last season, but he became a primary target near the goal line on a team with an injury-depleted receiving corps. He started every game and he ranked second among NFC tight ends in touchdown catches. The 22nd player chosen in the 1997 draft, LaFleur made his greatest impact as a blocker during his first two seasons. A backup as a rookie, LaFleur moved into the starting lineup in 1998 but caught just 20 passes and averaged only 8.8 yards per catch. In 1997, he finished strong with 10 receptions for 66 yards and two touchdowns in the final three games.

The skinny: LaFleur's role could expand in a more tight-end-friendly offense, but expecting another seven scores is a reach.

6 JAY RIEMERSMA / BILLS

YEAR	REC.	YARDS	AVG.	TDS	100+	GP/GS
1996	DNP					
1997	26	208	8.0	2	0	16/8
1998	25	288	11.5	6	0	16/3
1999	37	496	13.4	4	0	14/12

Comments: The Bills made re-signing Riemersma an offseason priority because he's a big, reliable target over the middle and an improved blocker. In 1999, Riemersma caught a career-high 37 passes, third most on the team. In 1998, he became Doug Flutie's go-to receiver near the goal line. He caught six touchdown passes that year to tie the team's tight end TD record. In 1997, he made the jump from a project to a contributor. A former quarterback who switched to tight end at the University of Michigan in 1994, Riemersma didn't play as a rookie in 1996. But in 1997 he scored a touchdown on his first career reception.

The skinny: Riemersma could be headed for a career year, but he probably never will surpass his 1998 touchdown total.

7 STEPHEN ALEXANDER / REDSKINS

YEAR	REC.	YARDS	AVG.	TDS	100+	GP/GS
1998	37	383	10.4	4	0	15/5
1999	29	324	11.2	3	0	15/15

Comments: Alexander was a surprising disappointment on a 1999 Redskins offense that was often unstoppable. He caught five passes for 86 yards and two touchdowns in Week 2, but then he failed to catch more than one pass in half of the remaining games. Alexander, who was slowed by back and hip injuries, finished fifth on the team in catches and tied for third in touchdown grabs. As a rookie in 1998, he caught 37 passes — fourth most on the team — despite playing in slightly more than half of the team's offensive plays. Alexander, who has good speed for a tight end, excels at making tough catches and gaining yards after the catch.

The skinny: Alexander should bounce back with a much better 2000 season.

8 FRANK WYCHECK / TITANS

YEAR	REC.	YARDS	AVG.	TDS	100+	GP/GS
1995	40	471	11.8	1	0	16/11
1996	53	511	9.6	6	0	16/16
1997	63	748	11.9	4	0	16/16
1998	70	768	11.0	2	0	16/16
1999	69	641	9.3	2	0	16/16

Comments: Wycheck is the focal point of the Titans' short, low-risk passing game. The team's leading receiver for four consecutive seasons, Wycheck has at least one reception in 55 consecutive regular-season games. He ranked second among 1999 tight ends with 69 receptions and tied a career high with 10 catches in one game. In 1998, Wycheck led all tight ends with 70 receptions for a team-record 768 yards. He was the lone bright spot amid a dismal group of pass receivers in 1997, and he caught six touchdown catches in 1996. Since being claimed off the waiver wire just before the 1995 season opener, he has 295 catches.

The skinny: Wycheck is much more valuable in performance scoring leagues, which reward his great reception and yardage productivity.

9 BEN COATES / CUT BY PATRIOTS

YEAR	REC.	YARDS	AVG.	TDS	100+	GP/GS
1995	84	915	10.9	6	1	16/15
1996	62	682	11.0	9	1	16/15
1997	66	737	11.2	8	0	16/16
1998	67	668	10.0	6	1	14/14
1999	32	370	11.6	2	0	16/15

Comments: Perhaps more than anyone else in the NFL, Coates appeared to grow old quickly in 1999. His production took a dive, he complained about his diminished role, and his high price made him expendable in the offseason. Coates caught 32 passes, his fewest in seven years. For six consecutive seasons from 1993 to '98, he scored at least six touchdowns and caught 50 or more passes. In 1997, Coates led tight ends with eight touchdown catches. His 1996 reception total of 62 was his lowest in three seasons, but he scored a career-high nine touchdowns. The ultimate third-down option, Coates in 1994 caught more passes (96) than any tight end in NFL history. He set a team single-season receiving record, and his 1,174 receiving yards ranked second in team history. He ranks second in Patriots history in receptions (490) and touchdown catches (50).

The skinny: Coates could still be a good fantasy starter, but he's no longer worth an early-round pick.

10 DAVID SLOAN / LIONS

YEAR	REC.	YARDS	AVG.	TDS	100+	GP/GS
1995	17	184	10.8	1	0	16/8
1996	7	51	7.3	0	0	4/4
1997	29	264	9.1	0	0	14/12
1998	11	146	10.2	1	0	10/2
1999	47	591	12.6	4	0	16/15

Comments: Good health has always been all Sloan needed to succeed in the NFL. He struggled through four injury-riddled seasons, but he stayed healthy and emerged as a Pro Bowler in 1999. At 6 feet 6, Sloan is a huge target, and he ranked third among NFC tight ends with 47 receptions. Sloan proved he also has speed when he outran Packers safety LeRoy Butler for a 74-yard touchdown run in Week 2. In 1998, a knee injury sidelined him for the first six games, then he backed up Walter Rasby and caught just 11 passes. In 1997, he ranked fourth on the Lions with 29 receptions, but he had never really fully recovered from a season-ending knee injury that he suffered in 1996.

The skinny: Sloan is worth a shot as your backup tight end, but he's a definite risk because he's injury-prone.

11 ERNIE CONWELL / RAMS

YEAR	REC.	YARDS	AVG.	TDS	100+	GP/GS
1996	15	164	10.9	0	0	10/8
1997	38	404	10.6	4	0	16/16
1998	15	105	7.0	0	0	7/7
1999	1	11	11.0	0	0	3/0

Comments: The Rams are confident Conwell has fully recovered from reconstructive knee surgery, so he was re-signed in the offseason. A serious knee injury ended Conwell's 1998 season in the seventh game. His slow recovery lingered into last season, and he played in three late-season games and in the playoffs and Super Bowl. Look for Conwell — a solid blocker and an adequate receiver — to regain the starting job. Conwell's promising 1997 campaign began with a tackle-breaking 46-yard TD grab in the opener that set the stage for his solid season — four touchdown catches and 38 receptions. As a rookie in 1996, Conwell made veteran Troy Drayton expendable.

The skinny: Conwell could prove to be a nice late-round sleeper.

12 MARK CHMURA / PACKERS

YEAR	REC.	YARDS	AVG.	TDS	100+	GP/GS
1995	54	679	12.6	7	2	16/15
1996	28	370	13.2	0	0	13/13
1997	38	417	11.0	6	0	15/14
1998	47	554	11.8	4	0	15/14
1999	5	55	11.0	0	0	2/2

Comments: Chmura appears confident that he can play again following a neck injury that ended his 1999 season in Week 2, but mid-April charges of rape might end those chances. His offseason rehabilitation and minicamp workouts went well. The 1999 Packers offense sorely missed Chmura, especially in the red zone. In 1998, he was the third-leading NFC tight end with 47 catches. In 1997, he regained his prominent role in the Packers' passing game. His six touchdown catches tied for the NFC lead among tight ends. In 1995, Chmura had the best season by a Packers tight end in 12 years. He led the NFL's tight ends with seven touchdown catches, and his 54 receptions were just two shy of the team tight end record.

The skinny: When healthy, Chmura is one of the best. But the Packers will probably cut him because of the rape charge. Where he ends up — and if he even plays again — is only conjecture.

13 TONY McGEE / BENGALS

YEAR	REC.	YARDS	AVG.	TDS	100+	GP/GS
1995	55	754	13.7	4	1	16/16
1996	38	446	11.7	4	0	16/16
1997	34	414	12.2	6	0	16/16
1998	22	363	16.5	1	0	16/16
1999	26	344	13.2	2	0	16/16

Comments: Underrated and underappreciated, McGee contributed more to the Bengals' ground game than to the passing game the past two seasons. In 1999, he had the Bengals' fifth-most receptions for the second-best average per catch. He scored both of his touchdowns in the first two games. After scoring 14 touchdowns in his three previous seasons, McGee scored just once in 1998. McGee led the Bengals and all NFL tight ends in average yards per catch (16.5). In 1997, McGee scored a career-high six touchdowns to rank third among NFL tight ends in scoring. Since McGee's rookie season of 1993, when he caught 44 passes, he has started 103 consecutive games.

The skinny: McGee is certainly capable, but he probably won't score much in this year's ground-oriented offense.

14 PETE MITCHELL / GIANTS

YEAR	REC.	YARDS	AVG.	TDS	100+	GP/GS
1995	41	527	12.9	2	1	16/4
1996	52	575	11.1	1	0	16/7
1997	35	380	10.9	4	0	16/12
1998	38	363	9.6	2	0	16/16
1999	58	520	9.0	3	0	15/6

Comments: Mitchell was the free-agent acquisition the Giants had hoped for when they signed him in 1999. A pass-catching specialist, Mitchell complemented blocker Howard Cross well in 1999. He caught 58 passes — the most by a Giants tight end in 13 years. He was slowed late in the season by sprained ankles but still finished fourth on the team in receptions and second in touchdown catches. Mitchell had 166 receptions in four seasons in Jacksonville, the most of any tight end drafted in 1995. He caught a pass in all but four games over that 64-game span. In 1997, Mitchell produced well (four touchdown catches) for a player who wasn't drafted in most fantasy leagues.

The skinny: For a guy who catches as many passes as Mitchell does, he doesn't score very often.

TIGHT ENDS

15 FREDDIE JONES / CHARGERS

YEAR	REC.	YARDS	AVG.	TDS	100+	GP/GS
1997	41	505	12.3	2	0	13/8
1998	57	602	10.6	3	0	16/16
1999	56	670	12.0	2	0	16/16

Comments: Jones consistently does less with more catches than any NFL tight end. He helps move the chains but averages only about one touchdown for every 30 receptions. Jones finished one shy of the team lead with 56 receptions in 1999, but he failed to break many tackles and make big plays. On a 1998 team that had woefully inadequate quarterbacking, Jones played remarkably well. He ranked fifth among AFC tight ends with a team-leading 57 receptions. The fourth tight end chosen in the 1997 draft, Jones has outproduced them all, with 154 receptions for 1,777 yards. He's the Chargers' best tight end since Kellen Winslow . . .

The skinny: . . . but don't waste a roster spot on this fantasy tease.

16 ANDREW GLOVER / SAINTS

YEAR	REC.	YARDS	AVG.	TDS	100+	GP/GS
1995	26	220	8.5	3	0	16/7
1996	9	101	11.2	1	0	14/4
1997	32	378	11.8	3	0	13/11
1998	35	522	14.9	5	0	16/12
1999	28	327	11.7	1	0	16/13

Comments: Glover became the forgotten man in the Vikings' offense of 1999, an afterthought when Jeff George replaced Randall Cunningham at quarterback. Glover caught just 10 passes in 10 games after the team's quarterback change. In 1998, Glover seemed to be uncovered and open on every pass play. He established career highs for catches, receiving yards, average per catch and touchdowns. In 1997, Glover had become an answer to a gaping hole in the Vikings' offense. Signed a month before the season opener, Glover ranked third on the team in receiving yards and touchdown catches. In 1996, he lost his starting job to rookie Rickey Dudley in Oakland.

The skinny: The Saints will utilize Glover more than the Vikings did last year, so he's a player to watch with Jeff Blake now at quarterback.

TIGHT ENDS

17 DAVE MOORE / BUCCANEERS

YEAR	REC.	YARDS	AVG.	TDS	100+	GP/GS
1995	13	102	7.9	0	0	16/9
1996	27	237	8.8	3	0	16/8
1997	19	217	11.4	4	0	16/7
1998	24	255	10.6	4	0	16/16
1999	23	276	12.0	5	0	16/16

Comments: Moore led the 1999 Buccaneers with five touchdown catches, but the team was searching to upgrade the position in the off-season with a playmaker, so he may be relegated to a part-time role. In 1998, Moore was the team's fourth-leading receiver with the second-most touchdown catches. He caught 22 catches in his first four seasons. Since then, he has 93 receptions and 16 touchdowns in four seasons. In 1997, his four touchdown catches tied for the team lead. Before 1996, he had switched back and forth between tight end and fullback.

The skinny: Moore is a steady performer, but his touchdown production will drop if he's benched.

18 KYLE BRADY / JAGUARS

YEAR	REC.	YARDS	AVG.	TDS	100+	GP/GS
1995	26	252	9.7	2	0	15/11
1996	15	144	9.6	1	0	16/16
1997	22	238	10.8	2	0	16/14
1998	30	315	10.5	5	0	16/15
1999	32	346	10.8	1	0	13/13

Comments: Brady is the top-rated run blocker the Jaguars sought when they made him the league's highest-paid tight end in 1999. But his receiving skills have never met the expectations of the first tight end taken in the 1995 draft. In 1999, Brady missed three games due to a knee injury, but he still caught a career-high 32 passes. Brady's only good fantasy football production came in 1998, when he scored five times and set career highs in virtually every receiving category. Brady failed to make the instant impact that was expected of him as a rookie, and his impact as a receiver was minimal in 1996 and '97, as well.

The skinny: Brady has 11 touchdowns in five seasons — hardly worth a fantasy pick.

19 DAMON JONES / JAGUARS

YEAR	REC.	YARDS	AVG.	TDS	100+	GP/GS
1997	5	87	17.4	2	0	11/3
1998	8	90	11.3	4	0	16/7
1999	19	221	11.6	4	0	15/8

Comments: Between the 20-yard lines, Jones contributes to the Jaguars' ground game as an effective blocker in two-tight-end sets. Inside the red zone, he becomes a secret weapon. In three seasons, Jones has scored on 10 of his 32 career receptions. In 1999, Jones set career highs in catches and receiving yards. In 1998, he started seven games in two-tight-end sets and scored on each of his first three catches. He broke into the starting lineup late in 1997 and caught two touchdown passes in the final four games of the season.

The skinny: Jones is worth a glance when you're looking for your backup in a late round.

20 MARCUS POLLARD / COLTS

YEAR	REC.	YARDS	AVG.	TDS	100+	GP/GS
1995	0	0	0.0	0	0	8/0
1996	6	86	14.3	1	0	16/4
1997	10	116	11.6	0	0	16/5
1998	24	309	12.9	4	0	16/11
1999	34	374	11.0	4	0	16/12

Comments: Pollard is a virtual unknown among most fans, but only seven tight ends have more touchdowns over the past two seasons. The other starter opposite Ken Dilger on a team that fully utilizes two-tight-end sets, Pollard has a flair for spectacular catches. Five of his catches covered 20 or more yards in 1999, when he was the Colts' fifth-leading receiver. In 1998, Pollard started 11 games and tied for third on the team with four touchdown catches (he also had a pair of two-point conversions). He played little in his first three seasons.

The skinny: Watch others in your league ask "Who?" if you draft Pollard in a late round to be your backup.

21   O. J. SANTIAGO / FALCONS

YEAR	REC.	YARDS	AVG.	TDS	100+	GP/GS
1997	17	217	12.8	2	0	11/11
1998	27	428	15.9	5	0	16/16
1999	15	174	11.6	0	0	14/14

Comments: A restricted free agent, Santiago is not going to be a part of the Falcons' plans for 2000. He started 14 games last season, but Reggie Kelly is his probable replacement. Santiago caught a 46-yard pass in the 1999 season opener, but he finished with just 15 catches for 174 yards. A huge target at 6 feet 7 and a deep threat, Santiago turned nine pass plays into gains of 20 or more yards in 1998. A third-round draft pick in 1997, Santiago immediately moved into the starting lineup as a rookie. He caught 17 passes and scored two touchdowns before suffering a fractured fibula in the 10th game.

The skinny: Santiago's season could be dependent on his next destination.

22   CAM CLEELAND / SAINTS

YEAR	REC.	YARDS	AVG.	TDS	100+	GP/GS
1998	54	684	12.7	6	0	16/16
1999	26	325	12.5	1	0	11/8

Comments: Cleeland played like a Pro Bowler as a rookie and he played like a rookie in 1999, his second season. A blocking liability, Cleeland made little impact in the passing game with just 26 catches and one touchdown. Sidelined for five games by hamstring, rib, shoulder and ankle injuries, Cleeland isn't very durable, so the Saints signed Andrew Glover in the offseason. Cleeland made an immediate impact as a rookie in 1998. He tied team rookie records with six touchdown catches and 54 receptions. He ranked second among NFC tight ends in touchdown grabs, and he led the Saints in receptions.

The skinny: The Saints' offense will be much improved in 2000, but Cleeland will have to share his receptions with Glover.

23 BYRON CHAMBERLAIN / BRONCOS

YEAR	REC.	YARDS	AVG.	TDS	100+	GP/GS
1995	1	11	11.0	0	0	10/10
1996	12	129	10.8	0	0	11/0
1997	2	18	9.0	0	0	10/0
1998	3	35	11.7	0	0	16/0
1999	32	488	15.3	2	1	16/0

Comments: Chamberlain helped make high-priced free agent Shannon Sharpe expendable with a solid 1999 season as a pass-receiving specialist. His role in the Broncos' passing game greatly expanded when Sharpe went down in the fifth game. Chamberlain led Broncos receivers with a 15.3-yard average per catch, and he ranked third on the team with 32 catches. In Game 6, he turned a shovel pass into an 88-yard gain. He's a solid receiver but a blocking liability.

The skinny: Look for a second consecutive career year from Chamberlain, especially now that Sharpe is gone.

24 LUTHER BROUGHTON / EAGLES

YEAR	REC.	YARDS	AVG.	TDS	100+	GP/GS
1997	0	0	0	0	0	0/0
1998	6	142	23.6	1	0	16/4
1999	26	295	11.3	4	0	16/3

Comments: Broughton was acquired in a trade just before the 1999 season opener, and he served a role as the Eagles' best pass-catching tight end. In just three starts (16 games played), he tied for the team lead with four touchdown catches and ranked fourth with 26 receptions. Broughton, who gained more than 25 yards with three of his catches last year, scored on a 68-yard touchdown play with the Panthers in 1998, so he has the ability to get downfield. But his blocking is average at best, so Chad Lewis and Jed Weaver earned more starts than Broughton did last season.

The skinny: Broughton bears watching; he has good speed and hands, and he's a primary target on what could be an improving team.

25 GREG CLARK / 49ERS

YEAR	REC.	YARDS	AVG.	TDS	100+	GP/GS
1997	8	96	12.0	1	0	15/4
1998	12	124	10.3	1	0	13/9
1999	34	347	10.2	0	0	12/11

Comments: An outstanding blocker and good pass catcher, Clark has a good shot at a Pro Bowl or two if he can stay healthy. In 1999, he missed the first three games due to a preseason rib injury, and he sat out a midseason game to mend a collapsed lung. He finished strong, with 23 receptions for 248 yards in the final eight games. In 1998, Clark was slowed by a foot injury and backed up Irv Smith for half of the season before moving into the starting lineup. A third-round draft choice of the 49ers in 1997, Clark subbed for the injured Brent Jones and contributed more as a blocker than as a receiver in his rookie season.

The skinny: Clark has great potential, but injuries and an unsettled quarterback situation could limit his production.

26 CHRISTIAN FAURIA / SEAHAWKS

YEAR	REC.	YARDS	AVG.	TDS	100+	GP/GS
1995	17	181	10.6	1	0	14/9
1996	18	214	11.9	1	0	10/9
1997	10	110	11.0	0	0	16/3
1998	37	377	10.2	2	0	16/15
1999	35	376	10.7	0	0	16/15

Comments: Fauria started the 1999 season slowly due to a preseason knee injury, but he finished strong and matched his career year of 1998. He caught nine passes for 108 yards in the final two regular-season games and gained the confidence of coach Mike Holmgren. In 1998, Fauria finally shed his reputation for being injury prone, and he tied a 22-year-old team tight end record with 37 receptions. A second-round pick in 1995, Fauria was slowed by ankle and knee injuries his first two seasons.

The skinny: Don't be surprised if Fauria breaks through with four or five scores this season in Holmgren's tight-end-friendly offense.

TIGHT ENDS

27 KEN DILGER / COLTS

YEAR	REC.	YARDS	AVG.	TDS	100+	GP/GS
1995	42	635	15.1	4	1	16/13
1996	42	503	12.0	4	1	16/16
1997	27	380	14.1	3	1	14/14
1998	31	303	9.8	1	0	16/16
1999	40	479	12.0	2	0	15/15

Comments: Re-signing Dilger was the Colts' biggest free-agent priority in the offseason. A solid blocker and steady receiver, he ranked fourth on the Colts in receiving with 40 catches in 1999. The previous season, a rookie quarterback and a desperate backfield situation combined to inhibit Dilger's production. Dilger averaged a career-low 9.8 yards per catch and scored just once. In 1995, he set a Colts record for rookie tight ends with 42 catches to surpass Hall of Famer John Mackey's 35 pass receptions in 1963. The fourth tight end taken in the '95 draft, Dilger had the best rookie season of them all.

The skinny: Dilger is much more valuable to the Colts than he is to your fantasy team.

28 ROLAND WILLIAMS / RAMS

YEAR	REC.	YARDS	AVG.	TDS	100+	GP/GS
1998	15	144	9.6	1	0	13/9
1999	25	226	9.0	6	0	16/15

Comments: With all of the weapons on the Rams' offense, the overlooked Williams quietly slipped underneath pass coverages for six touchdown grabs in 1999. A good receiver but suspect blocker, he moved into a starting role in 1998 due to an injury to Ernie Conwell. He started all but one game last season and excelled in the red zone. Williams tied for third on the team (and he ranked third among NFC tight ends) in touchdowns. In his rookie season of 1998, Williams's playing time was limited until Conwell was injured.

The skinny: Conwell's return will limit Williams's playing time this season, so don't expect more than three or four touchdown catches — if that.

29 MARK BRUENER / STEELERS

YEAR	REC.	YARDS	AVG.	TDS	100+	GP/GS
1995	26	238	9.2	3	0	16/13
1996	12	141	11.8	0	0	12/12
1997	18	117	6.5	6	0	16/16
1998	19	157	8.3	2	0	16/16
1999	18	176	9.8	0	0	14/14

Comments: Bruener is a victim of Pittsburgh's poor quarterbacking. Kordell Stewart rarely looks his way, so Bruener contributed primarily as a blocker in 1999. He did catch seven passes for 111 yards in three late-season games with Mike Tomczak at quarterback, but then he suffered a foot injury and missed the final two games. In 1998, Bruener didn't catch a pass in seven of his 16 starts. In 1997, he became the league's ultimate goal-line tight end by turning one-third of his receptions into touchdowns. His six scores tied for second in team history among tight ends.

The skinny: Forget about Bruener until the Steelers forget about Kordell.

30 TYRONE DAVIS / PACKERS

YEAR	REC.	YARDS	AVG.	TDS	100+	GP/GS
1995	1	9	9.0	0	0	4/0
1996	1	6	6.0	0	0	2/0
1997	2	28	14.0	1	0	13/0
1998	18	250	13.9	7	0	13/1
1999	20	204	10.2	2	0	16/13

Comments: Thrust into a starting role when Mark Chmura was injured two games into the 1999 season, Davis failed miserably. A converted wide receiver, he was a blocking liability. Even more disturbing, he dropped passes and botched assignments. Thus he is headed for a backup role in 2000. In 1998, Davis was by far the biggest surprise among tight ends. That season, he turned just 18 receptions into seven touchdowns — the most scores among NFC tight ends. Intrigued by his ability to get open downfield, the Packers signed Davis to a three-year contract after he flashed his potential in the 1997 season.

The skinny: A 1998 flash-in-the-pan, Davis will never again approach his seven-touchdown total.

31 TROY DRAYTON / CUT BY DOLPHINS

YEAR	REC.	YARDS	AVG.	TDS	100+	GP/GS
1995	47	458	9.7	4	1	3/3
1996	28	331	11.8	0	0	10/10
1997	39	558	14.3	4	0	16/15
1998	30	334	11.1	3	0	15/15
1999	32	299	9.3	1	0	14/13

Comments: The Dolphins gave up on Drayton and waived him following an uninspiring 1999 season. Bad knees plagued him in all four seasons in Miami, so he has never fulfilled the potential of a player who scored 10 touchdowns in his first two pro seasons. Last year, Drayton never gained more than 50 receiving yards in a game, and he failed to score after Week 2. He disappeared from the offense at times in 1998. The Dolphins' passing game bogged down in 1997, but Drayton led the team with four touchdown catches. With the Rams in 1995, Drayton was relatively productive with 47 catches and four TDs, and in 1994, he led the Rams with six TDs.

The skinny: Drayton is likely to find work with another team, but does he have many more pass routes in his legs?

32 JACKIE HARRIS / COWBOYS

YEAR	REC.	YARDS	AVG.	TDS	100+	GP/GS
1995	62	751	12.1	1	2	16/16
1996	30	349	11.6	1	0	13/12
1997	19	197	10.4	1	0	12/11
1998	43	412	9.6	2	0	16/16
1999	26	297	11.4	1	0	12/2

Comments: The Cowboys signed Harris to start opposite David LaFleur in their new two-tight-end offense. The highlight of his 1999 season was a 62-yard, against-the-grain score against Jacksonville. He was a good complement to Frank Wycheck in Tennessee, where they teamed to form the NFL's best tight end tandem in 1998. His 1996 and '97 seasons were cut short by injuries, and his reception totals dropped off sharply from those of his career year in 1995. That year, Harris tied for No. 1 among NFC tight ends with 62 catches (a Buccaneers record for tight ends). He moved into the forefront of tight ends with Green Bay in 1992, when he caught 55 passes.

The skinny: Do you really want to waste a draft pick on Harris, who has only six touchdowns in the past five seasons?

TIGHT ENDS

33 ERIC BJORNSON / PATRIOTS

YEAR	REC.	YARDS	AVG.	TDS	100+	GP/GS
1995	7	53	7.6	0	0	14/1
1996	48	388	8.1	3	0	14/10
1997	47	442	9.4	0	0	14/14
1998	15	218	14.5	1	0	16/4
1999	10	131	13.1	0	0	16/6

Comments: In the offseason, Bjornson was signed for two years to replace an aging Ben Coates as the Patriots' pass-catching specialist. After catching 95 passes in 1996 and '97, Bjornson practically disappeared from the Cowboys' offense the past two years due to the emergence of David LaFleur. A fractured fibula in Week 14 cut his 1997 season short, but Bjornson still caught 47 passes, second most on the team. In 1996, he made the most of his opportunity to fill in for injured Jay Novacek. Bjornson ranked second among NFC tight ends with 48 receptions.

The skinny: Bjornson can catch, but he seldom scores.

34 TERRY HARDY / CARDINALS

YEAR	REC.	YARDS	AVG.	TDS	100+	GP/GS
1998	0	0	0.0	0	0	9/0
1999	30	222	7.4	0	0	16/16

Comments: Hardy beat out Johnny McWilliams and Derek Brown for the starting job in 1999, and he started every game. His first start was his best, with five receptions for 49 yards in the season opener. He finished with 30 catches, fifth most on the team. Hardy is not a long-term solution as a starter, however.

The skinny: Expect the Cardinals to upgrade this position and return Hardy to a backup role.

35 DWAYNE CARSWELL / BRONCOS

YEAR	REC.	YARDS	AVG.	TDS	100+	GP/GS
1995	3	37	12.3	0	0	9/2
1996	15	85	5.7	0	0	16/2
1997	12	96	8.0	1	0	16/3
1998	4	51	12.8	0	0	16/1
1999	24	201	8.4	2	0	16/11

Comments: The 6-foot-3, 260-pound Carswell replaced the

injured Shannon Sharpe in the 1999 starting lineup because he's a good blocker. Carswell aided the Broncos' short passing game with 24 catches for 201 yards and two touchdowns, but Byron Chamberlain is the team's better receiving tight end. He scored just once in five previous seasons.

The skinny: Designated blockers such as Carswell don't score much.

36 REGGIE KELLY / FALCONS

YEAR	REC.	YARDS	AVG.	TDS	100+	GP/GS
1999	8	146	18.3	1	0	16/2

Comments: The Falcons wanted Kelly so badly last season that they traded this year's No. 1 draft pick to get him in the second round. They didn't pay such a high price to sit him on the bench, so expect Kelly to move into a starting role in 2000. Kelly was utilized primarily in short-yardage situations last season, but he did catch a 50-yard pass in Game 6, and his 18.3-yard average per catch tied for second on the team.

The skinny: Don't expect Kelly to play a major role in the passing game.

37 RYAN WETNIGHT / BEARS

YEAR	REC.	YARDS	AVG.	TDS	100+	GP/GS
1995	24	193	8.0	2	0	12/2
1996	21	223	10.6	1	0	11/5
1997	46	464	10.1	1	0	16/3
1998	23	168	7.3	2	0	15/3
1999	38	277	7.3	1	0	16/4

Comments: Wetnight has led Chicago tight ends in receiving in each of the past four years. But, in that time, he scored just five touchdowns. Last season, Wetnight started just four games (one at fullback), but he was a productive short-range target with 38 catches — fourth best among NFC tight ends. It's hard to believe, but in 1997 Wetnight had the most productive season by a Bears tight end since Mike Ditka caught 75 passes in 1964. Wetnight's 46 catches ranked third on the team. His playing time was limited in his first four NFL seasons.

The skinny: Even in this aerial circus of an offense, Wetnight won't score many touchdowns.

38 JAMIE ASHER / CUT BY EAGLES

YEAR	REC.	YARDS	AVG.	TDS	100+	GP/GS
1995	14	172	12.3	0	0	7/1
1996	42	481	11.5	4	0	16/12
1997	49	474	9.7	1	0	16/13
1998	28	294	10.5	0	0	9/7
1999	0	0	0.0	0	0	0/0

Comments: Asher missed the entire 1999 season due to a broken ankle, and he missed much of the 1998 season with a knee injury. When healthy, he's a proven pass-receiving specialist. The rapid development of Stephen Alexander made Asher expendable in Washington, where he emerged in 1996 with 42 catches — third most in the NFC. In 1997, Asher caught a pass in every game and he became the first tight end in 20 years to lead the Redskins in receiving.

The skinny: Asher appears to be out of the mix in Philadelphia, but he's talented enough to make a comeback if his legs hold up.

39 IRV SMITH / CUT BY BROWNS

YEAR	REC.	YARDS	AVG.	TDS	100+	GP/GS
1995	45	466	10.4	3	0	16/16
1996	15	144	9.6	0	0	7/7
1997	17	180	10.6	1	0	11/8
1998	25	266	10.6	5	0	16/8
1999	24	222	9.3	1	0	13/13

Comments: What a difference a quality offense makes. Smith makes an impact when he plays on a good offense. Smith scored five touchdowns on the high-flying 49ers offense of 1998, but he scored just once in 1999 with Cleveland, which had the league's worst offense. Smith, who scored just once with weak New Orleans offenses in 1996 and '97, has never quite lived up to the expectations of a 1993 first-round draft pick, though in 1994, his second season, he caught the most passes (41) of any Saints tight end in nine years.

The skinny: Don't count on much from Smith unless he gets another address change.

40 ERIC GREEN / CUT BY JETS

YEAR	REC.	YARDS	AVG.	TDS	100+	GP/GS
1995	43	499	11.6	3		14/14
1996	15	150	10.0	1	0	6/3
1997	65	601	9.2	5	0	16/15
1998	34	422	12.4	1	0	12/12
1999	7	37	5.3	2	0	10/8

Comments: Green's ailing knees might have reached the end of an underachieving career. In 1999, he started eight games but caught only seven passes and was benched by the Jets, who made him an expensive free-agent acquisition. Green, who missed four 1998 games due to three separate injuries, has always struggled to stay healthy. He had a remarkable comeback season in '97, when he played in every game for the first time in four years and finished with a career-high 65 catches. In 1995, Green provided far less than the Dolphins expected from their expensive free-agent investment. He had the most consistent season of his career in 1993, leading the Steelers in catches (63) and yards (942).

The skinny: Green scored 13 touchdowns in his first two NFL seasons — and just 23 in the past eight seasons.

LOOKING BACK AT TIGHT ENDS

The Best — Tony Gonzalez (Chiefs), Wesley Walls (Panthers)

Sure Bets — Rickey Dudley (Raiders), Shannon Sharpe (Ravens)

Top Sleepers — Ernie Conwell (Rams), Byron Chamberlain (Broncos), Eric Bjornson (Patriots), Kyle Brady (Jaguars), Luther Broughton (Eagles), Christian Fauria (Seahawks), Greg Clark (49ers)

Possible Busts — Roland Williams (Rams), Mark Chmura (Packers), Ben Coates (cut by Patriots)

Coming On — David LaFleur (Cowboys), David Sloan (Lions), Luther Broughton (Eagles)

Comeback Candidates — Shannon Sharpe (Ravens), Ernie Conwell (Rams), Ben Coates (cut by Patriots), Cam Cleeland (Saints), O. J. Santiago (Falcons)

Back to Earth After a Great 1999 — Roland Williams (Rams), David LaFleur (Cowboys)

In for a Career Year — Stephen Alexander (Redskins), Ernie Conwell (Rams), Byron Chamberlain (Broncos), Christian Fauria (Seahawks)

Top Rookies — Bubba Franks (Packers), Anthony Becht (Jets)
1999 Injured Players Who Will Be a Factor in '99 — Shannon Sharpe (Ravens), Ernie Conwell (Rams)
1999 Rookies Who Will Come On — Dan Campbell (Giants), Reggie Kelly (Falcons), Jerame Tuman (Steelers)
Top Players on a New Team — Shannon Sharpe (Ravens), Andrew Glover (Saints), Jackie Harris (Cowboys), Eric Bjornson (Patriots)
Late-Round Gambles — Stephen Alexander (Redskins), Luther Broughton (Eagles), Reggie Kelly (Falcons), Greg Clark (49ers), Christian Fauria (Seahawks), Byron Chamberlain (Broncos)
Best Deep Threats — Shannon Sharpe (Ravens), Tony McGee (Bengals), Byron Chamberlain (Broncos), Rickey Dudley (Raiders), Stephen Alexander (Redskins)

Best of the Rest

Chris Gedney, Cardinals	Alonzo Mayes, Bears
Brian Kozlowski, Falcons	Tony Johnson, Lions
Hunter Goodwin, Dolphins	Andrew Jordan, Vikings
Howard Cross, Giants	Greg DeLong, Ravens
Brian Kinchen, Panthers	Marco Battaglia, Bengals
Mitch Jacoby, Chiefs	Chad Fann, Vikings
Fred Baxter, Jets	Chad Lewis, Eagles
James Jenkins, Redskins	Jerame Tumane, Steelers
Jeff Thomason, Eagles	

TIGHT ENDS

Chapter 7

KICKERS

MIKE HOLLIS

Kickers are to fantasy football what a fan belt is to your car. They're cheap to obtain, but, boy, you'd better have one in good working order. With few exceptions, your starting kicker is the highest-scoring player on your fantasy team. And yet, they're not worth any more than a mid-round pick in your fantasy draft. In fact, in fantasy auctions, a good kicker can be had for a song.

Their price is low because their availability is high. While a 10-touchdown running back or receiver is at a premium, high-scoring kickers are relatively easy to find. Last season, 19 kickers scored more than 100 points.

Of those 19, 11 of them had reached the century point mark in 1998.

While some kickers last season complained that the new balls provided by the league were harder to kick, there was no noticeable difference in field goal accuracy from recent years.

As difficult as it is to predict the highest-scoring teams, it's even harder to anticipate which kicker will lead the league in field goals. Consider that Miami's Olindo Mare attempted just 27 field goals in 1998; with largely the same offense in '99, he set an NFL record with 39 field goals made in 46 attempts. Still, he finished one point behind Mike Vanderjagt for the league scoring title because the Colts were a much higher-scoring team.

The trick: Stay away from low-scoring teams (such as the Browns, Bengals and Eagles). Not only do their kickers score few extra points, but their weak offenses too seldom move into field-goal range.

Draft Tips for Choosing Kickers

■ Look at past performances, especially the last two or three seasons, rather than just last year. Far too often, a kicker's most recent season is not indicative of his true abilities (whether he had a good season or a bad one).

■ The biggest consideration for a kicker is the team he plays on. Therefore, be sure to draft those kickers who will get the most opportunities to score — not necessarily the team with the most touchdowns, such as St. Louis and Washington, but teams that bog down in the red zone and therefore attempt a lot of field goals (such as Miami, Tampa Bay and Seattle). The best guide here is a team's performance from the previous season.

■ Be sure to have a very good backup kicker who can take over if your starter is injured or is having a bad season. Don't be forced to go through the season with a kicker who is having an off year, and don't be afraid to make a quick transaction to replace a struggling kicker. In 1998, Richie Cunningham ranked among the league leaders in scoring and field-goal accuracy, Last year, his missed field goals cost the Cowboys some games and eventually cost Cunningham his job.

■ A kicker's longevity with a team is important, because some teams don't have much continuity at the position and thus change kickers often (even in midseason). If a kicker has played for the same team for several years, that team usually has a lot of confidence in him.

■ If your league's scoring system rewards long field goals, know which kickers are reliable on the long kicks (40 yards or longer). Jason Hanson and Jason Elam are two of the best long-range kickers.

■ Know which teams will enter training camp with unstable kicking situations. A hip injury ruined Jeff Jaeger's 1999 season in Chicago, and it remains to be seen if he'll get another chance. The Eagles, Patriots, Bills and Bengals may be due for an upgrade. Brad Daluiso's return from knee surgery made Cary Blanchard — who had an outstanding 1999 season — expendable. Will Daluiso reclaim his old job, and can Blanchard pick up where he left off and fill a long-standing gaping hole in Arizona? Do Morten Andersen and Gary Anderson, who both showed signs of aging last season, have another year left? Will either Martin Gramatica or Kris Brown struggle through a sophomore slump following excellent rookie seasons? Will Brett Conway, who had and up-and-down 1999 season, be placed on a short leash by an impatient owner?

1 MIKE HOLLIS / JAGUARS

YEAR	XP	XPA	FG	FGS	PTS	GP
1995	27	28	20	27	87	16
1996	27	27	30	36	117	16
1997	41	41	31	36	134	16
1998	45	45	21	26	108	16
1999	37	37	31	38	130	16

DISTANCE	1–19	20–29	30–39	40–49	50+
1999	0/0	12/13	8/9	10/15	1/1

Comments: Hollis wasn't among the league's best kickers last season, but he benefited from a high-scoring offense to rank fourth in the NFL in points. Only two kickers attempted more field goals than Hollis last season. He matched his career field goal percentage of 81.6, which ranks second in NFL history. He is even better in the postseason, with 16 field goals in 18 career attempts. In 1998, Hollis missed three of his first five field-goal tries and finished the year with a solid but not great 108 points. He followed a good 1996 season with a stellar Pro Bowl year in '97, when he won the NFL scoring title with 134 points. Hollis' rise to the top of the scoring charts began in the final seven regular-season games of 1996, when he led the league with 69 points, then added 30 points in the postseason.

The skinny: Hollis is exactly what you need — an accurate kicker on a high-scoring team.

2   JASON ELAM / BRONCOS

YEAR	XP	XPA	FG	FGS	PTS	GP
1995	39	39	31	38	132	16
1996	46	46	21	28	109	16
1997	46	46	26	36	124	15
1998	58	58	23	27	127	16
1999	29	29	29	36	116	16

DISTANCE	1–19	20–29	30–39	40–49	50+
1999	1/1	8/8	7/8	8/11	5/8

Comments: Elam is the best long-range kicker in the NFL, and he always ranks among the top scorers. His 1999 field goal percentage of 80.6 ranked 10th in the AFC, but that's because the average length of his field goal attempts and conversions was the most in the AFC. Elam, whose 63-yard field goal in 1998 tied an NFL record, led the league last year with five kicks made from 50 and beyond. He has never led the NFL in scoring, but his 846 points since 1993 is unmatched by any other kicker. In 1998, Elam made a career-best 85.2 percent of his field goals and tied for fifth in the NFL with 127 points. Since his career began in 1993, Elam has made 127 of 137 field goals from inside the 40-yard line, fourth best in the league. From beyond 50 yards, Elam is 61.1 percent (22 for 36). He is Denver's all-time scoring leader with 846 points.

The skinny: The safest kicker on your draft board, Elam is even more vaulable in performance fantasy leagues.

3   MIKE VANDERJAGT / COLTS

YEAR	XP	XPA	FG	FGS	PTS	GP
1998	23	23	27	31	104	14
1999	43	43	34	38	145	16

DISTANCE	1–19	20–29	30–39	40–49	50+
1999	2/2	10/10	11/13	10/11	1/2

Comments: Vanderjagt established himself as a quality kicker in 1998, and in 1999 he benefited from an explosive offense. Vanderjagt didn't lead the league in field goals or extra points, but he won the scoring title with 145 points. His 89.5 percent field-goal accuracy led the AFC and ranked second in the NFL. He made his final 26 field-goal attempts, a club record that ties the league's fifth-longest streak in history. In 1998, Vanderjagt won a preseason battle with veteran Cary Blanchard for the job, then quickly justified the team's decision by making his first eight field-goal tries, including a career-opening 51-yarder. That year, he tied a team record with a league-high six field goals from 50 yards and beyond.

The skinny: Vanderjagt will continue to thrive on this up-and-coming team.

4 AL DEL GRECO / TITANS

YEAR	XP	XPA	FG	FGS	PTS	GP
1995	33	33	27	31	114	16
1996	35	35	32	38	131	16
1997	32	32	27	35	113	16
1998	28	28	36	39	136	16
1999	43	43	21	25	106	16

DISTANCE	1–19	20–29	30–39	40–49	50+
1999	1/1	8/8	7/9	4/6	1/1

Comments: Del Greco ranks with Jason Elam as the steadiest kicker in fantasy football. In 1999, Del Greco attempted just 25 field goals — his fewest since 1994 — and he still extended his streak of 100-point seasons to six. His 84 percent field-goal accuracy was slightly above his team-record average and ranked seventh in the AFC. Del Greco, who has kicked a field goal in 20 consecutive regular-season games, gives fantasy players what they crave — consistent points. His 15th season was a career best in 1998, when he set team records for points (136), field-goal percentage (92.3) and consecutive games with a field goal (12). He owns 15 team records and five of the six most accurate kicking seasons in franchise history. In 1996, Del Greco set a team record with 131 points. He has made 20 of his 39 career field-goal tries from 50 and beyond.

The skinny: Tennessee's offense won't slip this season, and neither will Del Greco's points.

5 TODD PETERSON / SEAHAWKS

YEAR	XP	XPA	FG	FGS	PTS	GP
1995	40	40	23	28	109	16
1996	27	27	28	34	111	16
1997	37	37	22	28	103	16
1998	41	41	19	24	98	16
1999	32	32	34	40	134	16

DISTANCE	1–19	20–29	30–39	40–49	50+
1999	1/1	10/10	8/11	14/16	1/2

Comments: Peterson is still relatively unknown, but he should become a household name as he piles up points for Mike Holmgren's efficient offense. In 1998, Peterson was the league's third-highest scorer with a franchise record 134 points. His outstanding season included a team-record 16 consecutive field goals, and he ranked fourth in the AFC with an 85 percent field-goal-success rate. Peterson made the most three-pointers in the league from 40 or more yards out (15). His 1998 performance was hindered by an AFC-low 24 field goal attempts. In 1998, coming off three consecutive 100-point seasons, Peterson ranked 18th among kickers with 98 points, despite missing just one field-goal attempt from inside the 50. In 1997, Peterson became the only player in Seahawks history to score 100 points in three consecutive seasons.

The skinny: Peterson might be the best fantasy kicker available in rounds 8 through 10 of your draft.

6 JEFF WILKINS / RAMS

YEAR	XP	XPA	FG	FGS	PTS	GP
1995	27	29	12	13	63	7
1996	40	40	30	34	130	16
1997	32	32	25	37	107	16
1998	25	26	20	26	85	16
1999	64	64	20	28	124	16

DISTANCE	1–19	20–29	30–39	40–49	50+
1999	1/1	5/5	6/7	7/11	1/4

Comments: The 1999 Rams offense was so good that Wilkins scored more on extra points than he did on field goals, an NFL rarity. He set an NFL record with 64 extra points in 64 attempts, but 21 kickers were more accurate with their field goals. By contrast, in 1998

KICKERS

Wilkins's scoring chances (26 extra-point and 26 field-goal attempts) were limited by a bad Rams offense. He was a mediocre 76.9 percent on his field-goal accuracy, though he did kick a 57-yarder that set a career and franchise record. The Rams didn't get value for their big free-agent dollars in 1997, when Wilkins ranked 27th in field-goal accuracy with a bad 67.6 percentage. He had cashed in on the free-agent market after an outstanding '96 season in San Francisco when he scored 130 points to rank second in the NFC and fourth in the league.

The skinny: Expect fewer extra points, more field goals and about the same number of points from Wilkins in 2000.

7   OLINDO MARE / DOLPHINS

YEAR	XP	XPA	FG	FGS	PTS	GP
1996	0	0	0	0	0	0
1997	33	33	28	36	117	16
1998	33	34	22	27	99	16
1999	27	27	39	46	144	16

DISTANCE	1–19	20–29	30–39	40–49	50+
1999	1/1	9/9	17/17	9/14	3/5

Comments: Mare carried fantasy teams early in 1999, when he booted four or more field goals in four straight games, an NFL record. He shattered another league mark with 39 field goals and finished one point short of the league scoring title. All seven of his misses were from beyond the 40. Just 50 percent in field-goal attempts from 40 and beyond in his previous two seasons, Mare was 12 of 19 from that range last season, and his kickoffs were consistently deep. In 1998, Mare made 81.5 percent of his field-goal tries but scored just 99 points due to a struggling Miami offense. His career percentage of 81.7 percent is the best in Dolphins history. In 1997, his 117 points tied for fourth in the AFC, and his 28 field goals tied for the third most in team history.

The skinny: Don't expect a repeat performance from Mare this season, because the Miami offense is bound to struggle.

8   GARY ANDERSON / VIKINGS

YEAR	XP	XPA	FG	FGS	PTS	GP
1995	32	33	22	30	98	16
1996	40	40	25	29	115	16
1997	38	38	29	36	125	16
1998	59	59	35	35	164	16
1999	46	46	19	30	103	16

DISTANCE	1–19	20–29	30–39	40–49	50+
1999	0/0	6/8	9/11	4/9	0/2

Comments: Anderson exemplifies the fickle reality of an NFL kicker. Nearly perfect in an incomparable 1998 season, Anderson made just two of his first six attempts last year and finished with the third-worst field-goal percentage (63.3) in the NFL. His NFL-record streak of 40 straight field goals was broken in the season opener. On the league's fifth-highest-scoring team, Anderson scored fewer points than 18 other kickers. In 1998, he didn't miss a field goal until the playoffs, and his 164 points set an NFL record. Anderson was the first player to ever go an entire season without missing a kick (35 field goals and 59 extra points). He set an NFL playoff record with 16 consecutive field goals from 1989 to '95. Anderson now has an NFL-record 439 career field goals, and he is second on the all-time point list with 1,948. He has scored 100 or more points 12 times.

The skinny: At age 41, Anderson is approaching the end. But he may have one more high-scoring season left.

9   RYAN LONGWELL / PACKERS

YEAR	XP	XPA	FG	FGS	PTS	GP
1997	48	48	24	30	120	16
1998	41	43	29	33	128	16
1999	38	38	25	30	113	16

DISTANCE	1–19	20–29	30–39	40–49	50+
1999	0/0	8/9	8/9	8/10	1/2

Comments: Longwell was among the handful of Packers who actually had a good 1999 season. Other than a midseason streak in which he had a field-goal try blocked in three straight games, Longwell was nearly automatic. He ranked third in the NFC with 113 points and fifth in field goal accuracy (83.3 percent). He started the

1998 season by hitting 12 consecutive field goals, and he finished with an 87.9 percent accuracy rate that was the second highest in team history. Longwell entered the 1997 season as training camp fodder, but he replaced injured third-round draft pick Brett Conway and seized the opportunity with 120 points, the second most by a rookie in Packers history. He is the most accurate field goal kicker in team history (83.9 percent), and broke a team record with three consecutive 100-point seasons.

The skinny: The Packers still have the firepower to keep Longwell ranking among the league scoring leaders.

10 JASON HANSON / LIONS

YEAR	XP	XPA	FG	FGS	PTS	GP
1995	48	48	28	34	132	16
1996	36	36	12	17	72	16
1997	39	40	26	29	117	16
1998	27	29	29	33	114	16
1999	28	29	26	32	106	16

DISTANCE	1–19	20–29	30–39	40–49	50+
1999	0/0	8/8	4/4	10/12	4/8

Comments: Hanson is an exception to the rule that early-round draft picks underachieve at the kicker position. He's the most accurate kicker in NFL history from inside 50 yards (87.7 percent). In 1999, Hanson made all 15 of his attempts from inside the 46-yard line. He tied for fourth in the NFC with 106 points, and his 32 field-goal attempts averaged a league-high 41.6 yards in length. In 1998, Hanson broke his career pattern of good year/bad year. Coming off his Pro Bowl season of 1997, Hanson was the conference's fifth-leading scorer. It was the first time that the 1992 second-round pick strung together two straight high-scoring seasons. In 1996, Hanson had hit the skids with just 17 field-goal attempts and a career-low 72 points. In 1995, he booted a team-record 56-yard field goal and bounced back from a disappointing '94 season to lead the NFC with a team-record 132 points.

The skinny: Hanson's accuracy and range make him a solid pick in basic scoring leagues and an excellent pick in performance leagues.

11   BRET CONWAY / REDSKINS

YEAR	XP	XPA	FG	FGS	PTS	GP
1998	0	0	0	0	0	6
1999	49	50	22	32	115	16

DISTANCE	1–19	20–29	30–39	40–49	50+
1999	0/0	7/9	6/7	6/7	3/9

Comments: Conway hasn't yet lived up to expectations since he was drafted by the Packers in the third round of the 1997 draft. With Washington in 1999, he made his first seven field-goal attempts, then made just 15 of his next 25, though he was solid (19 of 23) from inside 50 yards. Only five kickers were worse than Conway's 68.8 percent field-goal accuracy because he attempted a league-high nine three-pointers from 50 yards and beyond. As a rookie in 1997, Conway struggled in the preseason, then injured a thigh and spent the year on injured reserve.

The skinny: The Redskins' win-now urgency is not conducive to job security and longevity for an inaccurate kicker.

12   MATT STOVER / RAVENS

YEAR	XP	XPA	FG	FGS	PTS	GP
1995	26	26	29	33	113	16
1996	34	35	19	25	91	16
1997	32	32	26	34	110	16
1998	24	24	21	28	87	16
1999	32	32	28	33	116	16

DISTANCE	1–19	20–29	30–39	40–49	50+
1999	4/4	9/9	6/8	7/7	2/5

Comments: The Brian Billick era has stepped up Stover's point production. In 1999, Stover quietly ranked sixth in the AFC with 116 points, his career high. He finished the season by making 18 consecutive field goals. Though he doesn't have a great leg, Stover made nine of 12 tries from 44 yards and beyond last season. After becoming at the time the NFL's all-time most accurate field-goal kicker in 1995, Stover posted three mediocre seasons before rebounding last year. In 1998, the Ravens' offense struggled and Stover scored just 87 points, 24th among NFL kickers. In 1995, Stover scored a career-high 113 points and he

KICKERS

made 29 of 33 attempts to rank second in the league with an 87.9 accuracy rate. He was even more accurate in 1994, when his 92.8 rate led the league. His career field goal percentage is 79.5.

The skinny: Stover is fantasy sleeper material, an excellent backup kicker for your team.

13 JOHN HALL / JETS

YEAR	XP	XPA	FG	FGS	PTS	GP
1997	36	36	28	41	120	16
1998	45	46	25	35	120	16
1999	27	29	27	33	108	16

DISTANCE	1–19	20–29	30–39	40–49	50+
1999	0/0	3/4	17/17	7/12	0/0

Comments: In 1999, Hall settled down and improved his short- and medium-range field-goal accuracy. Hall was just 20 of 30 from the 30- to 39-yard range in his first two seasons, but he was 17 of 17 from that range last year. Hall tied for 11th in the league with 108 points, and his 81.8 percent field-goal accuracy was eighth in the AFC. In his first two seasons, Hall was like a howitzer with a crooked barrel — a kicker with enormous range but little accuracy. Only two AFC kickers were less accurate than Hall in 1998. A rookie free agent in 1997, he scored a lot of points but missed a lot of field goals (he was 17 of 29 from 30-plus). He is among the league's best at booting long kickoffs.

The skinny: A more settled quarterback situation will help Hall turn in another high-scoring season.

14 JOHN KASAY / PANTHERS

YEAR	XP	XPA	FG	FGS	PTS	GP
1995	27	28	26	33	105	16
1996	34	35	37	45	145	16
1997	25	25	22	26	91	16
1998	35	37	19	26	92	16
1999	33	33	22	25	99	13

DISTANCE	1–19	20–29	30–39	40–49	50+
1999	1/1	8/8	6/6	5/6	2/4

Comments: Kasay's 1999 season ended in Week 14 when he tore the ACL in his kicking leg while covering a kickoff return. At the time, he ranked second among NFC kickers with 99 points. Kasay's 88 percent field goal accuracy was the league's third best in 1999. However, his return for the start of the 2000 season is in jeopardy. In 1998, Kasay made a personal-best four field goals from beyond the 50-yard line. Yet he ranked 21st among NFL kickers with just 92 points on a low-scoring team. In 1997, Kasay's only miss from inside 50 yards was blocked, but the Panthers ranked 27th in the NFL in points and failed to get him on the field often enough. A year earlier, the second-year expansion Panthers thrived and Kasay led the NFL with 145 points. That season, he connected on a then-NFL-record 37 field goals.

The skinny: Check Kasay's injury status as the regular season nears. Whoever kicks for this team should score plenty of points.

15 STEVE CHRISTIE / BILLS

YEAR	XP	XPA	FG	FGS	PTS	GP
1995	33	35	31	40	126	16
1996	33	33	24	29	105	16
1997	21	21	24	30	93	16
1998	41	41	33	41	140	16
1999	33	33	25	34	108	16

DISTANCE	1–19	20–29	30–39	40–49	50+
1999	2/2	10/10	7/10	3/9	3/3

Comments: Christie struggled through his worst season in six years in 1999. He was an unacceptable 10 of 19 on field-goal attempts from between the 30 and 49, and his kickoffs were short. Coming off a 93-point season in '97, Christie was the biggest surprise among fantasy kickers in 1998, when he won the AFC scoring title with a franchise-record 140 points. His 41 field-goal attempts led the league, and he ranked third in field goals with a team-record 33. In 1996, he logged his fifth straight 100-point season. In 1993, Christie was inconsistent and downright bad beyond the 50-yard line, despite hitting a 59-yard field goal that's tied for fourth longest in NFL history. He made 81 percent of his kicks with Tampa Bay in 1990 and '91. In eight seasons with Buffalo, he has 902 points.

The skinny: If the Bills bring some competition to training camp this year, don't be all that surprised if the high-priced and aging

Christie becomes a salary cap casualty.

16 ADAM VINATIERI / PATRIOTS

YEAR	XP	XPA	FG	FGS	PTS	GP
1996	39	42	27	35	120	16
1997	40	40	25	29	115	16
1998	32	32	31	39	127	16
1999	29	30	26	33	107	16

DISTANCE	1–19	20–29	30–39	40–49	50+
1999	1/1	14/14	5/7	5/9	1/2

Comments: Vinatieri has more than 100 points in each of his first four seasons, but he's not a lock to hold his job for the 2000 season. Last year, Vinatieri blew two field-goal kicks that could've put the Patriots into the playoffs, and his 78.8 percent field-goal accuracy ranked 11th in the AFC. In 1998, he was the conference's 10th-most-accurate field-goal kicker (79.5 percent), but he tied for fifth in the league in points with 127. Vinatieri booted the second-most field goals (31) in team history, including a pair of last-second game-winners. In 1997, he made his first 17 field goals to complete a club-record string of 25 consecutive field goals. As a rookie in 1996, Vinatieri started slowly but finished with 120 points, third most in the AFC. In four pro seasons, he has averaged 117 points a year and has a career field-goal percentage of 80.1.

The skinny: Vinatieri bears watching in the preseason, because he'll score well if he keeps his job.

17 MARTIN GRAMATICA / BUCCANEERS

YEAR	XP	XPA	FG	FGS	PTS	GP
1999	25	25	27	32	106	16

DISTANCE	1–19	20–29	30–39	40–49	50+
1999	0/0	8/8	10/12	6/8	3/4

Comments: Gramatica's post-field-goal theatrics are slightly annoying, but his rookie season exceeded expectations in 1999. Gramatica set single-season team records for points (106) and field goals (27). His point total led all NFL rookies and tied for fourth in the conference. His 84.4 percent field-goal accuracy was the NFC's fourth best and the second best in franchise history. A third-round draft pick, Gramatica made his first 10 field-goal tries and booted three of four from beyond the 50. At Kansas State, he kicked an NCAA no-tee-record 65-yard field goal.

The skinny: Gramatica is a good bet to score more in 2000 than he did last year.

18 PETE STOYANOVICH / CHIEFS

YEAR	XP	XPA	FG	FGS	PTS	GP
1995	37	37	27	34	118	16
1996	34	34	17	24	85	16
1997	35	36	26	27	113	16
1998	34	34	27	32	115	16
1999	45	45	21	28	108	16

DISTANCE	1–19	20–29	30–39	40–49	50+
1999	1/1	7/7	5/6	7/13	1/1

Comments: Stoyanovich is coming off a subpar 1999 season in which his field-goal percentage (75.0) was down, his kickoffs were short, and his blown 44-yarder in the season finale cost the Chiefs a playoff berth. Still, he tied for eighth in the AFC with 108 points, his ninth 100-point output in the past 10 seasons. In 1998, he posted his fourth-highest point total and second-highest field-goal percentage (84.4) of his career. In 1997, Stoyanovich made the Chiefs glad they traded a fifth-round pick for him the year before. In 110 regular-season games with Miami from 1989 to '94, he made 79.3 percent of his field-goal attempts. The sixth-most accurate field-goal kicker in history (80.2 percent), Stoyanovich has always been good from long range. His 65.6 field-goal percentage from beyond the 40 ranks second all-time.

The skinny: In the what-have-you-done-for-me-lately NFL, Stoyanovich could be gone if he struggles early this season.

19 JOHN CARNEY / CHARGERS

YEAR	XP	XPA	FG	FGS	PTS	GP
1995	32	33	21	26	95	16
1996	31	31	29	36	118	16
1997	5	5	7	7	26	4
1998	19	19	26	30	97	16
1999	22	23	31	36	115	16

DISTANCE	1–19	20–29	30–39	40–49	50+
1999	2/2	13/13	6/8	9/12	1/1

Comments: Carney was his usual reliable self in 1999. His field-goal accuracy (86.1 percent) was the AFC's third best, and he scored 115 points, the fourth-highest total of his exceptional 11-year career. High point totals haven't always accompanied Carney's great accuracy. The most accurate kicker in NFL history with an 81.66 field-goal percentage, Carney has just two 100-point seasons in the last five years. He was the AFC's third-most-accurate (86.7 percent) kicker in 1998, but he ranked 12th in the conference in scoring with 97 points. Carney's 1997 season was ruined by a strained medial collateral knee ligament in the fourth game. Carney led the league in scoring in '94 with 135 points. He is the Chargers' all-time leader in points (995) and successful field goals (243).

The skinny: Carney is a reliable kicker, but his point production is unreliable due to the Chargers' low-octane offense.

20 MORTEN ANDERSEN / FALCONS

YEAR	XP	XPA	FG	FGS	PTS	GP
1995	29	30	31	37	122	16
1996	31	31	22	29	97	16
1997	35	35	23	27	104	16
1998	51	52	23	28	120	16
1999	34	34	15	21	79	16

DISTANCE	1–19	20–29	30–39	40–49	50+
1999	1/1	5/5	5/8	4/6	0/1

Comments: Andersen was perhaps the biggest bust among fantasy kickers in 1999. His miserable start (he missed his first four field-goal tries) paralleled that of the team, and neither really recovered. Andersen made 15 of his next 17 tries, but his 79 points tied for last among full-time kickers in the NFC. In 1998, Andersen thrived on the NFL's Cinderella team. He scored the NFC's fourth-most points (120) and made 82.1 percent of his field goals. In 1995, Andersen had a record-setting season and tied for sixth among NFL kickers with 122 points. That year he booted an NFL-record eight field goals of 50 yards or longer, including an unprecedented three in one game. He owns NFL records for the most 100-point seasons (12), most game-winning kicks (25) and most consecutive games scored (253). The Saints let him get away to free agency in 1995, and he's now the third-leading scorer all-time with 1,840 points and ranks second with 417 career field goals.

The skinny: Andersen is bound to rebound, but the Falcons aren't going to be a high-scoring team, so don't expect more than 100 points.

21 WADE RICHEY / 49ERS

YEAR	XP	XPA	FG	FGS	PTS	GP
1998	49	51	18	27	103	16
1999	30	31	21	23	93	16

DISTANCE	1–19	20–29	30–39	40–49	50+
1999	1/1	7/7	7/8	5/6	1/1

Comments: Do you think college kicking success translates into NFL success? Richey made eight of 25 field-goal attempts at Louisiana State. In 1999, his second NFL season, he led the league with a field-goal percentage of 91.3. But a 49ers offense that was unparalleled in 1998 fell off a cliff last year, so Richey's scoring suffered. Coming off a shaky rookie season in 1998, he set a team record for field-goal accuracy. In '98, he missed two extra points and made just six of 13 field-goal tries from the 40-to-49-yard range. However, Richey benefited from a high-scoring team and scored 103 points. His poor 66.7 percent field-goal accuracy ranked 27th in the NFL.

The skinny: Richey's point total will suffer while the 49ers retool their aging, salary-cap-hindered team.

22 BRAD DALUISO / GIANTS

YEAR	XP	XPA	FG	FGS	PTS	GP
1995	28	28	20	28	88	16
1996	22	22	24	27	94	16
1997	27	29	22	32	93	16
1998	32	32	21	27	95	16
1999	9	9	7	9	30	6

DISTANCE	1–19	20–29	30–39	40–49	50+
1999	0/0	4/4	3/3	0/2	0/0

Comments: Daluiso tore the ACL in his nonkicking leg on the final play of the sixth game last season. He should be ready for the start of training camp, and the job is still his to lose. In 1998, his 77.8 percent accuracy ranked eighth in the NFC. Daluiso broke into the NFL with a reputation for deep kickoffs and long-range field goals, but he has hung around due to his short-range accuracy. In 1997, he booted his 39th consecutive field goal from inside the 40-yard line before the streak broke in the regular-season finale. However, he was just nine of 18 from beyond the 40. In 1996, he tied for the league lead with 20 touchbacks.

The skinny: In nine pro seasons, Daluiso has never scored 100 points.

23   DOUG BRIEN / SAINTS

YEAR	XP	XPA	FG	FGS	PTS	GP
1995	35	35	19	29	92	14
1996	18	18	21	25	81	16
1997	22	22	23	27	91	16
1998	31	31	20	22	91	16
1999	20	21	24	29	92	16

DISTANCE	1–19	20–29	30–39	40–49	50+
1999	0/0	9/11	6/7	7/9	2/2

Comments: Brien is a reliable kicker who has been stuck on low-scoring Saints teams for most of his six-year career. Last season, he missed a pair of chip shots and an extra point but still finished with a respectable 82.8 field-goal percentage, sixth best in the NFC. He was two of two from 50 yards and beyond and now ranks second all-time from that range with a 70 percent success rate. Brien had a nearly perfect 1998 season, but the Saints' weak offense dragged him down. His only two misses all year were from 53 and 54 yards. Brien tied for third in the NFC with an 85.2 percent field-goal accuracy in 1997, but he tied for ninth in the NFC in points on the league's lowest-scoring team. In 1995, Brien was waived after missing five of 12 field-goal tries in six games with the 49ers, then signed with the Saints. He's now the most accurate field-goal kicker in Saints history (83.3 percent).

The skinny: The Saints have completely retooled their offense, so Brien is at least worth consideration as your backup.

24 CARY BLANCHARD / CARDINALS

YEAR	XP	XPA	FG	FGS	PTS	GP
1995	25	25	19	24	82	12
1996	27	27	36	40	135	16
1997	21	21	32	41	117	16
1998	30	31	11	17	63	13
1999	19	19	18	21	73	10

DISTANCE	1–19	20–29	30–39	40–49	50+
1999	0/0	7/7	2/4	9/10	0/0

Comments: Blanchard is the latest attempt to fill a gaping hole on a team that has lacked adequate kicking since 1996. A career journeyman, Blanchard had an excellent 1999 season with the Giants after replacing the injured Brad Daluiso in Week 7. His 85.7 percent field-goal accuracy rate was the NFC's third-best mark. Blanchard, who was nine of 10 from 40 yards and beyond last season, replaces Chris Jacke, who was four of 10 from that range. In 1998, Blanchard was a stopgap replacement in Washington and ranked last in the NFC in field-goal accuracy (64.7 percent). On a lousy Indianapolis team that hit rock-bottom in 1997, Blanchard still managed to rank fourth in the AFC in scoring with 117 points. In 1996, Blanchard won the AFC scoring title and led the league with a 90 percent field-goal accuracy.

The skinny: Blanchard's career has been marked by inconsistency from season to season, so don't count on him to be your starter.

25 KRIS BROWN / STEELERS

YEAR	XP	XPA	FG	FGS	PTS	GP
1999	30	31	25	29	105	16

DISTANCE	1–19	20–29	30–39	40–49	50+
1999	2/2	5/5	9/10	8/11	1/1

Comments: A rookie in 1999, Brown got off to a rocky start in the preseason. Then he made some kicks, gained confidence and went on to turn in a special first season. He set an NFL record by converting on the first 13 field-goal attempts of his career. Brown scored 24 points in his first two games and finished the season with the AFC's second-best field-goal percentage (86.2). He missed just one field-goal try from inside the 44-yard line. Not bad for a seventh-round draft pick who was anything but assured the starting job entering camp.

The skinny: Brown's biggest obstacle appears to be the Steelers' struggling offense.

26 DAVID AKERS / EAGLES

YEAR	XP	XPA	FG	FGS	PTS	GP
1998	2	2	0	2	2	1
1999	2	2	3	6	11	16

DISTANCE	1–19	20–29	30–39	40–49	50+
1999	0/0	0/0	0/0	2/3	1/3

Comments: Akers showed the Eagles enough leg in limited playing time last season to probably earn the starting job in 2000. The team's kickoff specialist, Akers was utilized on long field-goal attempts in place of the aging Norm Johnson. He kicked 46-, 48- and 53-yard field goals and missed from 47, 51 and 59 yards out. Akers missed his only two field-goal attempts with the Redskins in 1998.

The skinny: Akers has the distance, but it remains to be seen whether he can be consistent kicking short-range field goals.

27 PHIL DAWSON / BROWNS

YEAR	XP	XPA	FG	FGS	PTS	GP
1999	23	24	8	12	53	15

DISTANCE	1–19	20–29	30–39	40–49	50+
1999	0/0	2/2	3/5	3/5	0/0

Comments: Rule No. 1: Never, ever draft a kicker from a first-year expansion team. The Browns were the league's lowest-scoring team in 1999, so Dawson's production was pathetic. He made just 67 percent of his 12 field-goal attempts to tie for last in the AFC in field-goal accuracy. At the University of Texas, Dawson made six straight field goals from beyond the 50-yard line, but he never even attempted one from that range last year. His 53-point total was the lowest of the decade by any full-time kicker in the NFL.

The skinny: There's only one way for Dawson and the Browns to go, but he's not worth your last-round draft pick.

28 DOUG PELFREY / BENGALS

YEAR	XP	XPA	FG	FGS	PTS	GP
1995	34	34	29	36	121	16
1996	41	41	23	28	110	16
1997	41	43	12	16	77	16
1998	21	21	19	27	78	16
1999	27	27	18	27	81	16

DISTANCE	1–19	20–29	30–39	40–49	50+
1999	1/1	9/11	7/12	0/2	1/1

Comments: The Bengals simply don't get enough scoring opportunities to afford to keep a placekicker who blows one-third of his 27 field-goal attempts. After two straight lousy seasons, don't be surprised if Pelfrey is not around for the 2000 season. Last year, he botched seven field-goal tries from inside the 39-yard line. A solid fantasy starter in the mid-1990s, Pelfrey has mirrored the struggles of the anemic Bengals the past three seasons. In 1998, he scored the fewest points (78) and had the second-worst field-goal percentage (70.4) among AFC kickers. In 1997, Pelfrey attempted a ridiculously low 16 field goals. He scored a team-record 121 points in 1995. Pelfrey is the Bengals' second-leading all-time scorer with 660 points.

The skinny: Because he'll get some strong competition from sixth-round draft pick Neil Rackers, Pelfrey might be scanning the want ads this summer.

29 JEFF JAEGER / BEARS

YEAR	XP	XPA	FG	FGS	PTS	GP
1995	22	22	13	18	61	11
1996	23	23	19	23	80	13
1997	20	20	21	26	83	16
1998	27	28	21	26	90	16
1999	7	7	2	8	13	3

DISTANCE	1–19	20–29	30–39	40–49	50+
1990	0/0	0/0	0/2	1/5	1/1

Comments: Jaeger never recovered from a hip injury suffered in 1999 training camp. He struggled through three painful games and was placed on injured reserve. In his first three seasons with the Bears, Jaeger made 81.3 percent of his field-goal attempts but averaged only

KICKERS

84 points on poor offensive teams. He is the first Bear in team history to record three consecutive seasons with better than 80 percent field-goal accuracy. With the Raiders prior to going to Chicago, Jaeger became the most accurate kicker in team history, with 152 field goals in 202 attempts for 75.2 percent. In 1993, Jaeger tied an NFL record with 35 field goals, and his 132 points led the entire league. But that's a long time ago, which is why the Bears drafted Paul Edinger in the sixth round.

The skinny: Reliable when healthy, Jaeger may get another shot this season, though he'll face some strong competition in training camp.

LOOKING BACK AT KICKERS

Sure Bets — Mike Hollis (Jaguars), Jason Elam (Broncos), Al Del Greco (Titans), Mike Vanderjagt (Colts)

Top Sleepers — Matt Stover (Ravens), Doug Brien (Saints), Brad Daluiso (Giants)

Possible Busts — Jeff Wilkins (Rams), Steve Christie (Bills), Brett Conway (Redskins)

Coming On — Martin Gramatica (Buccaneers), John Hall (Jets), Todd Peterson (Seahawks), Kris Brown (Steelers)

Comeback Candidates —Brad Daluiso (Giants), Jeff Jaeger (Bears), John Kasay (Panthers)

Back to Earth After a Great 1999 — Olindo Mare (Dolphins), Jeff Wilkins (Rams)

In for a Career Year — Mike Hollis (Jaguars)

Could Be Cut — Jeff Jaeger (Bears), Doug Pelfrey (Bengals)

Top Rookies — Sebastian Janikowski (Raiders), Paul Edinger (Bears), Neil Rackers (Bengals)

1999 Injured Players Who Will Be a Factor in '00 — John Kasay (Panthers), Brad Daluiso (Giants), Jeff Jaeger (Bears)

1999 Rookie Who Could Come On — Kris Brown (Steelers)

Top Player on a New Team — Cary Blanchard (Cardinals)

Late-Round Gambles — Brad Daluiso (Giants), Cary Blanchard (Cardinals), Doug Brien (Saints)

Best Over 50 Yards — Jason Elam (Broncos), Mike Vanderjagt (Colts), Jason Hanson (Lions), Doug Brien (Saints), Martin Gramatica (Buccaneers)

Worst Over 50 Yards — Cary Blanchard (Cardinals), Chris Jacke (Cardinals), Jeff Jaeger (Bears)

Best of the Rest

Richie Cunningham, cut by Panthers	Peter Elezovic, Redskins
Chris Boniol, free agent	Tim Sedler, Cowboys
Jaret Greaser, Cowboys	Michael Husted, cut by Raiders
Norm Johnson, cut by Steelers	Joe Nedney, cut by Raiders

KICKERS

Chapter 8
DEFENSES

Defense wins games. Just ask any football coach. And it's the same thing in fantasy football. Just as in the NFL, most weeks only a few points separate the winners and losers in a weekend of fantasy football. A touchdown, or even a safety, can be the difference between a win and a loss in both the NFL and in fantasy football. And that's why many fantasy leagues like to incorporate some form of defense into their game.

There are several commonly used methods for including defensive players in fantasy leagues.

The most common is to add an eighth "player" to each team in the form of a team defense (rather than choosing individual defensive players). If an entire defense is drafted, any score by any member of that defense counts. Points are awarded every time a player on a team's defense scores a touchdown on a fumble return or an interception, or when a player scores a safety (even a team safety, such as when an opposing punter steps out of the end zone). Most leagues also include touchdowns scored on blocked punts and field goals, since they are basically defensive scores, too.

Leagues can also draft special teams and award points for scores on punts and kickoff returns. Some leagues combine defensive scores and special-team scores.

Some leagues award points for other defensive categories, such as sacks and interceptions. A common scoring method is one point for a sack and two points for an interception that is not returned for a score.

But owners of teams in fantasy leagues can also draft individual defensive players. For example, every team can draft one defensive lineman, one linebacker and one defensive back (or more of each). The ways you can score points depend on your league and how detailed you want to get. But remember, as your league's scoring method gets more complicated, so does the work involved in determining the scores.

Believe it or not, there are some leagues that even count tackles. That's really getting complicated, perhaps overly complicated. The biggest problem with counting tackles is that they are unofficial statistics, and the quality of team statisticians ranges from conservative to liberal — for example, some teams' leading tacklers have 200 tackles, while other teams' top tacklers have only 100 or so. It's very subjective.

Papers such as *USA Today* include tackles and assists in their game summaries, but NFL coaches often change those figures drastically every Monday when they view the game film.

Also, if you draft individual players, it adds a lot of bookkeeping and score-tabulating chores for the commissioner.

So, if you want to include defense the easiest way, allow every team to draft a team defense and just count defensive scores — fumbles and interceptions returned for touchdowns, blocked kicks returned for touchdowns and safeties. This is the category that is most often pure luck. While you are looking to your quarterbacks, running backs and wide receivers for big scores, a defensive score is always a nice — and unexpected — bonus.

The average defensive team scored just over 20 points in 1999, which is the equivalent of only three touchdowns per team (though it's almost a field goal more than in '99). Eighteen or 20 points all season is not much at all, but you will think six points is a lot when it happens to your team.

It's almost impossible to predict which defenses will score the most points in any given season. Perennially good defenses don't always score a lot of points on defense. Since defensive scores are most often a result of luck, you can never figure which teams will improve. For example, the Chiefs are historically one of the highest-scoring defensive teams in the NFL, but they scored only eight points on defense in 1998 — sandwiched by 36 points in '97 and 54 points in '99. And the Eagles, who had just one safety (and not touchdowns) on defense in 1998 scored 34 points in '99. Need another example? The San Francisco 49ers scored no points on defense in 1998 and bounced back in '99 with 32 points (even though the defense was pretty miserable overall). You just never know, and there's not a lot of consistency. Just because a team might have scored four or five touchdowns on defense last year, that does not mean it will happen again this year.

One thing you can count on is that defenses will score a lot of points this year — at least compared to a decade ago. In recent years, the number of points being scored on defense has increased considerably. In 1995, 52 touchdowns were scored off interceptions; then there were only 41 such scores in '96 and 47 last season before increasing to 53 in '98 and 58 in '99. In 1996, only 24 touchdowns were scored off fumbles, but 36 were returned for scores in '99. The increase in defensive scores is because the strategy has changed in pro football these days — once players get the ball, they go for the end zone. But don't expect too many teams to score more than a couple of times on defense this

DEFENSES

year. Remember, luck is the biggest factor in defensive scores.

In drafting defenses, there are a lot of factors to take into consideration, such as which teams are most likely to make defensive scores (touchdowns on the returns of fumbles, interceptions or blocked kicks, and safeties).

If your league drafts individual defensive players, you will want to know which players get the most sacks and interceptions.

Also in this chapter, because an important factor in determining which offensive players you will play each week is the defenses your players will face in real NFL games, some defensive statistics are included (rushing touchdowns and yards allowed, passing touchdowns and yards allowed, total points allowed, sacks and takeaways).

And, also in this chapter, special-teams scores from 1999 (kickoffs and punts returned for touchdowns) are detailed.

Draft Tips for Choosing Defenses

■ Don't spend too much time analyzing the teams to decide which defense you want to draft. Defensive scores are so rare that they really should be considered a bonus, rather than points that you should expect.

■ Don't waste a pick drafting a defense high in your draft; wait until the last few rounds. While a defensive score could mean the difference between winning and losing any given week, it's too chancy, and you are much better off drafting players who have a better chance of scoring.

■ Draft a team with a strong defense. Those that force the most turnovers have the best chance of converting them into scores.

■ Look for opportunistic teams that convert turnovers into touchdowns, such as Seattle, Minnesota, Green Bay, Kansas City, Tennessee and the New York Jets. One team that would be a good pick to score more defensive points in 2000 than it did in '99 is New Orleans (with new head coach Jim Haslett).

1999 DEFENSIVE SCORES

		Fum. /TD	Int. /TD	Blk. Kick /TD	Saf.	Pts.	3-Year Avg.
1.	Kansas City	4	5	0	0	54	32.7
2.	St. Louis	1	7	0	1	50	24.7
3.	Jacksonville	1	3	1	3	36	22.0
4.	Philadelphia	0	5	0	2	34	16.0
5.	Dallas	1	4	0	1	32	21.3

	Team						
	San Francisco	3	2	0	1	32	16.7
7.	Baltimore	0	4	0	1	26	16.7
	Detroit	3	1	0	1	26	21.3
	N.Y. Jets	1	3	0	1	26	26.7
	Tennessee	2	1	0	4	26	24.7
11.	New England	2	2	0	0	24	22.7
	Seattle	1	2	1	0	24	36.7
	Washington	1	3	0	0	24	16.7
14.	Green Bay	2	1	0	1	20	25.3
	San Diego	2	0	1	1	20	21.3
16.	Arizona	0	3	0	0	18	16.7
	Indianapolis	2	1	0	0	18	16.7
	N.Y. Giants	1	2	0	0	18	20.7
	Oakland	1	1	1	0	18	22.7
20.	Denver	1	1	0	2	14	22.7
	Miami	1	1	0	1	14	16.0
	Tampa Bay	0	2	0	1	14	8.7
23.	Chicago	1	1	0	0	12	10.0
	New Orleans	2	0	0	0	12	25.3
	Pittsburgh	2	0	0	0	12	18.0
26.	Atlanta	0	1	0	1	8	15.3
	Minnesota	0	1	0	1	8	17.3
28.	Buffalo	1	0	0	0	6	7.3
	Cincinnati	0	1	0	0	6	8.0
30.	Carolina	0	0	0	0	0	6.7
	Cleveland	0	0	0	0	0	0.0

TEAM DEFENSES

One of the hardest — but most enjoyable — aspects of fantasy football is trying to decide whom to start each week.

For example, in the opening weekend of the season should you start the Jets' Curtis Martin against the tough Miami run defense (only 31 rushing TDs allowed in the last four seasons), or do you go with Baltimore's Jamal Lewis against the weak Cincinnati run defense (which allowed 22 rushing scores in 1999 alone)? Or, at wide receiver, do you go with the Bears' Marcus Robinson against the excellent Buccaneers secondary (an NFL-best 11 passing TDs allowed in '99), or do you choose St. Louis' Torry Holt versus the somewhat weak New Orleans secondary (34 TD

DEFENSES

passes given up in '99)? They are certainly things to consider.

The defensive charts that follow should help you decide. But remember, they are from the 1999 season (along with three-year averages of 1997 to '99), and the performance of each team's defense can change drastically from year to year (especially in this era of free agency with so many players changing teams).

1999 RUSHING TOUCHDOWNS ALLOWED

	Team	Rushing TDs Allowed	Three-Year Average
1.	St. Louis	4	8.3
2.	Baltimore	6	11.7
	Dallas	6	9.3
	Jacksonville	6	9.0
	Miami	6	7.0
	New England	6	10.0
7.	San Diego	8	10.7
	Tampa Bay	8	10.0
	Tennessee	8	9.7
10.	Buffalo	9	10.7
	Minnesota	9	11.3
	Seattle	9	10.7
13.	Kansas City	10	13.3
	Oakland	10	12.3
	Pittsburgh	10	7.7
16.	Chicago	11	13.7
	San Francisco	11	9.7
18.	Detroit	12	14.0
	Indianapolis	12	16.7
	Philadelphia	12	15.3
21.	Carolina	13	13.0
	New York Giants	13	14.3
23.	Denver	15	11.0
	New Orleans	15	13.0
25.	Green Bay	16	13.0
	New York Jets	16	12.0
	Washington	16	18.3
28.	Arizona	17	16.0
29.	Atlanta	18	14.3
30.	Cincinnati	22	20.0
31.	Cleveland	29	*29.0

Played only in 1999

DEFENSES

1999 RUSHING YARDS ALLOWED

	Team	Rushing Yards Allowed	Net Average Per Game
1.	St. Louis	1,189	74.3
2.	Baltimore	1,231	76.9
3.	San Diego	1,321	82.6
4.	Buffalo	1,370	85.8
5.	Tampa Bay	1,407	87.9
6.	Dallas	1,442	90.1
7.	Jacksonville	1,444	90.3
8.	Miami	1,476	92.3
9.	Detroit	1,531	96.7
10.	Tennessee	1,550	96.9
11.	Kansas City	1,557	97.3
12.	Oakland	1,559	97.4
13.	New York Giants	1,560	97.5
14.	Minnesota	1,617	101.1
15.	San Francisco	1,619	101.2
16.	Cincinnati	1,699	106.2
17.	New York Jets	1,703	106.4
18.	Indianapolis	1,715	107.2
19.	Denver	1,737	108.6
20.	New Orleans	1,774	110.9
21.	New England	1,795	112.2
22.	Green Bay	1,804	112.8
23.	Chicago	1,882	117.6
24.	Carolina	1,896	118.6
25.	Seattle	1,934	120.9
26.	Pittsburgh	1,958	122.4
27.	Washington	1,973	123.3
28.	Philadelphia	2,001	125.1
29.	Atlanta	2,072	129.5
30.	Arizona	2,265	141.6
31.	Cleveland	2,736	171.0

DEFENSES

1999 PASSING TOUCHDOWNS ALLOWED

	Team	Passing TDs Allowed	Three-Year Average
1.	Tampa Bay	11	13.0
2.	Buffalo	12	18.7
3.	New York Jets	16	18.3
4.	Cleveland	17	*17.0
	Denver	17	21.7
6.	Jacksonville	18	21.7
7.	Dallas	19	20.0
	Miami	19	19.7
	St. Louis	19	24.3
	Seattle	19	18.7
11.	Atlanta	20	22.0
	Baltimore	20	20.0
	Green Bay	20	17.7
	Minnesota	20	21.7
	New York Giants	20	15.7
	Pittsburgh	20	20.3
17.	Detroit	21	19.7
	Indianapolis	21	24.7
19.	Oakland	22	21.7
	Philadelphia	22	20.0
21.	Chicago	23	25.0
	New England	23	21.0
	Washington	23	19.3
24.	Kansas City	24	18.7
	San Diego	24	25.3
26.	Arizona	25	23.0
27.	Carolina	26	24.3
	Tennessee	26	23.7
29.	Cincinnati	28	27.0
30.	New Orleans	34	26.3
31.	San Francisco	36	28.0

Played only in 1999

1999 PASSING YARDS ALLOWED

	Team	Net Passing Yards Allowed	Net Average Per Game
1.	Buffalo	2,675	167.2
2.	Tampa Bay	2,873	179.6
3.	Jacksonville	2,890	180.6
4.	Pittsburgh	2,926	182.9
5.	Miami	2,928	183.0
6.	Denver	3,016	188.5
7.	Baltimore	2,991	186.9
8.	New England	3,013	188.3
9.	Atlanta	3,151	196.9
10.	Arizona	3,157	197.3
11.	Cleveland	3,310	206.9
12.	Oakland	3,321	207.6
13.	Dallas	3,398	212.4
14.	New York Giants	3,421	213.8
15.	Philadelphia	3,461	216.3
16.	Kansas City	3,482	217.6
17.	Seattle	3,492	218.3
18.	Green Bay	3,505	219.1
19.	Indianapolis	3,506	219.1
20.	St. Louis	3,509	219.3
21.	New Orleans	3,544	221.5
22.	San Diego	3,584	224.0
23.	Carolina	3,605	225.3
24.	New York Jets	3,676	229.8
25.	Tennessee	3,695	230.9
26.	Washington	3,732	233.3
27.	Detroit	3,760	235.0
28.	Cincinnati	3,798	237.4
29.	Chicago	3,822	238.9
30.	Minnesota	3,980	248.8
31.	San Francisco	4,068	254.3

DEFENSES

1999 TOTAL POINTS ALLOWED

	Team	Total Points Allowed	Points Per Game	Three-Year Average
1.	Jacksonville	217	13.6	18.2
2.	Buffalo	229	14.3	19.3
3.	Tampa Bay	235	14.7	16.5
4.	St. Louis	242	15.1	20.4
5.	Dallas	276	17.3	18.0
6.	Baltimore	277	17.3	19.9
7.	New England	284	17.8	18.8
8.	Seattle	298	18.6	20.2
9.	New York Jets	309	19.3	18.0
10.	San Diego	316	19.8	22.6
11.	Denver	318	19.9	19.0
12.	Pittsburgh	320	20.0	19.4
13.	Kansas City	322	20.1	19.1
14.	Detroit	323	20.2	21.0
15.	Tennessee	324	20.3	19.9
16.	Minnesota	325	20.3	20.4
17.	Oakland	329	20.6	23.0
18.	Indianapolis	333	20.8	24.5
19.	Miami	336	21.0	19.3
20.	Chicago	341	21.3	23.5
	Green Bay	341	21.3	19.6
22.	Philadelphia	357	22.3	22.4
23.	New York Giants	358	22.4	19.4
24.	Washington	377	23.6	22.6
25.	Atlanta	380	23.8	21.5
26.	Carolina	381	23.8	23.1
27.	Arizona	382	23.9	23.7
28.	New Orleans	434	27.1	23.3
29.	Cleveland	437	27.3	*27.3
30.	San Francisco	453	28.3	21.8
31.	Cincinnati	460	28.8	27.4

Played only in 1999

1999 SACKS

	Team	Sacks	Three-Year Average
1.	Jacksonville	57	45.0
2.	St. Louis	57	48.3
3.	Tennessee	54	39.7
4.	Denver	50	47.0
	Detroit	50	45.3
6.	Baltimore	49	43.3
7.	Minnesota	46	42.7
8.	New Orleans	45	50.3
9.	Oakland	44	39.0
10.	Tampa Bay	43	41.3
11.	New England	42	41.0
12.	Indianapolis	41	38.7
	San Diego	41	35.7
14.	Atlanta	40	44.3
	Kansas City	40	44.7
	Washington	40	36.7
17.	Miami	39	38.3
	Pittsburgh	39	42.7
19.	Seattle	38	44.3
20.	Buffalo	37	42.0
	Chicago	37	34.3
	Philadelphia	37	40.7
23.	Carolina	35	36.0
	Dallas	35	35.7
	Cincinnati	35	32.7
26.	Arizona	33	35.3
27.	New York Giants	32	46.7
	San Francisco	32	45.7
29.	Green Bay	30	40.3
30.	New York Jets	26	30.3
31.	Cleveland	25	*25.0

Played only in 1999

DEFENSES

1999 TAKEAWAYS

	Team	Fumbles	Int.	Total	Three-Year Average
1.	Philadelphia	18	28	46	29.7
2.	Kansas City	20	25	45	37.3
3.	Green Bay	15	26	41	32.0
4.	Tennessee	24	16	40	30.3
5.	Washington	13	24	37	29.3
6.	St. Louis	7	29	36	32.7
	Seattle	6	30	36	35.7
8.	New York Jets	11	24	35	30.0
9.	New Orleans	15	19	34	32.3
10.	Chicago	19	14	33	30.3
	Dallas	9	24	33	26.0
	Oakland	13	20	33	30.0
13.	Detroit	16	16	32	26.0
14.	Baltimore	10	21	31	27.3
	New England	15	16	31	31.7
	Tampa Bay	10	21	31	27.7
17.	Jacksonville	11	19	30	29.7
	Minnesota	18	12	30	30.3
19.	Carolina	14	15	29	28.0
20.	Miami	10	18	28	30.3
	Pittsburgh	14	14	28	30.3
22.	Arizona	10	17	27	28.7
	Cincinnati	15	12	27	23.3
	San Diego	12	15	27	26.7
25.	Denver	11	15	26	29.0
26.	New York Giants	7	17	24	31.3
27.	Indianapolis	13	10	23	22.3
28.	Buffalo	9	12	21	24.7
29.	Cleveland	12	8	20	*20.0
	San Francisco	7	13	20	31.3
31.	Atlanta	6	12	18	30.0

Played only in 1999

1999 SPECIAL-TEAMS SCORES

Some leagues like to award points for touchdown returns of kickoffs and punts. The NFL installed some new rules in 1994 that emphasized kick returns, and, in 1999, 17 of the 31 NFL teams scored a total of 28 touchdowns on returns. That's down a little from the 34 TDs scored in '98, but it's still quite a bit ahead of the 11 touchdowns scored on punt and kickoff returns in 1993. Maybe 28 touchowns is not much, but it is a nice bonus if you include special-teams touchdowns in your scoring.

Here are those scores for the 1999 season:

	Team	Punt Ret/TD	Kickoff Ret/TD	1999 Points	3-Year Total
1.	Cincinnati	2	1	18	36
	Minnesota	1	2	18	24
	St. Louis	1	2	18	30
4.	Atlanta	2	0	12	30
	Carolina	0	2	12	18
	Indianapolis	1	1	12	12
	Jacksonville	1	1	12	24
	Kansas City	2	0	12	24
9.	Buffalo	0	1	6	6
	Dallas	1	0	6	24
	Denver	1	0	6	30
	Detroit	1	0	6	18
	Green Bay	0	1	6	24
	New York Giants	1	0	6	18
	Philadelphia	0	1	6	12
	Seattle	1	0	6	24
	Washington	0	1	6	24
18.	Arizona	0	0	0	0
	Baltimore	0	0	0	36
	Chicago	0	0	0	18
	Cleveland	0	0	0	*0
	Miami	0	0	0	0
	New England	0	0	0	6
	New Orleans	0	0	0	12
	New York Jets	0	0	0	18
	Oakland	0	0	0	12
	Pittsburgh	0	0	0	6
	San Diego	0	0	0	24
	San Francisco	0	0	0	18
	Tampa Bay	0	0	0	18
	Tennessee	0	0	0	0

Played only in 1999

DEFENSES

Chapter 9

TEAM EVALUATIONS

ARIZONA CARDINALS

Who's New — First-round draft pick Thomas Jones takes over as the starting running back, whether he's ready or not. Tight end Chris Gedney is back after a year out of football because of an injury, though he's not a big factor. The new kicker is Cary Blanchard, who's been around the last few years.

Who's Gone — Underrated running back Adrian Murrell signed with Washington and could be missed. Kicker Chris Jacke will not be missed.

Quarterbacks — Jake Plummer can't possibly do any worse than last year, when he was the lowest-ranked starting quarterback in the league. He threw just nine touchdown passes and a league-high 24 interceptions behind a bad offensive line. The addition of Thomas Jones should help establish a ground game and keep defenses honest. Dave Brown did no better than Plummer last season, but he's an adequate backup.

Running Backs — Jones has been compared to Emmitt Smith, and if he's half that good, the Cardinals have found their answer to a ground game that ranked 29th in the league last year. Jones is a tough inside runner with good hands. Michael Pittman is built like a Greek god, but he has the durability of a china saucer. Mario Bates may be the best goal-line back in the NFL, but that's about it.

Wide Receivers — Rob Moore is coming off a subpar season that was largely a result of bad play by the quarterbacks and linemen. He should bounce back. Frank Sanders is an excellent possession receiver who seldom finds the end zone. David Boston is set to make a much bigger impact than he did as a rookie, though he'll probably settle for a No. 3 receiving role.

Tight Ends — Chris Gedney is back following colon surgery, but he has never stayed healthy for long. Terry Hardy caught 30 passes last year, but he's nothing special. Rookie Jay Tant, a good receiver, could become the starter before the season is over.

Kickers — Cary Blanchard had an outstanding 1999 season with the Giants in place of the injured Brad Daluiso, but he's had an inconsistent career. Still, he's better than the departed Chris Jacke.

Defense — In 1999, the Cardinals ranked 22nd in total defense and

30th vs. the run. They scored 18 points on defense off 27 takeaways (12 fewer than in 1998). You'd think they would be better with Vince Tobin as head coach, but mediocrity seems to be a way of life with the Cardinals. And that won't change much in 2000. Simeon Rice is one of the league's top sackers, finishing second with 16.5 sacks in 1999.

Who Gets the Ball — First-round draft pick running back Thomas Jones should be the main ballcarrier, but there's no guarantee he'll be all that he's cracked up to be in Arizona. Rob Moore is the primary pass receiver, but he needs to bounce back from a subpar 1999.

Best Players to Draft — Quarterback Jake Plummer and running back Thomas Jones.

ATLANTA FALCONS

Who's New — Wide receiver Shawn Jefferson should move into the starting lineup, which means Tim Dwight will be the No. 3 receiver and focus more on kick returns.

Who's Gone — Nobody at the skill positions.

Quarterbacks — This is a settled position as long as Chris Chandler stays healthy. He stayed on the field most of the time in his three seasons in Atlanta. Chandler nearly always throws at least one touchdown pass a game. There is a big drop-off if and when Chandler goes down, because the passing game would grind to a halt with Danny Kanell or Tony Graziani under center.

Running Backs — Here's the million-dollar question: Will Jamal Anderson come back 100 percent in 2000, or will he be a step slower so soon after knee surgery? Even if he's a step slower, he'll rush for 1,000 yards, because he's a relentless inside runner. Two years removed from Byron Hanspard's knee surgery, the Falcons hope he can provide the breakaway threat that was lacking in 1999. Bob Christian is a reliable pass-catching fullback; Ken Oxendine will be buried on the bench.

Wide Receivers — Shawn Jefferson will provide a deep threat that will help draw attention away from Terance Mathis, who remarkably caught 81 passes against double-teams last season. Tim Dwight is a gamebreaker who is best suited for a No. 3 receiving role due to his small size (and he's also an excellent kick returner). Jammi German is promising but inconsistent, and Eugene Baker is small and lacks great speed.

Tight Ends — O. J. Santiago is coming off a disappointing season, and the Falcons probably regret their decision to trade this year's first-round pick to take Reggie Kelly in the second round last year.

Kicker — Morten Andersen, who will turn 40 during training camp, is coming off a subpar season, but watch him come back strong. If the team puts him in position, he'll score 100-plus points.

Defense — The Atlanta defense fell apart in 1999, allowing 380 points and ranking 16th in total defense. Defenders scored only eight points last year, and nobody had more than four interceptions (the team had just six fumble recoveries and 18 takeaways — both last in the NFL). The only improvement was in sacks, going from 38 in 1998 to 40 in '99.

Who Gets the Ball — Running back Jamal Anderson, as long as he's 100 percent healthy, and wide receivers Terance Mathis and Shawn Jefferson.

Best Players to Draft — Running back Jamal Anderson, wide receiver Terance Mathis, quarterback Chris Chandler, and kicker Morten Andersen.

BALTIMORE RAVENS

Who's New — Two backup quarterbacks — Trent Dilfer (ex-Buccaneer) and Chris Redman (third-round draft pick). They'll both put pressure on Tony Banks to produce. Jamal Lewis, the surprise fifth overall pick in the draft, will be the new starter at running back, but he, too, isn't a sure thing. Another first-rounder, wide receiver Travis Taylor, will probably start, but he's not as good as the Ravens think he is. Ex-Bronco Shannon Sharpe is the new tight end, but he has to show he can bounce back after a subpar season that ended in injury.

Who's Gone — Starting running back Errict Rhett departed for Cleveland, while onetime starter at quarterback Scott Mitchell signed with Cincinnati.

Quarterbacks — Coach Brian Billick certainly resurrected Banks's career in 1999. Banks was the AFC's sixth-rated passer in 1999 when he jump-started a struggling offense with 17 touchdown passes in 12 games. But he's far from proven, and if he struggles he'll be replaced by Dilfer, who got the change of scenery he so desperately needed. Redman may be the quarterback of the future, but not the quarterback in 2000.

Running Backs — Jamal Lewis hasn't been the same since a 1998 knee injury, but the Ravens are counting on him returning to his spectacular 1997 form at the University of Tennessee, when he was an outstanding blend of speed and power. Priest Holmes broke free for runs of 72 and 64 yards late last season, and he gained 5.7 yards per carry.

Don't be too surprised if he replaces an injured or ineffective Lewis. Charles Evans is a useful pass-catching fullback, but that's about it.

Wide Receivers — The Ravens passed on Plaxico Burress with their fifth pick in the first round and took Taylor with the 10th pick. Taylor saved his best for the big games at the University of Florida. He should immediately start opposite Qadry Ismail, who is coming off a career season. Banks–to–Ismail became a great combination late in 1999. Justin Armour could become an effective possession receiver, and, although Jermaine Lewis appears to be a bad fit for Billick's offense, he has too much talent not to stage a comeback.

Tight Ends — Sharpe, a seven-time Pro Bowler, will improve the team's short and intermediate passing game, which should open things up deep for the wideouts. The Ravens practically ignored their tight ends last season, but Sharpe will be a primary target.

Kicker — Matt Stover has quietly carved out a solid career. He should match last year's surprising 116-point output.

Defense — The Ravens have the most underrated defense in the NFL. They ranked second in total defense in 1999, and the team's troubles cannot be attributed to its stout defense. It allowed only six rushing touchdowns and had 31 takeaways. Michael McCrary is one of the NFL's most unsung defenders. He had 11.5 sacks last season, while linebacker Rob Boulware had 10. Safety Rod Woodson tied for the league lead with seven interceptions in 1999.

Who Gets the Ball — The Ravens want No. 1 pick Jamal Lewis to be their every-down back. Whoever quarterbacks will look to tight end Shannon Sharpe and wide receivers Travis Taylor (a rookie) and Qadry Ismail.

Best Players to Draft — Quarterback Tony Banks is a boom-or-bust pick, but wide receiver Travis Taylor has great upside, tight end Shannon Sharpe should be a sure thing and kicker Matt Stover will score points. And rookie running back Jamal Lewis will be a great pick if he starts.

BUFFALO BILLS

Who's New — Just two late-round picks at wide receiver: Avion Black (fourth round) and Drew Haddad (seventh round).

Who's Gone — Two future Hall of Famers were cut: running back Thurman Thomas and wide receiver Andre Reed. Fullback Sam Gash was also let go, as was wideout/kick returner Kevin Williams.

Quarterbacks — One of the bigger surprises in the NFL last season was coach Wade Phillips's decision to bench Doug Flutie in favor of Rob Johnson for the regular-season finale and playoffs. But Johnson is a better passer, and he appears to have better rapport with his teammates. Flutie had a league-high 23 passes batted down in 1999. With Johnson starting, the Bills will improve on last year's 20th ranking in passing yardage . . . if he stays healthy, that is.

Running Backs — Will it be Antowain Smith or Jonathan Linton? Last season, Smith was the starter, but Linton is the one who got the most carries because he runs harder. Expect a wide-open battle in camp. Shawn Bryson, a third-round pick in 1999, was the hit of training camp before suffering a major knee injury. An undersized fullback at the University of Tennessee, Bryson has an outside shot to win the starting tailback job. The ground game will miss the departed Sam Gash, an outstanding lead blocker.

Wide Receivers — Eric Moulds is one of the best deep threats in the game, and he'll flourish with Johnson at quarterback. Second-year receiver Peerless Price moves into a starting role. He got off to a slow start as a rookie but finished with 18 catches in his final seven games when he caught on to the offense. There is no experienced depth behind the starters, so the team might be looking to add a veteran.

Tight Ends — The Bills made re-signing Jay Riemersma an off-season priority because he's a big target and an up-and-coming player.

Kicker — Steve Christie is coming off a bad year, so the team signed Dan Giancola, who made 48 of 61 field-goal tries in the CFL last year, to provide competition in camp.

Defense — Look at the numbers, and you'll see that the Buffalo defense allowed the fewest yards in the NFL in 1999 — ranking fourth vs. the run and first vs. the pass. The Bills allowed just 277 points, sixth in the league. But nobody had more than three interceptions and the entire team came up with just 21 takeaways. Those numbers have to improve.

Who Gets the Ball — Wide receiver Eric Moulds and tight end Jay Riemersma are the top pass receivers. There's sure to be a battle at running back between Jonathan Linton and Antowain Smith.

Best Players to Draft — Quarterback Rob Johnson will be a very good pick if he can stay in the lineup. Also, go for wide receiver Eric Moulds and tight end Jay Riemersma, and maybe take a flyer on wide receiver Peerless Price.

CAROLINA PANTHERS

Who's New — Running back Natrone Means will be the backup to

Tim Biakabutuka, though he hasn't had an injury-free season since 1994.

Who's Gone — A bunch of backups, such as quarterback Steve Bono (not re-signed) and running back Fred Lane (traded to Indianapolis). Richie Cunningham, who took over at kicker last year after John Kasay was injured, was let go, too.

Quarterbacks — Steve Beuerlein's 13th NFL season was by far his best. Beuerlein directed the second-most-prolific passing game in the league, and he threw 36 touchdown passes. Don't expect those numbers again, but Beuerlein should certainly throw at least 25 TD passes. Jeff Lewis faces a challenge from Dameyune Craig for the backup job.

Running Backs — Tim Biakabutuka provided the most explosive running in the franchise's five-year history in 1999, but he couldn't stay healthy. In the first quarter of one game, he rushed for 123 yards and three touchdowns on just five carries. Natrone Means, who is past his prime, has replaced Fred Lane as the backup. William Floyd is a quality, all-purpose fullback.

Wide Receivers — What a breakthrough season this position was in 1999 for Carolina. Muhsin Muhammad, who led the NFC in receiving, has developed into one of the best possession receivers in the game. Patrick Jeffers emerged as a dangerous complement to Muhammad. Jeffers caught eight touchdown passes in December alone. Donald Hayes caught five passes for 133 yards in his only start, but he's still a project.

Tight Ends — Wesley Walls is the best tight end in the NFC. In his 11th season, he led all tight ends with 12 touchdown catches. Walls is a focal point of this offense.

Kicker — John Kasay is recovering from a torn ACL in his kicking leg, but the team was confident enough in his recovery to drop his replacement, Richie Cunningham. Still, Kasay hasn't hit 100 points since 1996.

Defense — George Seifert needs to do with the Panthers' defense what he did in San Francisco a decade ago. In 1999, Carolina allowed 381 points, had no scores on defense and ranked 24th vs. the run and 23rd vs. the pass. Top sacker Kevin Greene retired and high-priced defenders such as Eric Davis and Sean Gilbert have yet to live up to their salaries. Ex-Falcon Chuck Smith will help make up for Green's loss.

Who Gets the Ball — Running back Tim Biakabutuka now carries the load, and the pass catchers are tight end Wesley Walls and wideouts Muhsin Muhammad and Patrick Jeffers.

Best Players to Draft — Quarterback Steve Beuerlein, wide receivers Muhsin Muhammad and Patrick Jeffers and tight end Wesley Walls.

CHICAGO BEARS

Who's New — Eddie Kennison was acquired in a trade with New Orleans, and Dez White was a steal in the draft's third round. There'll also be a new kicker, with sixth-round draft choice Paul Edinger competing with unproven Jaret Holmes and perhaps veteran Jeff Jaeger. Rookie sixth-round pick Frank Murphy will compete for the backup running back job.

Who's Gone — Kicker Jeff Jaeger might not be re-signed. One-time Pro Bowler Curtis Conway left for San Diego in free agency, and backup running back Edgar Bennett was let go. Shane Matthews, last year's opening-day starter at quarterback, may sign elsewhere.

Quarterbacks — The Bears took a lot of guff for cutting Erik Kramer last summer. Then they became the second team in NFL history with three 1,000-yard passers in the same season. Offensive coordinator Gary Crowton's wide-open offense resulted in career years for Shane Matthews and Jim Miller. The starting job is now Cade McNown's to lose following his erratic but promising rookie season. Miller, who played surprisingly well in five games last year, will start if McNown struggles.

Running Backs — Coming off knee surgery, Curtis Enis was slimmer, trimmer and yet slower in 1999. Two seasons after surgery, Enis has bulked back up in an attempt to take the pounding. He's due for a breakthrough season. Little-used backup James Allen has explosiveness; he'll be challenged by rookie Frank Murphy. Fullback is a moot position in Chicago's offense.

Wide Receivers — This is a position of strength and depth for the Bears. Marcus Robinson is a poor man's Randy Moss — big and fast, with great hands. Bobby Engram is a highly productive, reliable possession receiver who will be moved to the slot this season. Eddie Kennison's speed will complement Robinson. Second-year power wideout Marty Booker, third-round rookie Dex White and D'Wayne Bates will compete for playing time in an offense that regularly utilizes three- and four-receiver sets.

Tight Ends — Ryan Wetnight rarely starts, but he always leads the Bears' tight ends in receiving. Alonzo Mayes and John Allred have been disappointments.

Kicker — A wide-open battle following last year's disastrous 19-for-34 field-goal accuracy, which cost the team a shot at the playoffs. Look for draft choice Paul Edinger to win the job.

Defense — Head coach Dick Jauron needs to do a number on the Chicago defense. In 1999, the Bears ranked 29th in total defense, let up

341 points and made just 14 interceptions (though their 19 fumble recoveries led the NFC).

Who Gets the Ball — Running back Curtis Enis and receivers Marcus Robinson and Bobby Engram.

Best Player to Draft — Wide receiver Marcus Robinson and running back Curtis Enis.

CINCINNATI BENGALS

Who's New — There are two new wide receivers from Florida State: first-round draft choice Peter Warrick — who should be a star — and third-rounder Ron Dugans. Journeyman Scott Mitchell will be the backup quarterback (and could take over if Akili Smith falters). Fourth-round draft pick Curtis Keaton provides insurance in case running back Corey Dillon departs or holds out. Finally, sixth-round pick Neil Rackers will compete with veteran Doug Pelfrey for the placekicking duties.

Who's Gone — Running back Corey Dillon wanted out all offseason, but he'll most likely be back. Wide receiver Carl Pickens also wanted out, and he was likely to be granted his release before the start of training camp. Jeff Blake, who started at quarterback most of last season, signed with New Orleans as a free agent.

Quarterbacks — The third pick in the 1999 draft, Akili Smith is unquestionably the starter following a frustrating rookie season. He played fairly well in four starts but missed the final eight games due to a toe injury. With a full offseason and training camp behind him (he staged a 25-day holdout last year) and a full arsenal of offensive weapons, Smith should be improved. If not, he'll be looking over his shoulder at Scott Mitchell, who can play well for short stretches.

Running Backs — The Bengals have built a respectable offensive line, so Corey Dillon could have his best season yet if he stays. Last year's ground game tied for sixth in the league and carried the offense. Ki-Jana Carter suffered a dislocated kneecap in the offseason — yet another setback in a jinxed career. Michael Basnight, who averaged 5.0 yards per carry as a rookie last year, provides good depth.

Wide Receivers — Carl Pickens appears to be on his way out, but he has been a cancer to the team the past two seasons. Darnay Scott has become the team's go-to receiver, anyway. Rookie Peter Warrick is a playmaker, a touchdown producer and an instant starter. Ron Dugans is a possession receiver. The team is high on Craig Yeast, a promising second-year receiver.

Tight Ends — Tony McGee is the most durable tight end in the league, but he has been underutilized the past two seasons. He can do some things if they get him the ball.

Kicker — Incumbent Doug Pelfrey, who struggled with a new snapper and holder past year, faces a strong challenge from rookie sixth-round draft pick Neil Rackers. The team wants Rackers to win the job.

Defense — The Bengals allowed the most points in the NFL in 1999 — 460, even more than the woeful Browns. The team allowed 22 rushing TDs, 28 passing TDs and had just 27 takeaways. Nobody had more than six sacks or three interceptions. And things won't improve much in 2000, if at all.

Who Gets the Ball — Running back Corey Dillon (if he's still on the team) and wide receivers Peter Warrick and Darnay Scott.

Best Players to Draft — Running back Corey Dillon, and wide receivers Peter Warrick and Darnay Scott.

CLEVELAND BROWNS

Who's New — Errict Rhett was signed away from Baltimore and will start at running back, while third-round draft choice Travis Prentice could work his way into the lineup. Dennis Northcutt, a second-rounder, will battle for a starting role at wideout, and David Patten, the ex-Giant, will return kicks.

Who's Gone — Third-string quarterback Jamie Martin signed with Jacksonville, and wide receiver Leslie Shepherd, a failure in 1999, wasn't re-signed.

Quarterbacks — Tim Couch gained far more experience than the other highly touted rookie quarterbacks in 1999, and he played remarkably well for a team that finished 2–14. Even more remarkably, Couch stayed alive in front of an underachieving offensive line that surrendered 60 sacks in 1999. Surprisingly, the Browns didn't address their offensive line needs in the offseason. Ty Detmer is among the better backup quarterbacks in the league.

Running Backs — The Browns could certainly help Couch's development if they develop a running game. They signed hard-running Errict Rhett to beef up a ground game that was the league's worst last year. Terry Kirby, last year's starter, has a nose for the end zone, but he's better suited for a third-down role. The Browns were thrilled to grab Travis Prentice in the third round of the April draft.

Wide Receivers — Kevin Johnson was a pleasant surprise last year because he made an instant impact with eight touchdowns. So was rookie Darrin Chiaverini, who came on strong late to finish with 44 catches and four scores. Rookie Dennis Northcutt is a burner and a playmaker, and he could become an instant starter. New offensive coordinator Pete Carmichael wants to run four-receiver sets.

Tight Ends — Mark Campbell, who spent last season on injured reserve, is the starter until rookie Aaron Shea, a converted fullback, is ready.

Kickers — Don't be surprised if the Browns sign a veteran to challenge Phil Dawson, who made just eight of 12 field-goal attempts in 1999.

Defense — The Browns ranked last in total defense and last vs. the run in their first season back. Don't be fooled by the pass defense's 11th-best ranking — opponents knew they could run the ball and they took huge leads and just ran out the clock (in other words, they had no reason to throw). Only two teams allowed more points, and Cleveland's eight interceptions and 25 sacks were league lows. Still, there's some talent on this young defense, so things will improve, especially with Courtney Brown, the No.1 overall pick in the 2000 draft, and ex-Steeler Orpheus Roye added to the mix.

Who Gets the Ball — Running back Errict Rhett and wide receiver Kevin Johnson.

Best Players to Draft — Wide receiver Kevin Johnson is the only sure thing, though quarterback Tim Couch might be worth a late pick.

DALLAS COWBOYS

Who's New — The big acquisition was wide receiver Joey Galloway in a trade with Seattle. Jackie Harris will be the No. 2 tight end (which means he'll see lots of action), and Tim Sedler gets a shot to be the new kicker.

Who's Gone — In free agency, backup quarterback Jason Garrett signed with the Giants and tight end Eric Bjornson with New England. Wide receiver Ernie Mills was released. Also, wide receiver Michael Irvin and running back Daryl Johnston were expected to retire because of serious injuries.

Quarterbacks — Last year's conservative offense has been scrapped for an offense similar to the Super Bowl days of the early 1990s — and Troy Aikman couldn't be happier. Aikman is adept at hitting receivers in timing patterns, routes that were seldom used in 1999. They'll be utilized this year, though, so look for a very good season for Aikman. The backup job has been handed to journeyman Paul Justin, and if Aikman goes down, so will the Cowboys.

Running Backs — Emmitt Smith hasn't begun to slow down, and the Cowboys have an excellent line opening holes for him. Don't expect a drop-off from Smith and last year's sixth-ranked running game. The team's more wide-open offense will help spread the field for Smith to rumble between the tackles. The Cowboys have an exceptional backup in Chris Warren, who doubles as the third-down back.

Wide Receivers — Joey Galloway was an expensive trade acquisition (two first-round draft picks), but he's the No. 1 receiver the team desperately needed. With Galloway drawing extra attention, Raghib Ismail will flourish in the No. 2 receiving role. Wes Chandler, the team's new receivers coach, is grooming the team's young, inexperienced receivers, such as Jason Tucker and Wane McGarity. Michael Irvin is being forced to retire.

Tight Ends — David LaFleur, who scored seven touchdowns last season, may have an expanded role in a more tight-end-friendly offense. Ex-Titan Jackie Harris is the other starter in two-tight-end sets.

Kickers — Aging Eddie Murray or free agent Tim Sedler couldn't possibly do any worse than Richie Cunningham did last year. The kickers made a miserable 19 of 31 field-goal attempts in 1999.

Defense — Year after year, the Cowboys have a staunch defense, and new head coach Dave Campo will keep it that way. In 1999, Dallas gave up just 276 points (fifth best) and ranked ninth overall in yards allowed. The Cowboys scored 32 points on defense and made 24 interceptions (tied for sixth best).

Who Gets the Ball — Running back Emmitt Smith and wide receivers Joey Galloway and Raghib Ismail.

Best Players to Draft — Running back Emmitt Smith, wide receivers Joey Galloway and Raghib Ismail, and tight end David LaFleur.

DENVER BRONCOS

Who's New — Unless Steve Young signs with the Broncos, the offseason didn't bring many major changes. Gus Frerotte will battle with Brian Griese for the starting quarterback job (though he's not the long-term answer). Third-rounder Chris Cole was the fastest wide receiver in the draft and could be the No. 3 wideout.

Who's Gone — The two backup quarterbacks in 1999, Bubby Brister and Chris Miller, left town, tight end Shannon Sharpe was lost to Baltimore in free agency, and reserve running back Derek Loville was traded to St. Louis.

Quarterbacks — The Broncos have so little confidence in Brian Griese that they signed Gus Frerotte and sent out signs that they wanted to sign Steve Young to make one more Super Bowl run. Griese had a respectable second season in 1999, but the team obviously lacks confidence in him. If Denver doesn't get Young, Griese will feel pressure to play well immediately or give way to Frerotte. Griese led the league with 16 fumbles in 1999. Frerotte might be the better quarterback.

Running Backs — The Denver running game suffered but didn't fall apart when Terrell Davis went down in 1999. Olandis Gary, a Davis clone, rushed for 1,159 yards in just 11 games as a rookie last year. A full recovery is expected by Davis in 2000. Gary could be used to rest Davis, especially early in the season until Davis is completely comfortable running on his reconstructed knee.

Wide Receivers — Ed McCaffrey has 32 touchdowns in the last four seasons, and Rod Smith has 235 catches in the past three seasons. They form one of the best tandems in the league. The addition of rookie Chris Cole gives the Broncos a speed threat to stretch defenses. The team is high on Billy Miller, who is the favorite to become the No. 3 receiver. Miller was a sleeper seventh-round pick in 1999.

Tight Ends — Shannon Sharpe's unmatched production will be missed, though Byron Chamberlain and Dwayne Carswell are adequate. Carswell is the better blocker, while Chamberlain is the better receiver.

Kicker — Year after year, Jason Elam is good for at least 110 points. He's especially effective in performance scoring leagues because of his outstanding range.

Defense — The Denver defense had its problems in 1999, allowing 318 points, which is near the middle of the pack. Overall, it finished seventh in yards allowed and made 50 sacks (more than in their two Super Bowl years), but Denver had just 26 takeaways. Trevor Pryce was the league's fifth-leading sacker in 1999, getting 13.0 QB drops.

Who Gets the Ball — Terrell Davis and wideouts Rod Smith and Ed McCaffrey. The Broncos' tight end is no longer a key player in fantasy football.

Best Players to Draft — Running back Terrell Davis, kicker Jason Elam, and wide receivers Rod Smith and Ed McCaffrey.

DETROIT LIONS

Who's New — The big free-agent signing was $5 million man James Stewart, though he's not as good as you'd think for that kind of money. The new backup quarterbacks are Mike Tomczak and Steve Stenstrom, and ex-Saint Tony Johnson could figure at tight end.

Who's Gone — Backup quarterback Gus Frerotte, who started six games in 1999, signed with Denver as a free agent.

Quarterbacks — Charlie Batch's job just got easier. He already had an outstanding trio of receivers, and now he has a huge offensive line and a ground game to keep defenses honest. Batch missed five 1999 games due to a fractured right thumb, and he still posted respectable, low-risk numbers (13 touchdown passes, seven interceptions). Mike Tomczak is a reliable backup, not a threat to unseat Batch.

Running Backs — Stewart sweeps left for five, Stewart off right tackle for three, Stewart up the middle for two, first down. Opponents will get their fill of the Lions' expensive free-agent acquisition running behind an enormous line that averages 330 pounds. Stewart will immediately upgrade a ground game that ranked 28th last season, but he's never been very durable. Second-year player Sedrick Irvin and rookie Reuben Droughns will battle for the backup role.

Wide Receivers — The question is whether a healthy Herman Moore will start ahead of Germane Crowell and Johnnie Morton, who combined for 161 receptions, 11 100-yard receiving games and 12 touchdowns in 1999. It's hard to believe that Moore could be limited to a No. 3 receiving role, but he is in his 10th season. Crowell, one of the league's best young receivers, is a lock to start. Morton and Moore are likely to share playing time.

Tight Ends — David Sloan finally stayed healthy after four injury-filled seasons, and he emerged with 47 catches and four scores in 1999. The second tight end position is up for grabs.

Kicker — Jason Hanson is still one of the league's best long-range kickers, and he'll score at least 110 points.

Defense — The Lions never seem to have an outstanding defense, and 1999 was no exception. Detroit ranked 18th in yards allowed and gave up 323 points, just average numbers, and the offseason has not brought a major upgrade. Still, the Lions had 50 sacks, led by Robert Porcher, who was third in the NFL with 16. The defense scored 26 points.

Who Gets the Ball — Running back James Stewart, wide receivers Herman Moore, Germane Crowell and Johnnie Morton, and tight end David Sloan.

Best Players to Draft — Running back James Stewart, wide receivers Herman Moore, Germane Crowell and Johnnie Morton, tight end David Sloan and kicker Jason Hanson.

GREEN BAY PACKERS

Who's New — First-round draft choice Bubba Franks takes over as the new starting tight end. GM Ron Wolf loves running back Ahman Green, so he acquired him from the Seahawks in a trade. Look for Green to be a widely used backup.

Who's Gone — Tight end Mark Chmura will probably be let go because of his pending rape charge, and backup Jeff Thomason was traded to Philadelphia.

Quarterbacks — Brett Favre was nagged by a painful thumb injury on his throwing hand last season, but the bigger problem was an overall lack of team discipline, which was exemplified by Favre's careless play. The Packers plan to run a more structured, possession-type passing game, and Favre's play is bound to improve. Matt Hasselbeck might be the best backup quarterback you've never heard of.

Running Backs — The offense is heavily reliant on Dorsey Levens, who rushed for 1,034 yards, caught 71 passes and scored a team-high 10 touchdowns in 1999. Trade acquisition Ahman Green will steal some carries, but Levens is still the every-down back. Fullback William Henderson blocks well and he runs a nice screen pass play. De'Mond Parker added speed to the offense in 1999 before wrecking his knee.

Wide Receivers — Antonio Freeman and Bill Schroeder both caught 74 passes for more than 1,000 yards last season, but Freeman drops passes and Schroeder is better suited for a No. 3 role. Corey Bradford caught five touchdown passes last year, but he's a better special-teams player than receiver. Rookie Anthony Lucas could develop into a fourth-round find in time. The Packers are thin at this position.

Tight Ends — Rookie Bubba Franks fills a gaping hole and will start from Day One. Mark Chmura is probably going to be gone, and converted wide receiver Tyrone Davis is talented but unreliable.

Kickers — Ryan Longwell proves that you don't have to find kickers via the draft. As a 1997 free agent, Longwell won the job from third-round draft pick Brett Conway and has flourished ever since.

Defense — The Green Bay defense fell apart in 1999, ranking 19th in total defense and 20th in points allowed. Somehow the Packers were second in the league with 41 takeaways (26 interceptions, fourth in the league) and scored 20 points on defense. There's some young talent, especially at cornerback, so there's no reason this defense won't bounce back in '00, but don't expect another 41 takeaways.

Who Gets the Ball — Wide receivers Antonio Freeman and Bill Schroeder, running back Dorsey Levens and rookie tight end Bubba Franks.

Best Players to Draft — Quarterback Brett Favre, wide receiver Antonio Freeman, running back Dorsey Levens, tight end Bubba Franks and kicker Ryan Longwell.

INDIANAPOLIS COLTS

Who's New — Quarterback Pete Gonzalez, a third-stringer with Pittsburgh, was signed as a free agent, and running back Fred Lane was picked up in a trade with Carolina. Lane will be Edgerrin James's backup.

Who's Gone — Three backups: quarterback Steve Walsh, running back Darick Holmes and wide receiver Lake Dawson. None will be missed.

Quarterbacks — Peyton Manning couldn't ask for more. He has a great receiver, a great running back and an offensive line that led the league in sacks allowed in 1999. The Colts couldn't ask for more from Manning, who plays mature beyond his years. Pete Gonzalez will battle Kelly Holcomb for the backup job, but Manning has not missed a game in two seasons.

Running Backs — The Colts unloaded Marshall Faulk in 1999 but never missed him. Edgerrin James piled up 2,139 yards from scrimmage, the second most by a rookie in NFL history. An excellent all-purpose back, James led the league with 1,553 rushing yards and tied for the league lead with 17 touchdowns. Fred Lane, who was obtained in an off-season trade, will be the main backup if he can straighten out his act.

Wide Receivers — Manning–to–Marvin Harrison became the best combination of the NFL in 1999. Harrison's touchdown production tailed off after he scored 12 touchdowns in the first 10 games, but he still led the league in receiving yards. Terrence Wilkins, who scored seven touchdowns last season, proved to be the team's second-best receiver, but he's too small to last long. The Colts want injury-prone E. G. Green to step into the No. 2 receiving role rather than Jerome Pathon.

Tight Ends — Ken Dilger and Marcus Pollard form one of the best tight end tandems in the NFL. They combined for 74 catches and six scores in 1999.

Kickers — With the triplets (Manning, James and Harrison) moving the ball up and down the field, Mike Vanderjagt is certain to approach last year's league-leading 145-point output.

Defense — If the Colts want to improve upon last season's 13–3 record, they'll have to improve their defense. Indianapolis ranked 15th overall in 1999, allowing 333 points and making just 23 takeaways (the NFL's fourth-lowest total) and 10 interceptions (second fewest). Chad

Bratzke made 12 of the team's 41 sacks, tied for seventh in the NFL.

Who Gets the Ball — Running back Edgerrin James and wide receiver Marvin Harrison.

Best Players to Draft — Quarterback Peyton Manning, running back Edgerrin James, wide receiver Marvin Harrison and kicker Mike Vanderjagt.

JACKSONVILLE JAGUARS

Who's New — First-round draft choice R. Jay Soward will be the No. 3 wide receiver, and Jonathan Quinn will battle free-agent acquisition Jamie Martin for the backup quarterback job. There'll be a battle for the backup to Fred Taylor between Stacey Mack and Chris Howard and possibly seventh-round pick Shyrone Stith.

Who's Gone — Two backups left as free agents: quarterback Jay Fiedler and running back James Stewart.

Quarterbacks — Mark Brunell has proven to be a better NFL quarterback than fantasy quarterback, a low-interception guy who relies more on the ground game and less on his scrambling than he used to. Brunell has a 44–24 career winning record, but he still has to prove he can take his team to the next level. The Jaguars hope third-year pro Jonathan Quinn can take the next step and rightfully assume the No. 2 role. He has great size and a strong arm but struggles to read coverages and thinks too much rather than rely on his instrincts.

Running Backs — The Jaguars have the best ground game in the NFL in 1999, but that won't be repeated if Fred Taylor goes down again, because James Stewart is gone. If he stays healthy, the explosive Taylor could post Marshall Faulk–like numbers and have an MVP season. Taylor, who was in and out of last year's lineup due to a hamstring injury, will be utilized much more in the passing game. None of the backups have any experience to speak of, though the team is high on Stacey Mack.

Wide Receivers — Jimmy Smith produced one clutch catch after another last season. He led the league with 116 catches. Although Smith occasionally gets deep, he and Keenan McCardell are not big touchdown scorers. That's why the Jaguars drafted R. Jay Soward in the first round of the draft. Soward has great speed, and he'll try to stretch defenses from the No. 3 receiving position. Reggie Barlow and Alvis Whitted have failed to contribute to the passing game.

Tight Ends — Kyle Brady was overpaid in the 1999 free-agent market, but he is an excellent blocker whom the Jaguars are still very high on. Damon Jones is inconsistent, but he finds the end zone (he has 10 touchdown catches in three seasons).

Kicker — The second-most-accurate field-goal kicker in NFL history, Mike Hollis is certain to score more than 120 points on this team.

Defense — In their first year under defensive coordinator Dom Capers, the Jaguars ranked fourth on defense and first in fewest points allowed. With the addition of Hardy Nickerson at middle linebacker and no losses, they'll only be better in '00. They set a team record with 36 points on defense last year (five touchdowns and three safeties) and tied another with 30 takeaways. And three players, led by Tony Brackens (team-record 12.5), had 10 or more sacks, while the team set a record with 57, tying for the NFL lead.

Who Gets the Ball — Running back Fred Taylor and receivers Jimmy Smith and Keenan McCardell.

Best Players to Draft — Running back Fred Taylor, quarterback Mark Brunell, wide receiver Jimmy Smith and kicker Mike Hollis.

KANSAS CITY CHIEFS

Who's New — No. 1 draft pick Sylvester Morris could move straight into the starting lineup.

Who's Gone — Bam Morris and Tamarick Vanover both had off-season legal troubles and are no longer around. Wide receiver Joe Horn signed with New Orleans, while tight end Lonnie Johnson and wide receiver Andre Rison were let go.

Quarterbacks — Elvis Grbac came through with a much-improved 1999 season, and there are indications the Chiefs will pass more and run somewhat less in 2000. In 1999, Grbac shed his injury-prone label and started every game while throwing 22 touchdown passes. Warren Moon is much less likely to supplant Grbac, but if Grbac is injured, Moon can still carry an offense.

Running Backs — A wide-open battle will ensue in camp. Chiefs coach Gunther Cunningham wants to settle on one player, as opposed to last year's running-back-by-committee approach. Kimble Anders, who was injured last season, and hard-running Donnell Bennett are the favorites to start. But Tony Richardson proved last year that he could run as well as block. Mike Cloud, Rashaan Shehee and rookies Frank Moreau and Dante Hall further cloud the picture.

Wide Receivers — Derrick Alexander produced three plays of more than 80 yards last season, yet he was surprisingly unproductive.

Joe Horn — not Kevin Lockett — emerged last season, and Horn is gone. Rookie Sylvester Morris, who has ideal size but needs refinement, could become the team's best receiver right away.

Tight Ends — Tony Gonzalez was practically unstoppable near the goal line in the second half of the 1999 season. He stopped dropping passes, scored 11 touchdowns, and looks like a perennial Pro Bowler. This year, the Chiefs plan to play him in wide-receiver sets at times.

Kicker — Pete Stoyanovich is no longer a great long-range kicker, but he is reliable from short range. Consider him a fantasy backup this year.

Defense — The Chiefs were 14th in overall defense in 1999, letting up 20.1 points per game. However, they did lead the league with 54 points scored on defense (four off fumbles and five off interceptions), and their 45 takeaways were one shy of the league lead. Three players had five or more interceptions, led by cornerback James Hasty, who tied for the league lead with seven interceptions.

Who Gets the Ball — Tight end Tony Gonzalez is the only sure thing. Derrick Alexander is the top wide receiver, but running back is once again a toss-up between four or five contenders and pretenders.

Best Players to Draft — Tight end Tony Gonzalez and quarterback Elvis Grbac.

MIAMI DOLPHINS

Who's New — Jay Fiedler came from Jacksonville and will battle Damon Huard and Jim Druckenmiller for the starting quarterback job. Former Saint Lamar Smith and ex-Bill Thurman Thomas will be reserves in the backfield, and free agent wide receiver Bert Emanual was signed in May.

Who's Gone — Superstar quarterback Dan Marino retired, while troubled running back Cecil Collins and tight end Troy Drayton were released. Stanley Pritchett signed with the Eagles.

Quarterbacks — Damon Huard did well enough in limited playing time last year to enter the 2000 preseason as the starter. He actually outplayed Dan Marino by limiting mistakes and providing mobility that Marino lacked. Ex-Jaguar Jay Fiedler, a Dartmouth graduate, picks up offenses quickly and makes few mistakes. They're both likely to play in 2000. Jim Druckenmiller may never develop.

Running Backs — Jimmy Johnson failed in his annual attempt to build a strong ground game. Now new coach Dave Wannstedt will try to rely on talented but injury-prone J. J. Johnson, aged Thurman Thomas and journeyman Lamar Smith. They have a good lead blocker in rookie Deon Dyer and versatile fullback Rob Konrad, but don't expect much improvement on last year's No. 22 ranking in rushing yardage.

Wide Receivers — O. J. McDuffie is an excellent possession receiver, and Tony Martin can still go deep, though he disappeared for big stretches last season. Oronde Gadsden, a good end-zone target, will receive competition from Bert Emanuel for the third receiving position. Emanuel, an offseason free-agent acquisition, was an injury-plagued disappointment in two seasons with Tampa Bay.

Tight Ends — Troy Drayton was waived in a salary-cutting move, though he might be brought back because the Dolphins don't have much else. Miami may sign a veteran before camp starts.

Kicker — Olindo Mare will not match last year's dream season, when he kicked an NFL-record 39 field goals, but he might be the team's best offensive weapon for the second consecutive year.

Defense — Here's another team with a defense that was not as good as its rankings in 1999 — proven decisively by their 62–7 shellacking by Jacksonville in the playoffs. Miami ranked eighth against the run and fifth vs. the pass, but it allowed 21.0 points per game and had just 28 takeaways. One of the top cornerbacks in the NFL, Sam Madison tied for the league lead with seven interceptions. New head coach Dave Wannstedt is a defensive whiz who has his work cut out for him.

Who Gets the Ball — At least four players are serious contenders in the backfield, which means they'll all split time. At wide receiver, Oronde Gadsden, O. J. McDuffie and Tony Martin form a solid troika.

Best Players to Draft — With Dan Marino off this list, wide receiver Tony Martin and kicker Olindo Mare are the only sure things.

MINNESOTA VIKINGS

Who's New — The starting quarterback will be Daunte Culpepper, who didn't throw a pass as a rookie in 1999. Journeyman Bubby Brister is the insurance at quarterback, though he failed in his big chance as Denver's starter in 1999. Doug Chapman, a third-round pick, could see action in the backfield.

Who's Gone — Jeff George, who finished the season as the starting quarterback, signed to be Washington's backup, and look for Randall Cunningham to be released before camp begins. Two players signed with New Orleans: wide receiver Jake Reed and tight end Andrew Glover.

Quarterbacks — The Vikings failed to coerce Randall Cunningham into taking a pay cut. They failed to coax another season out of Dan Marino. They didn't offer Jeff George enough money, so he bolted for Washington. Finally, they settled on last year's No. 1 pick, Daunte Culpepper, who has yet to throw an NFL pass. The Vikings have just handed the keys of their Porsche to a boy who just got his driver's license. Culpepper had better brace himself for a barrage of blitzes. Journeyman Bubby Brister was signed to back up Culpepper, and he'll most likely see ample action.

Running Backs — The Vikings unloaded the power in their effective double-barrel ground game. With Leroy Hoard and his 10 1999 touchdowns gone, Robert Smith figures to get more red zone carries. Smith scored just twice last season, though he gained chunks of yards between the 20s. Hard-running rookie Doug Chapman could become the new goal-line back.

Wide Receivers — The only question is whether Culpepper can get these guys the ball. If so, Randy Moss will lead the league in touch-down catches, and Cris Carter will be right behind. If not, there could be a mutiny on the bounty. Talented Matthew Hatchette replaces Jake Reed as the No. 3 receiver, and there will be no drop-off there.

Tight Ends — Jim Kleinsasser, last year's second-round pick, was moved from tight end to fullback in the midseason. This year, the team wants to utilize him both as a blocking back and as an H-back. Carlester Crumpler is a blocker, not a receiving option.

Kicker — Coming off a perfect 1998 regular season, Gary Anderson struggled through a disappointing 1999, though he still scored 103 points on a high-scoring team. Expect him to bounce back.

Defense — Normally a team with a strong defense, the Vikings were not very good in 1999. Minnesota ranked 27th overall and 30th vs. the pass, allowing 20.3 points per game and forcing just 30 turnovers. Want a better indication? The Vikings can usually be counted upon to rank in the top tier of teams in points scored by their defense, but they had just eight points in 1999. A new staff of assistant coaches could help stem the tide, but salary cap problems didn't allow for much roster maneuvering in the offseason.

Who Gets the Ball — Wide receivers Cris Carter and Randy Moss catch lots of passes, and Robert Smith is the top runner.

Best Players to Draft — Wide receivers Cris Carter and Randy Moss, running back Robert Smith and kicker Gary Anderson.

NEW ENGLAND PATRIOTS

Who's New — The Patriots think Raymont Harris, who was out of football in 1999, will be their featured back, but then they drafted J.R. Redmond in the third round. They'll both battle Kevin Faulk for the job. Ex-Cowboy Eric Bjornson is the new tight end.

Who's Gone — Terry Allen, the 1999 starter at running back, was let go, as were backups Lamont Warren and Jerry Ellison and onetime star tight end Ben Coates. The biggest loss was No. 2 wide receiver Shawn Jefferson, who signed with Atlanta.

Quarterbacks — Put the heat on Drew Bledsoe, and he inevitably starts missing his receivers and throwing interceptions. The Patriots' biggest task for 2000 is rebuilding an offensive line that left Bledsoe bruised and battered under a barrage of 55 sacks last season. Bledsoe threw 13 touchdown passes and just four interceptions through eight games, then he fell apart with six touchdown throws and 17 interceptions in the last half of the season. His pass protection is vital to the team's welfare.

Running Backs — The search continues for a replacement for Robert Edwards, who blew out his knee in the 1999 offseason and isn't ready to return. Former Bear Raymont Harris wasn't the same after breaking his fibula, then he sat out last season. He's a risk, to say the least. Kevin Faulk, last year's top rookie, is too small to play on every down, though he can help on special teams and on third down. Rookie J. R. Redmond could become the starter, but he too may be better suited for a third-down role.

Wide Receivers — It's startling that the Patriots didn't address this deficiency in the offseason. New offensive coordinator Charlie Weis plans to spread the field with four and five receivers, but the Patriots don't have four or five good ones. Terry Glenn is both a talent and a head case. Troy Brown may replace Shawn Jefferson as the other starter, but he's better seeded for a No. 3 role. Tony Simmons is still raw and erratic.

Tight Ends — Eric Bjornson is a quality receiver but a weak blocker. Rod Rutledge is a better blocker. Rookie Dave Stachelski is a project. The Patriots will miss Ben Coates.

Kicker — Adam Vinatieri is adequate, not great. Don't expect much more than 100 points.

Defense — The Patriots ranked 21st vs. the run and seventh vs. the pass in 1999 (eighth overall). Although head coach Pete Carroll has been under fire for two years, his defense isn't much at fault. It scored 24 points, allowed just six rushing TDs and made 42 sacks, led by Willie McGinest (9.0). Still, there's no reason All-Pro DBs Ty Law and Lawyer Millow can't be more dominating and force more turnovers (the team had just 16 interceptions).

Who Gets the Ball — Raymont Harris, Kevin Faulk and rookie J. R. Redmond are competing for the featured-back role, and Terry

Glenn is the top wide receiver.

Best Players to Draft — Quarterback Drew Bledsoe, kicker Adam Vinatieri, and wide receiver Terry Glenn.

NEW ORLEANS SAINTS

Who's New — There are lots of new faces in the Jim Haslett and Randy Mueller era. Former Bengal Jeff Blake was handed the quarterback job after he signed as a free agent. Joe Horn (Chiefs) and Jake Reed (Vikings) might be the two new starting wideouts, and Andrew Glover (another former Viking) will play in two-tight-end sets.

Who's Gone — Quarterbacks Billy Joe Hobert and Danny Wuerffel, running back Lamar Smith, wide receivers Andre Hastings (because he wouldn't accept a salary cut) and Eddie Kennison (traded to Chicago), and tight end Tony Johnson.

Quarterbacks — No team overhauled its offense more this offseason than the Saints, who greatly upgraded their quarterback position by signing Jeff Blake. Although he's occasionally erratic, Blake has career totals of 93 touchdown passes and only 63 interceptions. He puts the deep pass back into the Saints' offense. Career journeyman Billy Joe Tolliver and hometown favorite Jake Delhomme are the backups, but they won't threaten Blake's job security.

Running Backs — Ricky Williams doesn't appear very determined to meet the enormous expectations heaped onto his shoulders. Injuries and a one-dimensional offense bogged down his rookie season. This year, he faces the task of rebuilding his bridges after ripping into his teammates, fans and the organization. Rookie Terrelle Smith is the lead-blocking fullback that Williams lacked in 1999.

Wide Receivers — Jake Reed and Joe Horn upgrade this from a position of weakness into a strength. Reed immediately becomes the No. 1 receiver, and Horn makes big plays and gets open deep. Look for big years from both. Keith Poole gets open and makes the most of his catches, though he's unlikely to match last year's six touchdown catches because he's now the No. 3 receiver.

Tight Ends — Cameron Cleeland regressed in 1999, his second season. Andrew Glover will push Cleeland, who hasn't proven to be durable. Glover, the forgotten man in the Vikings' offense last year, is a better blocker. The team has a good option in two-tight-end sets.

Kicker — Doug Brien's point production is bound to increase due to the much-improved offense. He scored 92 points in a solid 1999 season.

Defense — The New Orleans defense was pretty bad in 1999 — just like the rest of the team. It ranked 20th overall, but that's mostly due to opponents sitting on large leads. Only three teams allowed more points than the Saints (27.1 per game). New Orleans always makes a lot of sacks (45 in '99), but points scored on defense dropped from 58 in 1998 to 12 last year. With No. 1 draft pick Norman Hand and Joe Johnson's predicted comeback, the New Orleans defense will be improved.

Who Gets the Ball — Running back Ricky Williams is the only sure bet, though one of a big group of wideouts is sure to come through with Jeff Blake heaving the ball.

Best Player to Draft — Running back Ricky Williams, quarterback Jeff Blake and wide receiver Jake Reed.

NEW YORK GIANTS

Who's New — The biggest new face (in more ways than one) is No. 1 draft pick Ron Dayne, the Heisman Trophy winner who will be the new starter in the backfield. The other main acquisition was Jason Garrett, who signed from Dallas to be Kerry Collins's backup at quarterback.

Who's Gone — Backup quarterback Kent Graham signed with Pittsburgh, running back Gary Brown wasn't re-signed, wide receiver/kick returner David Patten signed with Cleveland, and kicker Cary Blanchard was no longer needed following Brad Daluiso's return from injury.

Quarterbacks — The Giants are banking on much-maligned Kerry Collins, who showed signs of resurrecting his career in 1999. In just 10 games (seven starts) last year, Collins engineered the team's best passing average in 37 years. However, he also short-circuited the offense with 11 interceptions and 11 fumbles. His backup, ex-Cowboy Jason Garrett, is just that — a backup — and not a threat to take over as the starter. The Giants will have their third opening-day starter in three years.

Running Backs — Rookie Ron Dayne certainly doesn't improve the team's overall lack of speed, but he's a power runner in the Jerome Bettis mold. Dayne hasn't always been durable, but he has always produced. Joe Montgomery, whose injury-plagued 1999 rookie season got off to a late start, promises to battle Dayne for the starting job, though he won't win. Third-down specialist Tiki Barber produced 1,639 all-purpose yards last year.

Wide Receivers — Amani Toomer and Ike Hilliard last year became the first pair of Giants receivers to combine for more than 2,100 yards in a season. Toomer is more of a big-play threat and Hilliard is a possession receiver. There isn't much depth behind them. The Giants may have reached on small-college receiver Ron Dixon in the third round of this year's draft.

Tight Ends — Pete Mitchell is the pass-catching specialist, and Howard Cross is an exceptional blocker. Mitchell, who caught 58 passes last year, is a primary target, but he's not much of a scorer.

Kicker — Brad Daluiso is back after an ACL tear ended his 1999 season after six games. He's solid, not great.

Defense — Here's another average defense that isn't going anywhere. In 1999, the Giants ranked 13th vs. the run and 14th vs. the pass and allowed 358 points. Totals for sacks (32) and takeaways (24) were below average, as was the 18 points scored on defense. Getting Michael Strahan (just 5.5 sacks in '99) back on track will help a lot.

Who Gets the Ball — Rookie running back Ron Dayne, wide receivers Ike Hilliard and Amani Toomer, and tight end Pete Mitchell.

Best Players to Draft — Running back Ron Dayne and wide receiver Amani Toomer.

NEW YORK JETS

Who's New — The first round of the draft brought tight end Anthony Becht and quarterback Chad Pennington, who will back up Vinny Testaverde. A possible steal in the third round was wideout Laveranues Coles, who could wind up starting.

Who's Gone — Star wide receiver Keyshawn Johnson was traded to Tampa Bay for two first-round picks, and neither tight end Eric Green nor backup quarterback Rick Mirer was re-signed.

Quarterbacks — Vinny Testaverde has made a complete comeback from a ruptured Achilles tendon. Now the key is keeping him healthy. It's hard to believe that, with Ray Lucas as the backup, the Jets would draft Chad Pennington in the first round, but Pennington was too good to pass up. Lucas had an exceptional 1999 season in place of Testaverde, but he's an overachiever. Pennington is the long-term solution.

Running Backs — Curtis Martin ran the ball 367 times in 1999, and he might get even more carries this season. Martin is productive and durable — two traits that make a back great. Richie Anderson is an undersized, versatile fullback who has kept promising Jerald Sowell on the bench. Martin's backup, Leon Johnson, may never be the same after tearing most of his knee ligaments in 1999.

Wide Receivers — The Jets will greatly miss Keyshawn Johnson. Wayne Chrebet now becomes the go-to receiver, though he's better-suited for a No. 2 role and it remains to be seen if he can beat double coverage. Dedric Ward is too small to be a starter, so don't be surprised if rookie Laveranues Coles becomes a starter. Coles has exceptional speed, but his commitment is dubious. Also, don't be surprised if the Jets sign a veteran receiver.

Tight Ends — Rookie Anthony Becht fills a gaping hole, so he'll start right away. Becht has well-rounded skills and a great combination of size and hands.

Kicker — John Hall greatly improved his consistency in 1999, his third season. He's one of the NFL's better long-range kickers.

Defense — Losing both Bill Parcells and Bill Belichick can only hurt the Jets' defense. In 1999, New York ranked 21st in total defense; they allowed 309 points, and only four teams gave up more rushing TDs. They also had just 26 sacks, one more than Cleveland's pitiful league low. Marcus Coleman led the team with six interceptions.

Who Gets the Ball — Running back Curtis Martin and wide receiver Wayne Chrebet.

Best Players to Draft — Running back Curtis Martin, quarterback Vinny Testaverde, wide receiver Wayne Chrebet and kicker John Hall.

OAKLAND RAIDERS

Who's New — The biggest surprise in the first round of the draft was Oakland's drafting of kicker Sebastian Janikowski. Otherwise, the offensive additions will be nonfactors.

Who's Gone — Kickers Michael Husted and Joe Nedney are history, and it's good riddance from Raiders fans. Backup quarterback Wade Wilson retired, and tight end Derrick Walker was cut.

Quarterbacks — Rich Gannon is an excellent fit for coach Jon Gruden's West Coast offense. Gannon provides mobility, good decision-making and creative playmaking — all vital traits given the team's shaky pass protection. He was slowed by injuries late last year, yet still finished with 24 touchdown passes. There's a big drop-off between Gannon and backup Bobby Hoying.

Running Backs — The Raiders couldn't have asked for more from this position in 1999. With Napoleon Kaufman better suited for a part-time role, the team signed Tyrone Wheatley midway through training camp. He injected power into the running game and complemented Kaufman perfectly. Fullback Jon Ritchie, an excellent lead blocker, was the team's second-leading receiver last year. The Raiders could use a third-down tailback with better pass-catching skills than Kaufman and Wheatley.

Wide Receivers — Tim Brown remains one of the league's elite receivers, as he is consistently durable and productive. One-dimensional James Jett is a bad fit for the offense. He could lose his starting job to special-teams standout Terry Mickens, Horace Copeland or Jerry Porter, a rookie. Porter is a tremendous but raw talent who may not be ready to play much this season.

Tight Ends — Rickey Dudley had the team concerned with his inconsistent play until the second half of the 1999 season, when he erupted with 26 catches for 370 yards and seven touchdowns. He isn't the steadiest tight end, but he's among the most dangerous.

Kickers — Sebastian Janikowski's booming kicks had NFL personnel directors drooling before the draft, but a rookie kicker is never a lock to succeed as a pro. He's a huge upgrade from last season's free-agent bust, Michael Husted, but don't expect Janikowski to be a franchise savior.

Defense — In 1999, the Raiders ranked 10th on defense (12th vs. both the rush and the pass) and allowed an average of 20.6 points per game — just average statistics. They did score three TDs off a total of 33 takeaways and had 44 sacks, led by Lance Johnstone (10.0) and Darrell Russell (9.5). But no player had more than three interceptions — including star cornerback Charles Woodson, who had just one.

Who Gets the Ball — Running back Tyrone Wheatley, wide receiver Tim Brown and tight end Rickey Dudley.

Best Players to Draft — Wide receiver Tim Brown and tight end Rickey Dudley.

PHILADELPHIA EAGLES

Who's New — Lots of players, but they're basically just a bunch of backups, with tight end Jeff Thomason (acquired in a trade with Green Bay) and running back Stanley Pritchett the most notable. David Akers, who had minimal playing time in 1999, will do the kicking.

Who's Gone — Several veterans were let go: running backs Eric Bieniemy and Kevin Turner, tight ends Jamie Asher and Kassem Sinceno, and kicker Norm Johnson. None was a big factor in 1999.

Quarterbacks — The Eagles patiently broke in McNabb in 1999. Now it's time to show why he was the No. 2 overall pick in the '99 draft. McNabb showed potential as a passer and elusive runner in six starts. He averaged 6.7 yards per carry and threw one more touchdown pass than interceptions. Doug Pederson, last year's opening-day starter, is marginal as a backup.

Running Backs — Duce Staley has almost been the entire Eagles offense for two seasons. Now the team needs to spread the wealth. Staley was the NFC's fourth-leading rusher and the team's second-leading receiver in 1999. Stanley Pritchett was signed to replace Kevin Turner at fullback. Pritchett, who caught 43 passes and scored five touchdowns for Miami last season, will be an often-used receiver in this offense.

Wide Receivers — Charles Johnson is a marginal No. 1 wideout, but he's the best option at a weak position. Don't be surprised if rookie Todd Pinkston replaces Torrance Small at the No. 2 receiving position. The skinny Pinkston needs to bulk up to take the pounding. Second-year player Na Brown is the favorite to become the fourth receiver.

Tight Ends — The Eagles are hoping that Luther Broughton develops into a solid pass receiver. Trade acquisition Jeff Thomason is a much better blocker than pass catcher.

Kicker — Last season, David Akers made three of six field goals, all from 46 yards and beyond, and he also handled kickoff duties. That was enough for the team to waive aging Norm Johnson and name Akers as their starter for this year, though he'll see some competition in training camp.

Defense — Talk about a defense that had its chances. In 1999, the Eagles led the NFL with 46 takeaways (18 fumble recoveries and 28 interceptions) and scored 34 points off five TD returns and two safeties. But they ranked 24th in yards allowed and gave up 357 points — though that was second fewest in the NFC East, believe it or not. Cornerback Troy Vincent tied for the league lead with seven interceptions, and defensive end Mike Mamula finally came through with 8.5 sacks. Defensive tackle Corey Simon, a first-round pick, might be the top rookie defender in 2000.

Who Gets the Ball — Running back Duce Staley. None of the receivers is guaranteed to catch a lot of passes.

Best Players to Draft — Running back Duce Staley (although he never really scores much).

PITTSBURGH STEELERS

Who's New — Kent Graham and late draftee Tee Martin will be the backups to Kordell Stewart at quarterback (and Graham will start if Stewart slumps). Two newcomers will factor in at wide receiver: first-rounder Plaxico Burress and fourth-round sleeper Danny Farmer.

Who's Gone — Both of last year's backup quarterbacks, Mike

Tomczak and Pete Gonzalez.

Quarterbacks — This is Kordell Stewart's final chance to quarterback the Steelers. After showing patience with Stewart during two straight disappointing seasons, the team will have a quick hook if he struggles early. Kent Graham is a journeyman, but he has proven that he can light a spark under a struggling offense. Anthony Wright, a second-year player with good running ability and a strong arm, might get a shot to play in 2001. Tee Martin was a long-term pick.

Running Backs — The Steelers still have plans for Jerome Bettis, even though they made re-signing explosive Richard Huntley an off-season priority. Bettis might be beginning a slow decline, and Huntley will steal some of his playing time. But the two of them form a formidable power/speed tandem. Fullback Jon Witman was a bad replacement last season for Tim Lester, Bettis's former lead blocker.

Wide Receivers — The Steelers have addressed this position with their most recent two first-round draft picks. Rookie Plaxico Burress has the ideal size and speed combination. He could be the Rookie of the Year or a monumental bust, depending on his questionable work ethic and the team's quarterbacking. Troy Edwards set the team's rookie receiving record last season. He's too small to be a true No. 1 receiver, but he can be a good complement to Burress. Hines Ward had a breakthrough 1999 season, but Burress will reduce his playing time.

Tight Ends — Kordell Stewart forgot to look for Mark Bruener in the end zone last season. Bruener was underutilized and probably will be again unless Kent Graham takes over.

Kicker — Kris Brown had an exceptional rookie season, especially given his horrible start in training camp. He scored 105 points and was the AFC's second-most-accurate kicker.

Defense — The Steel Curtain is no more, as too many years of players exiting via free agency have taken their toll. In 1999, the Pittsburgh defense ranked 11th in yards allowed (fourth vs. the pass but 26th against the run) and allowed 20.0 points per game. The defense totaled 39 drops of quarterbacks, but it came up with just 14 interceptions.

Who Gets the Ball — Running back Jerome Bettis. The wide receiving corps is deep, with rookie Plaxico Burress the favorite to be a star.

Best Player to Draft — Running back Jerome Bettis.

ST. LOUIS RAMS

Who's New — Quarterback Trent Green will be back from his injury. And there'll be a battle for the backup job to Marshall Faulk between former Bronco Derek Loville and No. 1 pick Trung Canidate.

Who's Gone — Other than head coach Dick Vermeil, nobody of significance. Amp Lee was the third-down back and Paul Justin was the backup quarterback, though he would've been No. 3 with the return of Trent Green.

Quarterbacks — Cinderella stories just don't get any better. Now Kurt Warner will prove that last season was no fluke. Once considered training camp fodder in Green Bay, Warner replaced the injured Trent Green late in the preseason and promptly threw the second-most touchdown passes in NFL history en route to league and Super Bowl MVP honors. Green is now the second-stringer, though he's certain to be highly sought-after trade bait after this season.

Running Backs — A year ago, the Rams pulled off one of the best trade steals in recent history — a second- and fifth-round draft pick for Marshall Faulk. He ran wild for an NFL-record 2,429 yards from scrimmage — MVP numbers in most seasons. Faulk was too quick and determined to be stopped. Now the Rams face the task of lessening Faulk's load. Dependable free-agent pickup Derek Loville and blazing-fast rookie Trung Canidate will get some carries.

Wide Receivers — The Rams have one of the best receiving trios in the league — as long as Isaac Bruce keeps his hamstrings stretched and not pulled. Torry Holt came on strong as a rookie in 1999. He was the team's most productive postseason receiver, and he'll get the ball more this season. Az-Zahir Hakim is a big-play maker who will have a hard time approaching last year's touchdown total of nine. Ricky Proehl, the No. 4 wideout, adds to an embarrassment of riches.

Tight Ends — Ernie Conwell, the 1998 starter before injuring his knee, figures to regain his starting job from Roland Williams, who filled in admirably last year. Williams is the better receiver, Conwell the better blocker.

Kicker — Had the Rams not done so well in 1999, Jeff Wilkins might have been out of work after making just 20 of 28 field-goal tries. As it is, he could face some competition in camp.

Defense — When you're the No. 1 defense vs. the run, you stand a good chance to go all the way, and the Rams did just that in 1999. The staunch St. Louis defense gave up a league-low four rushing TDs and 74.3 rushing yards per game. It tied for the NFL lead with 57 sacks and only five teams had more than the Rams' 36 takeaways (helped by an NFC-high 29 interceptions). Kevin Carter turned into one of the league's most-feared defenders, as he led the NFL with 17 sacks. The defense scored 50 points, second most in the league.

Who Gets the Ball — Running back Marshall Faulk and wide receivers Isaac Bruce, Torry Holt and Az-Zahir Hakim.

Best Players to Draft — Quarterback Kurt Warner, running back Marshall Faulk, wide receivers Isaac Bruce, Torry Holt and Az-Zahir Hakim, and kicker Jeff Wilkins.

SAN DIEGO CHARGERS

Who's New — Wide receiver Curtis Conway (if he has much left) and running back Robert Chancey (whom the team is high on).

Who's Gone — Two former starters — quarterback Erik Kramer and running back Natrone Means — are gone, but they had already been replaced.

Quarterbacks — Ryan Leaf may never play again — at least, not in San Diego. The Chargers are on the verge of writing him off and counting their enormous losses. Incredibly, untested two-year veteran Moses Mareno might be the opening-day starter. Jim Harbaugh apparently doesn't have enough in his battered body to last through an entire season, so he may end up the backup. Mareno has attempted just 50 career passes.

Running Backs — This is another largely untested area. Jermaine Fazande, who had one huge game as a rookie in 1999, is the starter. He's a 6-foot-2, 262-pound piledriver. Kenny Bynum, the team's top kickoff returner, produced 1,277 all-purpose yards last year, but he's not an every-down answer. Terrell Fletcher, the team's third-leading receiver last season, is a solid third-down back.

Wide Receivers — The Chargers are counting on the old Chicago Bears duo Curtis Conway and Jeff Graham. Conway is a deep threat who cannot stay healthy. Graham is much more productive, but he still drops too many passes. Mikhael Ricks failed to score with 40 catches last season — which is hard to believe from a 6-foot-5, 237-pound target. Charlie Jones, who was slowed by a dislocated hip last year, can get open deep.

Tight Ends — Freddie Jones is one of the league's top tight ends, but not one of the better fantasy tight ends because he doesn't score enough. In three seasons, he has 154 catches but only seven scores.

Kickers — On this sad 1999 offense, it's remarkable that John Carney scored 115 points. He's still one of the top kickers in the league, but it's risky to rely on the Chargers' kicker to be your fantasy starter.

Defense — The Chargers are a bad team, but they have a pretty good defense. In 1999, the Chargers ranked third vs. the run, though

22nd against the pass, and they gave up 19.8 points a game. They need to improve upon their 15 interceptions and 12 fumble recoveries.

Who Gets the Ball — Running back Jermaine Fazande, tight end Freddie Jones and wide receiver Jeff Graham.

Best Player to Draft — Kicker John Carney.

SAN FRANCISCO 49ERS

Who's New — Two rookie quarterbacks — Giovanni Carmazzi (third round) and Tim Rattay (seventh round) — get a chance to replace Steve Young.

Who's Gone — A bunch of backups, most notably quarterback Steve Stenstrom, running back Tommy Vardell and tight end Chad Fann. Quarterback Steve Young will probably retire or play in Denver

Quarterbacks — The minute Steve Young announces his retirement or signs with Denver, the 49ers' rebuilding process will officially begin. Young's presence could elevate the team into the playoff hunt, but Jeff Garcia will more than likely be the starter for at least one year while rookie Giovanni Carmazzi gains seasoning. Garcia spreads the ball around the offense, but he's better suited for a backup role.

Running Backs — Thought to be too fragile, Charlie Garner carried the league's second-most-productive ground game in 1999. He produced 1,764 yards of total offense. Garrison Hearst may fail in his comeback attempt from a broken leg and ligament damage suffered in the 1998 playoffs. Fullback Fred Beasley was a pleasant surprise in 1999, his second season. Beasley is quick through the hole for a fullback, and he has good hands.

Wide Receivers — Jerry Rice appears to be set to play at least one more year, but without Young in the lineup, Rice's production will be modest. Ditto for Terrell Owens and J. J. Stokes, who were underutilized in 1999. Owens became Young's favorite red zone target in 1998, but he was a huge fantasy disappointment last year. So far, at least, Stokes is a career underachiever.

Tight Ends — Greg Clark became increasingly involved in the offense in the second half of 1999, with 23 catches for 248 yards. An effective blocker and sure-handed receiver, Clark is an up-and-comer who needs to score more.

Kickers — Too bad the offense wasn't better. Wade Richey led the league in field-goal accuracy — but he scored just 93 points. Don't expect a big point increase unless Young returns.

Defense — Once the owners of a sturdy defense, the 49ers were awful in 1999. They allowed 453 points — the most ever by a San Francisco team — and ranked 28th in total defense and dead last vs. the pass. While the defense did score a very good total of 32 points, it came up with just 32 sacks and 20 takeaways (just 13 interceptions, six of them by Lance Shulters). The 49ers will never get back to a Super Bowl with this defense, so it can only get better.

Who Gets the Ball — Since Garrison Hearst is still rehabbing from a 1998 injury, pencil in Charlie Garner again at running back. The best wide receiver is still Jerry Rice, although Terrell Owens sees his share of passes, too.

Best Players to Draft — My, how the mighty have fallen! The 49ers used to be prime hunting ground for fantasy football players. There's no longer a sure thing. The best bets are wide receivers Jerry Rice and Terrell Owens and running back Charlie Garner, but none of them is a sure bet to score anywhere near 10 touchdowns.

SEATTLE SEAHAWKS

Who's New — No. 1 pick Shaun Alexander, although he won't replace Ricky Watters at running back just yet. Third-round pick Darrell Jackson and Dee Miller could press for playing time.

Who's Gone — Wide receiver Joey Galloway pretty much forced his way out of town (he was traded to Dallas), and backup running back Ahman Green was sent to Green Bay. Galloway will be missed, but the team did well when he was holding out in 1999.

Quarterbacks — Jon Kitna played like a Pro Bowler for more than half of the 1999 season, then he played like a rookie free agent. The jury is still out on Kitna, who could be pressed by Brock Huard this season. Teams blitzed Kitna heavily in the final six games, and under heavy pressure he threw 10 of his interceptions and just seven TD passes. Glenn Foley is a valuable backup, but coach Mike Holmgren is higher on Huard's ability.

Running Backs — Ricky Watters has proven to be the most durable back in the NFL, with 97 consecutive starts. But wear and tear is starting to slow him down and Shaun Alexander was drafted to be his eventual replacement. If he can pick up blitzes and hang on to the ball, Alexander will get some carries this year.

Wide Receivers — Everything was fine in 1999 — until Joey Galloway ended his holdout and weakened the good chemistry that had developed in the Seattle receiving corps. Derrick Mayes and Sean

TEAM EVALUATIONS

Dawkins both had career years. Mayes, who excels in the red zone, led the team in catches and touchdowns; Dawkins led the Seahawks in receiving yards. Mike Pritchard is the precise route runner who isn't afraid to go over the middle. Rookie Darrell Jackson could play in four-receiver sets.

Tight Ends — Christian Fauria and Itula Mili combined for just 40 catches and one touchdown in 1999 — very un-Holmgrenlike. Look for more production from this position this year.

Kicker — Todd Peterson was a fantasy sleeper with 134 points in 1999. He has scored at least 100 points in four of the last five seasons, and he'll do it again.

Defense — Now that Mike Holmgren has the Seattle offense on track, he needs to get to work on the defense. In 1999, the Seahawks ranked 23rd in defense, though they gave up just 18.6 points a game, not a bad average. Seattle had 38 sacks and came up with 36 takeaways — a league-high 30 of them off interceptions. Though the defense scored 24 points, that's way off their total of 60 in 1998.

Who Gets the Ball — Running back Ricky Watters will carry the load, although rookie first-rounder Shaun Alexander will get some playing time. At wide receiver, Sean Dawkins and Derrick Mayes are the top two, but there's no guarantee they'll repeat their 1999 successes.

Best Players to Draft — Kicker Todd Peterson is solid, while quarterback Jon Kitna, running back Ricky Watters and wide receivers Derrick Mayes and Sean Dawkins will get notice.

TAMPA BAY BUCCANEERS

Who's New — Wide receiver Keyshawn Johnson was the big acquisition, coming in a trade with the Jets for two first-round picks. A few other acquisitions will be backups: quarterback Joe Hamilton (seventh round), running back Jerry Ellison and tight ends Lovett Purnell and James Whalen.

Who's Gone — Quarterback Trent Dilfer signed with Baltimore as a free agent, and wide receiver Bert Emanuel was released.

Quarterbacks — A strong Super Bowl contender is relying on a green second-year quarterback. Shaun King did exceptionally well in six regular-season games and two postseason games as a rookie. However, he ran a low-risk, ultraconservative attack. Now he must assume a bigger role in the offense and get the ball to high-profile Keyshawn Johnson. Eric Zeier, who is capable of getting hot for a game or two, is the backup, but don't be startled if Randall Cunningham signs with the Bucs.

Running Backs — An upgraded line will open holes for a ground game that should rank among the league's best. Mike Alstott, who runs exceptionally hard, will again get more carries than Warrick Dunn, who does not run hard. Dunn, however, was the team's leading receiver in 1999, and he's a matchup nightmare for linebackers. Alstott is in line for his first career 1,000-yard season.

Wide Receivers — Tampa Bay's small, speedy receivers were not a good fit for the team's power-oriented, possession offense in 1999. Enter Keyshawn Johnson, who fits those needs perfectly, as long as Shaun King gets him the ball. Jacquez Green emerged as the team's best wideout in 1999, while Reidel Anthony and Bert Emanuel were disappointments. Darnell McDonald, a player to watch because he has the size the team needs, could push Anthony for the No. 3 receiving role.

Tight Ends — Dave Moore scored five touchdowns with just 23 receptions in 1999. A player often overlooked in fantasy drafts, he has 17 career scores.

Kicker — Martin Gramatica was as good as advertised as a rookie in 1999, and his point total should increase because the offense should improve this season.

Defense — The top defense in the NFC was the main reason the Buccaneers advanced all the way to the conference championship game a year ago. The Bucs ranked third in total defense (fifth vs. the run and second vs. the pass) and allowed the third-fewest points in the NFL. Still one of the top defensive tackles, Warren Sapp made 12.5 sacks in '99, sixth in the league. And cornerback Donnie Abraham tied for the league lead with seven interceptions in 1999.

Who Gets the Ball — Runners Warrick Dunn and Mike Alstott share the load in the backfield, and trade acquisition Keyshawn Johnson is easily the top wide receiver.

Best Players to Draft — Wide receiver Keyshawn Johnson, running back Mike Alstott and kicker Martin Gramatica.

TENNESSEE TITANS

Who's New — Erron Kinney, a third-round pick, will probably be the new No. 2 tight end. Otherwise, the Titans tried to keep the nucleus of their AFC championship team intact.

Who's Gone — Backup tight end Jackie Harris signed with Dallas.

Quarterbacks — Steve McNair proved that he can do more than hand the ball off and scramble for first downs. His leadership intangibles surfaced during the Super Bowl run. McNair won't ever lead the league in passing, but his touchdown runs make him a fantasy star. In eight games (five starts) in place of the injured McNair last year, Neil O'Donnell provided the low-risk underneath passing that fits the Titans like a glove.

Running Backs — When Eddie George gets on track, the Titans usually win. The team is 20–5 when George rushes for 100 or more yards. In four seasons, George has 5,365 yards. After scoring 21 TDs in his first three seasons, George scored 13 last year behind the lead blocking of Lorenzo Neal, an underrated 1999 free-agent pickup. Rodney Thomas is a good backup whose playing time is robbed by George's durability.

Wide Receivers — Kevin Dyson is due for a breakthrough year, but Yancey Thigpen can't stay healthy enough to make a big impact. Steve McNair failed to throw a touchdown pass in six consecutive games last season, and Thigpen missed five of them. He's still the team's top receiver. Chris Sanders still drops too many passes.

Tight Ends — Frank Wycheck, who excels at getting open underneath the coverage, is always the team's primary receiving target, though he doesn't score much. The departure of Jackie Harris prompted the team to draft Erron Kinney. He has great size and hands, and will play a key role as the No. 2 tight end.

Kicker — Al Del Greco is a high-percentage kicker who always scores well, even in years when the team's offense struggles.

Defense — The Titans may have been the AFC champions in 1999, but they didn't have close to the conference's best defense. They allowed 324 points — better than only five teams in the conference. In yardage, they were 17th overall (10th vs. the pass but 25th vs. the run). Still, there were some bright spots. They had 54 sacks (third in the NFL) and 40 takeaways (again third, and 13 of them from Jacksonville). "The Freak," Jevon Kearse, was the NFL's leading rookie sacker with 14.5 in 1999, fourth in the league.

Who Gets the Ball — Running back Eddie George, tight end Frank Wycheck and wide receivers Yancey Thigpen and Kevin Dyson.

Best Players to Draft — Running back Eddie George, quarterback Steve McNair, kicker Al Del Greco and tight end Frank Wycheck.

WASHINGTON REDSKINS

Who's New — Backup quarterback Jeff George (from Minnesota) and Adrian Murrell (from Arizona) could be valuable backups. Owner Daniel Snyder is breaking the bank in an effort to buy a Super Bowl title.

Who's Gone — Only backup quarterbacks Rodney Peete and

Casey Weldon, but their replacement (George) is a huge upgrade.

Quarterbacks — Fragile during his days with the Vikings, Brad Johnson stayed healthy in 1999. Not convinced he'll do it again, the Redskins signed Jeff George. Johnson had an excellent 1999 season, with 24 touchdown passes and 13 picks. But there is a sense of urgency to win right now, so you can bet there will be a quick hook should Johnson struggle at all. George stepped in for a struggling Randall Cunningham last season and helped rescue the Vikings.

Running Backs — The Redskins and Stephen Davis haggled over a long-term contract throughout the offseason. They signed Adrian Murrell as insurance in the unlikely but increasingly possible event of a Davis holdout. Last year, Davis beat out Skip Hicks in training camp for the starting job, then he proceeded to lead the NFL with 17 touchdown runs. Hicks, who scored eight touchdowns in 1998, is now a third-stringer. Fullback Larry Centers caught a team-high 69 passes last year, and the team wants to get him even more involved in the offense.

Wide Receivers — Michael Westbrook and Albert Connell are both coming off breakthrough seasons in which they gained more than 1,000 receiving yards. Connell is more of a deep threat, and Westbrook is a bigger target. The Redskins talked Irving Fryar out of retirement last year, and he'll return this season to the No. 3 receiving role.

Tight Ends — Stephen Alexander got off to a quick start but struggled through a disappointing 1999 season in which he practically disappeared from the offense. He should bounce back. James Jenkins is a blocker only.

Kicker — Brett Conway has never lived up to his potential, and he faces competition in camp from Peter Elezovic after making just 22 of 32 field goals in 1999. This battle bears close scruitiny, because who-ever kicks for this team should be a fantasy starter.

Defense — If the Redskins think they're ever going to go to the Super Bowl, they have to improve their defense — a lot. In 1999, they ranked 30th of 31 teams in yards allowed and gave up 377 points, fifth worst in the league. While they had 40 sacks, 37 takeaways and 24 defensive points — very good numbers — and the top rookie defender in cornerback Champ Bailey, they can't continue to give up so many points and keep winning. That's why the Redskins drafted Lavar Arrington, signed Bruce Smith and hired Ray Rhodes as the offensive coordinator.

Who Gets the Ball — Running back Stephen Davis, and wide receivers Michael Westbrook and Albert Connell

Best Players to Draft — Running back Stephen Davis, quarterback Brad Johnson, wide receivers Michael Westbrook and Albert Connell, and whoever wins the placekicking job.

Chapter 10

DEPTH CHARTS

Here are each team's depth charts as of mid-May. Some players are still listed with the teams they played for in 1999 if they have not yet signed with another team.

For example, the Cincinnati Bengals are most likely not going to have Carl Pickens back in 2000 because of his high salary (and after they drafted two top rookies). But because Pickens is one of the best wide receivers in the NFL, he's still listed in Cincinnati's roster because he should still be considered for most fantasy drafts (depending on what team he ends up with). ("R-1" designates a rookie drafted in the first round, etc.)

ARIZONA CARDINALS

Quarterbacks — Jake Plummer, Dave Brown, Chris Greisen
Running Backs — Thomas Jones (R-1), Mario Bates, Michael Pittman, Joel Makovicka, Dennis McKinley
Wide Receivers — Rob Moore, Frank Sanders, David Boston, Andy McCullough, Ronnie Anderson
Tight Ends — Chris Gedney, Terry Hardy, Johnny McWilliams, Derek Brown, Jay Tant (R-5)
Kicker — Cary Blanchard

ATLANTA FALCONS

Quarterbacks — Chris Chandler, Danny Kanell, Tony Graziani, Wally Richardson, Doug Johnson (R)
Running Backs — Jamal Anderson, Byron Hanspard, Ken Oxendine, Jeff Paulk, Bob Christian, Winslow Oliver
Wide Receivers — Terance Mathis, Shawn Jefferson, Tim Dwight, Chris Calloway, Ronnie Harris, Jammi German, Eugene Baker, Kamil Loud, Mareno Philyaw (R-6)
Tight Ends — O. J. Santiago, Reggie Kelly, Brian Kozlowski, Brian Saxton, Rod Monroe
Kicker — Morten Andersen

BALTIMORE RAVENS

Quarterbacks — Tony Banks, Trent Dilfer, Chris Redman (R-3), Stoney Case

Running Backs — Jamal Lewis (R-1), Priest Holmes, Jay Graham, Charles Evans

Wide Receivers — Travis Taylor (R-1), Qadry Ismail, Patrick Johnson, Jermaine Lewis, Brandon Stokley, Justin Armour, Billy Davis, James Roe, Ryan Collins

Tight Ends — Shannon Sharpe, Greg DeLong, A. J. Ofodile

Kicker — Matt Stover

BUFFALO BILLS

Quarterbacks — Rob Johnson, Doug Flutie, Alex Van Pelt

Running Backs — Antowain Smith, Jonathan Linton, Shawn Bryson, Lennox Gordon

Wide Receivers — Eric Moulds, Peerless Price, Avion Black (R-4), Drew Haddas (R-7), Jeremy McDaniel

Tight Ends — Jay Riemersma, Bobby Collins, Sheldon Jackson

Kicker — Steve Christie

CAROLINA PANTHERS

Quarterbacks — Steve Beuerlein, Jeff Lewis, Dameyune Craig

Running Backs — Tim Biakabutuka, Natrone Means, William Floyd, Anthony Johnson, Chris Hetherington

Wide Receivers — Muhsin Muhammad, Patrick Jeffers, Donald Hayes, Karl Hankton, Jim Turner

Tight Ends — Wesley Walls, Brian Kinchen, Kris Mangrum

Kicker — John Kasay

CHICAGO BEARS

Quarterbacks — Cade McNown, Jim Miller, Shane Matthews
Running Backs — Curtis Enis, James Allen, Glyn Milburn, Frank Murphy (R-6), Chad Levitt
Wide Receivers — Marcus Robinson, Bobby Engram, Dez White (R-3), Eddie Kennison, Macey Brooks, Marty Booker, D'Wayne Bates
Tight Ends — Alonzo Mayes, Ryan Wetnight, Dustin Lyman (R-3), John Allred
Kicker — Paul Edinger (R-6), Jaret Holmes, Jeff Jaeger

CINCINNATI BENGALS

Quarterbacks — Akili Smith, Scott Mitchell, Scott Covington, Eric Kresser
Running Backs — Corey Dillon, Ki-Jana Carter, Michael Basnight, Nick Williams, Sedrick Shaw, Custis Keaton (R-4)
Wide Receivers — Peter Warrick (R-1), Carl Pickens, Darnay Scott, Ron Dugans (R-3), James Hundon, Craig Yeast, Damon Griffin
Tight Ends — Tony McGee, Marco Battaglia, Brad St. Louis (R-7), Steve Bush
Kicker — Doug Pelfrey, Neil Rackers (R-6)

CLEVELAND BROWNS

Quarterbacks — Tim Couch, Ty Detmer, Spergon Wynn (R-6)
Running Backs — Errict Rhett, Terry Kirby, Travis Prentice (R-3), Marc Edwards, Madre Hill, Tarek Saleh
Wide Receivers — Kevin Johnson, Darrin Chiaverini, Dennis Northcutt (R-2), David Patten, JaJuan Dawson (R-3), Zola Davis, Damon Dunn
Tight Ends — Mark Campbell, Aaron Shea (R-4), James Dearth
Kicker — Phil Dawson

DALLAS COWBOYS

Quarterbacks — Troy Aikman, Paul Justin, Charles Puleri
Running Backs — Emmitt Smith, Chris Warren, Daryl Johnston (might retire or be cut), Robert Thomas, Beau Morgan
Wide Receivers — Joey Galloway, Raghib Ismail, Michael Irvin (will probably retire), Wane McGarity, Jeff Ogden, Jason Tucker, Michael Wiley (R-5), Morris Anderson
Tight Ends — David LaFleur, Jackie Harris, Brian Roche, Mike Lucky
Kicker — Tim Sedler, Jaret Greaser

DENVER BRONCOS

Quarterbacks — Brian Griese, Gus Frerotte, Jarious Jackson (R-7)
Running Backs — Terrell Davis, Olandis Gary, Howard Griffith, Detron Smith, Anthony Lynn, Mike Anderson (R-6)
Wide Receivers — Rod Smith, Ed McCaffrey, Chris Cole (R-3), Billy Miller, Andre Cooper, Travis McGriff, Muneer Moore (R-5), Chris Doering, Leroy Fields (R-7)
Tight Ends — Dwayne Carswell, Byron Chamberlain, Desmond Clark
Kicker — Jason Elam

DETROIT LIONS

Quarterbacks — Charlie Batch, Mike Tomczak, Steve Stenstrom, Cory Sauter
Running Backs — James Stewart, Cory Schlesinger, Sedrick Irvin, Reuben Droughns (R-3), Travis Reece
Wide Receivers — Herman Moore, Johnnie Morton, Germane Crowell, Desmond Howard, Iheanyi Uwaezuoke
Tight Ends — David Sloan, Tony Johnson, Walter Rasby, Pete Chryplewicz, Ed Smith
Kicker — Jason Hanson

GREEN BAY PACKERS

Quarterbacks — Brett Favre, Matt Hasselbeck, Aaron Brooks
Running Backs — Dorsey Levens, Ahman Green, DeMond Parker, William Henderson, Rondell Mealey (R-7), Basil Mitchell
Wide Receivers — Antonio Freeman, Bill Schroeder, Corey Bradford, Anthony Lucas (R-4), Joey Jamison (R-5), Charles Lee (R-7), Donald Driver
Tight Ends — Bubba Franks (R-1), Mark Chmura, Tyrone Davis, Kaseem Sinceno
Kickers — Ryan Longwell

INDIANAPOLIS COLTS

Quarterbacks — Peyton Manning, Pete Gonzalez, Kelly Holcomb
Running Backs — Edgerrin James, Fred Lane, Leeland McElroy, Keith Elias, Scott Greene, Paul Shields
Wide Receivers — Marvin Harrison, E. G. Green, Jerome Pathon, Terrence Wilkins, Chad Plummer, Isaac Jones
Tight Ends — Ken Dilger, Marcus Pollard, Bradford Banta
Kickers — Mike Vanderjagt

JACKSONVILLE JAGUARS

Quarterbacks — Mark Brunell, Jonathan Quinn, Jamie Martin
Running Backs — Fred Taylor, Stacey Mack, Chris Howard, Daimon Shelton, Shyrone Stith (R-7), Tavian Banks
Wide Receivers — Jimmy Smith, Keenan McCardell, R. Jay Soward (R-1), Reggie Barlow, Emanuel Smith (R-6), Alvis Whitted, Lenzie Jackson
Tight Ends — Kyle Brady, Damon Jones, Rich Griffith
Kicker — Mike Hollis

KANSAS CITY CHIEFS

Quarterbacks — Elvis Grbac, Warren Moon, Todd Collins, Ted White
Running Backs — Donnell Bennett, Mike Cloud, Rashaan Shehee, Kimble Anders, Frank Moreau (R-4), Dante Hall (R-5), Tony Richardson
Wide Receivers — Derrick Alexander, Sylvester Morris (R-1), Kevin Lockett, Larry Parker, Kirby Dar Dar, Desmond Kitchings (R-7)
Tight Ends — Tony Gonzales, Mitch Jacoby
Kicker — Pete Stoyanovich

MIAMI DOLPHINS

Quarterbacks — Damon Huard, Jay Fiedler, Jim Druckenmiller, Scott Zolak
Running Backs — J. J. Johnson, Thurman Thomas, Lamar Smith, Rob Konrad, Autry Denson, Brian Edwards, Deon Dyer (R-4)
Wide Receivers — Tony Martin, O. J. McDuffie, Oronde Gadsden, Bert Emanuel, Yatil Green, Lamar Thomas, Nate Jacquet, Kevin McKenzie
Tight Ends — Hunter Goodwin, Ed Perry, Hayward Clay
Kickers — Olindo Mare

MINNESOTA VIKINGS

Quarterbacks — Daunte Culpepper, Bubby Brister, Todd Bouman
Running Backs — Robert Smith, Moe Williams, Jim Kleinsasser, Doug Chapman (R-3), Harold Morrow, David Palmer, John Henry Mills
Wide Receivers — Randy Moss, Cris Carter, Matthew Hatchette, Chris Walsh, Troy Walters (R-5)
Tight Ends — Andrew Jordan, Chad Fann, Carlester Crumpler, Giles Cole (R-7)
Kickers — Gary Anderson

NEW ENGLAND PATRIOTS

Quarterbacks — Drew Bledsoe, John Friesz, Michael Bishop, Tom Brady (R-6)
Running Backs — Raymont Harris, Kevin Faulk, J. R. Redmond (R-3), Tony Carter, Chris Floyd, Patrick Pass (R-7)
Wide Receivers — Terry Glenn, Troy Brown, Tony Simmons, Vincent Brisby, Aaron Bailey, Sean Morey
Tight Ends — Eric Bjornson, Rod Rutledge, Dave Stachelski (R-5)
Kicker — Adam Vinatieri

NEW ORLEANS SAINTS

Quarterbacks — Jeff Blake, Billy Joe Tolliver, Jake Delhomme, Marc Bulger (R-6)
Running Backs — Ricky Williams, Troy Davis, Terrelle Smith (R-4), Chad Morton (R-5), Wilmont Perry, Dino Philyaw, Marvin Powell
Wide Receivers — Jake Reed, Joe Horn, Keith Poole, Sherrod Gideon (R-6), P. J. Franklin, Brett Bech, Danan Hughes, Ryan Thelwell, Robert Wilson
Tight Ends — Cam Cleeland, Andrew Glover, Scott Slutzker, Josh Wilcox, Austin Wheatley (R-5), Kevin Houser (R-7)
Kicker — Doug Brien

NEW YORK GIANTS

Quarterbacks — Kerry Collins, Jason Garrett, Mike Cherry
Running Backs — Ron Dayne (R-1), Joe Montgomery, Charles Way, Tiki Barber, Sean Bennett, Greg Comella, LeShon Johnson
Wide Receivers — Ike Hilliard, Amani Toomer, Ron Dixon (R-3), Joe Jurevicius, Brian Alford
Tight Ends — Pete Mitchell, Howard Cross, Dan Campbell
Kicker — Brad Daluiso

NEW YORK JETS

Quarterbacks — Vinny Testaverde, Chad Pennington (R-1), Ray Lucas, Tom Tupa, Jim Kubiak

Running Backs — Curtis Martin, Richie Anderson, Leon Johnson, Bernie Parmalee, Jerald Sowell

Wide Receivers — Wayne Chrebet, Laveranues Coles (R-3), Dedric Ward, Wendell Hayes (R-5), Quinn Early, Dwight Stone

Tight Ends — Anthony Becht (R-1), Fred Baxter, Blake Spence

Kicker — John Hall

OAKLAND RAIDERS

Quarterbacks — Rich Gannon, Bobby Hoying, Craig Whelihan, Scott Dreisbach

Running Backs — Tyrone Wheatley, Napoleon Kaufman, Zack Crockett, Jon Ritchie, Jerald Moore, Randy Jordan, Jermaine Williams

Wide Receivers — Tim Brown, James Jett, Jerry Porter (R-2), Terry Mickens, Horace Copeland, David Dunn, Larry Shannon, Kenny Shedd, Rodney Williams

Tight Ends — Rickey Dudley, Jeremy Brigham, John Burke, Chris Fontenot, Mondriel Fulcher (R-7)

Kicker — Sebastian Janikowski (R-1)

PHILADELPHIA EAGLES

Quarterbacks — Donovan McNabb, Doug Pederson, Koy Detmer, Ron Powlus

Running Backs — Duce Staley, Stanley Pritchett, Cecil Martin, Darnell Autry, Thomas Hamner (R-6), Edwin Watson

Wide Receivers — Charles Johnson, Todd Pinkston (R-2), Torrance Small, Gari Scott (R-4), Na Brown, Dietrich Jells, Troy Smith, Dameane Douglas

Tight Ends — Chad Lewis, Luther Broughton, Jeff Thomason, Jed Weaver, Mike Bartrum, Erik Stocz

Kicker — David Akers

PITTSBURGH STEELERS

Quarterbacks — Kordell Stewart, Kent Graham, Tee Martin (R-5), Anthony Wright

Running Backs — Jerome Bettis, Richard Huntley, Chris Fuamatu-Ma'afala, Amos Zereoue, Jon Witman

Wide Receivers — Plaxico Burress (R-1), Troy Edwards, Hines Ward, Danny Farmer (R-4), Will Blackwell, David Dunn, Bobby Shaw, Malcolm Johnson

Tight Ends — Mark Bruener, Mitch Lyons, Jerame Tuman, Jason Gavadza (R-6), Tony Cline, Matt Cushing

Kicker — Kris Brown

ST. LOUIS RAMS

Quarterbacks — Kurt Warner, Trent Green, Joe Germaine

Running Backs — Marshall Faulk, Trung Canidate (R-1), Derek Loville, Robert Holcombe, James Hodgins, Justin Watson

Wide Receivers — Isaac Bruce, Torry Holt, Az-zahir Hakim, Ricky Proehl, Tony Horne

Tight Ends — Ernie Conwell, Roland Williams, Jeff Robinson

Kicker — Jeff Wilkins

SAN DIEGO CHARGERS

Quarterbacks — Jim Harbaugh, Moses Moreno, Ryan Leaf, JaJuan Seider (R-6), Sherdrick Bonner

Running Backs — Jermaine Fazande, Terrell Fletcher, Kenny Bynum, Fred McCrary

Wide Receivers — Curtis Conway, Jeff Graham, Mikhael Ricks, Charlie Jones, Chris Penn, Trevor Gaylor (R-4)

Tight Ends — Freddie Jones, Steve Heiden

Kickers — John Carney

SAN FRANCISCO 49ERS

Quarterbacks — Jeff Garcia, Steve Young (will either retire or be traded), Giovanni Carmazzi (R-3), Tim Rattay (R-7), Pat Barnes

Running Backs — Garrison Hearst, Charlie Garner, Fred Beasley, Terry Jackson, Travis Jervey, Paul Smith (R-5)

Wide Receivers — Jerry Rice, Terrell Owens, J. J. Stokes, Mark Harris, Tai Streets

Tight Ends — Greg Clark, Shonn Bell, Brian Jennings (R-7), Joe Zelenka

Kickers — Wade Richey

SEATTLE SEAHAWKS

Quarterbacks — Jon Kitna, Glenn Foley, Brock Huard

Running Backs — Ricky Watters, Shaun Alexander (R-1), Mack Strong, Reggie Brown, Brian Milne

Wide Receivers — Sean Dawkins, Derrick Mayes, Mike Pritchard, Darrell Jackson (R-3), Fabien Bownes, James Williams (R-6), Karsten Bailey, Charlie Rogers

Tight Ends — Christian Fauria, Itula Mili, Deems May, Grant Williams

Kicker — Todd Peterson

TAMPA BAY BUCCANEERS

Quarterbacks — Shaun King, Eric Zeier, Joe Hamilton (R-7), Scott Milanovich

Running Backs — Warrick Dunn, Mike Alstott, Jerry Ellison, Fred McAfee, Kevin McLeod, Rabih Abdullah

Wide Receivers — Keyshawn Johnson, Reidel Anthony, Jacquez Green, Karl Williams, Darnell McDonald

Tight Ends — Dave Moore, Patrick Hape, John Davis, Lovett Purnell, James Whalen (R-5)

Kicker — Martin Gramatica

TENNESSEE OILERS

Quarterbacks — Steve McNair, Neil O'Donnell, Kevin Daft
Running Backs — Eddie George, Rodney Thomas, Lorenzo Neal, Spencer George, Mike Green (R-7)
Wide Receivers — Yancey Thigpen, Kevin Dyson, Chris Sanders, Isaac Byrd, Derrick Mason, Joey Kent
Tight Ends — Frank Wycheck, Erron Kinney (R-3), Michael Roan, Larry Brown
Kicker — Al Del Greco

WASHINGTON REDSKINS

Quarterbacks — Brad Johnson, Jeff George, Todd Husak (R-6)
Running Backs — Stephen Davis, Adrian Murrell, Skip Hicks, Larry Centers, Mike Sellers, Larry Bowie
Wide Receivers — Michael Westbrook, Albert Connell, Irving Fryar, James Thrash, Derrius Thompson, Ethan Howell (R-7)
Tight Ends — Stephen Alexander, James Jenkins
Kicker — Brett Conway, Peter Elezovic

BEST AVAILABLE PLAYERS

(1999 team listed in parentheses)

Quarterbacks — Randall Cunningham (Vikings), Rodney Peete (Redskins), Steve Walsh (Colts), Erik Kramer (Chargers), Billy Joe Hobert (Saints), Steve Bono (Panthers), Danny Wuerffel (Saints), Rick Mirer (Jets), Casey Weldon (Redskins)

Running Backs — Terry Allen (Patriots), Leroy Hoard (Vikings), Gary Brown (Giants), Sam Gash (Bills), Darick Holmes (Colts), Cecil Collins (Dolphins), Eric Bieniemy (Eagles), Amp Lee (Rams), Edgar Bennett (Bears), Kevin Turner (Eagles)

Wide Receivers — Leslie Shepherd (Browns), Andre Hastings (Saints), Ernie Mills (Cowboys), Andre Reed (Bills), Courtney Hawkins (Steelers), Eric Metcalf (Panthers), Willie Jackson (Bengals), Lake Dawson (Colts)

Tight Ends — Ben Coates (Patriots), Troy Drayton (Dolphins), Eric Green (Jets), Irv Smith (Browns), Jamie Asher (Eagles), Chad Fann (49ers)

Kicker — Richie Cunningham (Panthers), Chris Jacke (Cardinals), Norm Johnson (Eagles), Michael Husted (Raiders), Joe Nedney (Raiders)

Chapter 11

FANTASY RANKINGS

Pick a running back . . . and then pick a running back . . . and then draft another one just in case one of your starters bombs out or blows out his knee. OK, that's an exaggeration. But the point is vital. There is so much uncertainty and so little depth at running back this yar that the fate of your team largely hinges on your success at that position. Your odds of getting six touchdowns are much greater from the 30th-ranked wide receiver than from the 30th-ranked running back.

The quarterback position is top-heavy, with three sure bets and a large group of question marks and players with a skeleton in their closet. If you don't get Kurt Warner, Peyton Manning or Brett Favre, draft one or two running backs and a receiver before taking a quarterback.

It's worth drafting a tight end in the first four rounds — provided you get your hands on Tony Gonzalez, Wesley Walls, Rickey Dudley or Shannon Sharpe. Otherwise, wait until at least the sixth or seventh round. Don't get swept up into an early run on kickers — the guy you draft in Round 8 is nearly as likely to lead the league in scoring as the first kicker taken. Remember, in the 10 years of the 1990s, 10 different players were the highest-scoring kicker in the league.

Here is a look at the five positions, with the rankings made on the basis of a combined scoring system.

Quarterbacks — Kurt Warner won't do it again, you say? With all of those weapons in his arsenal, why can't he? He has three good receivers, the league's best all-purpose back and two good tight ends to pass to. Warner probably won't throw another 41 touchdown passes, but he's the most likely pick to lead the league in TD throws. Peyton Manning has thrown 26 touchdown passes in each of his first two seasons. He'd be right up there with Warner if the Colts had better receivers to complement Marvin Harrison. Brett Favre is the most durable quarterback in recent NFL history, but he's coming off a season in which he heaped too much pressure onto his own shoulders to carry an entire team. He doesn't have as many reliable receivers as he had during the Packers' Super Bowl years.

If you don't draft one of these three, wait to get your quarterback. This position might be the weakest it has been in a decade. Questions surround every other quarterback. Steve McNair gets the No. 4 ranking almost by default. McNair is durable and he's the top running quarterback, which raises his value a lot. In leagues that award three points per touchdown pass, one McNair touchdown run (he had eight last year) is worth two touchdown throws.

On the surface, Brad Johnson seems like a safe choice, but he plays for a meddlesome, impatient owner who might replace him with Jeff George if the team struggles early in the season. And, remember, Johnson had never been very durable before last year. Durability is a question which now accompanies Vinny Testaverde in his comeback from Achilles tendon surgery.

Drew Bledsoe is durable, but he has just one good receiver, Terry Glenn. That won't help him.

Steve Beuerlein won't repeat his career year of 1999, but he does run a passing offense with three fine receivers.

Jon Kitna could well be this year's Steve Beuerlein, with thirtysomething touchdown passes. Kitna, however, has not yet earned the confidence of coach Mike Holmgren. But he's a good gamble.

With a new offense and a new go-to receiver in Joey Galloway, Dallas' Troy Aikman appears headed for a career year.

If Steve Young goes to Denver, he's a top eight pick — much better than he would be if he rides along for one more year in San Francisco.

Strongly consider drafting a backup quarterback in a late round. Of the nine quarterbacks who threw 20 or more TD passes in 1999, seven of them (Warner, Beuerlein, George, Johnson, Elvis Grbac, Rich Gannon and Kitna) would not have been drafted as fantasy starters. And look what they did. That's why you don't have to draft a quarterback so early.

Running Backs — There's no such thing as a given — Terrell Davis and Jamal Anderson proved that last year. But Edgerrin James is highly likely to score more than 10 touchdowns. Fred Taylor will score 15 to 20 touchdowns if he stays healthy, something he failed to do in his first two pro seasons. Marshall Faulk and Emmitt Smith were two of the most durable, productive backs in the league in the 1990s, so they're safe picks, too.

Then the fun begins. Davis appears to be ready for a strong comeback season, but remember, he struggled before his 1999 injury because teams no longer had to worry about John Elway and stacked the line to stuff the run. Davis will need some help from his quarterbacks to share the offensive load.

Jamal Anderson — like Davis — is making a quick recovery from knee surgery, but will he be the workhorse he was before the injury?

Eddie George and Dorsey Levens are solid, reliable picks, especially in a performance or combined scoring league. But George averaged just seven touchdowns a season before last year, because Steve McNair is just as likely to run the ball near the goal line.

Stephen Davis's prospects are clouded by a potential holdout, though the Redskins appear determined to avoid that.

If only Corey Dillon and Duce Staley were on good teams . . . their stock would be much higher.

The running back position is deeper through about 18 players than in recent years, but after the top 24, it's a real crapshoot. In other words, load up early and often, and forget about your second and third receivers until you have two or three good backs.

Without Leroy Hoard around hogging all of the goal-line carries, Robert Smith should have a career year scoring-wise this year.

Finally, don't forget about the rookies — Thomas Jones, Jamal Lewis and Ron Dayne are almost certain to start from Week 1. If J. R. Redmond wins New England's starting job in camp, he could be a sleeper pick.

Wide Receivers — This is the deepest position in the draft, so use that to your advantage. There are a few sure bets to carry your team, several other solid picks, and then a large drop-off to a large group of about 35 or more players who could score anywhere from three to 10 TDs.

Why rank Marvin Harrison ahead of Randy Moss, who is unquestionably the better player? Because Peyton Manning is Harrison's quarterback, while untested Daunte Culpepper faces a monumental task trying to get the ball to Moss and Cris Carter enough. Case closed.

Consider a wide receiver's quarterback situation before drafting him. Shaun King to Keyshawn Johnson, and Culpepper to Carter and Moss? Please. Denver has a good pair of receivers in Ed McCaffrey and Rod Smith, but who's going to be the quarterback and will he be any good?

Thoughts to ponder: Will Jimmy Smith ever score 10 touchdowns? Will Isaac Bruce's hamstrings hold up for the second straight year. And who's the odd man out of Detroit's starting lineup — Herman Moore or Johnnie Morton?

Joey Galloway and Keyshawn Johnson are intriguing possibilities for Rounds 2 or 3 as they adjust to a new team.

Can Jerry Rice rebound (don't count him out yet, though he's in that third, big group of iffy receivers). Watch where Carl Pickens ends up (possibly with the Jets), because on the right team he is capable of a

10-touchdown, 1,000-yard season.

If only Peter Warrick were on a good team, he'd be an early-rounder.

Tight Ends — A moot point, you say? I play in a 16-team league that utilizes three starting wide receivers and no tight end position (a bad idea, I believe). With all of those receivers on rosters in 1999, nobody drafted Tony Gonzalez. I picked him up a few weeks into the season and rode him (and Emmitt Smith) into the championship game.

Gonzalez and Wesley Walls are clearly the top two, with Rickey Dudley and Shannon Sharpe not far behind. After that, don't expect more than a few scores from anybody, so don't draft any of them before Round 6 at the earliest. A couple of the others will score six or seven times, but it's only a guess which ones they'll be. If you're looking for a tight end in line for a breakout year, it's Stephen Alexander. Ernie Conwell — a player many fans forgot about because an injury sidelined most of his 1999 Super Bowl season — is worth a last-round gamble, because he'll start in a high-octane offense.

What about Mark Chmura and Ben Coates, two of the best in recent years? Follow Coates especially, because he might have a year or two left. As for Chmura, how do the color "orange" and prison dregs sound?

Kicker —What's the rush? Last season, 19 kickers scored 103 or more points. And the highest-scoring kicker of 1998 — Gary Anderson — was 19th. That tells you that this is a very deep, solid group and that it's a crapshoot trying to predict which guy will lead the league. Two of the most likely choices to lead the league — Mike Hollis and Jason Elam — could be outscored by the 15th-ranked kicker.

Nervertheless, don't wait too late in your draft to get a kicker. If you can get one of the top seven without reaching into the fifth or sixth round, go for it. Another strategy is to take two good ones in the middle to late rounds and play the odds every week. That adds an element of fun — and aggravation — to making out your weekly lineup.

Questions surround a few of the aging kickers, such as Gary Anderson, Morten Andersen and Jeff Jaeger. Don't forget about considering new kickers on high-scoring teams, such as Peter Elezovic (if he makes the Redskins) and Paul Edinger (Bears). Finally, don't reach for Sebastian Janikowski, as the Raiders did.

Overall — Bring a copy of the NFL schedule to your fantasy draft so that you can keep track of bye weeks. A bye week no longer includes several teams from the same division. With the byes now spread out over the course of the season, there is no reason to draft four or five players who will sit out the same week.

Most of all, pay attention in the middle and late rounds, when fantasy championships are won and lost.

Based upon 75% touchdowns, 25% yards and 5% distance

QUARTERBACKS	RUNNING BACKS
❏ 1. Kurt Warner, Rams	❏ 1. Edgerrin James, Colts
❏ 2. Peyton Manning, Colts	❏ 2. Fred Taylor, Jaguars
❏ 3. Brett Favre, Packers	❏ 3. Marshall Faulk, Rams
❏ 4. Steve McNair, Titans	❏ 4. Terrell Davis, Broncos
❏ 5. Brad Johnson, Redskins	❏ 5. Emmitt Smith, Cowboys
❏ 6. Steve Beuerlein, Panthers	❏ 6. Eddie George, Titans
❏ 7. Vinny Testaverde, Jets	❏ 7. Dorsey Levens, Packers
❏ 8. Mark Brunell, Jaguars	❏ 8. Jamal Anderson, Falcons
❏ 9. Drew Bledsoe, Patriots	❏ 9. Stephen Davis, Redskins
❏ 10. Jon Kitna, Seahawks	❏ 10. Curtis Martin, Jets
❏ 11. Rich Gannon, Raiders	❏ 11. Mike Alstott, Buccaneers
❏ 12. Rob Johnson, Bills	❏ 12. James Stewart, Lions
❏ 13. Troy Aikman, Cowboys	❏ 13. Ricky Watters, Seahawks
❏ 14. Elvis Grbac, Chiefs	❏ 14. Corey Dillon, Bengals
❏ 15. Chris Chandler, Falcons	❏ 15. Duce Staley, Eagles
❏ 16. Scott Mitchell, Ravens	❏ 16. Ricky Williams, Saints
❏ 17. Jeff Blake, Saints	❏ 17. Tyrone Wheatley, Raiders
❏ 18. Charlie Batch, Lions	❏ 18. Robert Smith, Vikings
❏ 19. Tim Couch, Browns	❏ 19. Ron Dayne, Giants (R)
❏ 20. Tony Banks, Ravens	❏ 20. Tim Biakabutuka, Panthers
❏ 21. Kerry Collins, Giants	❏ 21. Thomas Jones, Cardinals (R)
❏ 22. Cade McNown, Bears	❏ 22. Curtis Enis, Bears
❏ 23. Brian Griese, Broncos	❏ 23. Jerome Bettis, Steelers
❏ 24. Damon Huard, Dolphins	❏ 24. Charlie Garner, 49ers
❏ 25. Shaun King, Buccaneers	❏ 25. Errict Rhett, Browns
❏ 26. Akili Smith, Bengals	❏ 26. Jamal Lewis, Ravens (R)
❏ 27. Donovan McNabb, Eagles	❏ 27. Jonathan Linton, Bills
❏ 28. Jeff Garcia, 49ers	❏ 28. J. J. Johnson, Dolphins
❏ 29. Kordell Stewart, Steelers	❏ 29. Richard Huntley, Steelers
❏ 30. Jim Harbaugh, Chargers	❏ 30. Antowain Smith, Bills
❏ 31. Daunte Culpepper, Vikings	❏ 31. Mario Bates, Cardinals
	❏ 32. J. R. Redmond, Patriots (R)
Backups	❏ 33. Leroy Hoard, cut by Vikings
❏ 1b. Steve Young, 49ers	❏ 34. Donnell Bennett, Chiefs
❏ 2b. Trent Dilfer, Ravens	❏ 35. Warrick Dunn, Buccaneers
❏ 3b. Jeff George, Redskins	❏ 36. Jermaine Fazande, Chargers
❏ 4b. Gus Frerotte, Broncos	❏ 37. Napoleon Kaufman, Raiders
❏ 5b. Jay Fiedler, Dolphins	❏ 38. Kevin Faulk, Patriots
❏ 6b. Bubby Brister, Vikings	❏ 39. Kimble Anders, Chiefs
❏ 7b. Doug Flutie, Bills	❏ 40. Priest Holmes, Ravens
❏ 8b. Kent Graham, Steelers	❏ 41. Raymont Harris, Patriots
❏ 9b. Neil O'Donnell, Titans	❏ 42. Olandis Gary, Broncos
❏10b. Giovanni Carmazzi, 49ers (R)	❏ 43. Terry Kirby, Browns
❏11b. Trent Green, Rams	❏ 44. Tiki Barber, Giants
❏12b. Warren Moon, Chiefs	❏ 45. Chris Warren, Cowboys
❏13b. Jim Miller, Bears	❏ 46. Fred Beasley, 49ers
❏14b. Randall Cunningham, Vikings	❏ 47. Adrian Murrell, Redskins
❏15b. Jason Garrett, Giants	❏ 48. Natrone Means, Panthers
	❏ 49. Curtis Keaton, Bengals (R)
R = rookie	❏ 50. Terry Allen, cut by Patriots

FANTASY RANKINGS

285

WIDE RECEIVERS

- [ ] 1. Marvin Harrison, Colts
- [ ] 2. Randy Moss, Vikings
- [ ] 3. Antonio Freeman, Packers
- [ ] 4. Cris Carter, Vikings
- [ ] 5. Isaac Bruce, Rams
- [ ] 6. Joey Galloway, Cowboys
- [ ] 7. Jimmy Smith, Jaguars
- [ ] 8. Eric Moulds, Bills
- [ ] 9. Marcus Robinson, Bears
- [ ] 10. Keyshawn Johnson, Buccaneers
- [ ] 11. Tim Brown, Raiders
- [ ] 12. Ed McCaffrey, Broncos
- [ ] 13. Michael Westbrook, Redskins
- [ ] 14. Muhsin Muhammad, Panthers
- [ ] 15. Germaine Crowell, Lions
- [ ] 16. Patrick Jeffers, Panthers
- [ ] 17. Herman Moore, Lions
- [ ] 18. Terance Mathis, Falcons
- [ ] 19. Kevin Johnson, Browns
- [ ] 20. Jake Reed, Saints
- [ ] 21. Amani Toomer, Giants
- [ ] 22. Rod Smith, Broncos
- [ ] 23. Peter Warrick, Bengals (R)
- [ ] 24. Rob Moore, Cardinals
- [ ] 25. Carl Pickens, Bengals
- [ ] 26. Terrell Owens, 49ers
- [ ] 27. Darnay Scott, Bengals
- [ ] 28. Wayne Chrebet, Jets
- [ ] 29. Derrick Mayes, Seahawks
- [ ] 30. Terry Glenn, Patriots
- [ ] 31. Raghib Ismail, Cowboys
- [ ] 32. Tony Martin, Dolphins
- [ ] 33. Plaxico Burress, Steelers (R)
- [ ] 34. Torry Holt, Rams
- [ ] 35. Jerry Rice, 49ers
- [ ] 36. Qadry Ismail, Ravens
- [ ] 37. Az-Zahir Hakim, Rams
- [ ] 38. Johnnie Morton, Lions
- [ ] 39. Sean Dawkins, Seahawks
- [ ] 40. Bobby Engram, Bears
- [ ] 41. Travis Taylor, Ravens (R)
- [ ] 42. Yancey Thigpen, Titans
- [ ] 43. Keenan McCardell, Jaguars
- [ ] 44. Shawn Jefferson, Falcons
- [ ] 45. Oronde Gadsden, Dolphins
- [ ] 46. James Jett, Raiders
- [ ] 47. Jermaine Lewis, Ravens
- [ ] 48. Tim Dwight, Falcons
- [ ] 49. Curtis Conway, Chargers
- [ ] 50. Bill Schroeder, Packers

TIGHT ENDS

- [ ] 1. Tony Gonzalez, Chiefs
- [ ] 2. Wesley Walls, Panthers
- [ ] 3. Rickey Dudley, Raiders
- [ ] 4. Shannon Sharpe, Ravens
- [ ] 5. David LaFleur, Cowboys
- [ ] 6. Jay Riemersma, Bills
- [ ] 7. Stephen Alexander, Redskins
- [ ] 8. Bubba Franks, Packers (R)
- [ ] 9. Frank Wycheck, Titans
- [ ] 10. Ben Coates, cut by Patriots
- [ ] 11. David Sloan, Lions
- [ ] 12. Ernie Conwell, Rams
- [ ] 13. Mark Chmura, Packers
- [ ] 14. Tony McGee, Bengals
- [ ] 15. Pete Mitchell, Giants
- [ ] 16. Freddie Jones, Chargers
- [ ] 17. Andrew Glover, Saints
- [ ] 18. Dave Moore, Buccaneers
- [ ] 19. Kyle Brady, Jaguars
- [ ] 20. Anthony Becht, Jets (R)
- [ ] 21. Damon Jones, Jaguars
- [ ] 22. Marcus Pollard, Colts
- [ ] 23. O. J. Santiago, Falcons
- [ ] 24. Cam Cleeland, Saints
- [ ] 25. Byron Chamberlain, Broncos
- [ ] 26. Luther Broughton, Eagles
- [ ] 27. Greg Clark, 49ers
- [ ] 27. Christian Fauria, Seahawks
- [ ] 29. Ken Dilger, Colts
- [ ] 30. Roland Williams, Rams

KEEPER SLEEPERS

(These are lesser-name players who I believe have the upside potential to warrant consideration for a keeper league.)

- [ ] 1. Peerless Price, Bills
- [ ] 2. Olandis Gary, Broncos
- [ ] 3. Richard Huntley, Steelers
- [ ] 4. Ray Lucas, Jets
- [ ] 5. Shaun Alexander, Seahawks (R)
- [ ] 6. E. G. Green, Colts
- [ ] 7. Stephen Alexander, Redskins
- [ ] 8. Jermaine Fazande, Chargers
- [ ] 9. Tony Simmons, Patriots
- [ ] 10. David Boston, Cardinals
- [ ] 11. Matthew Hatchette, Vikings
- [ ] 12. Ernie Conwell, Rams
- [ ] 13. James Whalen, Buccaneers
- [ ] 14. Giovanni Carmazzi, 49ers
- [ ] 15. Travis Prentice, Browns

FANTASY RANKINGS

KICKERS

1. Mike Hollis, Jaguars
2. Jason Elam, Broncos
3. Mike Vanderjagt, Colts
4. Al Del Greco, Titans
5. Todd Peterson, Seahawks
6. Jeff Wilkins, Rams
7. Olindo Mare, Dolphins
8. Gary Anderson, Vikings
9. Ryan Longwell, Packers
10. Jason Hanson, Lions
11. Brett Conway, Redskins
12. Matt Stover, Ravens
13. John Hall, Jets
14. John Kasay, Panthers
15. Steve Christie, Bills
16. Adam Vinatieri, Patriots
17. Martin Gramatica, Buccaneers
18. Sebastian Janikowski, Raiders (R)
19. Pete Stoyanovich, Chiefs
20. John Carney, Chargers
21. Morten Andersen, Falcons
22. Wade Richey, 49ers
23. Brad Daluiso, Giants
24. Paul Edinger, Bears (R)
25. Doug Brien, Saints
26. Cary Blanchard, Cardinals
27. Kris Brown, Steelers
28. David Akers, Eagles
29. Phil Dawson, Browns
30. Doug Pelfrey, Bengals
31. Tim Sedler, Cowboys

DEFENSES

1. Seattle Seahawks
2. Kansas City Chiefs
3. St. Louis Rams
4. Jacksonville Jaguars
5. Tennessee Titans
6. New York Jets
7. Tampa Bay Buccaneers
8. New England Patriots
9. New Orleans Saints
10. Oakland Raiders

SLEEPERS

1. Joe Horn, WR, Saints
2. Troy Aikman, QB, Cowboys
3. Curtis Enis, RB, Bears
4. Stephen Alexander, TE, Redskins
5. Rob Johnson, QB, Bills
6. Richard Huntley, Steelers
7. Jeff Blake, QB, Saints
8. Matt Stover, K, Ravens
9. Jermaine Fazande, RB, Chargers
10. Peerless Price, WR, Bills
11. Luther Broughton, TE, Eagles
12. Tim Couch, QB, Browns
13. Brad Daluiso, K, Giants
14. Ernie Conwell, TE, Rams
15. David Boston, WR, Cardinals
16. Doug Brien, K, Saints
17. Ike Hilliard, WR, Giants
18. Byron Chamberlain, TE, Broncos
19. Charlie Batch, QB, Lions
20. Eric Bjornson, TE, Patriots
21. Eddie Kennison, WR, Bears
22. Raymont Harris, RB, Patriots
23. Whoever kicks for Bears
24. Whoever kicks for Cowboys
25. Christian Fauria, TE, Seahawks

POSSIBLE BUSTS

1. Jerome Bettis, RB, Steelers
2. Olindo Mare, K, Dolphins
3. Mark Chmura, TE, Packers
4. Patrick Jeffers, WR, Panthers
5. Charlie Garner, RB, 49ers
6. Tony Banks, QB, Ravens
7. Kordell Stewart, QB, Steelers
8. Curtis Conway, WR, Chargers
9. Steve Beuerlein, QB, Panthers
10. Jeff Wilkins, K, Rams
11. Mario Bates, RB, Cardinals
12. Sebastian Janikowski, K, Raiders
13. Antowain Smith, RB, Bills
14. Warrick Dunn, RB, Buccaneers
15. Brett Conway, K, Redskins
16. David LaFleur, TE, Cowboys
17. Errict Rhett, RB, Browns
18. Yancey Thigpen, WR, Titans
19. Brad Johnson, QB, Redskins
20. Az-Zahir-Hakim, WR, Rams
21. Steve Christie, K, Bills
22. Roland Williams, TE, Rams
23. Albert Connell, WR, Redskins
24. Donnell Bennett, RB, Chiefs
25. Doug Pelfrey, K, Bengals

TOP 100 PICKS

- 1. Edgerrin James, RB, Colts
- 2. Fred Taylor, RB, Jaguars
- 3. Marvin Harrison, WR, Colts
- 4. Marshall Faulk, RB, Rams
- 5. Randy Moss, WR, Vikings
- 6. Terrell Davis, RB, Broncos
- 7. Kurt Warner, QB, Rams
- 8. Emmitt Smith, RB, Cowboys
- 9. Antonio Freeman, WR, Packers
- 10. Peyton Manning, QB, Colts
- 11. Eddie George, RB, Titans
- 12. Brett Favre, QB, Packers
- 13. Cris Carter, WR, Vikings
- 14. Dorsey Levens, RB, Packers
- 15. Isaac Bruce, WR, Rams
- 16. Jamal Anderson, RB, Falcons
- 17. Joey Galloway, WR, Cowboys
- 18. Stephen Davis, RB, Redskins
- 19. Curtis Martin, RB, Jets
- 20. Tony Gonzalez, TE, Chiefs
- 21. Jimmy Smith, WR, Jaguars
- 22. Eric Moulds, WR, Bills
- 23. Mike Alstott, RB, Buccaneers
- 24. Wesley Walls, TE, Panthers
- 25. Marcus Robinson, WR, Bears
- 26. Keyshawn Johnson, WR, Bucs
- 27. Steve McNair, QB, Titans
- 28. James Stewart, RB, Lions
- 29. Tim Brown, WR, Raiders
- 30. Ricky Watters, RB, Seahawks
- 31. Brad Johnson, QB, Redskins
- 32. Steve Beuerlein, QB, Panthers
- 33. Ed McCaffrey, WR, Broncos
- 34. Vinny Testaverde, QB, Jets
- 35. Corey Dillon, RB, Bengals
- 36. Duce Staley, RB, Eagles
- 37. Michael Westbrook, WR, Redskins
- 38. Ricky Williams, RB, Saints
- 39. Tyrone Wheatley, RB, Raiders
- 40. Muhsin Muhammad, WR, Panthers
- 41. Robert Smith, RB, Vikings
- 42. Germaine Crowell, WR, Lions
- 43. Rickey Dudley, TE, Raiders
- 44. Ron Dayne, RB, Giants (R)
- 45. Patrick Jeffers, WR, Panthers
- 46. Mark Brunell, QB, Jaguars
- 47. Drew Bledsoe, QB, Patriots
- 48. Tim Biakabutuka, RB, Panthers
- 49. Jon Kitna, QB, Seahawks
- 50. Thomas Jones, RB, Cardinals (R)
- 51. Shannon Sharpe, TE, Ravens
- 52. Herman Moore, WR, Lions
- 53. Terrance Mathis, WR, Falcons
- 54. Curtis Enis, RB, Bears
- 55. Rich Gannon, QB, Raiders
- 56. Mike Hollis, K, Jaguars
- 57. Rob Johnson, QB, Bills
- 58. Jason Elam, K, Broncos
- 59. Kevin Johnson, WR, Browns
- 60. Jake Reed, WR, Saints
- 61. Troy Aikman, QB, Cowboys
- 62. Mike Vanderjagt, K, Colts
- 63. Al Del Greco, K, Titans
- 64. Todd Peterson, K, Seahawks
- 65. Jerome Bettis, RB, Steelers
- 66. Jeff Wilkins, K, Rams
- 67. Charlie Garner, RB, 49ers
- 68. Amani Toomer, WR, Giants
- 69. Elvis Grbac, QB, Chiefs
- 70. David LaFleur, TE, Cowboys
- 71. Rod Smith, WR, Broncos
- 72. Olindo Mare, K, Dolphins
- 73. Peter Warrick, WR, Bengals (R)
- 74. Gary Anderson, K, Vikings
- 75. Ryan Longwell, K, Packers
- 76. Rob Moore, WR, Cardinals
- 77. Errict Rhett, RB, Browns
- 78. Jason Hanson, K, Lions
- 79. Jay Riemersma, TE, Bills
- 80. Stephen Alexander, TE, Redskins
- 81. Jamal Lewis, RB, Ravens (R)
- 82. Carl Pickens, WR, Bengals
- 83. Jonathan Linton, RB, Bills
- 84. Brett Conway, K, Redskins
- 85. Bubba Franks, TE, Packers (R)
- 86. Terrell Owens, WR, 49ers
- 87. Matt Stover, K, Ravens
- 88. Frank Wycheck, TE, Titans
- 89. Chris Chandler, QB, Falcons
- 90. Darnay Scott, WR, Bengals
- 91. Jake Plummer, QB, Cardinals
- 92. Jeff Blake, QB, Saints
- 93. J. J. Johnson, RB, Dolphins
- 94. Richard Huntley, RB, Steelers
- 95. Charlie Batch, QB, Lions
- 96. Wayne Chrebet, WR, Jets
- 97. Antowain Smith, RB, Bills
- 98. Mario Bates, RB, Cardinals
- 99. Tim Couch, QB, Browns
- 100. Derrick Mayes, WR, Seahawks

KEEPER LEAGUES

It's not enough to consume yourself with worries about how Fred Taylor will do this year. Now you're gazing into a crystal ball to predict how he'll do for the next five seasons.

Welcome to keeper leagues, a way to incorporate a long-range approach to fantasy football. It takes an element out of your draft but keeps you interested and active throughout the offseason. The roster move or trade you make today could affect your franchise for the better part of a decade.

In a keeper league, you freeze one or more of the players on your roster for the next season. Some leagues freeze just one player, while other leagues freeze the majority of a roster. This obviously requires much foresight and planning, but I don't recommend it. Leagues that freeze most of their players take the fun out of the annual draft. If the pool of draftable players consists only of rookies, marginal players and washed-up veterans, there won't be much suspense on draft night.

Keeper leagues initiate a flurry of trading activity, especially late in the season, when some teams are fighting for the playoffs and a few teams are looking ahead to next year. Playoff-bound teams and bubble teams may need one player to fill a gaping hole in the lineup. A cellar-dweller, with nothing to lose this season, preys on a golden opportunity to stock up for the future. He trades a Pro Bowl player in exchange for a pair of prospects.

Keeper league strategy:

■ A player's age is more important than ever in a keeper league. Aging players such as Andre Reed or Emmitt Smith won't give you many years of service, while rookies are obviously in high demand.

■ Running backs (and, to a lesser extent, receivers) have a much shorter career than players at other positions because of the pounding they take. Conversely, quarterbacks and kickers often reach their prime in their 30s, and some play at a high level at age 40.

■ Look for backups who play behind an aging starter now but are likely to move into a starting role next year.

■ Look for young, up-and-coming players who are due for a career year, such as Jake Plummer, Jon Kitna, Kevin Dyson, Tim Biakabutuka and Stephen Alexander.

AUCTION LEAGUES

Time to put up or shut up.

Think your fantasy draft is exciting? Just try plunging into an auction league. The debate within your head about whether to draft Marvin Harrison or Terrell Davis is exciting, sure. But now imagine the butterflies in your stomach when you've just bid almost half of your total payroll on one player, Randy Moss.

A fantasy auction requires guts and careful planning. It's knowing when to drive up the price on a player you *don't* want in order to tap the resources of your competitors. If you're not careful, you'll get stuck with that player.

In an auction, each team has an imaginary payroll ($100 is the most common amount). You must fill all of your roster spots without exceeding your payroll.

A draft order is determined, but only for the sake of opening the bidding on a player. When it's your turn, you bid on the player of your choice. Bidding continues until one bidder remains. That amount is subtracted from the bidding winner's payroll.

If you haven't played in an auction league, I'd strongly recommend it, especially if you're in more than one league so that you could also enjoy a conventional league with a conventional draft. I wouldn't use the snowboarder-vs.-skier analogy by saying that once you try an auction league, you'll never go back. Just think of it as an excellent alternative that expands your fantasy insanity.

One of the best aspects of an auction is that every franchise owner has the opportunity to get every player. In a conventional draft, the owner who draws No. 10 has no shot at the top players. Of course, reversing the draft order after every round helps provide for equitable drafting. But the fact remains, your draft position largely dictates who's available, especially in the first few rounds.

In an auction, you could buy Edgerrin James and Antonio Freeman, though you'd have only enough money left to fill out the rest of your roster with leftovers that nobody else wants.

Strategies vary — and when you're in the heat of battle, reason sometimes goes out the window as you get swept up into a three-way bidding war.

To form an auction league, you need an auctioneer, preferably someone who is not one of the owners, to run the show. The auctioneer keeps track of bidding, logs each franchise's acquisitions, and keeps a running total of the available payroll. It's too much to ask of a franchise owner to keep track of the auction and try to assemble a good team.

As in any fantasy league, straighten out rules before beginning the auction. Establish a roster size and a salary cap. Keep bid amounts in whole dollars for the sake of simplicity and expediency. A fantasy auction won't last much longer than a conventional draft if you deal in whole dollars.

Every owner needs at least $1 left in the payroll for each unfilled roster spot. In other words, if you have purchased 10 players for a 14-player roster, you must have at least $4 remaining.

Auction strategy:

■ Place value amounts on each player and try to buy the guys you want for less than that value.

■ Buy most of your players late rather than early in your auction. Big-name players will command top dollar early. But two-thirds of the way through, when payrolls are dwindling, there are always some fantasy studs still available. The owners who hoarded their money early will be able to steal these players for half or even one-third of the amount they would have commanded an hour before.

■ Spend most of your money on running backs and receivers. Unless you can get one of the top three quarterbacks (Kurt Warner, Peyton Manning or Brett Favre) for a somewhat reasonable price, hold out for a QB late in your draft, when the other owners have already filled that position and can't afford to pay much for their backup. You'll get a quality starter for a backup-type price.

■ Pay very little on kickers. With so many good ones, and anybody's guess who will win the scoring title, you can still get a 110-point kicker for a buck or two late in the draft.

■ If there is a star player you just have to have, an option is to put him up for bid as soon as possible, and open the bidding very high (such as $40). In the first few minutes of the auction, many owners are gun-shy and will be scared off by that high bid. This certainly isn't bargain-shopping, but it might be worth it for a guy who scores 18 touchdowns.

■ Open the bidding for players you *don't* want. This strategy depletes the payroll of your rivals while wasting their roster spots on guys you believe won't have a good season.

AUCTION VALUES

(Based on a 10-team league with a $100 salary cap and 14 players per team.)

- ❏ 1. Edgerrin James, Colts, $42
- ❏ 2. Fred Taylor, Jaguars, $40
- ❏ 3. Marvin Harrison, Colts, $40
- ❏ 4. Marshall Faulk, Rams, $38
- ❏ 5. Randy Moss, Vikings, $37
- ❏ 6. Terrell Davis, Broncos, $35
- ❏ 7. Emmitt Smith, Cowboys, $35
- ❏ 8. Antonio Freeman, Packers, $33
- ❏ 9. Kurt Warner, Rams, $30
- ❏ 10. Eddie George, Titans, $30
- ❏ 11. Peyton Manning, Colts, $28
- ❏ 12. Brett Favre, Packers, $28
- ❏ 13. Cris Carter, Vikings, $26
- ❏ 14. Dorsey Levens, Packers, $26
- ❏ 15. Isaac Bruce, Rams, $25
- ❏ 16. Jamal Anderson, Falcons, $25
- ❏ 17. Joey Galloway, Cowboys, $24
- ❏ 18. Stephen Davis, Redskins, $23
- ❏ 19. Curtis Martin, Jets, $22
- ❏ 20. Jimmy Smith, Jaguars, $22
- ❏ 21. Eric Moulds, Bills, $21
- ❏ 22. Mike Alstott, Buccaneers, $20
- ❏ 23. Marcus Robinson, Bears, $20
- ❏ 24. Tony Gonzalez, Chiefs, $18
- ❏ 25. Wesley Walls, Panthers, $17
- ❏ 26. Keyshawn Johnson, Bucs, $15
- ❏ 27. Steve McNair, Titans, $14
- ❏ 28. James Stewart, Lions, $14
- ❏ 29. Tim Brown, Raiders, $13
- ❏ 30. Ricky Watters, Seahawks, $12
- ❏ 31. Brad Johnson, Redskins, $10
- ❏ 32. Steve Beuerlein, Panthers, $10
- ❏ 33. Ed McCaffrey, Broncos, $9
- ❏ 34. Vinny Testaverde, Jets, $9
- ❏ 35. Corey Dillon, Bengals, $8
- ❏ 36. Duce Staley, Eagles, $8
- ❏ 37. MichaelWestbrook, Redskins, $7
- ❏ 38. Ricky Williams, Saints, $7
- ❏ 39. Tyrone Wheatley, Raiders, $7
- ❏ 40. Muhsin Muhammad, Panthers, $6
- ❏ 41. Robert Smith, Vikings, $5
- ❏ 42. Germaine Crowell, Lions, $5
- ❏ 43. Rickey Dudley, Raiders, $5
- ❏ 44. Ron Dayne, Giants (R), $4
- ❏ 45. Patrick Jeffers, Panthers, $4
- ❏ 46. Mark Brunell, Jaguars, $4
- ❏ 47. Drew Bledsoe, Patriots, $4
- ❏ 48. Tim Biakabutuka, Panthers, $4
- ❏ 49. Jon Kitna, Seahawks, $4
- ❏ 50. Thomas Jones, Cardinals (R), $3
- ❏ 51. Shannon Sharpe, Ravens, $3
- ❏ 52. Herman Moore, Lions, $3
- ❏ 53. Terrance Mathis, Falcons, $3
- ❏ 54. Curtis Enis, Bears, $3
- ❏ 55. Rich Gannon, Raiders, $2
- ❏ 56. Mike Hollis, Jaguars, $2
- ❏ 57. Rob Johnson, Bills, $2
- ❏ 58. Jason Elam, Broncos, $2
- ❏ 59. Kevin Johnson, Browns, $2
- ❏ 60. Jake Reed, Saints, $2
- ❏ 61. Troy Aikman, Cowboys, $2
- ❏ 62. Mike Vanderjagt, Colts, $2
- ❏ 63. Al Del Greco, Titans, $2
- ❏ 64. Todd Peterson, Seahawks, $2
- ❏ 65. Jerome Bettis, Steelers, $2
- ❏ 66. Jeff Wilkins, Rams, $2
- ❏ 67. Charlie Garner, 49ers, $2
- ❏ 68. Amani Toomer, Giants, $2
- ❏ 69. Elvis Grbac, Chiefs, $2
- ❏ 70. David LaFleur, Cowboys, $2
- ❏ 71. Rod Smith, Broncos, $2
- ❏ 72. Olindo Mare, Dolphins, $2
- ❏ 73. Peter Warrick, Bengals (R), $2
- ❏ 74. Gary Anderson, Vikings, $2
- ❏ 75. Ryan Longwell, Packers, $2
- ❏ 76. Rob Moore, Cardinals, $2
- ❏ 77. Errict Rhett, Browns, $2
- ❏ 78. Jason Hanson, Lions, $2
- ❏ 79. Jay Riemersma, Bills, $2
- ❏ 80. Stephen Alexander, Redskins, $2
- ❏ 81. Jamal Lewis, Ravens (R), $1
- ❏ 82. Carl Pickens, Bengals, $1
- ❏ 83. Jonathan Linton, Bills, $1
- ❏ 84. Brett Conway, Redskins, $1
- ❏ 85. Bubba Franks, Packers (R), $1
- ❏ 86. Terrell Owens, 49ers, $1
- ❏ 87. Matt Stover, Ravens, $1
- ❏ 88. Frank Wycheck, Titans, $1
- ❏ 89. Chris Chandler, Falcons, $1
- ❏ 90. Darnay Scott, Bengals, $1
- ❏ 91. Jake Plummer, Cardinals, $1
- ❏ 92. Jeff Blake, Saints, $1
- ❏ 93. J. J. Johnson, Dolphins, $1
- ❏ 94. Richard Huntley, Steelers, $1
- ❏ 95. Charlie Batch, Lions, $1
- ❏ 96. Wayne Chrebet, Jets, $1
- ❏ 97. Antowain Smith, Bills, $1
- ❏ 98. Mario Bates, Cardinals, $1
- ❏ 99. Tim Couch, Browns, $1
- ❏ 100. Derrick Mayes, Seahawks, $1

FANTASY RANKINGS

Chapter 12

ROOKIE REPORT

The 1999 draft was the year of the quarterback. The 2000 draft brings the year of the wide receiver. This year's group of rookie receivers could rival the 1996 crop as one of the best ever.

The 1996 draft brought Marvin Harrison, Keyshawn Johnson, Eric Moulds, Amani Toomer, Terrell Owens, Muhsin Muhammad, Bobby Engram, Derrick Mayes, Eddie Kennison and Terry Glenn into the league.

This year, five receivers were drafted in the first round, three more were taken in Round 2, and 12 others were picked in Rounds 3 and 4. While all are expected to contribute eventually, only a handful are likely to make an impact this season. Quarterback and receiver are the two fantasy positions that require developmental time. Running backs and kickers (and, to a lesser extent, tight ends) often step right in and contribute as rookies. But last year's rookie wide receivers made modest contributions. For every Randy Moss who makes an instant impact, there are countless others — Will Blackwell, Pat Johnson, Marcus Nash and Yatil Green, to name a few — who are drafted in an early round but contribute little or nothing as rookies.

While four members of the Class of '96 — Glenn, Harrison, Johnson and Kennison — had exceptional years for rookies, nearly all of the other first-year wide receivers from that year didn't emerge right away. More than likely, only three or four of this year's rookie receivers, such as Peter Warrick, Travis Taylor, Plaxico Burress and Sylvester Morris, will make an instant fantasy impact.

In 1999, five quarterbacks were drafted in the first round. This year, only four were taken in the first five rounds. Don't expect any of them to make an impact as rookies.

By contrast, quite a few running backs will make a big impact this season. With the exception of blitz pickups, rookie runners manage to pick up most of the offense quickly, so they usually play right away. Teams such as the Patriots, Giants, Ravens, Cardinals and Browns were starved for an every-down running back, and they drafted to fill an immediate need.

Two tight ends who were drafted in the first round of the April draft, Green Bay's Bubba Franks and the Jets' Anthony Becht, will step in and start as rookies. And between one and three rookie kickers will win jobs this year.

QUARTERBACKS

1. CHAD PENNINGTON, Jets — The Jets didn't have a great need for a a quarterback, but Pennington was too good to pass up with the 18th pick in the first round. At 6 feet 3 and 230 pounds, Pennington has very good size and good speed. His deep passing is less than ideal, but he can throw on the run and place his passes well. An Academic All-America, Pennington passed for 14,000 yards and 123 touchdowns at Marshall. He'll sit on the bench this year unless Vinny Testaverde really struggles.

2. CHRIS REDMAN, Ravens — A slow time in the 40 dropped Redman to the third round, where the Ravens were thrilled to get him. A drop-back pocket passer with a quick release and a great arm but poor mobility, he'll stand and face the pressure rather than scramble, and that has led to spine/disc and knee injuries. Redman could become the starter as early as the 2001 season and could flourish in Brian Billick's offense.

3. GIOVANNI CARMAZZI, 49ers — Bill Walsh liked him enough to make him the second quarterback drafted, so that says something for Carmazzi. A big, intelligent player with good mobility, he needs time to develop because he played at the Division I-AA level. Carmazzi is advanced at reading coverages because he ran the run-and-shoot offense, though that didn't prepare him well for the pros.

4. TEE MARTIN, Steelers — Kordell Stewart hears footsteps, though they're from Kent Graham, not Martin. A proven winner and clutch performer at Tennessee, Martin could become a long-range solution. He shows flashes of brilliance but lacks consistency. He has good size (6-1, 228), though his accuracy is erratic.

RUNNING BACKS

1. THOMAS JONES, Cardinals — An Emmitt Smith–type back, Jones improved every year he was at Virginia. He rushed for 1,798 yards (including 164 against Florida State) and 16 touchdowns as a senior. He runs harder between the tackles than his 5-foot-9, 216-pound frame would suggest. Jones caught 71 passes and rushed for 36 touchdowns in college. He'll step right in and be an immediate starter, though he plays for a team that's not very good.

2. RON DAYNE, Giants — The most productive Division I college back ever, Dayne rushed for 7,125 yards and 71 touchdowns at Wisconsin. He also piled up 12 200-yard games. Although Dayne weighs close to 260, he has surprisingly nimble moves and quick feet. A Jerome Bettis–type battering ram, Dayne will start immediately. He is an unproven pass receiver, and his durability is a concern.

3. JAMAL LEWIS, Ravens — The first back taken in the draft, Lewis is a roll of the dice. He hasn't been the same since returning from a 1998 knee injury. If he returns to his pre-injury form, when he ran with outstanding power and speed, Lewis will be the best of this year's rookie backs. If not, he could become an injury-prone bust.

4. J. R. REDMOND, Patriots — An all-purpose back without great size or power, Redmond could play right away because the Patriots are desperate for a top back. A good receiver, he is a north-south runner with breakaway speed. He's a slashing, deceptive runner who rarely takes a square hit.

5. TRAVIS PRENTICE, Browns — Prentice could be an every-down back, though he'll probably share time with Errict Rhett this year. A productive 5-foot-11, 220-pound workhorse from Miami (Ohio), he rushed for 5,604 yards in college and never missed a practice or a game. He's a good receiver who doesn't fumble.

6. SHAUN ALEXANDER, Seahawks — The Seahawks traded away Ricky Watters's backup, Ahman Green, then drafted Alexander in the first round the next day. Watters's eventual replacement, Alexander should play some this season. He has a good size/speed ratio, excellent running skills, catches the ball well and excels in the fourth quarter. However, he's not a good inside runner.

7. TRUNG CANIDATE, Rams — A surprise first-round pick, Canidate fits the Rams' mold of exceptional quickness. One of fastest backs in the draft, he caught 30 passes as a senior and should replace Amp Lee as the team's change-of-pace third-down back. He averaged more than 50 yards per touchdown run in 1997 and '98.

8. CURTIS KEATON, Bengals — The team's instability at running back, with Corey Dillon possibly heading out and Ki-Jana Carter injured again, makes Keaton especially important. He has excellent speed and breakaway ability. He transferred from West Virginia and gained 1,719 yards at James Madison last season. Keaton isn't a physical runner.

9. FRANK MOREAU, Chiefs — Moreau is a typical power back preferred by the Chiefs. At 6 feet 1, 230, Moreau is big and durable, and he caught 38 passes as a senior at Louisville. Moreau is a hard runner, but he runs upright. He joins a crowded backfield.

10. SAMMY MORRIS, Bills — Morris is a tweener, a 6-foot, 222-pounder who isn't a very fast tailback and isn't a big fullback. He is very versatile, a good runner who can bounce outside and an excellent receiver. Morris gives the Bills good depth.

11. REUBEN DROUGHNS, Lions — Droughns will battle Sedrick Irvin for the backup job behind James Stewart. He had three 200-yard games at Oregon before breaking his fibula as a junior. He wasn't the same player as a senior, though he might now be back to his pre-injury form. He's a hard inside runner with a burst through the hole.

12. DOUG CHAPMAN, Vikings — A good receiver and goal-line runner, Chapman was productive in games, but he was injury-plagued and he was a bad practice player at Marshall. He runs hard and fast and sets up his blockers. He'll back up Robert Smith.

13. DEON DYER, Dolphins — Arguably the best fullback in the draft, this 265-pounder is best suited to be a blocking back, a much-utilized player in offensive coordinator Chan Gailey's power attack. Dyer probably won't get the ball much.

14. TERRELLE SMITH, Saints — A former defensive player who moved to fullback last season, Smith has a nasty disposition and he loves to hit. He'll be a special-teams contributor and the lead blocker for Ricky Williams. He can catch, but he isn't a very good runner.

WIDE RECEIVERS

1. PETER WARRICK, Bengals — Warrick isn't very big or fast, but he was the best playmaker in the draft. In Cincinnati, he can be part of a solution to a decade of losing. He has tremendous moves and rare ability to turn short routes into long gains, as well as great explosiveness and hands. A precise route runner and a touchdown maker in college, Warrick will start immediately. Although he's immature, Warrick won't be the latest bungled Bengals draft pick if Akili Smith can get him the ball.

2. TRAVIS TAYLOR, Ravens — Taylor is a polished receiver who has joined a passing team that is short on receivers, so, even though he skipped his senior season and has limited playing experience, he should get to play right from the start. He has good hands, the speed to get deep and the moves to break big plays. At Florida, Taylor was at his best for the biggest games.

3. PLAXICO BURRESS, Steelers — At 6 feet 5, 235 pounds, Burress has rare size, huge hands and the ability to get off the line against anyone. But he lacks concentration, hasn't always been motivated, his practice habits are poor and he runs sloppy pass routes. Burress needs coach Bill Cowher to light a fire under him. Perhaps the riskiest player in the draft, he could become an unstoppable force or a wasted head case.

4. SYLVESTER MORRIS, Chiefs — The Chiefs were desperate for a playmaking receiver, and Morris fills their need. The 6-foot-3, 210-pound Morris scored 30 touchdowns the past two seasons at Jackson State. A long strider with good speed for his size, he has great hands and the toughness to go over the middle, but he tends to round off patterns. Morris may need some time to develop.

5. R. JAY SOWARD, Jaguars — Soward fills an immediate need as a No. 3 receiver who can stretch a defense with deep routes and score from anywhere. He is small (5 feet 9, 177) and not very strong, but he has truly great speed. Soward was better as a sophomore and junior than he was his final season at USC. He's also a dangerous kickoff and punt returner.

6. DENNIS NORTHCUTT, Browns — A year after the Browns hit it big by taking Kevin Johnson with the first pick in the second round, they drafted Northcutt in the same exact spot. A former running back, cornerback and quarterback, he has exceptional versatility and good kick-return skills. A small but quick receiver, Northcutt is an elusive runner after the catch.

7. TODD PINKSTON, Eagles — At 6 feet 2, 168 pounds, one of Pinkston's biggest tasks will be to add meat to his skinny frame. He utilized his height well at Southern Mississippi. Despite his build, he is durable and unafraid of contact. Pinkston, who caught 11 passes for 163 yards against Nebraska, could play in the slot this year.

8. LAVERANUES COLES, Jets — Keyshawn Johnson's departure opens a spot for Coles as the second or third wideout. He has incredible speed but isn't polished and may need time to develop. Although he's a gamebreaker and a potentially explosive kick returner, Coles has been irresponsible and he carries the baggage of a checkered past.

9. JERRY PORTER, Raiders — Oakland needs a receiver to complement Tim Brown now, but Porter may be a year or two away. A converted defensive back and quarterback, Porter caught just 28 passes in limited playing time at receiver. He has incredible jumping ability and great size, but little experience. Expect him to be the No. 3 receiver in '00.

10. DEZ WHITE, Bears — One of the top athletes in the draft, White fell into the third round because of his suspect hands. However, he was very productive at Georgia Tech. The 6-foot-1, 218-pound White has the speed to get deep. White will return kicks and could contribute as a third or fourth receiver.

11. RON DUGANS, Bengals — Dugans can be a perfect complement to Peter Warrick and Darnay Scott, a 6-foot-1, 205-pound possession receiver. Though his speed isn't great, his hands are. He can make the tough catches in short and intermediate routes.

12. DANNY FARMER, Steelers — This crafty 6-foot-3, 217-pounder has been compared to Ed McCaffrey. He has natural pass-catching skills and he can go up and get the ball. A poor workout dropped his stock, but Farmer could help out this season.

13. TREVOR GAYLOR, Chargers — Gaylor is a 6-foot-3 burner who showed dramatic improvement as a senior and finished with 10 touchdown catches in his final six games at Miami (Ohio). He's frail, though he could play as a third or fourth receiver on a team that lacks depth.

14. CHRIS COLE, Broncos — Denver took a third-round gamble on one of the draft's fastest players. Cole has rare speed and can adjust to poorly thrown passes, but he is inconsistent. The Broncos need a third receiver now, but Cole probably isn't ready yet.

15. DARRELL JACKSON, Seahawks — Jackson has a good chance to become the No. 4 receiver in a passing offense. He runs routes well and sets up defenders. Jackson stepped up against top teams in 1999 and became Florida's top receiver when Travis Taylor was injured.

16. JAJUAN DAWSON, Browns — Dawson caught 234 passes in four years at Tulane. He's not a burner, but he is a productive possession receiver, and could step in and be the Browns' No. 4 wideout if he can learn to break through line jams.

17. RONALD DIXON, Giants — Considered to be a third-round reach, Dixon played at tiny Lambuth College in Tennessee. He was picked because of his great speed and big-play ability, though he's a raw developmental prospect who could return kicks this season.

TIGHT ENDS

1. BUBBA FRANKS, Packers — Franks will immediately start and fill Green Bay's most glaring need. He's not very fast, but he has soft, excellent hands, which he uses to make circus catches. At 6 feet 5 and 265 pounds, Franks gives Brett Favre a huge target down the middle. Franks caught 45 passes last season, and he scored 12 touchdowns in three seasons at Miami (Fla.). His blocking is nothing special, however.

2. ANTHONY BECHT, Jets — The Jets also had a gaping hole at tight end, and the 6-foot-5, 270-pound Becht may be the most complete tight end among rookies. He has good speed and agility for his size, and he isn't stiff for a big guy. An excellent in-line blocker, Becht is a good fit for the Jets' offense. He was an honor student who improved every year and has no real weaknesses in his game.

3. ERRON KINNEY, Titans — Tennessee lost Jackie Harris to free agency and drafted Kinney to start opposite Frank Wycheck. The 6-5, 272-pounder didn't block very well at Florida, and he caught only 39 passes in four seasons. But the Titans like his potential.

4. JAMES WHALEN, Buccaneers — Whalen could prove to be a sixth-round steal. An exceptional receiver, he dominated at Kentucky as a senior with 90 catches for 1,019 yards and 10 touchdowns. At 6-2, 228, he's more suited for an H-back role. He has a great feel for reading coverages and getting open, and he catches like a wide receiver.

5. JAY TANT, Cardinals — A fifth-round pick, Tant could join a wide-open battle for the starting job, especially if he improves his blocking. Tant is a solid receiver who runs good routes. He isn't very big and powerful.

6. DAVE STACHELSKI, Patriots — A converted defensive end, Stachelski could play right away because the Patriots lack tight ends. He's too stiff and still raw, but he has good size and speed. He came on as a senior at Boise State when he caught 31 passes as a senior.

7. AARON SHEA, Browns — A fullback and tight end at Michigan, Shea will play tight end and battle Mark Campbell for the starting role. The versatile Shea caught 31 passes as a senior. He has had shoulder problems, and he isn't a crushing blocker.

KICKERS

1. SEBASTIAN JANIKOWSKI, Raiders — Leave it to Al Davis to draft a kicker in the first round. The 260-pound Janikowski kicks the ball as hard and as far as anyone ever drafted. He gets great elevation on his field goals, and he drives his kickoffs into the end zone. But this free spirit is one arrest away from deportation to his native land, Poland. He could be an all-time best, or an all-time bust.

2. PAUL EDINGER, Bears — Edinger enters a wide-open battle, with Jaret Holmes and perhaps veteran Jeff Jaeger, for the job. Edinger converted 40 of 48 field goals the past two seasons at Michigan State. In his final college game, he kicked a 39-yard field goal to beat Florida in the Citrus Bowl. But he needs a higher trajectory on his kicks.

3. NEIL RACKERS, Bengals — Cincinnati hasn't been happy with Doug Pelfrey's kicking, so they drafted Rackers in the sixth round. He made 27 of 35 field-goal attempts in his final two seasons at Illinois. His kickoffs are long, but he's inconsistent.

Chapter 13

OFFSEASON UPDATE

THE NEW HEAD COACHES

Seven NFL teams have new head coaches this year, fewer than in 1999, when there were nine new head coaches. Here's a look at the new coaches and the effects each will have on their new teams:

BILL BELICHICK, Patriots — Belichick is an expert on defense, but he wasn't all that successful as head coach of the Cleveland Browns in the first half of the 1990s. The team's defense is fine; it's the offense that has struggled the last couple of seasons. Now the problem is that six of last year's key offensive players are gone. Charlie Weis has always been a sound position coach, but the quality of his play-calling is unknown. There's also just one quality receiver and nothing set in the backfield. In addition, the weak offensive line could spell problems for quarterback Drew Bledsoe (who suffered a career-high 53 sacks in 1999). The result should be low-scoring games.

DAVE CAMPO, Cowboys — Once again, Jerry Jones went seeking a new head coach, and once again he filled the opening the inexpensive way. Campo is a very sound defensive coach, but it remains to be seen what he does with the Cowboys' aging offense (especially with the meddling Jones). He will bring back some much-needed discipline, and the defense will remain the same. The offense, with new coordinator Jack Reilly, will be more of a vertical passing game (like the old Oakland Raiders). With Joey Galloway and Rocket Ismail at wide receiver, the new offense should succeed, and you can look for quarterback Troy Aikman to go downfield probably more than he has ever before in his career. Finally, Emmitt Smith may be aging, but he, too, should post some very good stats.

AL GROH, Jets — Al Groh has been a Bill Parcells disciple for years, and now he gets to run the show, and so far it has been a smooth transition. He should succeed as Parcells's replacement because he's a good communicator who has an air of confidence. However, the last two head coaches who replaced Parcells — Ray Handley with the Giants and Pete Carroll in New England — were noted failures, so only time will tell. The team's draft was questionable, but there's still ample talent on offense. Offensive coordinator Dan Henning has been around for a long time, but his résumé is filled with both successes and failures. Same thing on defense, where Mike Nolan is talented, but his defense in Washington last season was terrible. That's why Groh, a former head coach at Wake Forest, will oversee the defense. If Parcells remains as the head of football operations, he will have to stay in the background or else his presence could undermine Groh's authority with the players.

JIM HASLETT, Saints — The Saints are an inept franchise, and only the Jim Mora–Jim Finks regime could win games. Haslett, like most of the past New Orleans coaches, has a bright résumé, and new GM Randy Mueller hails from the Seahawks. They even had a very good offseason, bringing in nearly two dozen players who can really play. But they are the Aints, er, Saints. Things will be more organized than during the Mike Ditka era. The defense, under coordinator Ron Zook, will be opportunistic. And the offense might be able to score points with Jeff Blake at quarterback and Rickey Williams as the workhorse in the backfield. Offensive coordinator Mike McCarty has installed the West Coast offense, although short passes aren't exactly Blake's strength. All in all, don't be surprised if the Saints finish above the 49ers in 2000.

MIKE MARTZ, Rams — Less than 48 hours into their reign as the Super Bowl champions, the Rams had a major change when Dick Vermeil retired and offensive coordinator Mike Martz took over. The creative mind behind the No. 1 offense in the league in 1999 (400 yards a game and 526 points — the third-highest total in NFL history), Martz made numerous changes on the coaching staff. The Rams have some obstructions on their road back to the Super Bowl. As a result of their first place finish, they now face a more challenging schedule (they had a fifth-place schedule in '99). Martz also has to decide how to handle his quarterback situation between NFL MVP Kurt Warner and backup Trent Green, whom he had forged a strong relationship with in Washington in 1998. Also, Martz is not in charge of the entire football operation like Vermeil was. The Rams now have a three-headed hierarchy, and there are sure to be disagreements. Martz streamlined the coaching staff, getting rid of many of Vermeil's trusted aides, so there's a definite question whether or not the Rams can continue from where they were. The offense will stay the same, as Martz will continue to call plays, and all of the playmakers are back, too. The defense will remain the same, with Peter Giunta remaining as coordinator.

MIKE SHERMAN, Packers — After just one year of the Ray Rhodes regime, GM Ron Wolf realized the mistake (a lack of discipline, poor clock management and an out-of-sync offense) and brought in Mike Sherman for the new millennium. Sherman was largely an unknown both when he was the tight ends coach in Green Bay two years ago and last year in Seattle, where he was the offensive coordinator. But he had a good reference from Mike Holmgren, and Wolf was sold early in the interview process. Sherman should be able to get quarterback Brett Favre back on track, and Sherman knows how to run successful offenses. His coordinators — Tom Rossley on offense and Ed Donatell on defense — are longtime position coaches who have to make the step up. On the good side, some of the new position coaches, such as Bob Slowick, Ray Sherman and Kippy Brown, are experienced coordinators.

DAVE WANNSTEDT, Bears — Problems lie ahead in Miami, where Wannstedt has replaced his mentor, Jimmy Johnson. There's quite a bit of talent left, but there was quite a bit of it, too, in Chicago when Wannstedt took over for Mike Ditka in Chicago eight years ago. He's an excellent defensive coach, but he's not a good personnel expert and he dragged Chicago down into mediocrity. Look for Miami's defense to be one of the league's best. But, on offense, he's already shoved Dan Marino out the door, he (like Johnson) can't find a featured back out of a deep backfield, his receivers are aging and the offensive line isn't what it used to be. If Wannstedt makes the wrong choice at quarterback, it could be a long season in Miami.

THE INJURY REPORT

When preparing for a fantasy football draft, do not rely too much on last year's statistics. A lot of NFL players suffered injuries in 1999 that either lowered their statistics considerably or hampered them to the point where they didn't have typical seasons.

Here's a look at the players who were injured last season, as well as a report on their recovery as of mid-May.

Quarterbacks
CHARLIE BATCH, Lions — Batch missed all or parts of 14

games in 1999, including nine with a right thumb that was fractured on November 7 and then reinjured in the season finale. He didn't start tossing a ball until April, but he continues to make progress on his rehabilitation and will be fine for the start of the season.

STEVE BEUERLEIN, Panthers — He underwent offseason surgeries to fix a hernia, remove a bone spur from his right shoulder and bone spurs and chips from his left ankle, and to extract loose cartilage from his left knee. They were all minor procedures, and he's ready to go in 2000.

TIM COUCH, Browns — Couch suffered a severely sprained ankle in the next-to-last game of the season and missed the finale. He was back 100 percent by early spring.

JAY FIEDLER, Dolphins — He tweaked his elbow joint in the weightroom and missed the May minicamp. The team doesn't believe the injury is serious, and he will be slowed until training camp.

TRENT GREEN, Rams — Green suffered a torn ACL last August and missed the entire season and Super Bowl, leading the way to the Kurt Warner story. Green underwent another scope on his injured knee in early March but may not be quite 100 percent by August.

DANNY KANELL, Falcons — The team's third quarterback, he suffered a sprained MCL in his first start on December 19 and missed the rest of the year. He'll be OK.

ERIK KRAMER, cut by Chargers — He started four early games, then was replaced and eventually suffered a neck injury and went on I.R. on November 23. His career might be over.

RYAN LEAF, Chargers — Leaf underwent two arthroscopic surgeries on his shoulder in the last year and has been slow to recover (he also has missed most of the team's offseason conditioning program). He was to undergo an extensive rehab program last spring, but he still was not happy with the arm strength of his throwing shoulder and even was seeking other opinions in the spring. Figure him out, either for physical or mental reasons.

STEVE McNAIR, Titans — McNair had surgery on February 16 to remove a bone spur and a cyst from his left big toe. He had been slowed the past two seasons by a turf toe injury and wore a protective boot between playoff games last season. He's back to 100 percent.

JAKE PLUMMER, Cardinals — Plummer is completely healed from the thumb injury that hampered his passing in the 1999 season.

AKILI SMITH, Bengals — After gaining the starting job as a rookie, Smith suffered a severe right big toe sprain on October 31 and was inactive for the remaining eight games. He has recovered.

VINNY TESTAVERDE, Jets — Testaverde injured his Achilles tendon early in the first game of last season and missed the remainder of the year. He was running and throwing by spring, and there's no question that he will be 100 percent for the start of training camp.

STEVE YOUNG, 49ers — The big question is: Will Young be medically cleared to play? In 1999, he missed the last 13 games after suffering his fourth concussion in 35 months. His most recent MRI and diagnostic tests were all clear, and he was hoping to resume his career, although nearly everybody else told him to retire. He might be headed to Denver.

Running Backs

RABIH ABDULLAH, Falcons — Abdullah suffered a broken right thumb and sprained right wrist in the next-to-last game of 1999 but has rehabbed well.

KIMBLE ANDERS, Chiefs — After Anders finally gained the starting halfback job, his 1999 season ended with an Achilles tendon injury in the second game, but, even though he missed the spring minicamp, he should be ready for the start of training camp.

JAMAL ANDERSON, Falcons — Anderson played just one game before tearing the ACL in his right knee. He underwent reconstructive surgery on October 5 and was progressing very well in his rehab and is on schedule to be back for the 2000 regular season.

TAVIAN BANKS, Jaguars — Banks blew out his left knee (all three ligaments) at midseason, and it's most likely that he'll spend all of the 2000 season on injured reserve. He also has some nerve damage and a torn hamstring. Doctors said it was one of the worst injuries they had ever seen.

TIM BIAKABUTUKA, Panthers — Biakabutuka had left shoulder surgery in the offseason and missed the spring minicamp, but he will be fine for the start of training camp.

GARY BROWN, cut by Giants — Brown played in just three games for the Giants in 1999 and had season-ending arthroscopic knee surgery to repair extensive cartilage damage. He probably won't play football again.

SHAWN BRYSON, Bills — A third-round draft choice in 1999, he was having a terrific training camp before having a major knee injury. He is expected to be ready to go full speed by training camp.

KI-JANA CARTER, Bengals — Injured more than half of his

five-year career, Carter suffered a partial dislocation of his right kneecap while working out on April 13. He underwent arthroscopic surgery (which included a new procedure designed to hold the kneecap in place) five days later and says he'll play again. But he's a long shot to even practice in training camp, and there's no way he'll ever recover the abilities that made him the No. 1 overall pick in the 1995 draft.

BOB CHRISTIAN, Falcons — Christian was injured in the regular-season finale but didn't need surgery on his left knee.

STEPHEN DAVIS, Redskins — Davis is recovering from ankle and knee injuries suffered at the end of last season. He says he'll be 100 percent before the start of training camp.

TERRELL DAVIS, Broncos — Davis is expected to make a complete recovery from knee surgery. Broncos head coach Mike Shanahan has been raving about Davis's rehab, but it's only realistic to expect that Davis might be slowed a little early in the season. He tore his ACL and partially tore the MCL in the fourth game of last season, as well as sustaining cartilage damage.

GARY DOWNS, Falcons — Downs missed all of 1999 with a knee injury. He had reconstructive knee surgery in August and has made good progress in his rehab program.

ROBERT EDWARDS, Patriots — The 1998 Rookie of the Year who blew out his knee in a beach football game in January 1999, Edwards says the nerves in his surgically repaired knee have regenerated and is hopeful of making a comeback. That is unlikely to happen this year, however.

CURTIS ENIS, Bears — Enis played in 15 games last season but was slowed because he was still recovering from a 1998 knee injury. He is expected to be back with a fully healed ACL in 2000.

KEVIN FAULK, Patriots — A rookie in 1999, Faulk missed the last three games with a sprained ankle. He's perfectly healthy again.

BYRON HANSPARD, Falcons — In 1999, Hanspard was still recovering from a '98 knee injury, but he should be close to 100 percent in '00.

GARRISON HEARST, 49ers — Hearst broke his left fibula in the January 1999 playoffs, and then he developed a rare condition in which poor circulation caused part of the ankle bone to slowly decay. He spent most of last year trying to correct the ankle problem. But on May 6, Hearst underwent a second extensive surgery on his left ankle to try to save his career. The 49ers were originally hoping to have Hearst participate in the June minicamp, but now they might be lucky to have him at all this season, as his healing has been virtually nonexistent in 15 months.

DARICK HOLMES, cut by Colts — Holmes missed all of 1999 with a broken leg but was doing well in his rehab and was in search of a new team.

CHRIS HOWARD, Jaguars — Howard underwent surgery on February 16 to clean up cartilage in his knee. He's 100 percent.

J. J. JOHNSON, Dolphins — Johnson missed the final three games of 1999 with left calf and right hamstring injuries, but he has recovered.

LEON JOHNSON, Jets — Johnson suffered a torn ACL and MCL on the opening kickoff of the season opener and missed the remaining games. He took part in the April minicamp and will be just fine.

DARYL JOHNSTON, Cowboys — Johnston finished last season on injured reserve after a herniated disk was discovered in his neck just above the C-6–C-7 fusion that he received in 1997. He will very likely be cut after June 1.

DORSEY LEVENS, Packers — Levens injured the patella tendon in his knee on April 29 in the team's minicamp and was slowed the rest of the spring. However, he will be 100 percent by training camp.

NATRONE MEANS, Chargers — With San Diego in 1999, Means missed eight games with knee and ankle injuries. He was signed by Carolina as a free agent after undergoing surgery on his left knee and left ankle on March 2. He's optimistic he'll be ready to go at full speed for training camp. However, he hasn't played a full season since 1994, so he remains iffy.

DAVID PALMER, Vikings — Palmer suffered a knee injury and missed the last seven weeks of the season, but he should be OK.

De'MOND PARKER, Packers — Parker is recovering from torn knee ligaments suffered in the next-to-last game of '99 and may not be ready in time for camp. The injury is worrisome because speed and quickness are Parker's strengths and no one knows if he'll recover those fully.

MICHAEL PITTMAN, Cardinals — Pittman is a versatile talent who is always hurt (he missed six of the last seven games in 1999), and there is concern that he is injury-prone.

KEVIN TURNER, Eagles — Turner suffered two stingers in 1999 and might be forced to retire because of his neck injury.

CHARLES WAY, Giants — Way was slowed all of last season by an arthritic left knee that required surgery and was finally placed on I.R. for the final month of the year. He was scoped in early April and began running on his surgical right knee (cadaver cartilage, a first for an NFL player) in May. There are conflicting views on the stability of Way's knee, and team officials will wait until around training camp time to afford the veteran a sufficient recovery period. However, he might not play again.

Wide Receivers

BRETT BECH, Saints — Bech suffered an abdominal injury last November and missed the rest of the season. He's OK again.

WILL BLACKWELL, Steelers — Blackwell missed the final month of the season because of a severe midfoot sprain, but he's healthy again.

MACEY BROOKS, Bears — Brooks ruptured his left ACL last November 10 and is still rehabbing, but he'll be 100 percent.

CRIS CARTER, Vikings — After complaining of soreness in the spring (and playing on a bad ankle at the end of 1999), Carter had minor surgery on May 1 to remove bone spurs from his right ankle. He'll be fine.

CURTIS CONWAY, Chargers — With Chicago in 1999, Conway missed the final two games because of a strained left shoulder. He's healthy again and was signed by San Diego in the offseason as a free agent.

LAKE DAWSON, cut by Colts — Dawson finished the season on injured reserve, missing the final 11 games with an ankle injury. It was a very bad injury, and he might not play again for a while.

E. G. GREEN, Colts — Injuries continue to plague Green, who sustained a broken right leg in the playoffs. The team anticipates he will make a complete recovery, but it was a very serious fracture and he's no lock to make it back 100 percent. He might even require another surgery.

COURTNEY HAWKINS, Steelers — A high ankle sprain sidelined Hawkins for the final five games of 1999, but he has recovered.

MICHAEL IRVIN, Cowboys — Irvin has a congenital cervical stenosis condition in his spine. He could pass another team's physical, but his doctor recommends that he not play again. He still hopes to play again, but that's probably not going to happen, at least not in Dallas.

CHARLES JOHNSON, Eagles — The team's leading receiver at the time of his knee injury in the 11th game, Johnson is undergoing rehab and is doing very well.

CHARLIE JONES, Chargers — Jones fractured his hip in the preseason and played on it, though he was slowed and eventually placed on I.R. for the final six weeks. In the offseason, he had yet to regain his burst, but that should come in time.

TONY MARTIN, Dolphins — Martin twice had surgery to repair his shoulder this offseason, though he will be 100 percent for training camp.

O. J. McDUFFIE, Dolphins — McDuffie had surgery on his left big toe on February 16 and missed the offseason minicamps. He was slowed by the injury in 1999 and still wasn't running in early May, so keep an eye on his status.

WANE McGARITY, Cowboys — McGarity missed the April minicamp, but he was expected to be ready for the start of camp. He fractured the ring finger on his right hand December 8 and underwent surgery the next day to insert two screws. In late April he had the pins removed that held the bone together.

JAMES McKNIGHT, Cowboys — McKnight tore the anterior cruciate ligament in his left knee last August 5 and underwent surgery the next day. He missed the spring minicamp, but, in order to be safe, the club will limit McKnight's work early in training camp. Reportedly, he hasn't lost any of his speed.

MIKE PRITCHARD, Seahawks — Pritchard was bothered by a knee injury all of 1999, but he is healthy again.

LESLIE SHEPHERD, cut by Browns — Shepherd was hampered by injuries much of 1999, and when he was healthy he wasn't on the same page as Tim Couch, the quarterback. He missed the final six games and hasn't been signed by another team.

YANCEY THIGPEN, Titans — Thigpen suffered a broken right foot in the AFC Championship game against Jacksonville and missed the Super Bowl. His foot is pretty well healed, but in early May he had minor arthroscopic surgery on a troublesome left ankle that was originally injured on November 14. Check his status in August.

LAMAR THOMAS, Dolphins — Thomas missed all of 1999 with a left shoulder anterior subluxation suffered in the preseason. He underwent surgery on September 6 and has erased most of the doubts.

JASON TUCKER, Cowboys — Tucker underwent surgery on February 9 to remove bone spurs from the big toes of both feet. He didn't take part in any of the team's informal throwing sessions in the spring, but he was cleared to begin running routes in May.

MICHAEL WESTBROOK, Redskins — The team decided that Westbrook did not need surgery in the offseason to repair the broken wrist he suffered on November 14, so he should be fine.

ALVIS WHITTED, Jaguars — Whitted underwent surgery on February 16 to clean up cartilage in his knee. He's fine again.

Tight Ends

JAMIE ASHER, cut by Eagles —The oft-injured Asher missed all of last season with a broken left ankle suffered in a preseason game (he also missed half of 1998 with a knee injury). He'll probably be signed by another team as soon as he's 100 percent.

MARK BRUENER, Steelers — A midfoot sprain sidelined Bruener for the final two games of 1999, but he's healthy again.

MARK CAMPBELL, Browns — Campbell missed the final two games with an ankle injury. Now the team's starter, he's OK again.

DAN CAMPBELL, Giants — Campbell is a third-round draft choice in 1999 who showed promise before sitting out the final month with a hamstring injury. He's healthy.

PETE CHRYPLEWICZ, Lions — He is expected to be 100 percent by training camp after rehabbing from a torn ACL in his knee.

MARK CHMURA, Packers — Chmura is working out and is confident that the neck injury that put him on injured reserve for the final 15 weeks of 1999 is close to being healed. However, he now has rape charges hanging over his head and might be released. The team excused him from the late-April minicamp and was mum about his future.

HAYWARD CLAY, Cowboys — Clay suffered a torn ACL in his left knee during the preseason and was placed on I.R. on August 31, a day before undergoing surgery. He'll be slow in training camp, but he'll return.

CAM CLEELAND, Saints — Cleeland suffered through an injury-filled second season in 1999, missing five games. He's healthy again, but he has to learn to play through injuries more.

ERNIE CONWELL, Rams — Conwell played in only seven percent of the Rams' offensive plays last season as he recovered from reconstructive knee surgery, but by the Super Bowl it was clear that he was completely healthy. Don't worry about him; he'll start in 2000.

TROY DRAYTON, cut by Dolphins — Drayton had arthroscopic knee surgery in December and was still rehabbing in March. He is looking for a new team.

JOHN FARQUHAR, Saints — Farquhar missed all of 1999 with a knee injury suffered in the preseason. He's healthy again.

CHRIS GEDNEY, Cardinals — Gedney missed all of the 1999 season after undergoing two major colon surgeries (he had developed ulcerative colitis), but he regained his lost weight and passed a physical, making a remarkable recovery, because few people thought he'd play again.

ERIC GREEN, cut by Jets — Green had major neck surgery to repair a herniated disk. He expects to be healthy by training camp, although he is more likely to become a salary-cap casualty.

MITCH LYONS, Steelers — A backup, Lyons was having his best season until suffering a severe knee injury on December 18 and missing the rest of the year. He'll be 100 percent for the start of the season.

MICHAEL ROAN, Titans — Roan suffered a neck injury late in the season and missed the entire postseason. He should be fine.

SHANNON SHARPE, Ravens — Sharpe suffered a broken collarbone in 1999 while with Denver and missed the final 11 games. He's healthy again, which is why the Ravens signed him for big bucks.

DAVID SLOAN, Lions — The oft-injured Sloan had more off-season surgery (this time a toe). Considering his history of injuries, that's not encouraging, but he is supposed to be healthy.

SCOTT SLUTZKER, Saints — Slutzker missed the final two games because of a right knee sprain that has healed.

JERAME TUMANE, Steelers — Tumane suffered a season-ending knee injury on October 25 and had surgery on November 2. His rehab was going well in the spring.

WESLEY WALLS, Panthers — Walls had offseason surgery on his right knee and missed the spring minicamp but will be more than ready to go by the start of the season.

Kickers

BRAD DALUISO, Giants — Daluiso tore the ACL on his non-kicking leg in the sixth game of 1999 and was lost for the year. He's back to 100 percent.

JEFF JAEGER, Bears — Jaeger suffered a hip injury in the 1999 training camp and struggled early last season, playing in just three games before being placed on injured reserve. The Bears haven't decided whether or not they'll re-sign him, as they have two rookies ready to compete for the job.

JOHN KASAY, Panthers — Kasay suffered a torn ACL in his left (kicking) leg on December 12 when he tried to help make a tackle on a kickoff, and he underwent reconstructive knee surgery. There are rumors that he may not be sufficiently recovered in time for the start of the season. Watch this situation in training camp, because the Panthers will likely sign another kicker just in case.

ROSTER CHANGES

Like it or not, free agency is a fact of life in pro football, and it has a greater impact on the game than anyone thought it would. No longer can NFL teams build for the future, because the future is now! They cannot plan on developing players for several years, because those players might do their best for their next team. Players switch teams at an amazing pace each year, leaving many fans wondering, "When did *0* go there?"

That's why free agency was a prominent factor in the writing of this book: players were changing teams practically every day when this book went to press in mid-May. The free-agency period runs to July 15 every year, so there will undoubtedly be many changes that could not be included in this book (especially after June 1, when teams can release veterans and count half of their remaining prorated signing bonuses in 2000). These late changes will be reflected in the free Draft Day Update that is mailed in August (see the back of the book).

Free agency and the advent of a salary cap also have a big effect on how teams build their rosters. More than ever, teams are cutting high-salaried players throughout the offseason and signing players with lower salaries. Or, because of salary cap problems, teams are cutting players at some positions in order to sign big-name players at other positions. The net effect is major shakeups on most rosters.

However, for the fourth straight season since free agency began, not a lot of players changed teams through free agency (as compared to the first few years of free agency in the mid-1990s). NFL clubs seem to have figured out that it's best to keep their own players — and keep them happy, too.

From a fantasy football standpoint, the best players who changed teams this offseason were: quarterbacks Jeff Blake (from Cincinnati to New Orleans) and Jeff George (from Minnesota to Washington); running backs James Stewart (from Jacksonville to Detroit) and Thurman Thomas (from Buffalo to Miami); wide receivers Keyshawn Johnson (from the New York Jets to Tampa Bay), Jake Reed (from Minnesota to New Orleans) and Shawn Jefferson (from New England to Atlanta); tight ends Shannon Sharpe (from Denver to Baltimore) and Andrew Glover (from Minnesota to New Orleans); and kicker Cary Blanchard (from the New York Giants to Arizona).

Here's a list of the skill-position players who changed teams during the 2000 offseason (rookies and round drafted in are designated "R-1, etc."):

	Newcomers/Draft Picks	Losses
Arizona	RB Thomas Jones (R-1)	RB Adrian Murrell
	TE Derek Brown	K Chris Jacke
	TE Chris Gedney	
	TE Jay Tant (R-5)	
	K Cary Blanchard	

	Newcomers/Draft Picks	**Losses**
Atlanta	QB Wally Richardson WR Shawn Jefferson WR Kamil Loud TE Brian Saxton	None
Baltimore	QB Trent Dilfer QB Chris Redman (R-3) RB Jamal Lewis (R-1) WR Mareno Philyaw (R-6) WR Travis Taylor (R-1) TE Shannon Sharpe	QB Scott Mitchell RB Errict Rhett TE Aaron Pierce
Buffalo	WR Avion Black (R-4) WR Drew Haddad (R-7)	RB Sam Gash RB Thurman Thomas WR Kamil Loud WR Andre Reed WR Kevin Williams
Carolina	RB Natrone Means	QB Steve Bono RB Fred Lane RB Winslow Oliver K Richie Cunningham
Chicago	RB Chad Levitt RB Frank Murphy (R-6) WR Eddie Kennison WR Dez White (R-3) TE Dustin Lyman (R-3) K Paul Redinger (R-6) K Marshall Young	RB Edgar Bennett WR Curtis Conway
Cincinnati	QB Scott Mitchell RB Curtis Keaton (R-4) RB Sedrick Shaw WR Ron Dugans (R-3) WR Peter Warrick (R-1) TE Brad St. Louis (R-7) K Neil Rackers (R-6)	QB Jeff Blake

	Newcomers/Draft Picks	Losses
Cleveland	QB Spergon Wynn (R-6)	QB Jamie Martin
	RB Travis Prentice (R-3)	RB Sedrick Shaw
	RB Errict Rhett	WR Leslie Shepherd
	WR JaJuan Dawson (R-3)	
	WR Dennis Northcutt (R-2)	
	WR David Patten	
	TE Aaron Shea (R-4)	
Dallas	QB Paul Justin	QB Jason Garrett
	RB Robert Chancey	QB Mike Quinn
	WR Morris Anderson	RB Tarik Smith
	WR Joey Galloway	WR Ernie Mills
	WR Michael Wiley (R-5)	TE Eric Bjornson
	TE Jackie Harris	TE Hayward Clay
	TE Brian Roche	
	K Tim Sedler	
Denver	QB Gus Frerotte	QB Bubby Brister
	QB Jarious Jackson (R-7)	QB Chris Miller
	RB Mike Anderson (R-6)	RB Derek Loville
	WR Chris Cole (R-3)	TE Shannon Sharpe
	WR Leroy Fields (R-7)	
	WR Muneer Moore (R-5)	
Detroit	QB Steve Stenstrom	QB Jeff Fox
	QB Mike Tomczak	QB Gus Frerotte
	RB Reuben Droughns (R-3)	
	RB James Stewart	
	TE Tony Johnson	
Green Bay	RB Ahman Green	TE Jeff Thomason
	RB Rondell Mealey (R-7)	
	WR Joey Jamison (R-5)	
	WR Charles Lee (R-7)	
	WR Anthony Lucas (R-4)	
	TE Bubba Franks (R-1)	
	TE Kaseem Sinceno	
Indianapolis	QB Pete Gonzalez	QB Steve Walsh
	RB Fred Lane	RB Darick Holmes
		WR Lake Dawson

	Newcomers/Draft Picks	**Losses**
Jacksonville	QB Jamie Martin	QB Jay Fiedler
	RB Shyrone Stith (R-7)	RB James Stewart
	WR Emanuel Smith (R-6)	
	WR R. Jay Soward (R-1)	
Kansas City	RB Dante Hall (R-5)	RB Bam Morris
	RB Frank Moreau (R-4)	WR Joe Horn
	WR Kirby Dar Dar	WR Tamarick Vanover
	WR Desmond Kitchings (R-7)	TE Lonnie Johnson
	WR Sylvester Morris (R-1)	K Jon Baker
Miami	QB Jay Fiedler	QB Dan Marino
	RB Deon Dyer (R-4)	RB Kantroy Barber
	RB Lamar Smith	RB Cecil Collins
	RB Thurman Thomas	RB Stanley Pritchett
		WR Bert Emanuel
		TE Hayward Clay
		TE Troy Drayton
Minnesota	QB Bubby Brister	QB Jeff George
	RB Doug Chapman (R-3)	WR Jake Reed
	WR Chris Thomas	TE Andrew Glover
	WR Troy Walters (R-5)	
	TE Giles Cole (R-7)	
	TE Chad Fann	
New England	QB Tom Brady (R-6)	RB Terry Allen
	RB Raymont Harris	RB Derrick Cullors
	RB Patrick Pass (R-7)	RB Jerry Ellison
	RB J. R. Redmond (R-3)	RB Lamont Warren
	WR Aaron Bailey	WR Shawn Jefferson
	TE Eric Bjornson	TE Mike Bartrum
	TE Dave Stachelski (R-5)	TE Ben Coates
		TE Grant Williams

	Newcomers/Draft Picks	**Losses**
New Orleans	QB Jeff Blake	QB Billy Joe Hobert
	QB Marc Bulger (R-6)	QB Danny Wuerffel
	RB Chad Morton (R-5)	RB Lamar Smith
	RB Terrelle Smith (R-4)	WR Andre Hastings
	RB Robert Wilson	WR Eddie Kennison
	WR Sherrod Gideon (R-6)	TE Tony Johnson
	WR Joe Horn	
	WR Jake Reed	
	WR Ryan Thelwell	
	TE Andrew Glover	
	TE Kevin Houser (R-7)	
	TE Austin Wheatley (R-5)	
N.Y. Giants	QB Jason Garrett	QB Kent Graham
	QB Ron Powlus	RB Gary Brown
	RB Ron Dayne (R-1)	WR David Patten
	WR Ron Dixon (R-3)	WR Anthony Tucker
		K Cary Blanchard
N.Y. Jets	QB Chad Pennington (R-1)	QB Rick Mirer
	WR Laveraneus Coles (R-3)	WR Keyshawn Johnson
	WR Windrell Hayes (R-5)	TE Eric Green
	TE Anthony Becht (R-1)	
Oakland	RB Jerald Moore	QB Wade Wilson
	TE John Burke	TE Derrick Walker
	TE Chris Fontenot	K Michael Husted
	TE Mondriel Fulcher (R-7)	K Joe Nedney
	K Sebastian Janikowski (R-1)	
Philadelphia	RB Darnell Autry	RB Eric Bieniemy
	RB Thomas Hamner (R-6)	RB Kevin Turner
	RB Stanley Pritchett	TE Jamie Asher
	WR Todd Pinkston (R-2)	TE Kaseem Sinceno
	WR Gari Scott (R-4)	K Norm Johnson
	TE Mike Bartrum	
	TE Eric Stocz	
	TE Jeff Thomason	

OFFSEASON UPDATE

	Newcomers/Draft Picks	Losses
Pittsburgh	QB Kent Graham	QB Pete Gonzalez
	QB Tee Martin (R-5)	QB Mike Tomczak
	WR Danny Farmer (R-4)	WR Courtney Hawkins
	WR Plaxico Burress (R-1)	
	TE Jason Gavadza (R-6)	
St. Louis	RB Trung Canidate (R-1)	QB Paul Justin
	RB Derek Loville	RB Amp Lee
		RB Jerald Moore
		WR Chris Thomas
San Diego	QB JaJuan Seider (R-6)	QB Erik Kramer
	RB Robert Chancey	RB Natrone Means
	WR Curtis Conway	WR Ryan Thelwell
	WR Trevor Gaylor (R-4)	
San Francisco	QB Giovanni Carmazzi (R-3)	QB Steve Stenstrom
	QB Tim Rattay (R-7)	RB Tommy Vardell
	RB Paul Smith (R-5)	WR Morris Anderson
	TE Brian Jennings (R-7)	TE Chad Fann
Seattle	RB Shaun Alexander (R-1)	RB Ahman Green
	WR Darrell Jackson (R-3)	RB Robert Wilson
	WR Dee Miller	WR Joey Galloway
	WR James Williams (R-6)	
	TE Grant Williams	
Tampa Bay	QB Joe Hamilton (R-7)	QB Trent Dilfer
	RB Jerry Ellison	WR Bert Emanuel
	WR Keyshawn Johnson	
	WR Yo Murphy	
	TE Lovett Purnell	
	TE James Whalen (R-5)	
Tennessee	RB Mike Green (R-7)	TE Josh Bailey
	TE Erron Kinney (R-3)	TE Jackie Harris
Washington	QB Jeff George	QB Rodney Peete
	QB Todd Husak (R-6)	QB Casey Weldon
	RB Adrian Murrell	
	WR Ethan Howell (R-7)	
	PK Peter Elezovic	

TRADES

There were seven offseason trades involving eight skill-position players between the end of the 1999 season and mid-May — more than in most years. Here's the list:

Player	1999 Team	2000 Team
RB Ahman Green	Seattle	Green Bay
RB Fred Lane	Carolina	Indianapolis
RB Derek Loville	Denver	St. Louis
WR Joey Galloway	Seattle	Dallas
WR Keyshawn Johnson	N.Y. Jets	Tampa Bay
WR Eddie Kennison	New Orleans	Chicago
TE Kaseem Sinceno	Philadelphia	Green Bay
TE Jeff Thomason	Green Bay	Philadelphia

RETIREMENTS

The following veteran skill-position players retired during the off-season:

Player	Position	Team
Dan Marino	Quarterback	Miami
Chris Miller	Quarterback	Denver
Wade Wilson	Quarterback	Oakland
Bam Morris	Running Back	Kansas City
Tommy Vardell	Running Back	San Francisco
Aaron Pierce	Tight End	Baltimore

Chapter 14

10 QUESTIONS

1. You have the first pick in your draft. Whom do you take?

Congratulations. Now you can take any player you want. But who? If you botch the pick, it'll be disastrous. So you want a sure thing — a player who is going to have a great season in 2000. And that player is . . .

. . . Edgerrin James. As a rookie in 1999, the Indianapolis running back scored 17 touchdowns and had a season like few NFL rookies ever have. He's the No. 1 pick at running back because Fred Taylor is too injury-prone, and Terrell Davis and Jamal Anderson are coming off serious knee injuries. And he's a better choice for the overall No. 1 pick than wide receivers Marvin Harrison or Randy Moss *and* quarterbbacks Kurt Warner and Peyton Manning because he's a running back, which is the most crucial position in fantasy football. Go with James; you won't be disappointed.

2. Is the talent at some positions deeper than others?

Yes. This year, for the first time in a while, there are quite a few good running backs, but that position is only about 16 to 20 players deep. It's wide receivers and kickers that are deep in 2000. There's easily 20 to 25 kickers who could score 100-plus points, which is why they should not be drafted early. And, at wide receiver, there's easily 30 or more players who could score a half-dozen touchdowns or more. At running back, you start getting into backups about 20 players into the ranking list, while the top 60 wide receivers are almost all starters and No. 3 receivers who play nearly as much as starters.

3. Why are running backs always such a premium?

Because in any given year, more wide receivers score double-digit touchdowns than running backs. Also, running backs are more apt to be replaced during the course of the season than wide receivers. Finally, most teams have only one featured back, whereas at wide receiver every team plays two, and some teams have three or four good ones. That's why it's much more important that you have two solid runners on your fantasy team (and three is even better). In 2000, the best running backs are Edgerrin James, Fred Taylor, Marshall Faulk and Terrell Davis. Of that group, Taylor seems to be injury-prone (or else he'd be the No. 1 pick), and Davis is coming off an ACL injury. That's why James and Faulk are the more-sure picks. The next tier of top backs includes Emmitt Smith, Eddie George (who's finally scoring TDs), Dorsey Levens, Jamal Anderson (who's also coming off an ACL injury), Curtis Martin and Stephen Davis (who might be a holdout). And then there's a pretty big drop-off.

4. What position can be adequately filled in the later rounds of the draft?

Kicker. Never pick them in the first half of your draft. In 1999, the difference between the highest-scoring kicker (Miami's Olindo Mare with 145 points) and the 20th-highest-scoring kicker (John Kasay with 99 points) was 46 points. There's no other fantasy position where the 20th player on the scoring list managed nearly 70 percent of the output of the league leader. Also, kickers are subject to opportunity more than players at any other position. You don't want the last kicker, but you can safely sit out that seventh-round run on kickers (though it may be tempting to jump in), knowing that there will be a decent one available in the last three or four rounds. And make sure you get two good ones.

5. Who will be the top fantasy rookies in 2000?

Few rookies produce big numbers right away. You can take a chance on players such as Arizona's Thomas Jones, Cincinnati's Peter Warrick, Baltimore's Jamal Lewis, the Giants' Ron Dayne, Pittsburgh's Plaxico Burress, Kansas City's Sylvester Morris and Baltimore's Travis Taylor. But don't do it too early in your draft. Nearly every one of those players was drafted by a team that finished at or below .500 in 1999. And the best rookies are usually those on the top teams.

6. Why is Marvin Harrison a safer pick than Randy Moss?

Simple. Moss *is* better than Harrison. But look at it this way: Whom would you rather have throwing to your No. 1 receiver — Daunte Culpepper or Peyton Manning? Case closed. Manning is just short of superstar status; Culpepper never even threw a pass in 1999, his rookie season. Nobody knows if he's going to be any good or not, and there's a very strong chance he'll be replaced if he struggles and jeopardizes the Vikings' playoff hopes. After Harrison and Moss, the best bets are Antonio Freeman and Cris Carter, then a slight drop-off to Isaac Bruce and Joey Galloway.

7. Realistically, how many good quarterbacks are out there?

Just three: Kurt Warner, Peyton Manning and Brett Favre. Then there's quite a drop-off to the next tier of top passers: Drew Bledsoe, Vinny Testaverde, Steve McNair, Brad Johnson and Mark Brunell. Now, a couple of those players might have really fine seasons, but it's not a sure thing. The top three should throw 30 or more TD passes. If you can't get one of the top three, make sure that you have two very good starters, and then check the schedule every week and play your hunches. Also, be very wary of all of last year's rookies other than Tim Couch (Akili Smith, Shaun King, Donovan McNabb, Daunte Culpepper and Cade McNown). None of those five will be anywhere near as good as Peyton Manning was in 1999 (his second season). In fact, Culpepper and McNown might be replaced.

8. Is Tony Gonzalez really that good? Who are the other top tight ends?

Yes, Gonzalez is the best tight end, because he's like a cross between a tight end and a wide receiver — except that he's built like a tight end (as compared to Shannon Sharpe, who more resembles a wide-out). Gonzalez might not score 11 TDs this year, but he's certain to score a bundle of them. After him, Wesley Walls and Rickey Dudley are guaranteed to score quite a few TDs, and then there's Shannon Sharpe (though he needs to bounce back from a bad, injury-plagued year) and David LaFleur. If you get one of the top four or five tight ends, you'll have a decided advantage over your opponents. Following those five tight ends, there's some question marks about every other player. If any player is going to have a standout season, it's going to be Washington's Stephen Alexander.

9. Does a player's team matter much, or is individual talent all I should consider?

Talent is the most important consideration. But the quality of a team and its offensive system goes a long way toward determining a player's usefulness. Remember how bad Vinny Testaverde was for all those years that he languished on Tampa Bay? And imagine how good Cincinnati's Corey Dillon would be on a truly great team. Or Philadelphia's Duce Staley. But you also have to consider a player's surrounding cast. For example, Keyshawn Johnson is clearly one of the top half-dozen or so wide receivers. But he might struggle a bit this year with young Shaun King throwing to him. Some coaches know how to utilize their players better than others. Remember how Mike Shanahan got much more out of John Elway than Dan Reeves ever did? However, even some mediocre players can put up huge fantasy numbers in a system in which they are used correctly (like Arizona's Mario Bates in 1999, when he scored nine touchdowns).

10. Does a player's age matter in fantasy football?

Do you remember last year when players such as Dan Marino, Jerry Rice and Andre Rison seemed to age quickly and their production dropped? Thurman Thomas used to be a huge fantasy star; now he's struggling for a place on Miami's roster. Same thing with Randall Cunningham, who's looking for a job. This year, be careful when drafting players like Jerome Bettis, Ricky Watters and Natrone Means. Quarterbacks and kickers play the longest, then wide receivers, tight ends and running backs (in that order). Therefore, consider a player's age when you consider drafting running backs. Teams are always looking for a young stud to take over for a wise old buck who's carried the ball too many times and absorbed too much pounding.

Chapter 15

THE INTERNET

One of the biggest changes over the last few years is the availability of information on the Internet. If you have access to the Internet — and who doesn't these days? — learn to use it to your advantage to gain an edge on your competitors. There are many sources of information that can mean the difference between winning and losing in fantasy football. There's a lot out there, and much of it is free to use.

However, there are a lot of online services that serve as sources for fantasy football information put up by people who don't know very much about fantasy football — or football in general, for that matter. And, thus, a number of them are not very good.

In the entire country, there aren't more than a dozen or so people who make their living off fantasy football (about 10 of them work for *Fantasy Football Weekly* magazine, believe it or not, which is why its staff is so knowledgeable). In other words, there's a whole lot of people who think they know football but who are really just out to make a buck — they are more interested in getting your money than in helping you. In this chapter, you will learn which are the best Internet sites and what they offer in the way of information.

Most of these sites will help you once your draft is over and you have to set your lineup from week to week. There *is* a wealth of information waiting for you on the Internet, but be careful where you look. Spend some time learning which sites you like best, and you will be more knowledgeable when it comes to setting your lineup — and that can only help you win your league championship.

Fantasy Football Sites

Without a doubt, the best site devoted solely to fantasy football is fanball.com, which is run by the staff of *Fantasy Football Weekly* magazine. It has just about everything you could hope for — and all for free. It includes breaking news, injury updates, a chat room, free fantasy leagues, weekly online chats with NFL assistant coaches, Real Audio, and weekly contests — including a $1 million contest (that they're going to make easier to win in 2000).

Other good sites that pertain only to fantasy football or fantasy sports are: fantasyinsights.com, ffmastermind.com, kffl.com, thehuddle.com, rotonews.com/footbball, and about.com.

Most of these sites offer the same information as fanball.com, but they're not as complete and they're run by people as a side business. Still, they're pretty good. Check them out and see which ones you prefer to surf when you're on the Web.

You've probably heard a lot about rivals.com, but don't waste your time on it.

NFL News

There are lots of sources for NFL News. From the normal news outlets, the best Internet sites are cbssportsline.com and espn.com. If you're a sports fan and if you have access to the Internet, you know these two sites.

Another great up-and-coming site is nfltalk.com, which gives updates year-round and is getting a lot of looks in NFL front offices around the country.

Other good news sites are: cnnsi.com, sportingnews.com, foxsports.com, nfl.com and totalsports.net, but they're not as good as cbssportsline.com and espn.com.

Fantasy Football Services

Like I said, there are a lot of people who think they know fantasy football but who care more about making money. These sites offer their services for a fee, but very few of them are any good.

The best is allpropub.com, which is run by Jack Pullman, one of the dozen or so people in the country who make a living from fantasy football. Pullman is a great guy, and his service is very detailed and accurate. He has sources in every city. If you want to spend money, go with Pullman.

Two other good ones are fantasyguru.com and sandlotshrink.com. Again, you have to pay for these types of services. You might be better off surfing the Web to get the same information for free. That's for you to decide.

Newspaper Links

One of the best ways to get the latest news on the 31 teams is to read the metropolitan newspapers in those cities. The best links to those newspapers is via sportspages.com and newspapers.com. The two sites will link you to every newspaper in the country, large or small. That gives you access to each team via a beat writer who must dig out fresh stories each day.

At least three fantasy sites have their own links to newspapers: fantasyinsights.com (which has the most links), fantasyindex.com/pressbox and fspnet.com/links.

Any of these sites will put literally hundreds of fantasy and NFL information sites at your fingertips.

Injury Reports

The NFL releases its injury report every Wednesday and Thursday, but the categories of "Doubtful," "Questionable" and "Probable" are quite vague and leave most fantasy players wondering about the true status of players.

The best source is a service offered by espn.com that features injury updates by Steve Cohen, who is the executive producer of NFL programming on WFAN radio in New York and a producer for CBS Radio. He is easily the most connected person anywhere in regard to injuries, and he has excellent sources on each team. His "Pro Football News & Injury Report" is clearly the best. It is a yearly service that costs $49.95 to subscribe to, but it's worth it. During the season, Cohen offers postpractice reports on every team each Thursday, Friday and Saturday, as well as Sunday deactivations (yes, he even checks with the press box in every city 75 minutes before games).

Cohen's service includes NFL news provided by Jay Glazer of the *New York Post*. Reports are available by e-mail or fax. Cohen also provides injury information to *Fantasy Football Weekly* magazine.

Team Sites

The NFL's official site, nfl.com, will be different in 2000, with links to official sites of the 31 teams (yes, every team will have its own site this year). However, while most teams keep their rosters and depth charts updated on a weekly basis, these sites are not that good for fantasy news. In reality, there is very little insider access, although the clubs could do quite a bit if they wanted to.

The best site for real news might be bengals.com, which started in the spring and has a veteran sportswriter on staff who writes actual news stories.

Newsgroups and Chat Rooms

Many of the sites mentioned above have links to chatrooms. Two good ones are fanexfootball.com and the rec.sport.football fantasy newsgroup. Check them out sometime.

Weather

Need the latest weather at a game site before you set your lineup? Check with weather.com. It's the best of the weather sites.

Chapter 16

STATISTICS

1999 QUARTERBACKS

Player	Team	GP/GS	PASSING						RUSHING	
			ATT	CMP	YDS	TD	INT	RTG	YDS	TD
Warner, Kurt	St.L	16/16	499	325	4353	41	13	109.2	92	1
Beuerlein, Steve	Caro.	16/16	571	343	4436	36	15	94.6	124	2
George, Jeff	Minn.	12/10	329	191	2816	23	12	94.2	41	0
Manning, Peyton	Ind.	16/16	533	331	4135	26	15	90.7	73	2
Johnson, Brad	Wash.	16/16	519	316	4005	24	13	90.0	31	2
Gannon, Rich	Oak.	16/16	515	304	3840	24	14	86.5	298	2
Lucas, Ray	NYJ	9/9	272	161	1678	14	6	85.1	144	1
Batch, Charlie	Det.	11/10	270	151	1957	13	7	84.1	87	2
Frerotte, Gus	Det.	9/6	288	175	2117	9	7	83.6	33	0
Chandler, Chris	Atl.	12/12	307	174	2339	16	11	83.5	57	1
Brunell, Mark	Jax.	15/15	441	259	3060	14	9	82.0	208	1
Grbac, Elvis	K.C.	16/16	499	294	3389	22	15	81.7	10	0
Banks, Tony	Balt.	12/10	320	169	2136	17	8	81.2	93	0
Aikman, Troy	Dall.	14/14	442	263	2964	17	12	81.1	10	1
Matthews, Shane	Chi.	8/7	275	167	1645	10	6	80.6	31	0
McNair, Steve	Tenn.	11/11	331	187	2179	12	8	78.6	337	8
Garcia, Jeff	S.F.	13/10	375	225	2544	11	11	77.9	231	2
Kitna, Jon	Sea.	15/15	495	270	3346	23	16	77.7	56	0
Blake, Jeff	Cin.	14/12	389	215	2670	16	12	77.6	332	2
Dilfer, Trent	T.B.	10/10	244	146	1619	11	11	75.8	144	0
Tomczak, Mike	Pitt.	16/5	258	139	1625	12	8	75.8	19	0
Favre, Brett	G.B.	16/16	595	341	4091	22	23	74.7	142	0
Griese, Brian	Den.	14/13	452	261	3032	14	14	75.6	138	2
Bledsoe, Drew	N.E.	16/16	539	305	3985	19	21	75.6	101	0
Flutie, Doug	Buff.	15/15	478	264	3171	19	16	75.1	476	1
Graham, Kent	NYG	9/9	271	160	1697	9	9	74.6	132	1
Collins, Kerry	NYG	10/7	331	190	2318	8	11	73.3	36	2
Couch, Tim	Clev.	15/14	399	223	2447	15	13	73.2	267	1
Harbaugh, Jim	S.D.	14/12	434	249	2761	10	14	70.6	126	0
Marino, Dan	Mia.	11/11	369	204	2448	12	17	67.4	-6	0
McNown, Cade	Chi.	15/6	235	127	1465	8	10	66.7	160	0
Stewart, Kordell	Pitt.	16/12	275	160	1464	6	10	64.9	258	2
Pederson, Doug	Phil.	16/9	227	119	1276	7	9	62.9	33	0
Tolliver, Billy Joe	N.O.	10/7	268	139	1916	7	16	58.9	142	3
Plummer, Jake	Ariz	12/11	381	201	2111	9	24	50.8	121	2
Nonqualifiers										
Huard, Damon	Mia.	16/5	216	125	1288	8	4	79.8	124	0
McNabb, Donovan	Phil.	12/6	216	106	948	8	7	60.1	313	0
Cunningham, Randall	Minn.	6/6	200	124	1475	8	9	79.1	58	0
O'Donnell, Neil	Tenn.	8/5	195	116	1382	10	5	87.6	1	0
Mirer, Rick	NYJ	8/6	176	95	1062	5	9	60.4	89	1
Miller, Jim	Chi.	5/3	174	110	1242	7	6	83.5	9	0
Case, Stoney	Balt.	10/4	170	77	988	3	8	50.3	141	3
Brown, Dave	Ariz	8/5	169	84	944	2	6	55.9	49	0
Hobert, Billy Joe	N.O.	9/7	159	85	970	6	6	68.9	47	1

Smith, Akili	Cin.	7/4	153	80	805	2	6	55.6	114	1
King, Shaun	T.B.	6/5	146	89	875	7	4	82.4	38	0
Kramer, Erik	S.D.	6/4	141	78	788	2	10	46.6	1	0
Graziani, Tony	Atl.	11/3	118	62	759	2	4	64.2	11	0
Stenstrom, Steve	S.F.	6/3	100	54	536	0	4	52.8	15	0
Fiedler, Jay	Jax.	7/1	94	61	656	2	2	83.5	26	0
Detmer, Ty	Clev.	5/2	91	47	548	4	2	75.7	38	1
Kanell, Danny	Atl.	3/1	84	42	593	4	4	69.2		
Young, Steve	S.F.	3/3	84	45	446	3	4	60.9	57	0
Miller, Chris	Den.	3/3	81	46	527	2	1	79.6	40	0
Delhomme, Jake	N.O.	2/2	76	42	521	3	5	62.4	72	2
Garrett, Jason	Dall.	5/2	64	32	314	3	1	73.3	12	0
Mitchell, Scott	Balt.	2/2	56	24	236	1	4	31.5	1	0
Zeier, Eric	T.B.	2/1	55	32	270	0	1	63.4	7	0
Wuerffel, Danny	N.O.	4/0	48	22	191	0	3	30.8	29	1
Johnson, Rob	Buff.	2/1	34	25	298	2	0	119.5	61	0
Foley, Glenn	Sea.	3/1	30	18	283	2	0	113.6	-1	0
Detmer, Koy	Phil.	1/1	29	10	181	3	2	62.6	-2	0
Brister, Bubby	Den.	2/0	20	12	87	0	3	30.6	17	0
Peete, Rodney	Wash.	3/0	17	8	107	2	1	82.2	-1	0
Germaine, Joe	St.L	3/0	16	9	136	1	2	65.6	0	0
Testaverde, Vinny	NYJ	1/1	15	10	96	1	1	78.8		
Justin, Paul	St.L	10/0	14	9	91	0	0	82.7	-1	0
Walsh, Steve	Ind.	16/0	13	7	47	0	2	22.4		
Tupa, Tom	NYJ	16/0	11	6	165	2	0	139.2		
Hasselbeck, Matt	G.B.	16/0	10	3	41	1	0	77.5	15	0
Moreno, Moses	S.D.	1/0	7	5	78	0	0	108.0		
Greisen, Chris	Ariz	2/0	6	1	4	0	0	39.6		
Covington, Scott	Cin.	3/0	5	4	23	0	0	85.8	-4	0
Hoying, Bobby	Oak.	2/0	5	2	10	0	0	47.9	-3	0
Zolak, Scott	Mia.	1/0	4	0	0	0	0	39.6	-2	0
Lewis, Jeff	Caro.	2/0	3	2	11	0	0	72.9	1	0
Moon, Warren	K.C.	1/0	3	1	20	0	0	57.6		
Van Pelt, Alex	Buff.	1/0	1	1	9	0	0	104.2	-1	0
Gonzalez, Pete	Pitt.	1/0	1	1	8	0	0	100.0	-3	0
Bono, Steve	Caro.	2/0	1	0	0	0	0	39.6	-2	0

STATISTICS

1999 RUNNING BACKS

Player	Team	GP/GS	RUSHING ATT	RUSHING YDS	RUSHING TD	RECEIVING REC	RECEIVING YDS	RECEIVING TD
James, Edgerrin	Ind.	16/16	369	1553	13	62	586	4
Martin, Curtis	NYJ	16/16	367	1464	5	45	259	0
Davis, Stephen	Wash.	14/14	290	1405	17	23	111	0
Smith, Emmitt	Dall.	15/15	329	1397	11	27	119	2
Faulk, Marshall	St.L	16/16	253	1381	7	87	1,048	5
George, Eddie	Tenn.	16/16	320	1304	9	47	458	4
Staley, Duce	Phil.	16/16	325	1273	4	41	294	2
Garner, Charlie	S.F.	16/15	241	1229	4	56	535	2
Watters, Ricky	Sea.	16/16	325	1210	5	40	387	2
Dillon, Corey	Cin.	15/15	263	1200	5	31	290	1
Gary, Olandis	Den.	12/12	276	1159	7	21	159	0
Bettis, Jerome	Pitt.	16/16	299	1091	7	21	110	0
Levens, Dorsey	G.B.	14/14	279	1034	9	71	573	1
Smith, Robert	Minn.	13/12	221	1015	2	24	166	0
Alstott, Mike	T.B.	16/16	242	949	7	27	239	2
Wheatley, Tyrone	Oak.	16/9	242	936	8	21	196	3
Stewart, James	Jax.	14/7	249	931	13	21	108	0
Enis, Curtis	Chi.	15/12	287	916	3	45	340	2
Allen, Terry	N.E.	16/13	254	896	8	14	125	1
Williams, Ricky	N.O.	12/12	253	884	2	28	172	0
Rhett, Errict	Balt.	16/10	236	852	5	24	169	2
Taylor, Fred	Jax.	10/9	159	732	6	10	83	0
Biakabutuka, Tim	Caro.	11/11	138	718	6	23	189	0
Kaufman, Napoleon	Oak.	16/5	138	714	2	18	181	1
Linton, Jonathan	Buff.	16/2	205	695	5	29	228	1
Bennett, Donnell	K.C.	15/1	161	627	8	10	41	0
Dunn, Warrick	T.B.	15/15	195	616	0	64	589	2
Smith, Antowain	Buff.	14/11	165	614	6	2	32	0
Huntley, Richard	Pitt.	16/2	93	567	5	27	243	3
Johnson, J. J.	Mia.	13/4	164	558	4	15	100	0
Hoard, Leroy	Minn.	15/3	138	555	10	17	166	0
Murrell, Adrian	Ariz	16/12	193	553	0	49	335	0
Hill, Greg	Det.	14/8	144	542	2	13	77	0
Holmes, Priest	Balt.	9/4	89	506	1	13	104	1
Lane, Fred	Caro.	16/0	115	475	1	23	163	0
Kirby, Terry	Clev.	16/10	130	452	6	58	528	3
Oxendine, Ken	Atl.	12/9	141	452	1	17	172	1
Abdul-Jabbar, Karim	Mia.-Clev.	13/9	143	445	1	17	84	1
Collins, Cecil	Mia.	8/6	131	414	2	6	32	0
Morris, Bam	K.C.	12/8	120	414	3	7	37	0
Warren, Chris	Dall.	16/1	99	403	2	34	224	0
Richardson, Tony	K.C.	16/16	84	387	1	24	141	0
Hanspard, Byron	Atl.	12/4	136	383	1	10	93	0
Fazande, Jermaine	S.D.	7/3	91	365	2			
Montgomery, Joe	NYG	7/5	115	348	3			
Basnight, Michael	Cin.	13/1	62	308	0	16	172	0
Rivers, Ron	Det.	7/6	82	295	0	22	173	1
Holcombe, Robert	St.L	15/7	78	294	4	14	163	1
Pittman, Michael	Ariz	10/2	64	289	2	16	196	0
Bynum, Kenny	S.D.	6/5	92	287	1	16	209	2
Means, Natrone	S.D.	7/5	112	277	4	9	51	1
Beasley, Fred	S.F.	13/11	58	276	4	32	282	0
Barber, Tiki	NYG	16/1	62	258	0	66	609	2
Hicks, Skip	Wash.	10/2	78	257	3	8	72	0
Shehee, Rashaan	K.C.	9/5	65	238	1	18	136	0

Player	Team	G/S	No.	Yds	TD	No.	Yds	TD
Faulk, Kevin	N.E.	11/2	67	227	1	12	98	1
Mitchell, Brian	Wash.	16/0	40	220	1	31	305	0
Davis, Terrell	Den.	4/4	67	211	2	3	26	0
Smith, Lamar	N.O.	13/2	60	205	0	20	151	1
Loville, Derek	Den.	10/0	40	203	1	11	50	0
Bates, Mario	Ariz.	16/2	72	202	9	5	34	0
Parker, De'Mond	G.B.	11/0	36	184	2	4	15	0
Anders, Kimble	K.C.	2/2	32	181	0	2	14	0
Perry, Wilmont	N.O.	7/3	48	180	0	4	26	0
Watson, Justin	St.L	8/0	47	179	0			
Brown, Gary	NYG	3/2	55	177	0	2	2	0
Christian, Bob	Atl.	16/14	38	174	5	40	354	2
Thomas, Rodney	Tenn.	16/0	43	164	1	9	72	0
Pritchett, Stanley	Mia.	14/7	47	158	1	43	312	4
Thomas, Thurman	Buff.	5/3	36	152	0	3	37	1
Phillips, Lawrence	S.F.	8/0	30	144	2	15	152	0
Johnson, LeShon	NYG	16/4	61	143	2	12	86	1
Way, Charles	NYG	11/8	49	141	2	11	59	0
Evans, Chuck	Balt.	16/10	38	134	0	32	235	1
Parmalee, Bernie	NYJ	16/0	27	133	0	15	113	0
Irvin, Sedrick	Det.	14/0	36	133	4	25	233	0
Cloud, Mike	K.C.	11/0	35	128	0	3	25	0
Fletcher, Terrell	S.D.	15/2	48	126	0	45	360	0
Bennett, Sean	NYG	9/2	29	126	1	4	27	0
Schlesinger, Cory	Det.	16/11	43	124	0	21	151	1
Green, Ahman	Sea.	14/0	26	120	0			
Warren, Lamont	N.E.	16/2	35	120	0	29	262	1
Allen, James	Chi.	12/3	32	119	0	9	91	0
Mitchell, Basil	G.B.	16/2	29	117	0	6	48	0
Denson, Autry	Mia.	6/1	28	98	0	4	28	0
Crockett, Zack	Oak.	13/1	45	91	4	8	56	1
Anderson, Richie	NYJ	16/9	16	84	0	29	302	3
Banks, Tavian	Jax.	8/1	23	82	0	14	137	0
Floyd, William	Caro.	16/16	35	78	3	21	179	0
Bieniemy, Eric	Phil.	16/0	12	75	1	2	28	0
Jackson, Terry	S.F.	16/0	15	75	0	3	6	0
Johnson, Anthony	Caro.	16/0	25	72	0	13	103	0
Williams, Moe	Minn.	14/0	24	69	1	1	12	0
Griffith, Howard	Den.	16/16	17	66	1	26	192	1
Stephens, Tremayne	S.D.	11/2	24	61	3	18	133	1
Anderson, Jamal	Atl.	2/2	19	59	0	2	34	0
Chancey, Robert	Dall.	3/0	14	57	0			
Howard, Chris	Jax.	12/0	13	55	0	1	8	0
Centers, Larry	Wash.	16/12	13	51	0	69	544	3
Jervey, Travis	S.F.	8/0	6	49	1	1	2	0
Zereoue, Amos	Pitt.	8/0	18	48	0	2	17	0
Mack, Stacey	Jax.	12/0	7	40	0			
Craver, Aaron	N.O.	13/10	17	40	0	19	154	0
Brown, Reggie	Sea.	16/8	14	38	0	34	228	1
Gordon, Lennox	Buff.	8/0	11	38	0			
Edwards, Marc	Clev.	16/14	6	35	0	27	212	2
Thomas, Robert	Dall.	16/7	8	35	0	10	64	0
Jordan, Randy	Oak.	16/0	9	32	2	8	82	0
Davis, Troy	N.O.	16/2	20	32	0	7	53	0
Oliver, Winslow	Atl.	14/0	8	32	0	8	74	0
Milne, Brian	Cin.	1/1	3	30	0			
Williams, Nick	Cin.	11/0	10	30	0	10	96	0
Henderson, William	G.B.	16/13	7	29	2	30	203	1
Bennett, Edgar	Chi.	16/2	6	28	0	14	116	0
Elias, Keith	Ind.	14/0	13	28	0	4	16	0

STATISTICS

Name	Team	GP/GS	No.	Yds	TD	No.	Yds	TD
Carter, Tony	N.E.	16/14	6	26	0	20	108	0
Shaw, Harold	N.E.	8/0	9	23	0	2	31	0
Groce, Clif	Cin.	16/15	8	22	1	25	154	0
Shaw, Sedrick	Clev.-Cin.	4/0	7	22	1	3	4	0
Avery, John	Den.	6/0	5	21	0	4	24	0
Bostic, James	Phil.	16/0	5	19	0	5	8	0
Witman, Jon	Pitt.	16/11	6	18	0	12	106	0
Watson, Edwin	Phil.	6/0	4	17	0			
Philyaw, Dino	N.O.	13/0	4	16	0	2	23	0
Konrad, Rob	Mia.	15/9	9	16	0	34	251	1
Carter, Ki-Jana	Cin.	3/0	6	15	1	3	24	0
Jones, George	Clev.	6/0	8	15	0			
Turner, Kevin	Phil.	6/0	6	15	0	9	46	0
Floyd, Chris	N.E.	13/0	6	12	0	2	16	0
Ritchie, Jon	Oak.	16/14	5	12	0	45	408	1
Abdullah, Rabih	T.B.	15/1	5	12	0	2	11	0
Palmer, David	Minn.	8/2	3	12	0	4	25	0
Ellison, Jerry	N.E.	12/0	2	10	0	4	50	0
Hodgins, James	St.L	15/0	7	10	1			
Hetherington, Chris	Caro.	14/0	2	7	0	6	35	0
Makovicka, Joel	Ariz	16/10	8	7	0	10	70	1
Smith, Detron	Den.	16/0	1	7	0	4	23	0
Vardell, Tommy	S.F.	6/4	6	6	1	7	36	0
Sowell, Jerald	NYJ	16/0	3	5	0			
Fuamatu-Ma'afala, C.	Pitt.	10/0	1	4	0			
Tate, Robert	Minn.	16/1	1	4	0			
Lee, Amp	St.L	7/0	3	3	0	3	22	1
Martin, Cecil	Phil.	12/5	3	3	0	11	22	0
Johnson, Leon	NYJ	1/0	1	2	0			
Lynn, Anthony	Den.	16/0	2	2	0			
Salaam, Rashaan	Clev.	2/0	1	2	0			
Shelton, Daimon	Jax.	16/9	1	2	0	12	87	0
Neal, Lorenzo	Tenn.	16/14	2	1	1	7	27	2
Morrow, Harold	Minn.	16/0	2	1	0			
Olivo, Brock	Det.	14/0	1	1	0	4	24	0
Pope, Daniel	K.C.	16/0	1	0	0			
Strong, Mack	Sea.	14/1	1	0	0	1	5	0
Comella, Greg	NYG	16/3	1	0	0	8	39	0
McCrary, Fred	S.D.	16/14				37	201	1
Gash, Sam	Buff.	15/11				20	163	2
Kozlowski, Brian	Atl.	16/3				11	122	2
Sellers, Mike	Wash.	16/2				7	105	2
Hallock, Ty	Chi.	15/4				6	22	0
Kleinsasser, Jim	Minn.	13/7				6	13	0
Shields, Paul	Ind.	13/3				4	37	0
Lester, Tim	Dall.	5/1				2	9	0
McLeod, Kevin	T.B.	7/0				2	5	1
Williams, Jermaine	Oak.	15/0				1	20	0
Greene, Scott	Ind.	5/0				1	4	0
Johnston, Daryl	Dall.	1/0				1	4	0
McKinley, Dennis	Ariz.	16/0				1	4	0

STATISTICS

1999 WIDE RECEIVERS

Player	Team	GP/GS	RECEIVING			RUSHING		
			REC	YDS	TD	ATT	YDS	TD
Smith, Jimmy	Jax.	16/16	116	1636	6			
Harrison, Marvin	Ind.	16/16	115	1663	12	1	4	0
Muhammad, Muhsin	Caro.	15/15	96	1253	8			
Brown, Tim	Oak.	16/16	90	1344	6	1	4	0
Carter, Cris	Minn.	16/16	90	1241	13			
Johnson, Keyshawn	NYJ	16/16	89	1170	8	5	6	0
Engram, Bobby	Chi.	16/14	88	947	4	2	11	0
Robinson, Marcus	Chi.	16/11	84	1400	9			
Crowell, Germane	Det.	16/15	81	1338	7			
Mathis, Terance	Atl.	16/16	81	1016	6	1	0	0
Moss, Randy	Minn.	16/16	80	1413	11	4	43	0
Morton, Johnnie	Det.	16/12	80	1129	5			
Ismail, Raghib	Dall.	16/14	80	1097	6	13	110	1
Toomer, Amani	NYG	16/16	79	1183	6	1	4	0
Smith, Rod	Den.	15/15	79	1020	4			
Sanders, Frank	Ariz	16/16	79	954	1			
McCardell, Keenan	Jax.	16/15	78	891	5			
Bruce, Isaac	St.L	16/16	77	1165	12	5	28	1
Freeman, Antonio	G.B.	16/16	74	1074	6	1	-2	0
Schroeder, Bill	G.B.	16/16	74	1051	5			
Hilliard, Ike	NYG	16/16	72	996	3	3	16	0
McCaffrey, Ed	Den.	15/15	71	1018	7			
Glenn, Terry	N.E.	14/13	69	1147	4			
Ismail, Qadry	Balt.	16/16	68	1105	6	1	4	0
Scott, Darnay	Cin.	16/16	68	1022	7			
Martin, Tony	Mia.	16/13	67	1037	5	1	-6	0
Rice, Jerry	S.F.	16/16	67	830	5	2	13	0
Johnson, Kevin	Clev.	16/16	66	986	8	1	-6	0
Moulds, Eric	Buff.	14/14	65	994	7	1	1	0
Westbrook, Michael	Wash.	16/16	65	1191	9	7	35	0
Jeffers, Patrick	Caro.	15/10	63	1082	712	2	16	0
Connell, Albert	Wash.	15/14	62	1132	7	1	8	0
Mayes, Derrick	Sea.	16/15	62	829	10			
Kennison, Eddie	N.O.	16/16	61	835	4	3	20	0
Edwards, Troy	Pitt.	16/6	61	714	5			
Ward, Hines	Pitt.	16/14	61	638	7	2	-2	0
Owens, Terrell	S.F.	14/14	60	754	4			
Dawkins, Sean	Sea.	16/13	58	992	7			
Graham, Jeff	S.D.	16/11	57	968	2			
Pickens, Carl	Cin.	16/14	57	737	6			
Green, Jacquez	T.B.	16/10	56	791	3	3	8	0
Alexander, Derrick	K.C.	16/15	54	832	2	2	82	1
Dyson, Kevin	Tenn.	16/16	54	658	4	1	3	0
Holt, Torry	St.L	16/15	52	788	6	3	25	0
Reed, Andre	Buff.	16/16	52	536	1			
Small, Torrance	Phil.	15/15	49	655	4			
Gadsden, Oronde	Mia.	16/7	48	803	6			
Chrebet, Wayne	NYJ	11/11	48	631	3			
Reed, Jake	Minn.	16/8	44	643	2			
Chiaverini, Darrin	Clev.	16/8	44	487	4			
Conway, Curtis	Chi.	9/8	44	426	4	1	-2	0
McDuffie, O. J.	Mia.	12/10	43	516	2			
Poole, Keith	N.O.	15/15	42	796	6	1	14	0
Wilkins, Terrence	Ind.	16/11	42	565	4			
Jefferson, Shawn	N.E.	16/16	40	698	6			

STATISTICS

Hastings, Andre	N.O.	15/5	40	564	1	1	4	0
Boston, David	Ariz	16/8	40	473	2	5	0	0
Ricks, Mikhael	S.D.	16/15	40	429	0	2	11	0
Jett, James	Oak.	16/11	39	552	2			
Thigpen, Yancey	Tenn.	10/10	38	648	4			
Bradford, Corey	G.B.	16/2	37	637	5			
Moore, Rob	Ariz	14/10	37	621	5			
Armour, Justin	Balt.	15/7	37	538	4			
Hakim, Az-zahir	St.L	15/0	36	677	8	4	44	0
Brown, Troy	N.E.	13/1	36	471	1			
Horn, Joe	K.C.	16/1	35	586	6	2	15	0
Stokes, J. J.	S.F.	16/4	34	429	3			
Lockett, Kevin	K.C.	16/1	34	426	2			
Johnson, Charles	Phil.	11/11	34	414	1			
Proehl, Ricky	St.L	15/2	33	349	0			
Dwight, Tim	Atl.	12/8	32	669	7	5	28	0
Price, Peerless	Buff.	16/4	31	393	3	1	-7	0
Williams, Kevin	Buff.	16/0	31	381	0	1	13	0
Jackson, Willie	Cin.	16/2	31	369	2			
Mills, Ernie	Dall.	11/7	30	325	0	1	-1	0
Anthony, Reidel	T.B.	13/7	30	296	1	1	2	0
Hawkins, Courtney	Pitt.	11/11	30	285	0			
Johnson, Pat	Balt.	10/6	29	526	3	1	12	0
Shaw, Bobby	Pitt.	15/1	28	387	3			
Pritchard, Mike	Sea.	14/5	26	375	2			
Fryar, Irving	Wash.	16/1	26	254	2			
Lewis, Jermaine	Balt.	15/6	25	281	2	5	11	0
Tucker, Jason	Dall.	15/4	23	439	2	1	8	0
Shepherd, Leslie	Clev.	9/8	23	274	0	1	5	0
Galloway, Joey	Sea.	8/4	22	335	1	1	-1	0
Ward, Dedric	NYJ	16/2	22	325	3	1	-1	0
Calloway, Chris	Atl.	11/6	22	314	1			
Emanuel, Bert	T.B.	11/10	22	238	1			
Green, E. G.	Ind.	11/4	21	287	0			
Rison, Andre	K.C.	15/14	21	218	0			
Williams, Karl	T.B.	13/4	21	176	0			
Sanders, Chris	Tenn.	16/0	20	336	1			
Mickens, Terry	Oak.	16/3	20	261	0			
Blackwell, Will	Pitt.	11/1	20	186	0			
Milburn, Glyn	Chi.	16/1	20	151	0	16	102	1
Simmons, Tony	N.E.	15/1	19	276	2			
Booker, Marty	Chi.	9/4	19	219	3	1	8	0
Jurevicius, Joe	NYG	16/1	18	318	1			
Brisby, Vincent	N.E.	12/1	18	266	0			
Brown, Na	Phil.	12/5	18	188	1			
Green, Yatil	Mia.	8/1	18	234	0			
Penn, Chris	S.D.	16/3	17	257	1			
Barlow, Reggie	Jax.	14/2	16	202	0			
Moore, Herman	Det.	8/4	16	197	2			
Dawsey, Lawrence	N.O.	10/0	16	196	1			
Byrd, Isaac	Tenn.	12/6	14	261	2			
Carruth, Rae	Caro.	5/5	14	200	0	1	4	0
Pathon, Jerome	Ind.	10/2	14	163	0			
Brooks, Macey	Chi.	9/2	14	160	0	1	7	0
German, Jammi	Atl.	14/0	12	219	3			
Ogden, Jeff	Dall.	15/0	12	144	0			
Metcalf, Eric	Caro.	16/1	11	133	0	2	20	0
Stablein, Brian	Det.	16/2	11	119	1			
Jells, Dietrich	Phil.	14/3	10	180	2			
Irvin, Michael	Dall.	4/4	10	167	3			

STATISTICS

Name	Team							
Harris, Ronnie	Atl.	13/0	10	164	0			
Still, Bryan	S.D.-Atl.	7/1	10	110	0			
Jones, Charlie	S.D.	8/1	10	90	1	1	-8	0
Hatchette, Matt	Minn.	13/0	9	180	2			
Patten, David	NYG	16/0	9	115	0	1	27	0
Cooper, Andre	Den.	10/1	9	98	0			
McDonald, Darnell	T.B.	8/0	9	96	1			
Mason, Derrick	Tenn.	13/0	8	89	0			
Douglas, Dameane	Phil.	14/0	8	79	1			
Baker, Eugene	Atl.	3/1	7	118	0			
McGarity, Wane	Dall.	5/1	7	70	0			
Davis, Billy	Balt.	16/0	6	121	0			
Early, Quinn	NYJ	16/3	6	83	0			
Cody, Mac	Ariz.	13/0	6	60	1			
Loud, Kamil	Buff.	7/0	6	66	0			
Brazzell, Chris	Dall.	5/0	5	114	0			
Miller, Billy	Den.	10/0	5	59	0			
Bownes, Fabien	Sea.	15/0	4	68	1	1	-14	0
Bech, Brett	N.O.	8/0	4	65	1			
Murphy, Yo	T.B.	7/0	4	28	0			
Sanders, Deion	Dall.	14/14	4	24	0			
Jordan, Charles	Sea.-G.B.	8/1	3	60	0			
McCullough, Andy	Ariz	2/0	3	45	0			
Thrash, James	Wash.	16/0	3	44	0	1	37	0
Kent, Joey	Tenn.	8/0	3	42	0			
McGriff, Travis	Den.	14/0	3	37	0			
Driver, Donald	G.B.	6/0	3	31	1			
Doering, Chris	Den.	3/0	3	22	0			
Yeast, Craig	Cin.	9/0	3	20	0	2	-16	0
Davis, Zola	Clev.	6/1	2	38	0			
Streets, Tai	S.F.	2/0	2	25	0			
Walsh, Chris	Minn.	16/1	2	24	1			
Johnson, Malcolm	Pitt.	6/0	2	23	0			
Finneran, Brian	Phil.	3/0	2	21	0			
Bates, D'Wayne	Chi.	7/1	2	19	0			
McKenzie, Kevin	Mia.	1/0	2	18	0			
Franklin, P.J.	N.O.	3/0	2	13	0	1	0	0
Powell, Ronnie	Clev.	14/0	1	45	0	1	-14	0
Stokley, Brandon	Balt.	2/0	1	28	1			
Jacquet, Nate	Mia.	13/0	1	18	0	1	4	0
Smith, Troy	Phil.	1/0	1	14	0			
Jones, Isaac	Ind.	1/1	1	8	0			
Thomas, Chris	St.L	6/0	1	6	0			
Hundon, James	Cin.	6/0	1	5	0			
Uwaezuoke, Iheanyi	Det.	10/0	1	5	0			
Dunn, David	Clev.	1/0	1	4	0			
Tate, Robert	Minn.	16/1	1	3	0			
Bates, Michael	Caro.	16/0	1	2	0	3	12	0
Stone, Dwight	NYJ	10/0				2	27	0
Whitted, Alvis	Jax.	14/1				1	9	0
Powell, Marvin	N.O.	9/0				1	1	0

334   **STATISTICS**

1999 TIGHT ENDS

Player	Team	GP/GS	RECEIVING			RUSHING		
			REC	YDS	TD	ATT	YDS	TD
Gonzalez, Tony	K.C.	15/15	76	849	11			
Wycheck, Frank	Tenn.	16/16	69	641	2			
Walls, Wesley	Caro.	16/16	63	822	12			
Mitchell, Pete	NYG	15/6	58	520	3			
Jones, Freddie	S.D.	16/16	56	670	2			
Sloan, David	Det.	15/15	47	591	4			
Dilger, Ken	Ind.	15/15	40	479	2			
Dudley, Rickey	Oak.	16/16	39	555	9			
Wetnight, Ryan	Chi.	16/4	38	277	1			
Riemersma, Jay	Buff.	14/11	37	496	4			
Fauria, Christian	Sea.	16/16	35	376	0			
LaFleur, David	Dall.	16/16	35	322	7			
Pollard, Marcus	Ind.	16/12	34	374	4			
Clark, Greg	S.F.	12/11	34	347	0			
Chamberlain, Byron	Den.	16/0	32	488	2			
Coates, Ben	N.E.	16/15	32	370	2			
Brady, Kyle	Jax.	13/12	32	346	1			
Drayton, Troy	Mia.	14/13	32	299	1			
Hardy, Terry	Ariz	16/16	30	222	0			
Alexander, Stephen	Wash.	15/15	29	324	3			
Glover, Andrew	Minn.	16/13	28	327	1			
McGee, Tony	Cin.	16/16	26	344	2			
Cleeland, Cameron	N.O.	11/8	26	325	1			
Harris, Jackie	Tenn.	12/1	26	297	1			
Broughton, Luther	Phil.	16/3	26	295	4			
Williams, Roland	St.L	16/15	25	226	6			
Smith, Irv	Clev.	13/13	24	222	1			
Carswell, Dwayne	Den.	16/11	24	201	2			
Moore, Dave	T.B.	16/16	23	276	5			
Sharpe, Shannon	Den.	5/5	23	224	0			
Davis, Tyrone	G.B.	16/13	20	204	2			
Jones, Damon	Jax.	15/8	19	221	4			
Bruener, Mark	Pitt.	14/14	18	176	0			
Santiago, O. J.	Atl.	14/14	15	174	0			
Battaglia, Marco	Cin.	16/0	14	153	0			
Thomason, Jeff	G.B.	14/2	14	140	2			
Allred, John	Chi.	16/5	13	102	1			
DeLong, Greg	Balt.	16/7	13	52	1			
Davis, Reggie	S.D.	16/3	12	137	1			
Griffin, Damon	Cin.	13/0	12	112	0			
Hayes, Donald	Caro.	13/1	11	270	2			
Slutzker, Scott	N.O.	11/2	11	164	1			
Pierce, Aaron	Balt.	10/8	11	102	0			
Weaver, Jed	Phil.	16/10	11	91	0			
McWilliams, Johnny	Ariz	15/4	11	71	1			
Bjornson, Eric	Dall.	16/7	10	131	0	1	20	0
Johnson, Lonnie	K.C.	14/2	10	98	1			
Campbell, Mark	Clev.	14/4	9	131	0			
Collins, Bobby	Buff.	14/4	9	124	2			
Roan, Michael	Tenn.	11/1	9	93	3			
Cross, Howard	NYG	16.15	9	55	0			
Kelly, Reggie	Atl.	16/2	8	146	0			
Brigham, Jeremy	Oak.	16/2	8	108	0			
Lewis, Chad	St.L-Phil.	12/4	8	88	3			
Mayes, Alonzo	Chi.	16/9	8	82	1			

Lyons, Mitch	Pitt.	14/2	8	81	0
Baxter, Fred	NYJ	14/8	8	66	2
Goodwin, Hunter	Mia.	15/5	8	55	0
Walker, Derrick	Oak.	11/3	7	71	1
Rutledge, Rod	N.E.	16/2	7	66	0
Green, Eric	NYJ	10/7	7	37	2
Robinson, Jeff	St.L	16/9	6	76	2
Harris, Mark	S.F.	16/2	6	66	0
Wilcox, Josh	N.O.	8/4	6	61	0
Chmura, Mark	G.B.	2/2	5	55	0
Kinchen, Brian	Caro.	16/0	5	45	2
Jordan, Andrew	Minn.	11/1	5	40	1
Mili, Itula	Sea.	16/1	5	28	1
Lucky, Mike	Dall.	14/4	5	25	0
Hape, Patrick	T.B.	15/1	5	12	1
Collins, Ryan	Balt.	4/3	4	62	0
Cline, Tony	S.F.	8/0	4	45	0
Jackson, Sheldon	Buff.	13/4	4	34	0
Ofodile, A. J.	Balt.	7/3	4	25	0
Pupunu, Alfred	S.D.	8/0	4	17	0
Hall, Lamont	G.B.	14/0	3	33	0
Mills, John Henry	Minn.	15/0	3	30	0
Rasby, Walter	Det.	16/6	3	19	1
Spence, Blake	NYJ	10/0	3	15	1
Perry, Ed	Mia.	16/1	3	8	1
Crumpler, Carlester	Minn.	11/1	2	35	1
Cushing, Matt	Pitt.	7/1	2	29	0
Chryplewicz, Pete	Det.	11/1	2	18	0
Purnell, Lovett	Balt.	2/0	2	10	0
Fann, Chad	S.F.	16/3	2	8	0
Davis, John	T.B.	16/0	2	7	1
Jenkins, James	Wash.	16/4	1	30	0
Conwell, Ernie	St.L	3/0	1	11	0
Monroe, Rodrick	Atl.	2/0	1	8	0
Alford, Brian	NYG	2/0	1	7	1
Mangum, Kris	Caro.	11/0	1	6	0
Jacoby, Mitch	K.C.	5/0	1	6	0
Clark, Desmond	Den.	9/0	1	5	0
Bush, Steve	Cin.	13/0	1	4	0
Bartrum, Mike	N.E.	16/0	1	1	1

STATISTICS

1999 KICKERS

Player	Team	GP	XP	XPA	FG	FGA	PCT	PTS
Vanderjagt, Mike	Ind.	16	43	43	34	38	.895	145
Mare, Olindo	Mia.	16	27	27	39	46	.848	144
Peterson, Todd	Sea.	16	32	32	34	40	.850	134
Hollis, Mike	Jax.	16	37	37	31	38	.816	130
Wilkins, Jeff	St.L	16	64	64	20	28	.714	124
Elam, Jason	Den.	16	29	29	29	36	.806	116
Stover, Matt	Balt.	16	32	32	28	33	.848	116
Carney, John	S.D.	16	22	23	31	36	.861	115
Conway, Brett	Wash.	16	49	50	22	32	.688	115
Longwell, Ryan	G.B.	16	38	38	25	30	.833	113
Christie, Steve	Buff.	16	33	33	25	34	.735	108
Hall, John	NYJ	16	27	29	27	33	.818	108
Stoyanovich, Pete	K.C.	16	45	45	21	28	.750	108
Vinatieri, Adam	N.E.	16	29	30	26	33	.788	107
Del Greco, Al	Tenn.	16	43	43	21	25	.840	106
Gramatica, Martin	T.B.	16	25	25	27	32	.844	106
Hanson, Jason	Det.	16	28	29	26	32	.813	106
Brown, Kris	Pitt.	16	30	31	25	29	.862	105
Anderson, Gary	Minn.	16	46	46	19	30	.633	103
Kasay, John	Caro.	13	33	33	22	25	.880	99
Richey, Wade	S.F.	16	30	31	21	23	.913	93
Brien, Doug	N.O.	16	20	21	24	29	.828	92
Husted, Michael	Oak.	13	30	30	20	31	.645	90
Cunningham, Richie	Dall.-Caro.	15	44	45	15	25	.600	89
Jacke, Chris	Ariz	16	26	26	19	27	.704	83
Pelfrey, Doug	Cin.	16	27	27	18	27	.667	81
Andersen, Morten	Atl.	16	34	34	15	21	.714	79
Johnson, Norm	Phil.	15	25	25	18	25	.720	79
Blanchard, Cary	NYG	10	19	19	18	21	.857	73
Dawson, Phil	Clev.	15	23	24	8	12	.667	#53
Boniol, Chris	Chi.	10	17	18	11	18	.611	50
Murray, Eddie	Dall.	4	10	10	7	9	.778	31
Daluiso, Brad	NYG	6	9	9	7	9	.778	30
Nedney, Joe	Oak.	3	13	13	5	7	.714	28
Gowins, Brian	Chi.	2	3	3	4	6	.667	15
Jaeger, Jeff	Chi.	3	7	7	2	8	.250	13
Akers, David	Phil.	16	2	2	3	6	.500	11
Holmes, Jaret	Chi.	3	0	0	2	2	1.000	6

Also scored one touchdown.

300-YARD PASSERS

No. of Games	Player	Team
9	Kurt Warner	St. L.
6	Brett Favre	G.B.
5	Steve Beuerlein	Caro.
4	Drew Bledsoe	N.E.
4	Brad Johnson	Wash.
	(one 400-yard game)	
3	Mark Brunell	Jax.
3	Jeff Garcia	S.F.
	(one 400-yard game)	
3	Dan Marino	Mia.
2	Chris Chandler	Atl.
2	Kerry Collins	NYG
2	Randall Cunningham	Minn.
2	Gus Frerotte	Det.
2	Rich Gannon	Oak.
2	Jeff George	Minn.
2	Brian Griese	Den.
2	Jim Harbaugh	S.D.
	(one 400-yard game)	
2	Peyton Manning	Ind.
	(one 400-yard game)	
2	Jim Miller	Chi.
	(one 400-yard game)	
2	Neil O'Donnell	Tenn.
1	Troy Aikman	Dall.
1	Tony Banks	Balt.
1	Jeff Blake	Cin.
1	Trent Dilfer	T.B.
1	Jay Fiedler	Jax.
1	Doug Flutie	Buff.
1	Elvis Grbac	K.C.
1	Steve McNair	Tenn.
1	Cade McNown	Chi.
1	Jake Plummer	Ariz.
1	Billy Joe Tolliver	N.O.
1	Mike Tomczak	Pitt.

100-YARD RUSHERS

No. of Games	Player	Team
10	Edgerrin James	Ind.
9	Emmitt Smith	Dall.
7	Marshall Faulk	Ind.
	(also one 100-yard receiving game)	
6	Stephen Davis	Wash.
6	Curtis Martin	NYJ
5	Corey Dillon	Cin.
5	Eddie George	Tenn.
5	Duce Staley	Phil.
4	Olandis Gary	Den.
4	Errict Rhett	Balt.
4	Robert Smith	Minn.
4	Ricky Watters	Sea.
3	Charlie Garner	S.F.
3	Dorsey Levens	G.B.
3	Fred Taylor	Jax.
2	Terry Allen	N.E.
2	Mike Alstott	T.B.
2	Jerome Bettis	Pitt.
2	Tim Biakabutuka	Caro.
2	Priest Holmes	Balt.
2	Antowain Smith	Buff.
2	James Stewart	Jax.
2	Tyrone Wheatley	Oak.
2	Ricky Williams	N.O.
1	Kimble Anders	K.C.
1	Bryan Hanspard	Atl.
1	Leroy Hoard	Minn.
1	J.J. Johnson	Mia.
1	Jermaine Fazande	S.D.
1	Greg Hill	Det.
1	Napoleon Kaufman	Oak.
1	Joe Montgomery	NYG
1	De'Mond Parker	G.B.
1	Lawrence Phillips	S.F.
1	Michael Pittman	Ariz.
0	Tiki Barber	NYG
	(one 100-yard receiving game)	
0	Warrick Dunn	T.B.
	(one 100-yard receiving game)	

STATISTICS

100-YARD RECEIVERS

No. of Games	Player	Team
9	Marvin Harrison	Ind.
9	Jimmy Smith	Jax.
	(one 200-yard game)	
7	Randy Moss	Minn.
	(one 200-yard game)	
6	Tim Brown	Oak.
6	Germane Crowell	Det.
5	Cris Carter	Minn.
5	Patrick Jeffers	Caro.
5	Tony Martin	Mia.
5	Johnnie Morton	Det.
5	Muhsin Muhhamad	Car.
5	Marcus Robinson	Chi.
5	Michael Westbrook	Wash.
4	Derrick Alexander	K.C.
4	Isaac Bruce	St.L.
4	Albert Connell	Wash.
4	Terry Glenn	N.E.
	(one 200-yard game)	
4	Jeff Graham	S.D.
4	Ed McCaffrey	Den.
4	Amani Toomer	NYG
3	Antonio Freeman	G.B.
3	Oronde Gadsden	Mia.
3	Ike Hilliard	NYG
3	Raghib Ismail	Dall.
3	Qadry Ismail	Balt.
	(one 200-yard game)	
3	Keenan McCardell	Jax.
3	Eric Moulds	Buff.
2	Sean Dawkins	Sea.
2	Tim Dwight	Atl.
2	Bobby Engram	Chi.
2	Jacquez Green	T.B.
2	Torry Holt	St. L.
2	Kevin Johnson	Clev.
2	Keyshawn Johnson	NYJ
2	Derrick Mayes	Sea.
2	Rob Moore	Ariz.
2	Terrell Owens	S.F.
2	Carl Pickens	Cin.
2	Jake Reed	Minn.
2	Jerry Rice	S.F.
2	Frank Sanders	Ariz.
2	Darnay Scott	Cin.
2	Jason Tucker	Dall.
1	Kevin Dyson	Tenn.
1	Corey Bradford	G.B.
1	Byron Chamberlain (TE)	Den.
1	Marshall Faulk (RB)	Ind.
	(one 200-yard game)	
1	Tiki Barber (RB)	NYG
1	Marty Booker	Chi.
1	David Boston	Ariz.
1	Troy Brown	N.E.
1	Darren Chiaverini	Clev.
1	Wayne Chrebet	NYJ
1	Curtis Conway	Chi.
1	Warrick Dunn (RB)	T.B.
1	E. G. Green	Ind.
1	Az-Zahir Hakim	St.L.
1	Andre Hastings	N.O.
1	Donald Hayes	Caro.
1	Michael Irvin	Dall.
1	Shawn Jefferson	N.E.
1	Patrick Johnson	Balt.
1	Eddie Kennison	N.O.
1	Keith Poole	N.O.
1	Peerless Price	Buff.
1	Terance Mathis	Atl.
1	Chris Sanders	Tenn.
1	Bill Schroeder	G.B.
1	Bobby Shaw	Pitt.
1	Tony Simmons	N.E.
1	Torrance Small	Phil.
1	J. J. Stokes	S.F.
1	Yancey Thigpen	Tenn.
1	Terrence Wilkins	Ind.

50-YARD FIELD GOALS

No. of 50+	Player	Team
5	Jason Elam	Den.
4	Jason Hanson	Det.
3	Steve Christie	Buff.
3	Brett Conway	Wash.
3	Martin Gramatica	T.B.
3	Olindo Mare	Mia.
2	Doug Brien	N.O.
2	John Kasay	Car.
2	Matt Stover	Balt.
1	David Akers	Phil.
1	Kris Brown	Pitt.
1	John Carney	S.D.
1	Al Del Greco	Tenn.
1	Mike Hollis	Jax.
1	Jeff Jaeger	Chi.
1	Ryan Longwell	G.B.
1	Joe Nedney	Oak.
1	Doug Pelfrey	Cin.
1	Todd Peterson	Sea.
1	Wade Richey	S.F.
1	Pete Stoyanovich	K.C.
1	Mike Vanderjagt	Ind.
1	Adam Vinatieri	N.E.
1	Jeff Wilkins	St.L.

1999 RANKINGS

	Offense			Defense		
	Total	Rush	Pass	Total	Rush	Pass
Arizona	29	29	27	22	30	10
Atlanta	27	30	17	16	29	9
Baltimore	24	16	25	2	2	6
Buffalo	11	8	19T	*1	4	*1
Carolina	6	20	2	26	24	23
Chicago	8	26	3	29	23	29
Cincinnati	15	T6	23	25	16	28
Cleveland	31	31	29	31	31	11
Dallas	16	T6	24	9	6	13
Denver	14	12	15	7	19	8
Detroit	21	28	9	18	9	27
Green Bay	9	21	7	19	22	18
Indianapolis	4	19	4	15	18	19
Jacksonville	7	2	12	4	7	3
Kansas City	12	4	22	14	11	16
Miami	20	22	T13	5	8	5
Minnesota	3	14	5	27	14	30
New England	18	23	10	8	21	7
New Orleans	19	18	T19	20	20	21
New York Giants	17	T24	8	13	13	14
New York Jets	25	11	28	21	17	24
Oakland	5	3	11	10	12	12
Philadelphia	30	17	31	24	28	15
Pittsburgh	22	10	26	11	26	4
St. Louis	*1	5	*1	6	*1	20
San Diego	26	27	18	12	3	22
San Francisco	10	*1	21	28	15	31
Seattle	23	T24	16	23	25	17
Tampa Bay	28	15	30	3	5	2
Tennessee	13	13	T13	17	10	25
Washington	2	9	6	30	27	26

STATISTICS

APPENDIX

2000 NFL SCHEDULE
(All times local)

WEEK 1
(Open date: Cincinnati)
Sunday, Sept. 3

Arizona at New York Giants	1:00
Baltimore at Pittsburgh	1:00
Carolina at Washington	1:00
Chicago at Minnesota	12:00
Detroit at New Orleans	12:00
Indianapolis at Kansas City	12:00
Jacksonville at Cleveland	1:00
New York Jets at Green Bay	3:15
Philadelphia at Dallas	3:05
San Diego at Oakland	1:15
San Francisco at Atlanta	1:00
Seattle at Miami	4:15
Tampa Bay at New England	1:00
Tennessee at Buffalo	8:35
Monday, Sept. 4	
Denver at St. Louis	8:00

WEEK 2
Sunday, Sept. 10
(Open date: Pittsburgh)

Atlanta at Denver	2:15
Carolina at San Francisco	1:15
Chicago at Tampa Bay	1:00
Cleveland at Cincinnati	1:00
Green Bay at Buffalo	1:00
Jacksonville at Baltimore	1:00
Kansas City at Tennessee	12:00
Miami at Minnesota	12:00
New Orleans at San Diego	1:15
New York Giants at Philadelphia	1:00
Oakland at Indianapolis	12:00
St. Louis at Seattle	1:15
Washington at Detroit	4:15
Dallas at Arizona	5:35
Monday, Sept. 11	
New England at New York Jets	9:00

WEEK 3
(Open dates: Arizona, Indianapolis, Tennessee)
Sunday, Sept. 17

Atlanta at Carolina	1:00
Buffalo at New York Jets	1:00
Cincinnati at Jacksonville	1:00
Denver at Oakland	1:05
Minnesota at New England	4:15
New Orleans at Seattle	1:15
New York Giants at Chicago	3:15
Philadelphia at Green Bay	12:00
Pittsburgh at Cleveland	1:00
San Diego at Kansas City	12:00
San Francisco at St. Louis	12:00
Tampa Bay at Detroit	1:00
Baltimore at Miami	8:35
Monday, Sept. 18	
Dallas at Washington	9:00

WEEK 4
(Open dates: Buffalo, Carolina, Minnesota)
Sunday, Sept. 24

Cincinnati at Baltimore	1:00
Cleveland at Oakland	1:15
Detroit at Chicago	12:00
Green Bay at Arizona	1:05
Kansas City at Denver	2:15
New England at Miami	1:00
New York Jets at Tampa Bay	4:15
Philadelphia at New Orleans	12:00
St. Louis at Atlanta	1:00
San Francisco at Dallas	12:00
Seattle at San Diego	1:15
Tennessee at Pittsburgh	1:00
Washington at New York Giants	8:35
Monday, Sept. 25	
Jacksonville at Indianapolis	8:00

WEEK 5
(Open dates: New Orleans, New York Jets, Oakland)
Sunday, Oct. 1

Arizona at San Francisco	1:15
Baltimore at Cleveland	1:00
Chicago at Green Bay	3:15
Dallas at Carolina	1:00
Indianapolis at Buffalo	1:00
Miami at Cincinnati	4:05
Minnesota at Detroit	1:00
New England at Denver	2:05
New York Giants at Tennessee	12:00
Pittsburgh at Jacksonville	1:00
San Diego at St. Louis	12:00
Tampa Bay at Washington	4:15
Atlanta at Philadelphia	8:35
Monday, Oct. 2	
Seattle at Kansas City	8:00

WEEK 6
(Open dates: Dallas, Kansas City, St. Louis)
Sunday, Oct. 8

Buffalo at Miami	1:00
Cleveland at Arizona	1:15
Denver at San Diego	1:15
Green Bay at Detroit	1:00
Indianapolis at New England	1:00
New Orleans at Chicago	12:00
New York Giants at Atlanta	4:05
Oakland at San Francisco	1:15
Pittsburgh at New York Jets	1:00
Seattle at Carolina	4:15
Tennessee at Cincinnati	1:00
Washington at Philadelphia	1:00
Baltimore at Jacksonville	8:35
Monday, Oct. 9	
Tampa Bay at Minnesota	8:00

WEEK 7

(Open dates: Detroit, Miami, Tampa Bay)
Sunday, Oct. 15

Atlanta at St. Louis	12:00
Baltimore at Washington	1:00
Carolina at New Orleans	12:00
Cincinnati at Pittsburgh	1:00
Cleveland at Denver	2:05
Dallas at New York Giants	1:00
Indianapolis at Seattle	1:05
New York Jets at New England	4:05
Oakland at Kansas City	12:00
Philadelphia at Arizona	1:15
San Diego at Buffalo	1:00
San Francisco at Green Bay	3:15
Minnesota at Chicago	7:35

Monday, Oct. 16

Jacksonville at Tennessee	8:00

WEEK 8

(Open dates: Green Bay, New York Giants, San Diego)
Thursday, Oct. 19

Detroit at Tampa Bay	8:35

Sunday, Oct. 22

Arizona at Dallas	12:00
Buffalo at Minnesota	12:00
Chicago at Philadelphia	1:00
Cleveland at Pittsburgh	1:00
Denver at Cincinnati	1:00
New England at Indianapolis	12:00
New Orleans at Atlanta	1:00
St. Louis at Kansas City	12:00
San Francisco at Carolina	1:00
Seattle at Oakland	1:05
Tennessee at Baltimore	1:00
Washington at Jacksonville	4:15

Monday, Oct. 23

Miami at New York Jets	9:00

WEEK 9

(Open dates: Chicago, Denver, New England)
Sunday, Oct. 29

Carolina at Atlanta	1:00
Cincinnati at Cleveland	1:00
Detroit at Indianapolis	1:00
Green Bay at Miami	1:00
Jacksonville at Dallas	3:15
Kansas City at Seattle	1:15
Minnesota at Tampa Bay	1:00
New Orleans at Arizona	2:05
New York Jets at Buffalo	1:00
Philadelphia at New York Giants	4:05
Pittsburgh at Baltimore	1:00
St. Louis at San Francisco	1:05
Oakland at San Diego	5:35

Monday, Oct. 30

Tennessee at Washington	9:00

WEEK 10

(Open date: Jacksonville)
Sunday, Nov. 5

Baltimore at Cincinnati	1:00
Buffalo at New England	1:00
Dallas at Philadelphia	1:00
Denver at New York Jets	4:15
Indianapolis at Chicago	12:00
Kansas City at Oakland	1:15
Miami at Detroit	1:00
New York Giants at Cleveland	1:00
Pittsburgh at Tennessee	12:00
San Diego at Seattle	1:15
San Francisco at New Orleans	12:00
Tampa Bay at Atlanta	1:00
Washington at Arizona	2:05
Carolina at St. Louis	7:35

Monday, Nov. 6

Minnesota at Green Bay	8:00

WEEK 11

(Open date: Washington)
Sunday, Nov. 12

Arizona at Minnesota	12:00
Atlanta at Detroit	1:00
Baltimore at Tennessee	12:00
Chicago at Buffalo	1:00
Cincinnati at Dallas	12:00
Green Bay at Tampa Bay	4:15
Kansas City at San Francisco	1:05
Miami at San Diego	1:05
New England at Cleveland	1:00
New Orleans at Carolina	1:00
Philadelphia at Pittsburgh	1:00
St. Louis at New York Giants	4:15
Seattle at Jacksonville	1:00
New York Jets at Indianapolis	8:35

Monday, Nov. 13

Oakland at Denver	7:00

WEEK 12

(Open date: Seattle)
Sunday, Nov. 19

Arizona at Philadelphia	1:00
Atlanta at San Francisco	1:15
Buffalo at Kansas City	12:00
Carolina at Minnesota	12:00
Cincinnati at New England	1:00
Cleveland at Tennessee	12:00
Dallas at Baltimore	4:15
Detroit at New York Giants	1:00
Indianapolis at Green Bay	12:00
New York Jets at Miami	4:05
Oakland at New Orleans	12:00
San Diego at Denver	2:05
Tampa Bay at Chicago	12:00
Jacksonville at Pittsburgh	8:35

Monday, Nov. 20

Washington at St. Louis	8:00

APPENDIX

WEEK 13
(Open date: San Francisco)
Thursday, Nov. 23
Minnesota at Dallas	3:05
New England at Detroit	12:30

Sunday, Nov. 26
Atlanta at Oakland	1:05
Buffalo at Tampa Bay	1:00
Chicago at New York Jets	1:00
Cleveland at Baltimore	1:00
Denver at Seattle	1:15
Kansas City at San Diego	1:15
Miami at Indianapolis	1:00
New Orleans at St. Louis	12:00
Philadelphia at Washington	1:00
Pittsburgh at Cincinnati	1:00
Tennessee at Jacksonville	4:15
New York Giants at Arizona	6:35

Monday, Nov. 27
Green Bay at Carolina	9:00

WEEK 14
(Open date: Baltimore)
Thursday, Nov. 30
Detroit at Minnesota	7:20p

Sunday, Dec. 3
Arizona at Cincinnati	1:00
Cleveland at Jacksonville	4:15
Dallas at Tampa Bay	1:00
Denver at New Orleans	12:00
Indianapolis at New York Jets	4:15
Miami at Buffalo	1:00
New York Giants at Washington	1:00
Oakland at Pittsburgh	1:00
St. Louis at Carolina	1:00
San Francisco at San Diego	1:05
Seattle at Atlanta	1:00
Tennessee at Philadelphia	1:00
Green Bay at Chicago	7:35

Monday, Dec. 4
Kansas City at New England	9:00

WEEK 15
(Open date: Atlanta)
Sunday, Dec. 10
Arizona at Jacksonville	1:00
Carolina at Kansas City	12:00
Cincinnati at Tennessee	12:00
Detroit at Green Bay	12:00
Minnesota at St. Louis	12:00
New England at Chicago	12:00
New Orleans at San Francisco	1:15
Philadelphia at Cleveland	1:00
Pittsburgh at New York Giants	1:00
San Diego at Baltimore	1:00
Seattle at Denver	2:05
Tampa Bay at Miami	1:00
Washington at Dallas	3:15
New York Jets at Oakland	5:35

Monday, Dec. 11
Buffalo at Indianapolis	9:00

WEEK 16
(Open date: Philadelphia)
Saturday, Dec. 16
Washington at Pittsburgh	12:30
Oakland at Seattle	1:05

Sunday, Dec. 17
Atlanta at New Orleans	12:00
Baltimore at Arizona	2:15
Chicago at San Francisco	1:05
Denver at Kansas City	12:00
Detroit at New York Jets	1:00
Green Bay at Minnesota	12:00
Indianapolis at Miami	4:15
Jacksonville at Cincinnati	1:00
New England at Buffalo	1:00
San Diego at Carolina	1:00
Tennessee at Cleveland	1:00
New York Giants at Dallas	7:35

Monday, Dec. 18
St. Louis at Tampa Bay	9:00

WEEK 17
(Open date: Cleveland)
Saturday, Dec. 23
Jacksonville at New York Giants	12:30
San Francisco at Denver	2:15
Buffalo at Seattle	5:35

Sunday, Dec. 24
Arizona at Washington	1:00
Carolina at Oakland	1:15
Chicago at Detroit	1:00
Cincinnati at Philadelphia	1:00
Kansas City at Atlanta	1:00
Miami at New England	1:00
Minnesota at Indianapolis	4:15
New York Jets at Baltimore	1:00
Pittsburgh at San Diego	1:05
St. Louis at New Orleans	12:00
Tampa Bay at Green Bay	12:00

Monday, Dec. 25
Dallas at Tennessee	8:00

POSTSEASON
Saturday, December 30
AFC and NFC Wild-Card Games
Sunday, December 31
AFC and NFC Wild-Card Games
Saturday, January 6
AFC and NFC Divisional Playoffs
Sunday, January 7
AFC and NFC Divisional Playoffs
Sunday, January 14
AFC and NFC Championship Games
Sunday, January 28
Super Bowl XXXV at Tampa, Florida
Sunday, Febuary 4
Pro Bowl at Honolulu, Hawaii

APPENDIX   343

FANTASY FOOTBALL SCHEDULES
Six-Team Leagues

Team #	1	2	3	4	5	6
Week #						
1	2	1	4	3	6	5
2	3	6	1	5	4	2
3	4	5	6	1	2	3
4	5	3	2	6	1	4
5	6	4	5	2	3	1
6	2	1	4	3	6	5
7	3	6	1	5	4	2
8	4	5	6	1	2	3
9	5	3	2	6	1	4
10	6	4	5	2	3	1
11	2	1	4	3	6	5
12	3	6	1	5	4	2
13	4	5	6	1	2	3
14	5	3	2	6	1	4
15	6	4	5	2	3	1
16	Playoffs					
17	Championship Game					

Eight-Team Leagues

Team #	1	2	3	4	5	6	7	8
Week #								
1	2	1	4	3	6	5	8	7
2	3	4	1	2	8	7	6	5
3	4	8	6	1	7	3	5	2
4	5	6	8	7	1	2	4	3
5	6	5	7	8	2	1	3	4
6	7	3	2	5	4	8	1	6
7	8	7	5	6	3	4	2	1
8	2	1	4	3	6	5	8	7
9	3	4	1	2	8	7	6	5
10	4	8	6	1	7	3	5	2
11	5	6	8	7	1	2	4	3
12	6	5	7	8	2	1	3	4
13	7	3	2	5	4	8	1	6
14	8	7	5	6	3	4	2	1
15	Playoffs							
16	Championship Game							
17	(Season over)							

APPENDIX

10-Team Leagues

Team #	1	2	3	4	5	6	7	8	9	10
Week #										
1	2	1	4	3	10	7	6	9	8	5
2	4	5	8	1	2	9	10	3	6	7
3	6	3	2	5	4	1	8	7	10	9
4	9	10	6	7	8	3	4	5	1	2
5	2	1	5	9	3	7	6	10	4	8
6	5	7	4	3	1	10	2	9	8	6
7	10	6	7	8	9	2	3	4	5	1
8	4	3	2	1	10	9	8	7	6	5
9	3	5	1	9	2	8	10	6	4	7
10	5	4	8	2	1	10	9	3	7	6
11	8	9	10	6	7	4	5	1	2	3
12	7	8	9	10	6	5	1	2	3	4
13	3	7	1	5	4	8	2	6	10	9
14	6	4	5	2	3	1	9	10	7	8
15	10	6	7	8	9	2	3	4	5	1
16	Playoffs									
17	Championship Game									

12-Team Leagues

Team #	1	2	3	4	5	6	7	8	9	10	11	12
Week #												
1	2	1	4	3	6	5	8	7	10	9	12	11
2	3	4	1	2	7	8	5	6	11	12	9	10
3	4	3	2	1	8	7	6	5	12	11	10	9
4	5	6	11	12	1	2	9	10	7	8	3	4
5	6	7	9	10	11	1	2	12	3	4	5	8
6	12	11	8	6	9	4	10	3	5	7	2	1
7	11	10	6	5	4	3	12	9	8	2	1	7
8	7	8	12	9	10	11	1	2	4	5	6	3
9	8	9	7	11	12	10	3	1	2	6	4	5
10	10	12	5	7	3	9	4	11	6	1	8	2
11	9	5	10	8	2	12	11	4	1	3	7	6
12	2	1	4	3	6	5	8	7	10	9	12	11
13	3	4	1	2	7	8	5	6	11	12	9	10
14	4	3	2	1	8	7	6	5	12	11	10	9
15	Playoffs											
16	Championship Game											
17	(Season over)											

INDEX

INDEX

ABOUT THE AUTHOR

Joseph Korch is the sports editor of the Marinette Menominee *EagleHerald*, a daily newspaper. Korch has received 11 awards from the Wisconsin and Illinois Press Associations for sportswriting, sports page design, newswriting and feature writing, and outdoor writing.

A lifelong National Football League junkie, Korch is single and lives near Marinette, Wisconsin.

He is the brother of Rick Korch, who was the author of the first four editions of this book. Rick Korch now works for the Jacksonville Jaguars.

SUGGESTIONS

Anyone wishing to write to the author with comments or suggestions for next year's edition of this book, please do so. Write to:

Joseph Korch
N8298 Island View Road
Porterfield, WI 54159

Or E-mail him at:
jody@cybrzn.com